METHUEN'S
MANUALS OF MODERN PSYCHOLOGY

General Editor: H. J. Butcher

Fact and Fantasy in Freudian Theory

Fact and Fantasy in Freudian Theory

PAUL KLINE

METHUEN & CO LTD
11 New Fetter Lane London EC4

First published 1972
© 1972 Paul Kline
Printed in Great Britain by
T & A Constable Ltd
Edinburgh

SBN 416 15060 8

Distributed in the USA
by Barnes & Noble Inc

*To the memory of
the late Professor F. W. Warburton*

Contents

Contents

Introduction

The aim of this book is relatively simple – to establish what parts of Freudian theory have been confirmed or, at least, could be confirmed by objective, scientific psychological research. In short, to establish psychoanalysis as a true science. This is necessary because Freudian theory, so far as it is dependent on data at all, rests on data which by the criteria of scientific methodology are totally inadequate. These data are, for the most part, the free associations of patients undergoing therapy and their dream reports, and both of these sources are unquantifiable and riddled with subjective interpretation. The achievement of such an aim seems worthwhile if only because the influence of Freud's ideas has been so pervasive. Art and literature as well as psychiatry and other fields associated with mental health have been radically affected. Yet academic psychology has tended to disregard psychoanalytic theory or even to consider it as a positively baleful influence on precise scientific thought.

Thus the first chapter of the book is devoted to a brief statement of what the scientific method is and how it may be applied to a study of psychoanalytic theory. It is not intended to be a comprehensive study of scientific methodology or the philosophy of science, subjects demanding books to themselves. It does, however, deal with the particular problems of validating Freudian hypotheses.

Based on this analysis the rest of the book is devoted to a study of specific hypotheses to be found in the writings of Freud. It would be idle to pretend that every empirical proposition in his voluminous output (24 volumes of collected papers) has been examined. What has been attempted, however, is a careful scrutiny of the scientific evidence, as defined in our opening chapter, which bears upon his major hypotheses. Thus, for example, chapters are devoted to the Oedipus and castration complex, to psychosexual personality syndromes and to defence mechanisms.

A serious difficulty in the study of psychoanalysis lies in the emotional attitudes it arouses both in its adherents and its opponents – feelings which are not conducive to a rational appraisal of its value. Psychoanalysts, at the earliest stages in the development of the theory, frequently argued that any opposition to the ideas was a form of resistance – a mechanism of defence against the unpalatable truths it contained. As Medawar (1969) has recently pointed out, this is contrary to all the canons of scientific investigation and he consequently dismisses the *whole* theory as unscientific, a rejection with which Eysenck would thoroughly agree. A further barrier is the psychoanalytic claim that only those who have undergone an analysis themselves can understand the ideas. These arguments have been entirely ignored throughout this book.

In accord with the concept of psychoanalysis as many theories rather than one, each chapter is devoted to a study of the objective scientific evidence relevant to one of the basic postulates in psychoanalytic theory. For many such postulates the amount of good evidence is small. This has enabled us to discuss the researches at greater length than is often found in surveys of this type. Great attention has been paid to the quality of the measurements and the experimental design of the investigations. This is of vital importance since a mere description of an investigation and a statement of results can be totally misleading in areas where the methodology is complex and there is no single agreed procedure among psychologists. Our discussion of the research has therefore been designed to allow the reader to judge for himself the extent to which the Freudian theory has been confirmed, and to enable him, if he wishes, to disagree with our interpretation. Without this discussion, however, the book would consist of dogmatic assertions of necessarily little weight.

In some cases, however, the amount of experimental evidence is enormous. To review all this in detail would be impossible in a book of this size and equally arduous for both writer and reader. Here the method used has been to review first the methodological problems involved in testing the theory and then to examine only those studies which meet these criteria.

The subject matter of the chapters follows a logical developmental sequence: the first chapters are concerned with the Freudian hypotheses concerning child development which lead to his structured hypotheses of mental provinces, defence mechanisms and the contents of the unconscious, as revealed in dreams. This in turn leads on to the hypotheses concerning neuroses, the success of psychoanalytic therapy and a brief study of neo-Freudian theories in the light of the experimental evidence. Lastly, in the final chapter, we review those parts of psychoanalytic theory which have been supported and assess the status of the theory. Nevertheless despite this sequential arrangement of chapters, each is self-contained and can be read on its own by readers interested in one particular part of Freudian theory.

Psychoanalytic theory has never been drab or uninteresting. It is our hope that this book will help to put psychoanalysis back among the sciences and encourage imaginative researchers to investigate with methodological precision those areas of human thought and behaviour that Freudian theory has attempted to illuminate and which behaviouristic psychologies seem unwilling to study or even to contemplate.

I

Freudian theory and scientific method

Eysenck (1953) answering his own question – 'What is wrong with psycho-analysis ?'– claims that the answer is simple:'Psychoanalysis is unscientific'. First, therefore, it is necessary to clarify the meaning of the term scientific as applied to a theory.

THE MEANING OF SCIENTIFIC

Marx (1963) in a definition that would seem agreeable to the majority of philo-sophers of science argues that there are three fundamental elements of all scientific theory construction:

1. *Observations* – which must be under *controlled* conditions (that is eliminate the role of extraneous variables)
2. *Constructs* – which must be *operational* (that is have clearly specified and identifiable empirical referents)
3. *Hypotheses* – which must be *testable* (that is clearly disconfirmable).

It is certainly true to say that on all these criteria much of Freudian theory is open to criticism.

OBSERVATIONS

The observations on which Freudian theory rests are made by psychoanalysts during therapy. The raw data of psychoanalytic theory consist of the free associ-ations of the patient and the reports of dreams to which further free associations are elicited. These raw data are not even recorded as spoken but are recalled later by the analyst. Thus there is no quantification, no control group, nor indeed any check on the reliability of the analyst's memory.

CONSTRUCTS

Many of the constructs in psychoanalytic theory are vague and difficult to relate to any external referent: for example, the concepts of eros and thanatos, the life and death instincts. Thus Freud (1920) in 'Beyond the pleasure principle' writes that there are two kinds of instinct: 'Those which seek to lead what is living to death and others, the sensual instincts, which are perpetually attempting and achieving a renewal of life'. It is, obviously, no simple matter to operationalise these terms.

I

HYPOTHESES

It is inevitably the case that if the constructs of a theory are themselves unclear, any hypotheses of which they form a part must be difficult to refute. Even worse, they may be impossible to test. For example, the anal character (Freud, 1908) is considered in psychoanalytic theory to be the result of repressed anal erotism. Although at present this hypothesis is not testable because there are no adequate measures of anal erotism (an example of a vague construct) or repression, it may be tested in principle at least. Until recently the back of the moon could not be observed, yet the statement or hypothesis that the back of the moon was made of cheese was testable and refutable in principle and hence scientific. However, the Freudian theory of the anal character cannot easily be refuted. Thus if parsimony, a sublimation of the retentive desire, were not found to be part of the anal character, the Freudian theorist can point to Jones (1923) and argue that generosity too may be included, being a reaction-formation against the retentive desire.

These examples make it clear that on these criteria of scientific theories Eysenck (1953) is correct. Psychoanalytic theory is open to serious criticism. However psychoanalytic theory is of such a kind that these criticisms are not necessarily entirely destructive.

THE NATURE OF PSYCHOANALYTIC THEORY

Rapaport and Gill (1959) have attempted to impose a four-fold hierarchical structure upon psychoanalytic theory which is exceedingly useful for the clarification of the theory. This structure with the examples given by the authors is set out below.

1. *Empirical proposition.* Around the fourth year of life boys regard their fathers as rivals.
2. *Specific psychoanalytic proposition.* The solution of the Oedipal situation is a decisive determinant of character formation and pathology.
3. *General psychoanalytic proposition.* Structure formation by means of identifications and anti-cathexes explains theoretically the consequences of the 'decline of the Oedipus complex'.
4. *Metapsychological proposition.* The propositions of the general psychoanalytic theory which explain the Oedipal situation and the decline of the Oedipus complex involve dynamic, economic, structural, genetic and adaptive assumptions.

This taxonomy is the basis for the argument, suggested above, that the failure of psychoanalytic theory to stand scrutiny against the normal criteria of science is not necessarily destructive. The criticisms raised by Eysenck (1953) are directed against the top of the hierarchical structure – general psychoanalytic propositions and metapsychological propositions: they do not apply with the same force to the empirical basis – empirical and specific psychoanalytic propositions. Indeed the problem of the scientific validity of psychoanalysis in terms of this structure turns about this question. Are the empirical propositions and specific psychoanalytic propositions true? In other words, the first concern is with the observations. Indeed it seems pointless to criticise the metapsychology of psychoanalytic theory on the grounds of internal inconsistency, or untestability of the hypotheses, before establishing whether or not the empirical data, which the metapsychology seeks to subsume, are well founded or not. This is the approach adopted in this book. Psychoanalytic theory has been carefully examined in order to set out as precisely as possible the empirical or specific psychoanalytic propositions. The psychological literature has then been reviewed to see whether or not these propositions may be regarded as true. This procedure, it should be noted, has been objected to by Martin (1964) who argues that to restate the theory in this way is to alter it. Nevertheless, if one proceeds with care this need not be the case.

There is a further characteristic of psychoanalytic theory which is relevant to its viability as a scientific theory. This is that it is not a unified theory but a collection of parts (Farrell, 1961). This means that even if certain psychoanalytic hypotheses are shown to be false it does not destroy the whole of psychoanalysis. Thus, for example, even if dreams do not express wishes, the castration complex might well lie behind homosexuality. Farrell (1951, 1961, 1964) has, of course, been long interested in the problem under discussion – the scientific validity of Freudian theory – and he makes a number of points which deserve mention.

1. He agrees with Eysenck (1953) that psychoanalytic theory cannot be called scientific because the evidence on which it is based is not of established validity. In addition its terms are not clearly enough defined. These criticisms relate to the observation and constructs of Marx (1963).

2. However, he refuses (1964) to consider psychoanalytic theory as a myth, as suggested by Popper (1959), on the grounds that it is not considered to be, even by its most hostile opponents, purely fictitious, it invokes no supernatural persons and does not make use of 'popular' ideas. Nor indeed is it a pre-scientific theory in that unlike, for example, *De Rerum Natura* it can be used for something – psychotherapy.

3. He thus concludes (1964) that psychoanalytic theory cannot be said to be true; for the data on which it is based are not well established. On the other hand it cannot be said to be false – because no collection of evidence has, as yet, falsified the entire complex. Finally there is no acceptable alternative to the theory. This last argument has been much stressed by Conant (1947) who argues that theories are not deposed by facts that do not fit them, but by alternative superior theories. In summary, Farrell describes psychoanalytic theory as a premature empirical synthesis offered in advance of the evidence.

This is the view of psychoanalytic theory accepted in this book. The theory is regarded as a huge collection of empirical hypotheses and propositions some of which may be true. Certainly the metapsychology is unscientific but equally certainly the implicit empirical propositions, in the sense that they are testable, are not. Because the theory is not unified, the disproof of some or even most of the propositions is not fatal to the whole theory – a view proposed strongly also by Sherwood (1969).

THE TESTING OF THE EMPIRICAL PROPOSITIONS

As Eysenck (1965) says, the reason why psychoanalysis 'has never been taken very seriously by people with some regard for the principles of scientific method' resides in the nature of the data on which psychoanalytic theory is based. The fact is that the psychoanalytic method is not the scientific method (Farrell, 1964). This means that the effort to establish the empirical propositions of psychoanalysis scientifically must largely depend on the work of psychologists. The data from psychoanalytic sessions have not done this, nor are they likely to do so for some time. Thus Crown (1968), a psychoanalyst writing on psychoanalysis and the scientific method, categorically states that analysts are not prepared to use methods appropriate to the sciences because these distort the data.

ACCEPTABLE DATA FOR PSYCHOANALYTIC THEORY

In this book the objective evidence for psychoanalytic theory is reviewed and discussed. Only investigations where the data had any claims to scientific respectability have been examined. Thus, for example, if tests were used they had to be tests with some evidence for their validity. This has meant that the majority of studies with the Rorschach have not been considered. Eysenck (1961) succinctly puts the case against the Rorschach technique, namely that in studies of its validity there is an inverse correlation between positive results and methodological excellence! Other projective techniques are open to similar criticisms but their results have been used where evidence for the validity of the particular score was presented.

If Freudian hypotheses concerning special groups were under examination, then control groups were regarded as essential. After all, the Freudian claim that paranoid-schizophrenia is caused by repressed homosexuality is not proven by demonstrating that homosexuality is repressed in paranoids unless it be shown also that such homosexuality does not occur in non-paranoid schizophrenics. This is a matter of simple logic.

A third constraint on the types of study examined was that there has to be some form of statistical analysis of results so that non-significant fluctuations of scores would not be seized on as evidence for or against the theory. The judgement of the statistical excellence of the analysis naturally involved a consideration of the sampling techniques.

The final consideration given to all studies was whether the results were in fact relevant to psychoanalytic theory. This to some extent constitutes a value judgement but where the empirical propositions were clear the problem was not so difficult. Where they are not, then the results of objective studies can be used to clarify the theory itself. This difficulty of deciding the relevance of an investigation to Freudian theory was partly overcome by examining only those studies where the hypothesis tested was clearly stated and deliberately related by the author to Freudian theory. Alternative and perhaps more parsimonious explanations of the results were also discussed. In summary, for the type of data that can put psychoanalytic propositions upon a scientific basis, the following criteria were considered important:

1. Stringency of sampling procedures and use of adequate control groups
2. Validity of tests used
3. Quality of the statistical analysis of results
4. Relevance of the conclusions to psychoanalytic theory and possible alternative hypotheses.

At this point it should strike the reader that such studies are no different from the normal procedures of respectable scientific disciplines. If, therefore, the results of any such studies support psychoanalytic theory, there is no reason at all why that part of it that is supported should not be scientifically acceptable.

THE PROBLEM OF REFUTATION

As has been stated earlier, refutability is essential if a theory is to be regarded as scientific. This raises a peculiar difficulty in the objective study of psychoanalysis. If the theory is supported and there is no other viable explanation of the results, it seems fair to argue that this is evidence in favour of psychoanalysis. If, on the other hand, the theory is not supported, the results do not necessarily refute the theory. This is simply because in many cases the validity of the tests is not perfect. This means that if the results are positive they can be accepted, since error is random and likely to spoil rather than to improve the results in any systematic way. If they are negative it *may be* because the tests are faulty. Thus refutation of psychoanalytic theory is not easy.

2

The Freudian theory of psychosexual development

'Sexual life does not begin only at puberty but starts with clear manifestations soon after birth' (Freud, 1940). 'Sexual life comprises the function of obtaining pleasure from zones of the body – a function which is subsequently brought into the service of that of reproduction' (*Ibid.*). This sexual drive first manifests itself through the mouth during the first year of the infant's life. This is the *oral phase*. Around the third year the erotogenic zone of the anus comes to the fore – the *anal phase*. Third comes the *phallic phase*, around the age of four, where the chief erotogenic zone is the penis (in the case of the girl – the clitoris). The final phase of sexual organisation is the *genital phase* established after puberty. At this stage all the previous phases are organised and subordinated to the adult sexual aim of pleasure in the reproductive function (Freud, 1933 and 1940). The pleasure derived from stimulation of the erotogenic zones, which plays a part in mature sexual behaviour, is known as oral erotism, anal erotism and phallic erotism respectively.

According to psychosexual theory this infantile sexuality is crucial to the personality development of the individual because it cannot always be directly expressed. The clearest example of this is the adult anal character – a triad of traits, parsimony, orderliness and obstinacy – which is derived from repressed anal erotism (Freud, 1908). In the concluding paragraph of this paper, Freud states that 'The permanent character traits are either unchanging perpetuations of the original impulse, sublimations of them or reaction-formations against them'. As an example of the process, kissing may be regarded as a perpetuation of oral erotism, orderliness a reaction formation against anal erotism (the desire to smear the faeces) and parsimony as a sublimation of anal erotism (desire to retain the faeces). From this outline of the theory it is clear that character traits can be derived from all these infantile pregenital stages of sexuality. Indeed Fenichel (1945) points out that such correlations of personality and infantile sexual development were the first discovery of psychoanalytic characterology.

Adult personality is therefore related to infantile sexuality. The extent to which oral erotism, for example, is directly expressed or sublimated in any individual depends upon two further factors. One is constitutional – each zone is differentially capable of excitation (Freud, 1905). The other is environmental – in this example, the duration and nature of the feeding and weaning process. Excessive satisfaction at feeding means that the individual is loth to renounce oral erotism. Similarly excessive frustration (e.g. too rapid and early weaning) produces the

6

same effect. This refusal to renounce the pleasure from a particular erotogenic zone is known as fixation. Freud (1916-17) likens fixation and regression to an advancing army in enemy territory leaving occupation troops at all important points. The stronger the occupation troops left behind (fixation) the weaker is the army that marches on. If the latter meets a too powerful enemy force (e.g. toilet training) it may retreat to those points (regression) where it had previously left the strongest occupation troops. The stronger a fixation the more easily will regression take place if difficulties arise. Fixations most frequently are rooted, according to Fenichel (1945), in satisfactions which simultaneously gave reassurances against some anxiety or helped in the repression of some feared impulse. Variations in adult personality, therefore, are linked, according to this theory, to fixations at and regressions to these psychosexual stages. Such fixations are themselves related to child-rearing procedures as well as to constitutional factors.

IMPORTANCE OF THE THEORY

There can be no doubt that this is an important theory in psychoanalysis: much has been made of its implications. Berkley-Hill (1921), for example, attributed the character and behaviour of Hindus to repressed anal erotism, a factor which was employed by Spitzer (1947) and Gorer (1943) in the clarification of Japanese culture. Freud (1913) regarded fixation at the anal phase as important in the development of obsessional neurosis while Abraham (1916) related depression to the oral phase. Sexual repressions also are considered to spring from fixations at various phases. If this be insufficient evidence, Roheim (1934) regarded the whole of Western culture as anal and Menninger (1943) considered the anal phase as 'without doubt the most important period in the development of not only individuals but whole cultures as well'. Freudian psychosexual theory gives insight into the nature and causes of personality development and implicitly suggests how desired behaviour patterns might be produced. It implies, also, possible alleviation of disorders in that the conflicts resulting in fixation may be resolvable under psychoanalytic therapy. It is from this theory that the first five years of life are considered crucial for adult behaviour. For, as has been indicated, normal personality variations, neuroses, cultural differences and sexual anomalies are based upon psychosexual development within this period.

THE HYPOTHESES

At this point it should be evident that within this theory there are implied three independent sets of hypotheses of which two, at least, are open to empirical validation. These hypotheses may be thus expressed:

1. that there exist in mature adults certain constellations of personality traits,
2. that certain constellations of personality traits are related to child-rearing procedures,
3. that the mouth, the anus and the phallus are erotogenic zones in early childhood.

The first hypothesis is basic to the whole theory. If, for example, it could be shown that the anal traits of obstinacy, parsimony and orderliness do not in fact occur together (to a greater extent than would be expected by chance) i.e. that no such syndrome as the anal character exists, then psychosexual theory breaks down. Thus the first empirical test must be to discover whether such constellations of traits as the oral, the anal and the phallic character do occur. If they do not, Freudian theory is refuted. If they do, a small part, and perhaps the most interesting part, of psychosexual theory is supported. Clearly it could well be the case that such syndromes do exist but that they are unrelated to infantile sexuality and child-rearing procedures.

If it can be shown that such syndromes exist, the second hypothesis becomes crucial. Are such syndromes related, as the theory implies, to child-rearing procedures ? Clearly longitudinal child studies and cross-cultural investigations will be necessary to confirm or refute this second hypothesis. However, such empirical tests, although difficult to execute, are conceptually clear.

The third hypothesis, on the other hand, is more difficult to confirm. The problem is to know what observations would confirm or refute the theory. Does, for example, frequent thumbsucking, as Freud (1905) supposes, constitute evidence for the mouth being an erotogenic zone ? These problems will be fully considered in the relevant chapter.

Before any examination of the evidence relevant to these three hypotheses, it is necessary to define the theory more precisely. The remaining section of this chapter will be concerned, therefore, with the psychoanalytic descriptions of the character syndromes and the child-rearing procedures and erotogenic zones implicated in their development.

SOURCES

Whereas the original psychosexual theory may be found in Freud, as is evident from the outline, the detailed descriptions of the personalities are to be found elsewhere. These sources will now be quoted, since what follows is a summary of their texts.

1. Oral character – Abraham (1924) and Glover (1924a, 1924b)
2. Anal character – Freud (1908, 1917), Abraham (1921), E. Jones (1923) and Menninger (1943)
3. Urethral traits – E. Jones (1933)
4. Phallic traits – Reich (1945) and E. Jones (1915).

Fenichel (1945) contains useful information on all these stages.

1. The oral character

Most authorities distinguish between traits derived from the first phase – sucking – and the later oral-sadistic stage – biting. A distinction is drawn, too, between traits derived from over-indulgence and frustration. It is to be noted that more direct expression of oral erotism is permissible in Western society than of anal erotism. All agree that oral characteristics are to some extent mixed with later anal influences (Fenichel, 1945).

Summary of descriptions of the oral character

Trait	Source – sucking or biting	Frustration or satisfaction (where clearly stated)
(a) Found in Abraham (1924)		
Optimism	S	S
Dependency and inactivity: feeling that people will do things for them	S	S
Pessimism	S	F
Desire for a regular income	S	S
Dependency = Demanding attitudes: 'clinging like a leech'	S	F
Impatience	S	F
Hostility and cruelty: 'clinging like vampires'	S	F
Need to give (often by way of mouth)	S	—
Talkativeness	S	—
Feeling of an inexhaustible flow of ideas	S	—
High valuation on own ideas	S	—
Hostile, sarcastic, biting speech patterns	B	—
Generosity	S	S
Envy, hostility	B	F
Jealousy	B	F
Cheerfulness, sociability	S	S
Malice	B	F
Accessibility to new ideas	S	—
Ambition	—	—
Love of soft foods	S	—
Love of hard foods	B	—
Curiosity and delight in observation	—	—
(b) Found in Glover (1924a and 1924b) but not in Abraham		
Rhythmic character of oral reactions	—	—
Quick motor movements	—	—
Buying drinks to produce intoxication in others	B	—
Generous presents of advice	S	F
Tooth grinding	—	—
(c) Found in Fenichel (1945)		
Voracious reading	—	—

Glover (1924a) summarised oral characteristics under the oral triad of impatience, envy and ambition. 'He hankers after the plums and yet behind it all is a feeling that the silver spoon is, or ought to have been, in the mouth.'

2. The anal character

The anal triad – obstinacy, parsimony and orderliness – was the first discovery (Freud, 1905) in Freudian psychosexual theory. It has been the most extensively studied both by psychoanalysts and by academic psychologists. Part of its interest lies in the prima facie absurdity of linking such traits to anal erotism repressed by pot training. As has been indicated, anal erotism is regarded as a very powerful influence on personality in psychoanalysis because almost none of it can be directly expressed in Western society. It therefore emerges in the character as reaction-formations or sublimations.

Summary of Psychoanalytic Description of the Anal Character – Parsimony, Orderliness and Obstinacy (Freud, 1908)

A. *Traits found in Jones (1923)*:
Procrastination followed by intense concentration, boring persistence
self-willed independence – a belief that nobody can do anything as well as oneself
inability to depute work
minute attention to detail
intolerant insistence to do things one way
strong drive to clean things (routine chores)
profound interest in handwriting
opposition to any attempt to guide one's conduct
resentment of any thwarting
resentment of advice
standing on rights and dignity
strong feelings at any injustice
dislike of time being used up against one's will
irritability and vindictive desires of revenge (symptoms of above)
highly individualistic
pleasure spoiled by small things out of place
love of self-control
interest in the backs of things.
(All the above derive from interest in the act itself. Those below derive from interest in the product of the act.)

a. (sublimation of retaining tendency):
parsimony – avarice and meanness, especially copro-symbols – money, time, food, books – 'all collectors are anal erotic'
pleasure in finding things
tenderness to children
tendency to domineer.

b. (reaction-formation to retaining tendency):
orderliness – love of symmetry
pedantry, love of exactitude, delight in organising
reliability
hatred of waste.

c. (sublimation of the impulse to give – not part of the anal character):
useful for finding what anals are not

d. (reaction-formation of the impulse to give):
strictly not part of the anal character but having certain traits in the triad already mentioned above.

These last two sections represent fixation at the anal expulsive level and are outside the strictly Freudian concept of the anal character.

B. *Traits found in Abraham (1921) but not in Jones:*
Pleasure in possessing something rare or unusual
pleasure in statistics and tables – Bradshaw's, etc.
critical of others, generally malcontent
dislike of spending money on perishable things
simultaneous performance of more than one activity
pleasure in looking at one's own mental creations
dislike of new subjects
delight in meticulous planning, orderly rooms but untidy cupboards
dislike of feeling obliged to anyone, love of doing the opposite of most, e.g. curious tastes in food, clothes.

3. Characters derived from fixation at other psychosexual levels

Oral and anal characteristics are far more important in psychoanalytic personality theory than characteristics derived from fixation at other levels. Jones (1915 and 1933) has described urethral and phallic characters and Reich (1945) has discussed the phallic personality. However there are far less detailed pictures of these available than is the case with the oral and anal character. Consequently, a very brief description of each will be given below. Such brevity is also due to the fact that very few objective studies of these characters exist, so that a lengthy description would be irrelevant.

The Urethral Character

Ambition is the dominant trait, derived from infantile competition in respect of urination (Fenichel, 1945). Indeed, Glover (1924a) refers to the urinary character. Unnatural pleasure in fire is also claimed to be a related trait (Freud, 1932).

The Phallic Character

Typical traits are recklessness, self-assurance and resolute courage. There is often intense pride and vanity.

   Such then are the descriptions of the personality characteristics considered by psychoanalysis to be derived from fixation at various psychosexual levels. It will be clear that these descriptions and theories enable the first two hypotheses to be put to the empirical test – do such constellations of traits in fact occur and, if they do, are they related to child-rearing procedures and psychosexual stages? In the next chapter the objective evidence bearing on the first hypothesis will be considered – the evidence from personality measurement.

3

The objective evidence concerning psychosexual personality syndromes

INTRODUCTION

In this chapter investigations of the first of the hypotheses implicit in Freudian psychosexual theory will be discussed: are constellations of personality traits, as described in psychoanalytic theory, in fact observable? Only those studies *deliberately* aimed at defining these syndromes will be examined. More general studies of personality which incidentally confirm or refute these hypotheses will be reviewed in a later chapter.

THE NATURE OF THE EVIDENCE

Clinical studies of small numbers of individuals are inherently irrelevant to the Freudian hypotheses. By the laws of probability certain traits would be found occurring together in certain individuals. What is required therefore are investigations of large populations such that the magnitude of observed correlations can be reliably estimated. It is also essential that reliable and valid measuring instruments be used. Thus clinical impressions and rating scales in general carry less weight as evidence than personality inventories and, best of all, objective personality tests. Consequently, as befits the problem, the majority of the researches discussed below will be psychometric studies of these personality syndromes. Generally, the review will be arranged chronologically except where a particular investigation bears directly on the problem under discussion and is therefore better discussed out of sequence.

THE GOLDMAN-EISLER STUDIES OF THE ORAL CHARACTER

Goldman-Eisler reported in three papers (1948, 1950 and 1951) an investigation into the oral character. Her first study (1948) sought to establish the existence of two typical oral personality patterns – the oral pessimist and the oral optimist. Her other two papers investigated the aetiology of such characteristics and will be discussed in the chapter devoted to the aetiological hypotheses in Freudian psychosexual theory, although the 1951 paper gives further details of the tests used. The relevant parts of these papers will be discussed together since they represent one investigation.

Brief description of the study

A sample of 115 middle-class adults, age range 18-35, completed rating scales for the 19 traits, mentioned in the psychoanalytic literature under the titles of

13

oral optimist and oral pessimist. Profiles based on the top 20 and bottom 20 subjects closely fitted the psychoanalytic descriptions and a factor analysis of the scores (Burt's simple summation method) revealed a factor of oral pessimism which was similar to the Freudian picture except that it did not load on compulsion, aggression or autonomy. From this Goldman-Eisler concluded that there was a syndrome of oral pessimism but that the psychoanalytic description which emphasises aggression and compulsion should be modified. She suggested tentatively that there were two kinds of oral pessimists: (a) the placid kind, and (b) the impulsive and aggressive kind who would go to psychoanalysts for treatment, whereas the others would not. This speculation would account for the inclusion of aggression and impulsion as oral characteristics.

Comments and conclusions

Although the sample was somewhat homogeneous, this cannot be held to invalidate the results for it would tend to depress not raise the correlations. The rating scales were reliable (mean split-half r was ·56) but the only evidence for their validity was face validity – the items appeared to refer to oral traits. Face validity is not considered to be satisfactory for personality tests (Cattell and Warburton, 1967), especially since in this study there was no check on the major response sets of acquiescence or social desirability which Cronbach (1946, 1950) and Jackson and Messick (1961) regard as an important souce of variance in personality testing.

Another point to be noted is that the factor-analysis was not rotated to simple structure and another more elegant solution, not fitting Freudian theory, might be possible.

In view of these points the claim that there are two oral syndromes of optimism and pessimism must be treated with caution. These results give tentative rather than definitive support for psychoanalytic theory although the profiles based on extreme scorers were strikingly clear. The second part of this study relating oral characteristics to weaning will be reviewed in Chapter 5.

BARNES' (1952) STUDY OF PSYCHOSEXUAL THEORY

Barnes (1952) examined the whole Freudian theory of psychosexual development in a factor-analytic study of questionnaire items. Items apparently pertaining to various levels of psychosexuality were given to a sample of 266 male students, median age 23 years. These subjects had also completed the Guilford-Zimmerman Temperament Survey, the scores from which were used as markers to identify the factors emerging from the tetrachoric intercorrelations of the Freudian scales. Were the Freudian theory correct, oral, anal and phallic factors would be expected to emerge as well as, perhaps, a general genital factor. Since the Guilford factors were not intended to measure any such variables and since there is nothing from their description which suggests any congruence with these Freudian concepts, these factors ought to be independent of the hypothesised Freudian factors. It is of course possible, as Barnes points out, that even more Freudian factors might be predicted, e.g. oral dependent and oral sadistic, anal expulsive and anal retentive, and, if the item writing were sufficiently sensitive, urethral and phallic factors. From the orthogonal rotation of the centroid analysis, however, 11 factors emerged, none of which could be reasonably identified with the predicted psychosexual factors. The first factor Barnes claimed was meticulousness, which might possibly be identified as anal in that all its loadings were on anal tests although not all the anal tests loaded on it. Of the other factors only one, factor 6, independent self-sufficiency, even faintly resembled a Freudian factor, in this case orality, although factor 11, masculine dominance, could possibly be regarded as phallic. The other factors emerging were: externalised aggression, impatient exhibitionism, a factor with loadings on tests at all levels of psychosexual development, puritanical anti-feminism, optimistic self-confidence (identified as very similar to Guilford's I), flexible ascendance, very similar to Guilford's S, mild anti-feminism and liking for routine together with two factors which could not be identified from the pattern of their loadings.

Comments and conclusions

These results cannot be considered to refute the psychoanalytic theory for a number of reasons. The original correlations were tetrachoric. Guilford (1958) has shown that these have a standard error about twice as large as that of product-moment correlations and that they are unduly affected by the evenness of the dichotomy. This means that the reliability of the factor analysis must be in doubt.

As with the previous investigation, there is no evidence for the validity of the scales except face validity and no checks against response sets. Furthermore, the reliability of the scales cannot have been high since they contained either 5 or 10 items and reliability is related to length. Thus this study neither refutes psychoanalytic theory nor supports it.

STUDIES WITH THE KROUT PERSONAL PREFERENCE SCALE (KPPS)

Krout and Krout (1954), Stagner, Lawson and Moffit (1955) and Stagner and Moffit (1956) have conducted studies of Freudian psychosexual personality syndromes, using the KPPS as their instrument of measurement. The test itself has also been investigated by Snider (1959) and Littman, Nidorf and Sundberg (1961) whose findings must be considered in the appraisal of results achieved with these scales.

(a) The KPPS

This scale purports to measure (Krout and Krout, 1954) 10 developmental levels of personality growth – infantile passive, prenatal, oral sucking, oral sadistic, anal retentive, anal expulsive, narcissistic, feminine, masculine, intro-familial sublimation and social sublimation. From this it can be seen that the test goes beyond orthodox Freudian psychosexual theory, although if valid it would still be useful for testing classical psychosexual theory. Each scale contains 10 items to which subjects indicate like or dislike.

Validity

Krout and Krout were not content to rely on face validity for these scales. First they demonstrated that the scales were independent of the Bell Adjustment Inventory (Bell, 1938) as they ought to be from the nature of the variables in both tests. This alone is not sufficient evidence of course since, for example, intelligence would be equally unrelated to the Bell Inventory. In addition small samples of normals and neurotics were compared. Although there were differences on certain scales – e.g. normals were higher on the anal retentive scale – it is difficult to substantiate the validity of the test by this method without knowing the nosological category of the neurotics. Thus, for example, obsessional neurotics would not be hypothesised to be lower on an anal scale, and depressives ought to be more oral than normals. Finally the scores from 14 pairs of twins were examined, together with ratings by observers. Although little more than anecdotal the differences observed do support the validity of the scales. In general these validity studies support the validity of the KPPS and thus the existence of the psychosexual personality syndromes.

Reliability

Split-half reliabilities for such short scales were very high – all between ·89 and ·98. Inter-scale correlations were low showing that the sub-tests were independent and that acquiescence could not be a major factor in the results. There appears to have been no check on the effects of social desirability.

Conclusions

From this paper it is clear that the KPPS is a reliable measure of 10 independent variables. The face validity of the items is good and the validity studies presented, although not definitive, strongly suggest that the scales are valid and thus by implication that the Freudian personality syndromes in fact exist.

(b) Studies using the KPPS

Stagner, Lawson and Moffit (1956) and Stagner and Moffit (1956)

Stagner *et al.* selected the three best items (by item analysis) from each scale of KPPS and then subjected the inter-item correlation to an oblique (Quartimax) factor analysis on a sample of 200 male and 200 female students. Although 10 factors emerged, as would be expected from the low inter-correlations of the scales, the pregenital scales, which are of closest relevance to this chapter, did not form clear factors although the later scales (extensions of psychoanalytic theory) did.

With only three items per factor and with the size of inter-item correlations being dependent on item splits, the rather poor results of this factor analysis are not unexpected. Indeed, that there were 10 factors is in itself encouraging. In fact, in 1956 Stagner and Moffit investigated the problem further.

In this more rigorous study of Freudian psychosexual theory with the KPPS these authors argued that if a type is a functional organised unity, then individuals classified into one type should show greater similarities to one another than to persons classified into other types. To test this hypothesis, three men were chosen on the basis of KPPS scores to represent each of the 10 types. The inter-correlations between all the 30 subjects selected were calculated and an analysis of variance was computed to compare the mean within-type correlation with the mean between-type correlation. If the theory were correct, within-type correlations should be greater than between-type correlations. In fact there were no significant differences. From these results Stagner and Moffit (1956) argued that a typological organisation of personality is not the best way of representing the functional relationships of these particular responses. They cast doubt on the general Freudian psychosexual theory. To the argument that only rare cases exemplify the types and that these are probably neurotics, these authors reply that such rare instances may be only those special combinations of varying trends which must be expected to occur occasionally in any population in accordance with probability theory. Such cases would not justify a 'type' theory of personality organisation. Oral, phallic and anal types are only extremes of a continuum. They conclude by arguing that even if a subject is high on oral erotism this knowledge does not provide a good basis for predicting other personality traits.

Comments

1. The typology suggested by Stagner does not seem implicit in Freudian theory. The anal character may be legitimately regarded, in theory, as the extreme of a continuum – just as is the extravert and introvert as measured by the EPI (Eysenck and Eysenck, 1964). Severe pot training of a person with strong anal erotism produces the full range of anal characteristics. A less severe training produces fewer traits. At the other extreme is the person of weak anal erotism and gentle training. He shows very few anal characteristics.

2. The last point, that knowledge that a person is high on oral erotism provides no basis for predicting other features of his personality is in fact a denial that *syndromes* of traits are derived from fixation at psychosexual phases. Stagner (1956) claims that the behaviour due to fixation is extremely restricted in nature with little generalisation. However, the weakness of the argument is in the data. Since the scales are uncorrelated, individuals chosen to represent one type would not be expected to be more alike than those representing another *on these scales*. What should have been done was to find degrees of similarity on other variables. Then it would be possible to argue about predicting other traits of personality.

Conclusions

It does not appear that the conclusions drawn by Stagner are supported by the data. On the other hand these findings do not support psychosexual theory but are, rather, irrelevant to it. In fact Stagner and Moffit (1956) were not really testing Freudian theory at all – despite their intentions.

The work of Snider (1959) and Littman *et al.* (1961)

As part of a research into marriage Snider gave the KPPS to 152 stable married couples. The men scored more highly than the neurotic group in the manual to the test, and the women were more like neurotics than normals.

Comments on Snider

This throws doubt on the validity of the scales in the test and the adequacy of the normative data reported by Krout and Krout (1954) on which the validity of the test was based.

Littman *et al.* investigated the patterns of norms and the correlations between the KPPS scales on a sample of around 300 Oregon students. They found sex differences on six of the scales and concluded that the unities postulated by Krout and Krout did not exist. Although they used a later revision of the test with a trichotomous response (the earlier studies used a dichotomous response scale), so that the results are not entirely comparable, they concluded that the earlier findings did not apply to the Oregon sample. They considered the test to be invalid rather than the Freudian theory at fault.

Comments on Littman et al.

With a test of this sort it is impossible to tell whether the theory or the test is at fault. If the test results are not in accord with theory the test cannot be valid for this is its only criterion of validity. If however the theory is untrue, a valid test cannot be constructed. Consequently in examining the evidence for psycho-analytic personality theory, it is necessary to consider the results of researches simultaneously rather than each research in isolation. If tests of the syndromes can be constructed in accord with theory, this is good evidence for the validity of the theory. But if large numbers of tests fail to show themselves valid with no technical, psychometric reasons for failure, the theory must be rejected.

Conclusions from the studies with the KPPS

One of the apparent advantages of the KPPS was that Krout and Krout (1954) had offered some evidence for its validity. The work of Snider (1959) and Littman *et al.* (1961) suggests, however, that much of this evidence is of dubious value and that the test is invalid. If this be the case the studies of Stagner are not useful. In any case, it has been shown that Stagner's conclusions (Stagner and Moffit,

1956) are not supported by his data. What may be concluded from these studies, therefore, is that they failed to support Freudian theory probably because the KPPS is not a valid measuring instrument for psychosexual personality levels. The results may certainly not be used to refute the theory.

THE DYNAMIC PERSONALITY INVENTORY (GRYGIER, 1961)

This test was developed from the KPPS which, as has been shown, is not a satisfactory instrument for the measurement of psychosexual personality constellations. The DPI, according to the test manual (Grygier, 1961), purports to measure 'tendencies, sublimations, reaction-formations and defence mechanisms associated with the various patterns of psychosexual development'. If therefore the scales could be shown to be valid, the psychosexual personality syndromes would be shown to exist and the first set of hypotheses in the theory would be supported. As with the KPPS, therefore, this test deserves most careful scrutiny.

Description of the DPI

There are 33 scales in the DPI so that it goes very far beyond orthodox psychosexual theory. This is because Freudian theory was regarded as a stimulus for the construction of this test rather than a rigid framework. Nevertheless, as is to be expected all the classical Freudian psychosexual patterns have scales purporting to measure them – 5 oral scales, 6 anal scales and several relevant to fixation at the phallic level. A descriptive list of the 33 variables is set out below:

H   Hypocrisy: self-satisfaction with own moral standards, lack of insight.
Wp Passivity: liking for comfort, warmth and mild sensual impression.
Ws Seclusion and introspection as a defence against social anxiety.
O   Orality: interest in food; liking for sweet creamy food.
Oa Oral aggression: pleasure in biting and crunching, liking for strong drinks and savoury foods: suggestion of free floating aggression and anxiety about its control.
Od Oral dependence, especially on parents and parental substitutes.
Om Need for freedom of movement and emotional independence; a reaction-formation against oral dependence.
Ov Verbal aggression: verbally and/or intellectually aggressive behaviour.
Oi Impulsiveness, changeability, spontaneity, reactive speed, emotional expressiveness.
Ou Unconventionality of outlook.
Ah Hoarding behaviour: anxious possessiveness, stubborn, clinging persistence.
Ad Attention to details: orderliness, conscientiousness and perfectionism.

Ac Conservatism, rigidity and tendency to stick to routine.
Aa Submissiveness to authority and order.
As Anal sadism: emphasis on strong authority, cruel laws and discipline.
Ai Insularity: reserve and mistrust, social and racial prejudice.

These 'A' scales from their description appear to be the anal scales of the DPI. Only the last of these, *Ai*, does not seem relevant to the psychoanalytic picture.

P   Interest in objects of phallic symbol significance.
Pn Narcissism: concern with clothes and appearance: sensuous enjoyment of luxury.
Pe Exhibitionism: conscious enjoyment of attention and admiration.
Pa Active Icarus complex: psycho-physical drive, drive for achievement.
Ph Fascination by height, space and distance: aspirations at the fantasy level.
Pf Fascination by fire, winds, storms and explosions: vivid imagination.
Pi Icarian exploits: interest in active exploration, a love of adventure.
S   Sexuality: conscious acceptance of sexual impulses.
Ti Enjoyment of tactile impressions, interest in handicrafts and creative manipulation of objects.
Ci Creative, intellectual and artistic interests.
M   Masculine sexual identification, masculine interests, attitudes and roles.
                                    or
F   Feminine sexual identification, feminine interests, attitudes and roles.
MF Tendency to seek roles regardless of their sexual identification.
Sa Interest in social activities.
C   Interest in children, need to give affection.
EP Ego-defensive persistence: tendency to act with renewed effort in the face of difficulties.
Ei Initiative, self-reliance and a tendency to plan, manage and organise.

Evidence for the validity of the DPI

Grygier claims in the manual to the test that concurrent validity has been assessed by 'correlating both test profiles and individual scale scores with several hundred independent measures such as cognitive and personality tests, experimental procedures, inventories, psychiatric assessments, rating scales and Q sorts.'! Since the average internal split-half reliability of the scales is ·75 and test-retest reliability is ·80, we are forced to agree with Sells (1965) that, were these claims true, the DPI would be the most outstanding test of personality (of any sort) ever devised. Unfortunately, Grygier gives no details either of these correlations, the names of the tests used or even any references to published results.

Most of the studies published with this test, e.g. the study of student nurses by Grygier (1956) or the study of insularity by Grygier (1957), simply assume the scales to be valid and thus throw no light on their validity. This also applies to the study of homosexuals with this scale by Grygier (1957a, 1958). In an effort to remedy this lack of evidence Kline (1968a) investigated the validity of the Dynamic Personality Inventory.

Kline's study of the DPI

Kline (1968a) subjected the scores on the DPI of students at two colleges of education to a Varimax orthogonal rotation of a principal components analysis. The rationale for this validity study was simple. Since the construction of 33 scales is an extension of psychoanalytic theory, for those scales which have no obvious theoretical basis there ought to be strong statistical justification in terms of clear factorial pattern. For the scales relevant to psychosexual theory factor loadings may be predicted, e.g. an oral factor with loadings on the oral scales, an anal factor and a phallic factor with loadings on phallic interest, Icarus complex, fascination by heights, fascination by fire, liking for adventure and narcissism (see the description of the phallic character in Fenichel, 1945).

Results

Eleven factors emerged from the Varimax analysis. However, only the first was in accordance with psychosexual theory – it was clearly an anal or a super-ego factor. The second factor appeared to be masculine interests and was perhaps interpretable in Freudian terms as a phallic factor. The third was feminine interests but was not in accord with the psychoanalytic theory. None of the other factors was interpretable in terms of psychosexual theory. Indeed 3 factors could not be meaningfully named in relation to the scales loading on them. It was concluded from these results that the construct validity of the DPI was not high. Only the anal scales *could* be valid in that they were measuring a common factor. The difficulty of naming the factors, even in non-Freudian terms, suggests that the scales are not valid.

Comments and conclusions

The sample size, 70, was perhaps smaller than desirable for a factor-analytic study. Nevertheless it is clear that the scales do not fit their underlying theory or have any strong statistical justification. It must be noted that in a study of this sort congruence of factors to hypothesis is only evidence that the scales *could* be valid (the factors would have to be further identified). Failure to conform to prediction, however, is evidence of invalidity. From this study it must be concluded that, without strong supporting evidence, the validity of these DPI scales, other than the anal ones, cannot be taken on trust. The anal scales could be valid (thus providing evidence for the anal character). Later in this chapter some evidence concerning their validity will be presented.

FURTHER STUDIES OF THE ORAL AND ANAL CHARACTER

Studies of the anal character by Farber (1955) and Rabinowitz (1957)

Farber and Rabinowitz published two papers on the anal character which, owing to methodological imperfections, will receive the briefest description. Farber examined the relationship between anal characteristics and political aggression in a sample of 130 students; he found a positive significant relationship between the variables of ·37. Such a finding of course implies the existence of the anal syndrome.

Comments

His scale to measure the anal character consisted of five items all keyed 'Yes'. The only evidence for their validity other than item content was the fact that each item correlated with the total score. This of course indicates only that the scale was measuring a common factor, not what that factor was. Furthermore, two of the items referred to professors, e.g. 'I get terribly annoyed with the professor who . . .'. No evidence was presented concerning the reliability of this scale. The political aggression scale was equally short and again keyed 'Yes'. Rabinowitz (1957) argued that the scales probably measured acquiescence rather than anal characteristics – hence the positive correlation. He therefore wrote 5 anal items keyed 'No' and 5 political aggression items keyed 'No'. The new 10-item scales failed to correlate significantly. However when they were scored for acquiescence the correlation again became significant – ·27. From this Rabinowitz concluded that the anal scale was a measure of acquiescence. Farber (1958) attempted to answer the criticism by criticising the anal items of Rabinowitz in terms of content. Certainly item 2 of the new scale (concerned with sleeping habits) did not seem particularly relevant to the anal triad. Indeed Rabinowitz stated that his concept of anality was taken from the summary of Farber's (1955) original paper!

Conclusions

It seems highly unlikely, both in terms of item content and test length, that either of these two anal scales was valid. Certainly no evidence for validity was presented. These findings are probably best ignored as they clearly cannot be regarded as sound evidence for the existence of an anal syndrome.

The Beloff study (1957)

Beloff investigated the structure and origin of the anal character in a study which therefore dealt with two of the hypotheses implicit in psychosexual theory. In this chapter only the first part of the investigation – concerned with the syndrome of anal characteristics – will be considered.

Summary

Questionnaire items were constructed from a search of the psychoanalytic descriptions of the anal character and administered to a sample of just over 100 students. The item inter-correlations were factor-analysed and a general factor appeared – considered by Beloff to be an anal factor. From the emergence of this factor it was argued that anality was a meaningful dimension of personality. An examination of the factor loadings of the individual items persuaded Beloff that the emphasis given in the literature to certain traits, notably cleanliness and parsimony, was perhaps wrong – they had small loadings on the general factor. Two attempts were made to demonstrate the validity of the scale. First, self-report responses were correlated with ratings by peers. In this way an estimate of how self-reports corresponded to observed behaviour was obtained. The correlation was satisfactory (·48). Furthermore, scores on the anal test were correlated with the Guilford personality factors. Here the results were inconclusive. There was a small but significant correlation with T (thinking introversion) of ·34, which fits the hypothesis that the anal character is due to over-learning, which itself is typical of introverts (Eysenck, 1953b). However, contrary to hypothesis, there was no correlation with S (social introversion) or R (freedom from care). From this first part of her paper Beloff concluded that the anal character does exist – the first hypothesis was supported.

Comments and conclusions

Of the studies so far reviewed this one offers by far the best evidence for the psychoanalytic theory so that it deserves careful examination. There are a number of points that must be made.

The emergence of a general factor among the items is not *ipso facto* evidence for the anal character. It is still necessary to demonstrate what this general factor is. The content of the items, i.e. the face validity, suggests that it is the anal character, and the fact that the scale fails to correlate with the Guilford scales is further indirect support for its validity. Furthermore, the correlation between self and peer ratings indicates that the test reflects observed behaviour and this eliminates the possible influence of response sets. Nevertheless the only positive evidence for the validity of the scale lies in its item content.

As with the study by Barnes (1952), the correlations were tetrachoric. As was pointed out in the discussion of that study, these are not reliable and if they are to be factored Guilford (1958) suggests that a sample size of 300 or more is desirable. Beloff's small sample size would not have been a serious defect if she had not *compared* item loadings on her general factor and then attempted to argue from their values that the emphasis in the literature was wrong. This interpretation is far too precise bearing in mind the unreliability of these factor loadings which only accounted, anyway, for 43% of the variance.

However, despite these statistical caveats which limit the possible interpretations and the lack of clear evidence of validity, this study by Beloff may be regarded as sound evidence for the anal character.

B

The Gottheil studies

Gottheil (1965b) conducted an empirical study of oral and anal characteristics on a group of 200 soldiers. Personality questionnaire items were written from a study of the psychoanalytic literature and subjected to item analysis. Item analysis revealed that items tended to form a scale in the hypothesised manner. The correlation between the two scales was − ·22. From this it was concluded that oral and anal syndromes did in fact occur.

The validity of the scales

To a certain extent the validity of these scales had been endorsed in a previous study by the author (Gottheil, 1965a). Fifteen psychiatrists and 5 psychologists had been asked to predict the responses of oral and anal characters to these questionnaires. There was good agreement in both cases, especially so for the anal character. This study at least demonstrated beyond reasonable doubt that the item content of the scales was relevant to the syndromes concerned.

Comments and conclusions

Apart from this demonstration of face validity and homogeneity (item analysis) there was no further attempt to demonstrate the validity of these scales. Without this the identification of common factors as oral and anal must remain doubtful.

Although these studies appear to support Freudian theory, before the results can be accepted more convincing evidence for the validity of the scales must be forthcoming.

The work of Lazare, Klerman and Armor

Lazare, Klerman and Armor (1966) carried out a factor-analytic study of the oral, obsessive and hysterical personality patterns. In this study a 200 item, 20 trait, personality questionnaire was constructed. The oral items were mostly the same as those used by Goldman-Eisler (1948, 1950 and 1951). The oral character was measured by 7 traits – pessimism, passivity, oral aggression, rejection of others, aggression dependence and parsimony. The obsessive character was measured by orderliness, obstinacy, parsimony, rejection of others, emotional constriction, self-doubt, severe super-ego, rigidity and perseverance. This description makes it clear that the obsessive character as defined here is identical with that of the anal character. In a later chapter in this book, concerned with the bearing of more general personality studies on Freudian psychosexual theory, the similarity between these two concepts will be examined. A major source of information on this point is the paper by Delay, Pichot and Perse (1962). The hysterical character is not relevant to the theory and will not be discussed here. These tests were then given to 90 female neurotic patients and the results were subjected to an orthogonal Varimax rotated factor analysis.

Results

Three clear factors emerged. Factor 1 was identified as hysterical. Factor 3 was identified as anal and was very clear with loadings on orderliness (·74), severe super-ego (·62) and perseverance and obstinacy (·54). The second factor was more tentatively labelled oral, but did not so closely fit the psychoanalytic picture with loadings of dependence (·66), pessimism (·65) and passivity (·61). Parsimony and aggression failed to load on this factor. Nevertheless it was concluded that oral and anal syndromes did occur in accordance with psychoanalytic theory.

Comments and conclusions

Although the sample was somewhat restricted, being female neurotics, this factor analysis is good support for the oral and anal syndromes although it is plain that the oral constellation is not clear cut. The evidence of three factors rather rules out response sets as accounting for the results since these would have tended to produce a general factor. Although there are no external studies of validity relating these scales to other tests, the fact that the scales load on factors, as expected, is good evidence for their validity – a different matter from illustrating that items in one scale load on *one* common factor – which fails to show what that factor is. It is noteworthy that these authors claim that their results are similar to those of Goldman-Eisler (1948, 1950 and 1951). This, however, is hardly surprising since they used the same items.

To what extent this study may be generalised to a normal population is not clear.

The work of Kline on the anal character

Kline (e.g. 1967, 1968b, 1969) has made several studies of the anal character using a 30 item personality test, Ai3, as a measure of anal characteristics. The paper relevant to this chapter is Kline (1969) where the evidence for the validity of the scale is summarised This paper claims to demonstrate the existence of an anal syndrome within a normal population.

The validity of Ai3 as a measure of the anal character

(a) *Construction of Ai3.* As with many of the scales discussed in this chapter the items for Ai3 were written from a search of the psychoanalytic descriptions of the anal character. Items were submitted to item analysis and to checks for acquiescence (the percentage of anal responses keyed 'Yes' endorsed by subjects was compared with the percentage keyed 'No': clearly these ought to be the same). Social desirability was checked upon by examining the proportions of the sample responding 'Yes' to each item. An item with an even split can hardly be said to be socially desirable. In the light of these three checks items were rewritten and again submitted to item analysis. The 30 best items were selected covering the whole range of the anal triad in respect of content. These items were then submitted to further item analyses on different samples. The majority of items had a correlation with the total scale beyond ·4.

(*b*) *Reliability of Ai3*. In three separate studies the internal consistency of Ai3 was ·67.

(*c*) *Discriminatory power*. The discriminatory power of the test was very high – Ferguson Delta ·97 (Ferguson, 1949).

At this point the study reported in Kline (1969) diverged from those previously reviewed in this chapter in that attempts were made to validate the scale. Face validity and homogeneity of items were not regarded as proof of validity. Three factor analytic construct validity studies were carried out and one concurrent validity study was made.

Construct validity study 1

A Varimax rotation of Ai3 with the Cattell 16 PF test and Eysenck's EPI was computed on a sample of Ghanaian students. This study strongly supported the validity of Ai3 in that it was independent of all the personality scales in terms of correlation yet loaded on the Cattell second-order super-ego factor. This factor may be better identified as one of defence mechanisms since id-pressure (Q4) has a negative loading on it. This result is in accord with psychoanalytic theory of defence mechanisms against anal erotism repressed into the id.

Construct validity study 2

A Varimax rotation of Ai3 with the MMPI and the Beloff (1957) and Hazari (1957) scales was computed on a further sample of students. Again the validity of Ai3 was supported. It did not correlate with any of the MMPI scales but had positive correlations with the Beloff measure of the anal character and the Hazari scale of obsessional traits. In addition it did not load on the first general factor of emotionality, which runs through the MMPI scales, but loaded on the second factor identified as obsessional traits. This analysis, therefore, supported the symptom-trait dichotomy in obsessional disorder (Foulds, 1965; Sandler and Hazari, 1960).

Construct validity study 3

Ai3 was given together with the DPI to a sample of students. The results were subjected to a Varimax rotation. Here the validity of Ai3 was again supported since a clear anal or super-ego factor emerged (see Kline, 1968a) on which Ai3 and the DPI anal scales loaded. However Ai3 appeared superior to the anal scales of the DPI in that it was more factor-pure.

Concurrent validity study

Ai3 was given to a sample of students who were rated by their tutors for anal characteristics. An analysis of variance of the scores on Ai3 of those rated high and those rated low was significant at the ·01 level. This fourth study was regarded as important, despite the crudity of the five point rating scale, because it indicated that responses to Ai3 were related to observed behaviour.

From these studies Kline (1969) concluded that Ai3 was a valid measure of the anal character and that the anal character was a meaningful dimension of personality within a normal population.

Comments and conclusions

Construct validity is regarded by the main authors of the concept (Cronbach and Meehl, 1955) as the establishment of a nomothetic network round the variables concerned. Of course it is just this which it is very difficult to do with any precision in the case of psychoanalytic constructs. Nevertheless what is impressive about Ai3 is the way in which it correlates with other similar variables yet remains independent of the scales in the most widely used personality questionnaires – the MMPI and the Cattell 16 PF test. It could be objected in the first study of the construct validity that perhaps none of the tests was valid in this Ghanaian population. However the validity of all these tests has been demonstrated with this population in Kline (1966, 1969).

It must be concluded from these earlier studies that Ai3 is a valid measure of the anal character. This of course inevitably implies that the anal character exists within a normal and indeed a Ghanaian population.

The work of Stringer

Stringer (1970) subjected Kline's factor analysis of the Dynamic Personality Inventory to an oblique factor analysis followed by the extraction of second-order factors. However, the eleven oblique factors emerging from this study were still not a close fit to psychoanalytic psychosexual theory. Stringer described the four second-order factors as being consistent with the theory. He identified a factor of masculine identification ('despite the intrusions of elements of orality'), a bipolar oral-anal factor, feminine identification and a phallic factor (with unexpected loadings on anal scales). It seems to us that this second-order analysis of the Dynamic Personality Inventory is still a long way short of confirming psychosexual theory. We should expect oral, anal and phallic factors as was hypothesised by Barnes (1952) in his early study.

Stringer argues that one of the difficulties in the original study by Kline (1968b) was the small size of his sample. He therefore subjected to another oblique rotation the scores on the DPI of 357 male students. Eleven factors were again extracted. Again Stringer claims that these results support psychosexual theory: three bipolar oral-anal factors, an anal singlet, three phallic factors, two factors of feminine identification, a post-genital social sublimation factor and a prenatal early oral factor. Reference to our outline of psychosexual theory must make it clear that these results cannot be regarded as confirmatory. Two oral factors, erotism and sadism, two anal factors, expulsive and retentive, can be predicted from the theory. There seems to be no room for three. Nor is the bi-polarity of orality and anality expected since, as Abraham (1921) points out, oral and anal fixations are often related. To argue that this factor analysis supports psychosexual theory is to make that theory so vague as to be entirely worthless.

Comments and conclusions

We conclude from this study by Stringer (1970), which certainly overcomes the technical shortcomings of the study by Kline (1968b), that the Dynamic Personality Inventory is not a valid measure of Freudian psychosexual theory. Its scales are not related in accordance with prediction. Whether this be due to the invalidity of the scales or the theory cannot be settled from studies of this type. Stringer thus supports the previous findings by Kline.

CONCLUSIONS FROM ALL THE STUDIES

As must now be clear, the methodology of many of these studies is flawed. It seems that the investigators of this problem view their results with hope rather than precision. Indeed the flaws may be easily summarised:

1. There has been far too much reliance on item content, i.e. face validity. Barnes (1952) and Krout and Krout (1954) are examples of this.

2. There has been little effort made to overcome the problems of response sets. Edwards (1957) has shown in detail the influence of social desirability and acquiescence has been recognised as a source of error since Cronbach (1946). Beloff (1957) and Grygier (1961), as well as the two authors already cited, exemplify this fault.

3. Related to this there has been correspondingly little attempt to demonstrate the validity of the scales used.

4. The fourth error is the assumption that the demonstration of a common factor accounting for item variance, either by factor analysis or item analysis, is evidence of validity. As has been pointed out it is not: the factor must still be identified.

Nevertheless, when all these studies are considered together, despite their collective shortcomings the weight of the evidence enables certain conclusions to be drawn.

(a) There does appear to be an anal character

A syndrome of traits similar to that described by psychoanalysis is discernible in normal and abnormal populations. Beloff (1957), Grygier (1961) and Kline (1969) have produced measures of this with significant positive correlations between each other. Kline's scale, Ai3, has also been shown to have construct validity. In an abnormal population the study of Lazare *et al.* (1966) lends support to this syndrome. Lesser support comes from the work of Gottheil (1965) and from Barnes (1952) – the meticulousness factor.

(*b*) The oral character, although less well vindicated, has reasonable support

Goldman-Eisler (1948, 1950, 1951) in a normal population, and Lazare *et al.* (1966) with an abnormal sample, used a scale which they identified as oral. Goldman-Eisler found extreme scorers closely resembled the psychoanalytic picture of the oral optimist and the oral pessimist. The factorisation of the scale by Lazare was not so clear-cut. On the other hand Barnes (1952), Krout and Krout (1954) and Grygier (1961) have produced little firm evidence for the oral character. The Gottheil (1965) scale was at least homogeneous, although only face valid.

(*c*) There is no evidence in favour of other psychosexual personality syndromes

The complex scales of Barnes (1952), Krout and Krout (1954) and Grygier (1961) have entirely failed to support the psychoanalytic hypotheses.

LIMITS OF THE CHAPTER

(*a*) Theoretical

It must be stressed that this chapter is concerned only with the evidence for the existence of the hypothesised psychosexual personality syndromes. It is not concerned with their relationship to psychosexual phases of childhood and child-rearing procedures, which was the second of the hypotheses implicit in Freudian psychosexual theory. Thus in the conclusions above the claim that there is an anal character refers only to the existence of the syndrome. The term anal is used because it is the Freudian term not because it is implied that the syndrome is related to or stems from anal erotism.

(*b*) Empirical

Furthermore, the evidence from more general personality studies must be reviewed – evidence which incidentally confirms or refutes these hypotheses.

SUMMARY

1. This chapter has reviewed those studies aimed at verifying the first set of hypotheses implicit in psychosexual theory, namely that certain personality patterns are observable in adults.

2. The relevant studies have been summarised and discussed in the light of Freudian theory and experimental procedures.

3. It was concluded that there is firm evidence for the anal character and moderate support for the oral character. The other syndromes were not supported.

Tabular summary of results

Syndrome	Result	Studies
The anal character	Strong support	Beloff (1957)
		Grygier (1961)
		Kline (1969)
		Lazare *et al.* (1966)
The oral character	Support	Goldman-Eisler (1948, 1950, 1951)
		Lazare *et al.* (1966)
Other syndromes	No support	Barnes (1952)
		Krout and Krout (1954)
		Grygier (1961)

4

Psychometric studies of personality

THE WORK OF CATTELL

Cattell (1957) makes the grandiose claim that the 16 factors of his 16 PF test account for the major part of the variance of personality. If such a claim were true it would not be unreasonable to expect his test to measure psychosexual personality syndromes, if such exist.

THE BASIC DATA OF CATTELL'S WORK

There are three sources of data for the factorial studies of Cattell:

(a) *L data:* These are based on correlations of ratings made by trained observers of subjects in life situations. These correlations have then been subjected to factor analysis.

(b) *Q data:* These are based on the factorisation of responses to personality questionnaires designed, as far as possible, to tap the traits and factors found in L data.

(c) *T data:* These derive from the factor analysis of objective test devices. Although at an early stage of development and beset by the low reliability of the tests in their present form, Cattell regards these data as potentially the best in personality assessment. This is because they are free from distortion both deliberate and accidental, such as that caused by response sets.

Nevertheless, since the compendium of objective test devices (Cattell and Warburton, 1967) clearly indicates that as yet most of the factors emerging from T data cannot be clearly identified, despite their advantages, much of the discussion in this section must centre on the more clearly defined and closely studied L and Q factors. As will be seen these two sets of factors are well matched.

Description of factors

1. *T Factors*

Since, as has been stated, these factors based on the scores from objective tests have not been clearly identified, only those factors which appear relevant to the psychosexual syndromes will be discussed. The descriptions are to be found in Cattell and Warburton (1967).

UI19. Independence *v.* subduedness. This is characterised by conscientiousness, exacting criticalness, reliability, restraint, control, concern for accuracy and standards, independence and refusal to make errors. The high UI19 person is better with machines and ideas than people, is perfectionist and does not relax easily.

Descriptively, there is a considerable resemblance in this factor to the anal character. Indeed if parsimony were present, the identification would be complete. Since, as yet, none of the 800 objective tests contain such a measure this lack is easily explicable. As it stands, however, this factor supports the Freudian claim for an anal character.

UI33. Reactive dismay (pessimism) *v.* sanguine poise. The person high on UI33 is pessimistic, believes that most events will affect him unfavourably, is slow in warming to new tasks, is inhibited, compulsive but tends to have good intellectual achievement.

Although not as obvious as UI19, the resemblance to oral pessimism, the claimed result of frustration at the oral level, is clear. Particularly interesting, in view of the claims of Fenichel (1945) that anal and oral influences are linked, is the presence of certain anal components, e.g. compulsion. This factor may be regarded with great caution, as tenuous support for an oral syndrome.

None of the other T factors appears relevant to psychosexual syndromes.

Conclusions. Despite the difficulties with T factors mainly because they are not vet fully developed, UI19 and UI33 do offer some support for the existence of oral and anal syndromes.

2. *Q Factors (in the 16PF test)*

A Cyclothymia *v.* schizothymia: warm-hearted, easy-going, impulsive contrasted with obstructive, cool, cautious.

B Intelligence: (as it affects personality).

C Ego strength *v.* proneness to neuroticism: stable and calm contrasted with emotional and excitable.

E Dominance *v.* submissiveness: confident, boastful, aggressive contrasted with submissive, modest, complaisant.

F Surgency *v.* desurgency: cheerful, sociable, energetic contrasted with depressed, subdued.

G Super-ego strength: persevering, conscientious, stable, contrasted with fickle, unscrupulous, unstable. There can be little doubt that in this factor, descriptively as well as theoretically, there are elements, at least, of the obsessional personality.

H Parmia *v.* threctia: adventurous, gregarious, frank contrasted with shy, aloof, secretive.

I Premsia *v.* harria: impatient, kindly, sensitive contrasted with mature, hard, practical.

L Paranoid trends *v.* inner relaxation: suspicious, jealous, withdrawn contrasted with trustful, understanding, composed.

M Autia *v.* praxernia: unconventional, intellectual, imaginative, contrasted with conventional, narrower interests, practical.
N Shrewdness *v.* naïvety: polished, cool, insightful, regarding self and others contrasted with awkward, company seeking, lacking insight.
O Guilt-proneness *v.* confidence: worrying, suspicious, discouraged contrasted with self-confident, accepting, spirited.

These 12 factors in the 16 PF test have also been found in life data. Four other factors however have been identified in the questionnaire realm only:

Q1 Radicalism *v.* conservatism
Q2 Self-sufficiency
Q3 Will control *v.* slothful lack of dependability
Q4 Id demand or conflict pressure.

It is clear from the description of each of these factors that none of them is measuring any of the psychosexual personality syndromes. Nevertheless Q2, F and E could well be related to orality and G, Q3 and Q4 might be related to the anal character. In brief, as it stands the 16 PF does not appear to provide a measure of the psychosexual syndromes but it is possible that measures might be developed from it if clear criterion groups were available.

Cattell second-order factors. Because these primary factors are themselves inter-correlated it is possible to factor the correlations and obtain second-order factors from them. The main second-order factors are:

Anxiety. This factor is concerned with anxiety in the generally accepted sense – worry over problems and difficulties, feelings of guilt and tenseness.
Extraversion. A high score indicates an outgoing, uninhibited person, a good mixer. The introvert on the other hand is shy and self-contained.
These first two are much the most important second-order factors.
Radicalism. The high scorer is aggressive, independent, self-directing.
Tendermindedness. Sensitivity, liability to frustration and emotionally controlled conduct.
Super-ego. This second-order factor loads alone on factor G which has already been described. This factor is implicated in the anal syndrome.

It is clear that only the second-order factor G is at all related to any of the psychosexual syndromes. The relationship of G, as has already been discussed, is not sufficient to allow that it be used as a measure of and evidence for the anal character. These second-order factors, therefore, may not be regarded as evidence for the existence of psychosexual personality syndromes.

3. *L Factors (not also in the 16PF test)*
D Excitability *v.* insecurity (not found in all studies).
J Vigour, activity *v.* slowness in action, control. (This factor J appears in the

children's versions of the 16 PF test.) Cattell (1957) claims that it is heavily implicated in the anal character.

K Conformity to *v.* rejection of cultural standards.

Factor J is clearly of great interest since Cattell claims that it is implicated in the anal character. The first point to notice is that if he were correct then his own adult personality test, the 16 PF test, is unable to measure the anal character since it has no factor J in it. This is because, so far, items have not been found which load in the required manner. Further and perhaps more important is the fact that Cattell recognises the existence of the syndrome. Indeed he goes on to argue that 'the anal erotic pattern is a syndrome of two or more factors (maybe J, A and G ...' (1957, p. 138). This 'maybe' indicates, of course, that as yet Cattell is unable to measure it. Since this is the case the question must arise as to the grounds for Cattell's belief that the anal character exists. After all the whole basis of Cattell's enormous output has been the faith that measurement is essential to a scientific psychology. This question involves two points:

(*a*) the nature of these Cattellian factors,
(*b*) the nature of the original data on which they were based.

The factors as source traits

The factors which have been described are regarded by Cattell as source traits. These source traits are defined as structures responsible for a pattern of behaviour appearing as a factor. This is in contrast to surface traits which may not be due to single sources of variance. Surface traits consist of syndromes of trait elements of descriptive value, as in psychiatric syndromes, for example, but accountable in terms of factors. According to Cattell, surface traits are not as useful for personality measurement as source traits because they are very numerous and not clearly separated. It is to be noted, however, that if, as is the case with the anal character, source traits cannot adequately measure surface traits or syndromes, they cannot be regarded as substitutes for them as regards measurement.

The nature of the original data: surface traits

The original data from which all factors – source traits – and surface traits were derived, were ratings for trait elements in normal populations. These trait elements were themselves defined after searching the dictionary for words describing behaviour and after synonyms had been eliminated. The fact that all these terms were in the analysis thus enables Cattell to claim that his 16 factors, which account for the variance among these ratings, account for the major variance of personality. This is also the reason that Cattell (1946, 1957) can state categorically that there are 50 surface traits that may be reliably defined. Cluster analysis of the correlations between these ratings for trait elements defined 50 surface traits or syndromes among them. To form a surface trait, the elements must correlate at least ·4 with each other. It is these surface traits that the 16 factors underlie. Therefore, since it has been shown that the factors do not, in all cases, adequately measure the surface traits, it is necessary to examine these empirically defined surface traits to see to what extent any of them correspond to the hypothesised Freudian psychosexual syndromes.

Surface traits

Of the 50 surface traits defined in normal populations the following appear relevant to psychosexual syndromes:

AA2 Conscientious effort *v.* quitting, incoherence. This embraces nuclear traits, persevering, pedantic, painstaking, conscientious, thoughtful.

AB4 Infantile, demanding *v.* emotional maturity, frustration tolerance.

CB3 Lack of restraint, adventurousness *v.* general inhibition, fearfulness. This includes the traits bold, enterprising, assertive, sociable, incontinent.

D2   Sociability, sentimentalism, warmth *v.* independence, hostility, aloofness. This includes the traits responsive, affectionate, sentimental, social interests, family interests, dependent, friendly, frank, genial, tough.

D5   Cheerful, enthusiastic, witty *v.* coldhearted, sour, mirthless. This embraces the traits, cheerful, enthusiastic, optimistic, laughterful, witty.

F1   Gratefulness, geniality *v.* hardness, vindictiveness, coldheartedness.

F2   Gratefulness, kindness *v.* hostility, cynicism. This includes the traits grateful, idealistic, self-denying, friendly.

F3   Friendliness, generosity, co-operativeness *v.* hostility, meanness, obstructiveness.

H1   Thrift, tidiness, obstinacy *v.* lability, curiosity, intuition. The following descriptions are included – habit-bound, thrifty, logical, pedantic.

These are the surface traits which appear to be relevant to the psychosexual syndromes. AA2 and H1 are clearly implicated in the anal character. Cattell indeed identifies H1 as the anal erotic complex. The oral character would appear to be caught by the surface traits AB4, D2, F1, 2 and 3. The surface trait CB3 resembles the phallic character. It is encouraging for Freudian theory that these surface traits based on the intercorrelation of ratings should thus appear. As with the studies reported in the previous chapter, the clearest syndrome is that of the anal character.

CONCLUSIONS FROM THE WORK OF CATTELL

T factor source traits, UI19 and UI33, offer some evidence for the existence of oral and anal syndromes. Factors F, E and Q2, from questionnaire data, could well be implicated in the oral character and from this same realm factors G, Q3 and Q4 may be related to the anal character. Factor H, adventurousness, is related to the phallic character. As regards L factors, J is claimed by Cattell to be relevant to the anal character. However, it is clear from this that none of the source traits is able on its own to provide a measure of and thus evidence for psychosexual syndromes. Surface traits, on the other hand, representing observable syndromes, are more likely to provide such evidence and in fact the anal character is clearly supported by H1 and AA2 while there is less clear support for the oral character (AB4, D5 and F1, 2, 3) and the phallic syndrome (CB3).

THE WORK OF EYSENCK

As is the case with Cattell, Eysenck considers that the whole sphere of personality may be factorially defined. From a review of all the relevant literature Eysenck (1964) concludes that two factors are sufficient to do this – extraversion-introversion and neuroticism. The uniqueness of an individual's personality is therefore determined by his position on these two factors. The test devised for this purpose, measuring both these variables, is the EPI (Eysenck and Eysenck, 1964), a development of the previous MPI. There can be little doubt that these two factors are essentially similar to the two major second-order factors of Cattell. Indeed Adcock (1965) points out that the main difference between the results of Cattell with 16 primary factors and second-order factors dependent on these, and the results of Eysenck where two major factors are taken out, is that the 16 factors, not unnaturally, account for more variance than two. In fact Kline (1967) found a substantial positive correlation between these two tests – the 16 PF test and the EPI.

Since it has already been shown that the Cattell second-order factors of anxiety and extraversion have little relevance to Freudian psychosexual syndromes, it is inevitable also that the two factors of Eysenck will not be relevant. A short description of each, taken from the manual (Eysenck and Eysenck, 1964) to the EPI will demonstrate this point.

Extraversion. The typical high scorer is sociable, gay, expressive and fond of excitement whereas the introvert is quiet, retiring, calm, controlled and a lover of books rather than people.

Neuroticism. This is defined in terms of worry, anxiety, instability and moodiness.

There can be little doubt that these variables are not to be identified with psychosexual syndromes.

THE MMPI

Unlike the personality inventories previously discussed in this chapter, which were developed by factor analysis, the MMPI was developed by criterion keying. Items were selected for scales because they were able to discriminate criterion groups from a control group of normals. The criterion groups consisted of patients classified by psychiatrists into the well-known Kraepelinian categories. If, therefore, oral, anal, and phallic characteristics formed important syndromes of personality, the MMPI scales might be expected to cover these, especially since these Freudian categories were originally discovered in clinical patients.

The nine MMPI standard clinical scales are set out below so that it is possible to see to what extent these variables are related to the Freudian psychosexual syndromes. The scales are:

Hs The hypochondriasis scale is a measure of the amount of abnormal concern over bodily function.

D The depression scale measures the depth of the clinically recognised symptom complex, depression.

Hy The hysteria scale measures the degree of resemblance to patients who have developed conversion symptoms.

Pd The psychopathic deviate scale measures the similarity of the subject to a group of persons whose main difficulty lies in their absence of deep emotional response, their inability to profit from experience and their disregard for social mores.

Mf The masculinity scale measures the tendency towards masculinity or femininity of interest pattern.

Pa The paranoia scale measures the paranoid (suspicious, brooding, with delusional persecutory feelings) tendencies in the subjects.

Pt The psychasthenia scale measures the similarity of the subject to psychiatric patients who are troubled by phobias or compulsions – the obsessional neurotics.

Sc The schizophrenia scale measures the similarity of the subject to those diagnosed as schizophrenic.

Ma the hypomania scale measures the personality factor characteristic of persons with marked overproductivity of thought and action.

In addition there is the Si, social introversion, scale, which measures the tendency to withdraw from others and is thus similar to the Eysenckian introversion variable.

Even this brief description of the standard clinical scales of the MMPI is sufficient to indicate that they do not directly measure under another name any of the Freudian psychosexual syndromes. Nevertheless it is possible that the D depression scale is related to the oral pessimism syndrome. Although the Pt scale, psychasthenia, is frequently referred to as an obsessional symptom scale, this does not imply that it is a measure of the anal or obsessional character. Apart from the fact that Ai3 – a measure of the anal character (Kline, 1969) – was shown to be independent of the Pt scale, there is a distinction drawn between obsessional symptoms and obsessional traits. Foulds (1965) and Sandler and Hazari (1960) make this point explicit: traits are ego-syntonic, often a source of pride to the subject and relatively enduring. Symptoms, on the other hand, are egodystonic, a source of misery to the subject and his relatives and friends, and are frequently transient. From this it is clear that none of the standard MMPI scales could be used as a measure of psychosexual level and thus they do not support the existence of the syndromes.

OTHER MMPI SCALES

Hathaway and McKinley (1951) are careful to point out that in addition to the standard clinical scales many other scales may be empirically derived from the MMPI. Indeed the MMPI may be regarded as an item pool. In fact over 200 scales may have been constructed from the MMPI items (Dahlstrom and Welsh, 1960). The majority of these are not relevant to psychosexual syndromes so that it would be pointless to even list their names. Those that are relevant however will be discussed in that section where further investigations with other tests are reviewed.

THE GUILFORD SCALES

The main objective of the Guilford inventories is to provide scores for separate factors of personality. In most cases items designed to indicate various well-known dimensions of personality, for example introversion-extraversion, were subjected to factor analysis on the hypothesis that such dimensions really represented more than one primary trait or factor of personality (Guilford, 1959).

First, three separate personality inventories appeared, identified by the factors they measured:

(a) Inventory of Factors   STDCR
(b) Inventory of Factors   GAMIN
(c) Personnel Inventory.

However, since some of these original factors were themselves highly correlated and since it was clearly desirable to produce one inventory rather than three, the Guilford-Zimmerman Temperament Survey was constructed which measured ten independent factors from these tests. These ten factors and a short description will be shown below so that it will be possible to see to what extent this personality inventory measures Freudian psychosexual syndromes.

VARIABLES IN THE GZTS (GUILFORD AND ZIMMERMAN, 1949)

G General activity
R Restraint *v.* rhathymia
A Ascendance
S Sociability
E Emotional stability (factors D and C)
O Objectivity
F Friendliness
T Thoughtfulness or thinking introversion
P Personal relations
M Masculine emotions and interests

As was the case with the MMPI test and the EPI, it is clear that none of these factors would provide, either in itself or in combination with others, measures of the Freudian syndromes. Eysenck and Eysenck (1969) have recently produced a study of the Cattell, Eysenck and Guilford scales combined. These tests were administered to 1,200 training college students, and the inter-correlations between the items were subjected to factor analysis. As was perhaps predictable the Cattell primary factors and the Guilford factors did not emerge. However the second-order factors of neuroticism and extraversion were clearly to be seen, thus confirming the validity of the relatively simple approach adopted by Eysenck in his EPI. This study, therefore, supports two dimensions rather than sixteen. However, careful examination of the items in this combined study reveals that 114 items from Eysenck's scales went into the analysis compared, for example, with only 99 from Cattell's scales which were spread over 16 factors! Thus the factor analysis was somewhat weighted to produce two main factors of extraversion and neuroticism and it is little wonder that the Guilford and Cattell scales failed to factor clearly.

Thus before rejecting the Cattell and Guilford scales, a replication of this study with more items from these tests is needed. We eagerly await the riposte from Illinois.

FURTHER INVESTIGATIONS

The evidence from what were called the major essays into personality measurement has now been reviewed. It remains, therefore, to examine those studies which, although less ambitious in scope, have also thrown light on the problems of psychosexual personality traits. As was pointed out in the discussion of the MMPI, studies using non-standard scales (where the MMPI becomes an item pool for the construction of new scales) will be considered in this section.

THE WORK OF FINNEY

Finney (e.g. 1961a, 1963, 1966) has produced a number of papers on the structure of personality and its childhood antecedents. Thus he has provided evidence relevant to two of the empirical hypotheses implicit in Freudian psychosexual theory. Naturally only the work on character structure will be discussed in this chapter.

The 1961a study

Finney administered a 600 item inventory, composed of items from the MMPI, the Gough scale (Gough, 1957) and the F scale of the authoritarian personality (Adorno *et al.*, 1950) to a sample of 50 men and 50 women, mainly neurotics. The scores were subjected to a centroid factor analysis and then to an objective, oblique simple structure rotation. From this oblique rotation Finney identified the following factors:

1. *Anal compulsive character or reaction-formation.* On this factor there were

substantial loadings on orderliness (·61), stinginess (·41) and stubbornness (·30). Gough's (1957) rigidity scale loaded ·70 on this factor, while a score comprised of all these scales loaded ·78. The authoritarian F scale loaded ·24. It should be observed at this point that the loadings quoted refer to the combined oblique analysis on 100 subjects. Finney identifies this factor confidently as the anal character and suggests from the loadings that its most prominent feature is rigidity. This factor accounted for the largest portion of the variance.

From the face validity of the scales there is little doubt that this factor is an anal factor. Although each scale has no proven validity, the fact that they fall together as suggested by theory is in itself some evidence for their validity. The Gough scale of rigidity has some construct validity in the work of Rokeach (1960). This factor must be regarded as sound evidence for the existence of an anal dimension within an abnormal population.

Other factors in this study were:

2. *Hysterical character or repression.*
3. *Paranoid character or projection.*
4. *Conversion.*
5. *Oral aggression and delinquency.* This factor had loadings on the following scales Pd (MMPI) ·58, Gough-Petersen delinquency ·52. High scorers on this last scale were described by Gough (1957) as demanding and exhibitionistic.

Finney admits that his identification was only tentative and that it is not a well-defined factor. It cannot be regarded on the evidence of these loadings as firm support for the oral character.

6. *Obsessive worrying.*

These six factors were the ones that appeared in all three analyses – men alone, women alone and combined. The other factors, which were not replicated, will not be considered since the factorisation of 59 variables on 50 subjects leads to loadings of considerable unreliability.

Conclusions

From the viewpoint of psychosexual theory this study provides firm evidence for the existence of the anal character as a dimension of personality in abnormal populations. It also provides interesting evidence concerning defence mechanisms and will, therefore, be again considered from that point of view in a later chapter.

THE WORK OF PICHOT AND PERSE

Pichot and Perse (1967) carried out a factorial study of the concept of sub-validité on a sample of 260 male neurotics. The concept of sub-validité has been identified by Sjobring (1963) and is closely related to what has been called asthenia, neurasthenia and psychasthenia. The subject high on the dimension of sub-validité is characterised by doubt and difficulty in making decisions as well as other obsessional symptoms. In this study the following tests were used and subjected to a Varimax orthogonal rotation of a principal components analysis:

Hazari obsessional trait scale (Hazari, 1957).
Hazari obsessional symptom scale.
Finney An scale (Finney, 1961b). A measure of the anal character.
Finney Rep scale. A measure of repression or hysterical character.
Sub-validité scale of Marke and Nyman (1960).
MMPI scales, Hy, Pa and Pd both subtle and obvious scales (Wiener, 1948).

Three significant factors emerged:

(a) Clear pathology. This is not relevant to this chapter.
(b) Anal character. The loadings on this factor were: ·883 An, ·844 Hazari traits, ·552 Rep, and − ·565 MMPI Pd.
(c) Defensive tendency. Again this factor is not relevant to the chapter.

Comments and conclusions

Factor (b) is yet again evidence for the existence of an anal syndrome in an abnormal population. In the previous study examined, that of Finney (1961b), the An scale loaded on an anal factor and provided evidence of an anal syndrome. This study reinforces that conclusion. It also suggests that the Hazari A scale of obsessional traits is measuring the anal character which is further evidence for its existence. The negative loading on Pd is impressive, since psychopathy can be regarded in psychoanalytic theory as due to defective super-ego. Super-ego is, of course, important in the development of the anal character. Only the loading on the Rep scale is unexpected.

This study is good support for the existence of the anal syndrome in an abnormal male population. It also supports the validity of the An scale and the Hazari trait scale with an abnormal population.

It is now clear that the work of Hazari on obsessional traits and symptoms must be reviewed.

THE WORK OF HAZARI AND SANDLER AND HAZARI

Hazari (1957) in his doctoral thesis and Sandler and Hazari (1960) in the paper derived from that study, investigated the distinction between obsessional symptoms and obsessional traits among 50 male and 50 female neurotics. To this end, items from the Tavistock Self-Assessment Inventory (Sandler, 1954) were selected if they appeared to be relevant to either obsessional traits or obsessional symptoms. Traits were regarded as ego-syntonic and enduring features of the personality whereas symptoms were considered to be ego-dystonic and of a more transient nature. A factor analysis of the item inter-correlations revealed two factors, one loading on items pertaining to traits, the other on items pertaining to symptoms. This first factor identified as obsessional character was regarded by the authors as evidence for the existence of an obsessional character among this population.

Comments

The interest of this investigation, from the viewpoint of this chapter, lies in the identification of the obsessional character. This is because many writers regard the obsessional character as identical to the anal character. Thus Delay, Pichot and Perse (1962), for example, in a truly excellent study of the relation of obsessional symptoms and obsessional traits, argue that the obsessional character is the psychiatric term for the anal character. Such a term allows the existence of the syndrome but makes no reference to the exclusively Freudian aetiology of repressed anal erotism. Nevertheless examination of psychiatric as distinct from psychoanalytic texts, e.g. Mayer-Gross, Slater and Roth (1961), Henderson and Gillespie (1956), reveals one major difference between the obsessional and the anal character. Parsimony, part of the anal triad, is not part of the obsessional character. Nevertheless there is a considerable similiarity between the two syndromes.

Examination of the item content of the Hazari scale reveals that there are no items relevant to parsimony. However, if the anal character is a true syndrome the scale could still be used as a valid measure of the anal character.

Evidence for the validity of the scale

Apart from item content and homogeneity there is no evidence presented for the validity of this scale. Indeed since all items are keyed 'yes' acquiescence could well play a part in the variance. So too could social desirability since many of the items appear liable to this form of bias. For example:

I am a punctual sort of person.
I have a higher standard of cleanliness than the average person.

However, in his thesis Hazari (1957) presented case studies of the subjects and these showed, to some extent at least, that the scale was valid. If the evidence presented by Hazari (1957) and Sandler and Hazari (1960) as regards validity is not entirely convincing, the work of Pichot and Perse (1967) where it loaded on the same factor as the An scale of Finney (1961b) and the validity study of Kline (1969) where it correlated with the Beloff scale (Beloff, 1957) and Ai3 (Kline, 1969) provides further empirical evidence.

Conclusions

The work of Sandler and Hazari shows that in an abnormal population an obsessional syndrome of traits appears to be a dimension of personality. Further empirical work with their scale gives some evidence for its validity, while the theoretical approach of Delay, Pichot and Perse (1962) indicates that essentially the obsessional and the anal character are the same. The Sandler and Hazari studies, therefore, must be regarded as support for the existence of an anal syndrome. This is especially true when further studies with the Hazari scale are taken into account.

THE WORK OF COMREY

Comrey (1961, 1962, 1965, 1966) and Comrey and Jamison (1966) have conducted a series of factor analytic studies of personality variables. Since their technique is novel it must be briefly described. Instead of relying on items to measure factors Comrey uses the inter-correlations between *groups of items* to define his factors – groups which he labels 'factored homogeneous item dimensions'. Most FHIDs have six items each and most factors are defined by 6 FHIDs. Another novelty is that in an attempt to avoid contamination from response sets a nine-point response scale is used rather than the simple yes/no dichotomy. Since the results of these studies largely replicate themselves – part of their strength, of course – it will be convenient to examine that by Comrey and Jamison (1966). This investigation conducted on 153 females and 121 males verified 6 personality factors – shyness, dependence, empathy, neuroticism, compulsion and hostility. It is evident that two of these factors, compulsion and dependence, resemble the anal and oral characters of Freudian theory. Thus on the dependence factor loaded the following FHIDs: succorance, lack of self-sufficiency, deference, conformity, need for approval and affiliation. On the compulsion factor loaded: grooming, cautiousness, rhathymia (neg.), order, love of routine, meticulousness and drive to finish. Both these factors appear in the other studies by this author. Although, for example, the compulsion factor contains no measure of parsimony so that it cannot be regarded as a close fit to the anal character, these studies do provide some evidence for Freudian psycho-sexual theory. However it must be stressed that the only validity for these scales consists of face validity and construct validity in as much as they fall into meaningful factors.

Nevertheless these studies provide yet more evidence of an objective nature for the existence of oral and anal personality constellations.

CONCLUSIONS FROM ALL THE STUDIES

There is little support for the existence of these psychosexual syndromes from the major questionnaire studies of personality. The scales of Guilford and Eysenck and the clinical scales of the MMPI do not appear to measure similar variables. The basic source traits of Cattell are also not relevant although it is possible that certain combinations of these might be developed to provide measures of them. T objective test factors are, however, more promising: UI19 is, descriptively, not unlike the anal character. Cattell's surface traits do resemble psychosexual syndromes to some extent and H1 is identified by him as being the anal character. This must be regarded as good evidence for its existence. It is to be noted that it is a failing of his source traits that, as yet, they are unable to account for all the surface traits.

Finney (1961) and Pichot and Perse (1967) together provide further good evidence for the existence of an anal syndrome, this time within abnormal populations. Hazari (1957) and Sandler and Hazari (1960) also support the existence of the anal character with their obsessional trait scale. Comrey, in his studies, provides support for both the anal character, his compulsion factor, and the oral character, the dependence factor, although it must be admitted that further evidence is needed concerning the validity of these scales.

In the previous chapter concerning studies deliberately aimed at providing objective evidence for psychosexual personality theory, it was concluded that there was good evidence for the anal character and some less clear evidence for the oral character. The evidence for more general studies of personality points the same way.

The conclusions may be thus summarised:

1. **There is good evidence for the anal character.** This is supported by Cattell (surface trait, H1), Finney (1961b), Pichot and Perse (1967) with the An scale, and Hazari (1957) and Sandler and Hazari (1960). To a less extent Comrey's studies provide evidence.

2. **There is some evidence for the oral character.** This is supported, to some extent at least, by the surface traits of Cattell and by the work of Comrey. It is by no means as clear as the anal character.

3. **There is almost no support for other psychosexual syndromes.** Cattell's factor H and surface trait CB3 are the only evidence that can be offered.

5

The relation of psychosexual personality syndromes to infantile experiences

As was pointed out in the opening chapter, psychosexual theory has implicit in it three basic empirical propositions:

1. that certain adult personality syndromes may be observed,
2. that these are related to infant rearing procedures, and
3. that pregenital erotism may be observed in infants.

Since the effects of child-rearing procedures are created through repression or frustration of this pre-genital erotism, propositions two and three are related. The two previous chapters have considered the evidence for the first proposition. In this chapter we shall examine the objective studies of the last two hypotheses. That this is a worthwhile procedure has been demonstrated by the findings already discussed – that some of these hypothesised personality syndromes do seem to exist.

A study of the objective evidence reveals that four different approaches have been used by the investigators, and these, which are set out below, will be discussed and evaluated in separate sections in this chapter. The five methods are:

1. Retrospective studies of the infantile experiences of adults.
2. Cross-cultural studies.
3. Current and longitudinal studies of children.
4. Studies with the Blacky Pictures (Blum, 1949).
5. Other techniques.

These five methods have been used because each method has certain specific problems (or indeed faults).

PROBLEMS OF THE DIFFERENT METHODS

1. Retrospective studies of adults

The difficulty here is simple – recollection. The fact is that the majority of adults are unable to recollect with any accuracy early childhood events. Freud, of course, used the fact of infantile amnesia as one of his arguments to support the concept of repression of infantile sexuality and the Oedipus complex. Robbins (1963), in a most interesting investigation, showed that parents' recollections of the details of how they had weaned and pot trained their children were not closely related to records of these events made at the time as part of a longitudinal study. Newson and Newson (1963) in Nottingham found, in their study of parental child-rearing practices and attitudes, that recall of training milestones became inaccurate after an interval of more than a year. This means that the child-rearing data in such studies are likely to be of dubious validity. The advantage of this approach lies in the fact that adult personality tests of the psychosexual syndromes have been developed so that criterion populations can be compared.

2. Cross-cultural studies

This approach involves severe problems of measurement in alien cultures. Biesheuvel (1962) has discussed these difficulties which may be insuperable in some societies. On the other hand the attraction of cross-cultural studies resides in the opportunities to study the effects of truly diverse child-training procedures.

3. Current and longitudinal studies of children

Current studies of children are beset with the difficulty of obtaining adequate measures of personality. Eysenck and Eysenck (1969) show clearly, for example, that their Junior EPI is not viable below the age of nine. Furthermore, interpretative measures such as doll-play do not have high validity. On the other hand, child-training data can be accurate. However it must be observed that very often such current studies still use retrospective data concerning infant experience. These studies may well have the disadvantages, therefore, of both this and the first method.

4. The Blacky Pictures (Blum, 1949)

Some investigators have used this projective technique, specifically designed to test Freudian psychosexual hypotheses, in an attempt to measure infantile experiences indirectly and thus overcome the problems discussed above. Their validity is not obvious however, and evidence for the validity of this technique and the results achieved with it are discussed in the relevant section.

1. RETROSPECTIVE STUDIES OF CHILD-REARING PROCEDURES AND ADULT PERSONALITY

INTRODUCTION

Despite the problems of the validity of the data on child-rearing procedures when these are recalled by adults (remember that in the study by Newson and Newson (1963) a gap of one year was sufficient to blur the memory), a number of such studies has been conducted. The general plan of these investigations is to select subjects, typical of the personality syndrome claimed to be derived from oral or anal fixation in childhood (usually by means of psychometric tests), and then to investigate how they were weaned or pot trained. In this section those investigations where fixation was measured by the Blacky Pictures (Blum, 1949) will not be considered. The validity and reliability of the Blacky Pictures and the work done with them are separately examined (see p. 80). It should now be obvious that many of these investigations have already been discussed in the previous chapter – for the support they bring to the first of the empirical propositions implicit in Freudian psychosexual theory that the hypothesised personality syndromes do in fact exist. These studies will now be examined again but this time in relation to the second empirical proposition of the theory – are these personality syndromes related to repressed pregenital erotism and specific child-rearing procedures ?

THE WORK OF GOLDMAN-EISLER ON THE ORAL CHARACTER

Goldman-Eisler (1950, 1951) attempted to relate the scores on a personality questionnaire designed to measure oral optimism and oral pessimism to the weaning procedures of the subjects taking the test.

Sample and validity of scales. In Chapter 2 the validity of these scales for selecting oral optimists and oral pessimists was fully discussed. It was concluded that although these scales had face validity and were reliable, further evidence for their validity was necessary before the results of this study could be regarded as definitive evidence for the existence of the syndromes. The samples, too, were considered somewhat homogeneous but this was not a serious fault in that correlations would tend to be depressed rather than boosted. Positive results, therefore, would hardly be likely to be artificial.

Feeding data. The feeding data was obtained from the subjects themselves – many of whom were students. It was thus retrospective data at least 15 years old. Furthermore, as Hoffman and Hoffman (1964) point out, no data were obtained concerning feeding procedures after weaning from the breast. This is important since bottle feeding of orange juice after weaning on to solid food gives sucking gratification which is clearly relevant to the repression of oral erotism. Similarly whether milk was fed by cup or bottle is another relevant factor.

Results. In the 1951 study early weaning was related to oral pessimism but in this oral factor it was noted that there was little impulsion aggression or autonomy. These traits tended to cluster together and were not related to early weaning.

Comments

The fact that early weaning was related to oral pessimism, even though this factor did not embrace the whole gamut of oral characteristics as portrayed in the psychoanalytic delineation (see p. 8), does support Freudian theory. When the dubious nature of both the feeding data and the validity of the scales is taken into account the fact that any correlation at all was observed is remarkable.

It must be remembered in these studies that when the data are not ideal, unless it can be shown that the measures are not only in error but actually measuring some other factor any correlation is still support for the theory. Error would lead to no correlation by definition (being randomly distributed). No correlation, on the other hand, for this same reason of error variance, cannot necessarily be held to refute the theory.

Conclusions

The unproven validity of the scales and the fact that the oral factor, related to early weaning, was not a precise match to the Freudian description means that this study cannot be regarded as convincing evidence for the hypothesised aetiology of the oral character. In addition it must be pointed out that the design of this study does not constitute a true test of psychoanalytic psychosexual theory. In the delineation of psychosexual theory (p. 6), it will be remembered, Freud (1905) drew attention to the genetic aspects of the psychosexual constitution: that is, oral, anal and phallic erotism is of differing intensity in each individual. This means that the same weaning process or toilet-training procedure will produce differing degrees of fixation in each individual – quite a mild weaning might severely traumatise an infant whose oral erotism was intense.

For all these reasons, therefore, this correlation between a factor of oral pessimism and early weaning is considered to be some support for the Freudian position. It cannot be considered as proof or as very strong evidence. On the other hand, and this is most important, these Goldman-Eisler studies cannot, by any stretch of the imagination, be used to refute Freudian theory. To the present writer it seems that Goldman-Eisler has better supported the existence of the oral syndrome than its hypothesised aetiology.

THE WORK OF THURSTON AND MUSSEN (1951)

Thurston and Mussen investigated the relationship between infant feeding gratification and adult personality. This study was not discussed in the previous chapter because no measure of the oral character was used.

Tests. The group form of the TAT was used from which measures of oral traits were derived.

Infant-feeding data. These were gathered from questionnaires sent to the mothers of the subjects in the sample.

Sample. 91 male undergraduates (students of psychology).

Results. No significant relationship was found between infant feeding gratification and oral traits. Freudian psychosexual theory was not considered to be supported.

Comments

The first point to be discussed concerns the validity of the TAT as a measure of oral traits. There appears to be no sound evidence that the TAT is a valid measure of these traits. As with many projective techniques, it is relatively easy to derive face-valid indices from the responses. Nevertheless firm evidence must be supplied before the score is used. Without this it thus seems highly doubtful whether in fact orality was being measured in the study. In addition, again in common with many other projective techniques, the reliability of such oral scores (not only test-retest but also repeated marking by the same markers) must be dubious. Such unreliability would again lead to low validity. It is therefore concluded that without good evidence of validity TAT measures cannot be accepted.

The second point is similar to that raised in the discussion of the work of Goldman-Eisler (1951) – the validity of the data on infant feeding. The discussion will not be repeated. Suffice it to say that it is most unlikely that such retrospective data is valid.

Conclusions

Since in this investigation both the test of oral personality and the measure of infant-feeding gratification are of dubious value, the final result of no significant correlations is not unexpected. Again the design of the investigation fails to take into account the psychosexual constitution of the subjects and this must be regarded as a weakness. Consequently it is concluded that while the results of this study in no way support psychoanalytic theory, equally they do not refute it.

BELOFF (1957)

This study by Beloff of the anal character has been fully discussed in the previous chapter. There it was concluded that her scale was in all probability a valid measure of the anal factor, although the emergence of a general factor running through the items and a high face validity are not of themselves sufficient to demonstrate validity.

Sample. 120 college students.

Infant-training data. Interview material from the mothers of the subjects.

Tests. Guilford scales and the Beloff anal scale.

Results. There was no correlation between the severity of pot training as judged by the age of completion (the earlier the more severe it was held to be) and scores on the anal questionnaire. There was, however, a correlation between the scores on the anal scale of mothers and their children. Beloff concluded from these results that the psychoanalytic aetiology was not valid.

Comments and conclusions

In common with the other studies, using retrospective data on child-rearing procedures, no account was taken of the psychosexual constitution of the subject. Inevitably, too, for reasons that have already been discussed the validity of this pot-training data cannot be considered high simply because it was gathered so long after toilet training was completed. The anal test however does appear to be valid. Thus it is possible to argue that the failure to obtain positive correlations was due to the inadequacy of the pot-training data. This view is, perhaps, supported by the fact that Beloff identified early completion of training with severity – an arguable but not necessarily correct identification.

The conclusion from this study therefore must be that it fails to support the Freudian theory. It cannot, however, be held to refute it.

CONCLUSIONS FROM THE THREE RETROSPECTIVE STUDIES

Owing to the doubts concerning the validity of the data on child-rearing in all these investigations, the fact that two of them failed to support Freudian theory cannot be regarded as a refutation of it. Since, too, in all these studies the personality measures are of unproven validity (although there is some evidence for the Beloff anal scale) there is further cause for confusion. The theoretical weakness of the design, in that no account was taken of the psychosexual constitution of the subjects, can also be used to explain the failure of these studies to corroborate psychoanalytic theory. In all fairness to these researchers it should be said that as yet there is no measure of psychosexual constitution which they might have used and it could be argued that any such differences would be randomly distributed throughout a sample so that the effects would be cancelled out. Actually this argument is unlikely in terms of psychoanalytic theory in that it is probable that intensity of oral or anal erotism is an important factor in causing fixation since it increases the *perceived* severity of the weaning or toilet training.

In short, therefore, two of these investigations, Thurston and Mussen (1951) and Beloff (1957), fail to support Freudian theory. The work of Goldman-Eisler (1951) gives some support. None of them, however, refutes psychoanalytic psychosexual theory.

2. CROSS-CULTURAL STUDIES

INTRODUCTION

If we disregard the difficulty of the individual's psychosexual constitution, cross-cultural studies of child-rearing practices and adult personality are clearly of great interest in the elucidation of these psychoanalytic aetiological hypotheses. For in cultures different from our own, diverse infant-training procedures can be observed such that a real test of the Freudian hypotheses may be made. An additional advantage, especially in more traditional cultures than that of Europe, lies in the homogeneity of many customs due to the fact that deviation from the cultural norm is regarded as bad. Psychoanalysts and psychoanalytically oriented anthropologists have not failed to see the implications of these different culture patterns for their theories. Thus Berkley-Hill (1921) attributed much of the religion, philosophy and character of the Hindus to repressed anal erotism and similar arguments have been invoked concerning the Japanese personality by Gorer (1943), La Barre (1945) and Spitzer (1947). Devereux (e.g. 1947 and 1951) has written a series of papers linking the personality of the Mohave Indians to oral and anal erotism repressed and fostered by their child-rearing practices. None of these studies was, however, quantitative or experimental. They were, on the contrary, speculative and impressionistic and as such they fall outside the scope of this book.

However, Whiting and Child (1953), in the course of their reading of the relevant anthropological literature for their classic investigation of child training and personality, rated 75 primitive societies for a large number of child-training procedures. They were thus able to use quantitative methods for relating these procedures to personality traits similarly quantified from the literature. Their findings, therefore, in so much as they bear on the aetiological hypotheses, will be examined below.

Yet another approach in the study of cross-cultural psychological variables is to use tests and measures standardised in the West (including America) and to make statistical comparisons of the results. This method, unfortunately, is beset with problems, especially where measures of personality are involved. Nevertheless cross-cultural studies have been carried out with, for example, the Cattell 16 PF personality test (see p. 31) in France (Cattell, Pichot and Rennes, 1961), Germany (Cattell, Pawlik and Nesselrode, 1965), Japan (Tsujioka and Cattell, 1965) and Ghana (Kline, 1967).

CROSS-CULTURAL PROBLEMS IN TESTS

Cattell (1957) distinguishes, in the study of personality, culture-free and culture-bound personal characteristics. Intelligence and anxiety level, for example, might be included among the former; among the latter sentiment for sport or science. This same distinction may also be applied to items within scales. In the MMPI can be found an item concerned with the enjoyment of Drop the Handkerchief (item 70). This is certainly a culture-bound item, whereas the item in Eysenck's MMQ, 'Have you ever been made unconscious for two hours or more by an accident or blow?' appears to be virtually culture-free. Such items are extreme instances of a distinction which is often difficult to draw. In addition there is the problem of whether in two different cultures the same behaviour has the same motivation. Indeed Biesheuvel (1962) argues that the relevance of items in different cultures constitutes the main problem in the cross-cultural testing of personality. Therefore before any tests can be used satisfactorily, the items must be subjected to item analysis in the new population and the validity of the test must also be demonstrated. Needless to say, in addition to the problem of item content there are the difficulties of translation and the administration of tests to non-literate non-English-speaking samples. It must be concluded, therefore, that the problems of the validity of self-report tests in non-Western cultures, together with the difficulties of administration, make the interpretation of results extremely complex. Obviously good evidence that such tests are working as designed must be advanced before results may be taken at their face value.

One apparent way round such difficulties is to use projective material. Here, in response to the TAT or Rorschach, subjects can fantasise freely in their own languages. However the reliability and validity of these tests in normal use is not high and to attempt, therefore, to interpret responses from such subjects seems a dubious procedure. In this writer's view little weight could be attached to data of this type.

Despite these problems cross-cultural studies of child-rearing procedures and adult personality have been conducted. It is arguable that the difficulties discussed above are less than those associated with the testing of adults in our culture and trying to obtain pot training or weaning data retrospectively. The studies relevant to Freudian psychosexual aetiological hypotheses will now be examined.

THE WORKS OF WHITING AND CHILD (1953)

Kardiner (1945), in *The Psychological Frontiers of Society*, makes a distinction between Primary and Secondary Institutions. *Primary Institutions* comprise those aspects of culture, especially child-training practices, which in his opinion produce the basic personality structure of members of a society and have an important influence on other aspects of culture – the *Secondary Institutions*. Whiting and Child (1953) claim that this is their basic approach. Whereas, for example, Gorer (1943) and La Barre (1945) assumed that toilet training affected personality and interpreted the Japanese personality in the light of this assumption, Kardiner claims that his approach allows the hypotheses to be tested as they arise. Consequently, following Kardiner, Whiting and Child do attempt to put the Freudian hypotheses to the test. It should be clear that the concepts themselves of Primary and Secondary Institutions are, if not derived from, certainly influenced by psychoanalytic psychosexual theory.

Sample. 75 primitive societies, and an American middle-class reference group (N = 50) as used by Davis and Havinghurst (1946, 1947).

Raw data. Ethnographic reports of these societies.

Dimensions of measurement. Five dimensions: oral, anal, sexual, dependent and aggressive. For the sexual dimension sub-systems were used: immodesty, masturbation, heterosexual play and homosexual play. For the aggressive dimension, the sub-systems were: temper trantrums, physical aggression, verbal aggression, property damage and disobedience.

For all these dimensions the child-training practices of each society were examined for:

1. initial satisfaction
2. socialisation anxiety
3. age of socialisation.

Method of measurement. Three independent judges rated the literature on a seven-point scale (e.g. degree of anxiety). Then within each society the 5 dimensions were ranked. The reliability of these judgements ran from ·55 - ·95.

Reliability of ratings. The median r of the ratings for the three judges was ·85 (confident ratings). For their doubtful ratings it fell to ·61.

This rater reliability is very satisfactory – as high as the reliability of many psychological tests. But no matter how skilful the ratings, all is wasted if the original ethnographic material is inaccurate. Without extensive and precise observation of the individual societies it is clearly impossible to say how accurate each of these reports is. It is to be noted that a dimension was not rated if the particular report contained no relevant information. Although only distinguished reports were used, the validity of these rating scales must remain enigmatic and interpretation of the results must be accordingly cautious. Such were the measures of child-training procedures.

The personality measures

Whiting and Child (1953) argue from a combination of what they describe as Psychoanalytic and Hullian drive theory that fixation due to excessive indulgence is positive fixation whereas negative fixation is derived from excessive severity. In the anal sphere, for example, a love of defaecation would be regarded as positive fixation and extreme modesty about secretion as negative fixation (Fenichel, 1945). So the personality measures were resolved into indices of positive and negative fixation based on the ethnographic reports.

Explanations of illness and disease will concentrate around areas of negative fixation. Thus the index is the occurrence of this kind of explanation. If therapeutic value is attached to responses in any area, this is regarded as an index of positive fixation.

Both these indices are related to the generalisation of anxiety. Thus the belief that kissing is a source of infection is considered to be anxiety derived from oral anxiety and the belief that it is a cure for toothache is considered to be euphoria derived from general oral euphoria. It is clear that such arguments are not so easily applicable in a society where the causes and treatments of illness are more thoroughly understood.

Thus the Freudian hypothesis that negative fixation is produced by excessive severity of socialisation and positive fixation by excessive indulgence can now be put to the test.

A. *Negative fixation*

The greater the *socialisation anxiety* in any area, the more will *explanations of illness concentrate round that area*, in any society.

Results

Oral and *aggressive* dimensions *strongly confirmed* (t sig. ·0005 and ·005).
Dependence dimension *confirmed* (t sig. ·05).

Anal dimension slight confirmation (t sig. ·03).

Sexual dimension no confirmation.

Curiously enough it was also found that negative fixation in the *dependent and aggressive* dimensions was related to initial satisfaction in these areas. These findings demonstrate that, except in the last two areas, positive and negative fixation are indeed different.

B. *Positive fixation*

The greater *the initial satisfaction in any area, the greater will be deemed the therapeutic value of the responses* related to that area, in any society.

Results. No significant differences in any area except the *sexual dimension* (t sig. ·01 level). *Progressive satisfaction* was then substituted for initial satisfaction. Then positive fixation in the oral dimensions was related (·05 sig.) but the anal dimension was related in the wrong direction. Whiting and Child (1953) conclude from this that there is no evidence for positive fixation.

Comments

As the results stand, the position is that Whiting and Child have provided evidence from the study of these 75 primitive societies that negative fixation is related to severity of socialisation training, at least in some areas (supporting Freudian theory). They have failed to find evidence that positive fixation is related to indulgence and they thus refute Freudian theory. However the question of the validity of these most ingenious personality measures must be examined. First, it must be said that there is no evidence that they are valid. Their validity depends on the chain of reasoning mentioned above concerning the generalisation of anxiety. All that can be said is that the reasoning appears sound (in fact brilliant); however it must have empirical support. The only empirical support these measures could have would be if they correlated with the child-training procedures, because they would thus fit their (Freudian) constructs, i.e. have construct validity. When they fail to fit, as do the measures of positive fixation, it is impossible to tell whether the measure or the theory is at fault.

Whiting and Child themselves admit this point in their discussion of the negative results of their positive identification hypothesis. In addition, the point raised in discussion of the child-rearing data must not be forgotten – that the validity of those measures depends upon the accuracy of the ethnographic literature. It is interesting to note that in further studies not relevant to the problem of the childhood origins of the oral and anal personality, no correlations whatever were established with the anal dimension. This fact strongly suggests that in this sphere the reports may have been faulty – with random error no correlations would have been expected. In addition it would be peculiarly ironic if the anal dimension, so strongly stressed in psychoanalysis and certainly the first (Freud, 1908) to be developed into the implicit psychosexual theory, were in fact the dimension of child rearing which had no effect on adult personality. What then of Menninger's claim (1943) that the anal phase of childhood was undoubtedly the most important not only in the development of individual personality but of cultures as well, and Roheim's claim (1934) that the whole of Western culture was anal? To substantiate this on the basis of indirect measures such as those of Whiting and Child would be possible, since on no other theory could such results be understood, but to refute them on such measures without demonstrated validity is hardly possible.

There is one other point. Some readers may perhaps be wondering what relationship these personality measures have with the oral and anal syndromes. In fact the oral pessimist and the anal character are the results of negative fixation at the oral and anal phase respectively; the oral optimist the result of positive fixation.

Conclusions

The main conclusions have in effect been made clear in the discussion. Despite the problems of measurement and the possible faults in the original material, Whiting and Child (1953) have provided good evidence for the concept of negative fixation. There seems no other convincing explanation of the results. They have, on the other hand, failed to support positive fixation. This may be due to faults in psychoanalytic theory or it could be due to errors of measurement. Thus this finding does not refute psychosexual theory.

Perhaps even more important than these results are the possibilities this quantitative method of analysis opens up in the cross-cultural elucidation of psychoanalytic hypotheses (and indeed in the study of many other hypotheses). From this point of view, *Child Training and Personality* is a most impressive and brilliant work. Later in this book some of their other findings, as well as further work by their colleagues, will be discussed.

In summary, Whiting and Child (1953) have provided impressive support for negative fixation but failed to confirm positive fixation among a large number of primitive societies.

THE STUDY BY KERLINGER (1953)

Kerlinger wrote a brief critique of the studies of Japanese personality by Gorer (1943) and La Barre (1945). As has been made clear, these investigations were not considered to be within the scope of this section because of their impressionistic approach and the lack of any precisely defined data. Kerlinger makes the point that many of the so called facts assumed by these writers concerning child-rearing practices are simply not true. This severely underlines the danger of studies not empirically based on precise observation. It does, however, support the fact that these and similar highly interesting and speculative investigators have not been seriously considered.

C

THE WORK OF STRAUSS (1957)

Strauss examined the relationship between anal and oral fixation and personality in a Sinhalese sample. Before examining this study in further detail one point needs to be emphasised. The sample consisted of third-grade children (around 9-10 years). These were, therefore, in the latency period according to the Freudian theory. Now the oral and anal characters were observed in adults, not children, and the fact that sexual strivings tend to die down in the latency period may well mean that in children of this age the typical personality traits do not appear. This argument will be further discussed later in this chapter when the empirical work with children is scrutinised (see p. 60).

Sample. 34 children in grade 3 of a highland village school (all in the grade). 39 children in grade 3 of a city school ($\frac{1}{3}$ of the grade). (Both these rural and urban schools were, of course, in Ceylon.)

Tests

(*a*) Personality – the California Test of Personality and the Rorschach. A Sinhalese translation was used for the Californian Test.

(*b*) Oral and anal frustration indices – based on interviews with mothers of the subjects as to their infant-training procedures.

Statistical analysis. A Chi-square method was used: the children were split into three groups on the oral and anal frustration index, and two groups on the personality tests.

Results. There were no significant associations between infant training and personality traits in this study and Freudian psychosexual theory was not supported.

Comments

The methodology of this study is beset with problems. The validity of the Rorschach test is by no means agreed upon, even when used in the West. Eysenck (1959) has made a severe attack upon it which still remains to be answered. The Sinhalese version of the California Personality Test has not been validated either, so that the two measures of personality cannot be regarded as trustworthy. Furthermore, as was pointed out in the discussion of the problems of obtaining satisfactory data on child-rearing procedures, interviewing of parents some years after the completion of the training in question is not likely to produce accurate recall. The fact that data for both personality and child-rearing processes are so liable to error obviates the need for a more subtle statistical analysis than that chosen for this study. Finally the sample, although both urban and rural, is probably too small to be truly representative.

Conclusions

Although conducted in a non-Western culture, this study is in fact hardly cross-cultural in that no use of the cultural differences was made. Indeed being in

Ceylon may well have hindered the results. It does become cross-cultural, however, if the argument is then produced that Freudian theory does not work in Ceylon!

The conclusion to be drawn from this study is that *Freudian theory was not confirmed*, a finding which may have been due to the methodological problems involved in testing in Ceylon. On account of these problems the negative findings cannot be considered to refute psychosexual theory.

THE WORK OF SCOFIELD AND SUN (1960)

Scofield and Sun studied the effect on personality of Chinese and American child-training practices.

Sample. 40 Chinese students at Oklahoma University.

Tests. Cattell 16 PF test.

Infant-training. The system of Whiting and Child (1953) was followed. Oral, anal, sexual, dependent and aggressive dimensions were rated as more or less severe than American middle-class norms by three graduate students.

Results. The 16PF test was able to discriminate the Chinese from American students since the coefficient of pattern similarity (rp) was only ·11 which was not significant. Since, according to the ratings of infant training, the Chinese were *not* more severe on the anal dimension, it was hypothesised that there would be no difference on the anal traits of compulsivity and rigidity of control. This was confirmed. Scofield and Sun (1960) consider this finding to confirm Freudian psychosexual theory.

Comments

This is not a convincing study for a number of reasons. First, 40 Chinese students at an American University can only, at best, be a representative sample of Chinese students studying in America. These may have very different backgrounds from other Chinese. Even more important is the claim that there were no differences in compulsivity or rigidity of control on the 16 PF test. The fact is that the 16 PF has no real measures of this. Q3, self-control, is the nearest factor to it but, as Cattell (1957) himself makes clear, the 16 PF contains no scale for anal traits. This was empirically demonstrated by Kline (1969). A full discussion of the relation of the 16 PF factors to Freudian psychosexual syndromes may be found in Chapter 4. Finally, mention must be made of the use of Whiting and Child's (1953) rating system. To use it on 75 societies, where in effect 75 measurements are made, does much to obviate errors. To use it on one society as was done in this study is probably to exceed its capacity. Reliability strongly affects the use of tests with individuals on account of the standard error of measurement being related to it. Thus the use of this scale on one society is not likely to yield a valid result.

Conclusions

The size and homogeneity of the sample, the nature of both the personality test and the measure of infant training used, all mean that the results of this study must be treated with great caution. It can only be regarded as but the most tenuous support for psychoanalytic theory.

THE WORK OF KLINE (1969)

Kline carried out a cross-cultural study of the anal character in Ghana, using a sample of Ghanaian students.

Sample. 123 Ghanaian students at the University of Cape Coast, Ghana. Mean age 30 years.

Tests. Ai3, a measure of the anal character, the EPI and the 16 PF test (Cattell).

Statistical analysis. T test, between Ghanaian sample and comparable British samples, of scores on Ai3.

Results. The Ghanaians were significantly more anal than their British counterparts (t = 5·06 sig. beyond the ·01 level).

Discussion and comments

There can be little doubt that the sample was representative of Ghanaian students since Wyllie (1966) has shown that there are few social differences between students at Cape Coast and those at Legon – the largest of the three Ghanaian universities. The high mean age is also typical of Ghanaian students. This is almost certainly due to the fact that many Ghanaian students have to study on their own in the evenings to reach the entrance standard of the universities (Peil, 1965).

The validity of Ai3 has already been discussed in a previous chapter. It appears to be a valid measure in Britain. In Ghana too, somewhat surprisingly, it still works efficiently. In an earlier study (Kline, 1967) the EPI and the 16 PF test were shown to be valid with this Ghanaian sample. Ai3 factored out as predicted with these tests – good evidence for its validity. Furthermore an item analysis showed only a few items in the scale to be inefficient so that it can be concluded that Ai3 was valid in Ghana.

Thus, from the point of view of sample and test, this cross-cultural study is satisfactory even if limited to students. The result, therefore, that Ghanaian students were more anal than their British contemporaries must imply, if Freudian theory be correct, that Ghanaian pot training is more severe than British.

Studies of Ghanaian pot training

Pot-training data were derived, in this investigation, from the literature relevant to it. It was not considered feasible to question the subjects, who were unused to psychological research and whose first glimpse of a psychometric test occurred in the present study. Furthermore the ordinary problems of retrospective data on child-rearing procedures were considered sufficiently overwhelming.

Unfortunately the evidence concerning Ghanaian pot training was scanty and untrustworthy. Field (1940, 1960), Lystad (1958) and Tait (1961) make no mention of it. Kaye (1962) devotes a chapter to it in his book on child development in Ghana. The data, however, were collected by students untrained in the social sciences and give the impression of referring to ideal rather than actual behaviour. The general conclusion to emerge from Kaye is that throughout Ghana there may be found a considerable variety of pot-training methods, as regards age of starting, severity of training and expected age of completion of training. Whiting and Child (1953) rated the Ghanaian Ashanti tribe, some of whose members are included in the sample in the present investigation, as severe in their pot training as their middle-class American reference group. Since it could be argued from the work of Sears, Maccoby and Levin (1957) in America and of Newson and Newson (1963) in this country that British and American methods are similar, it follows that the anal training of the Ashanti and Nottingham mothers is similar.

From these tenuous arguments, if anal training is related to the anal personality, a greater variance might be expected among the Ghanaians than among the British and the mean scores should be the same. These can only be tentative hypotheses because, as should be clear, not enough is known about Ghanaian pot training. Indeed, the same could also be said of British child-rearing practices. Thus, as a cross-cultural study designed to elucidate the aetiology of the anal character, this investigation by Kline (1969) must be regarded as a failure.

However, the result that the Ghanaian sample was significantly more anal than the British one, even if it failed to elucidate the aetiology of the anal character, did support the concept of the anal character. For, as was mentioned earlier, many of these Ghanaian students had been forced to study in the evenings after work, often for many years, to obtain entrance qualifications. Such efforts undoubtedly demand considerable persistence – one of the anal triad of characteristics. Orderliness, too, over such a long period of study and planning would all enter into such an effort so that the result, in terms of this special sample, makes good psychological sense and confirms the validity of Ai3 in Ghana.

Conclusions

This study by Kline (1969) underlines the problems involved in the cross-cultural study of these Freudian hypotheses. Although the validity of the personality test, Ai3, was established the study floundered through the paucity of accurate data on toilet-training practices.

It must be concluded, therefore, that this study fails either to support or refute the aetiology of the anal character, although it does support its existence.

CONCLUSIONS FROM ALL THESE CROSS-CULTURAL STUDIES

In terms of results these cross-cultural studies have yielded little concerning the aetiological hypotheses of psychosexual theory. Indeed all that has been demonstrated is the phenomenon of negative fixation (Whiting and Child, 1953). In terms of methodology however the position is different. Here the work of Whiting and Child offers enormous possibilities in the hands of imaginative researchers. In other chapters of this book we shall examine some of the fruits of their work.

Nevertheless an appraisal of the results, as far as psychosexual aetiological theory is concerned, strongly suggests that cross-cultural studies are, alas, the Sirens of the researcher into psychoanalysis.

3. CURRENT AND LONGITUDINAL STUDIES OF CHILDREN

INTRODUCTION

As we have seen, the problem in retrospective studies of adults, aimed at elucidating Freudian psychosexual hypotheses, lies in the dubious validity of recollections about infant-training procedures. Obviously current and longitudinal studies avoid this pitfall. Nevertheless these too are beset with difficulties. These problems will be briefly discussed below so that the investigations to be discussed in this section may be usefully evaluated.

INFANT-REARING DATA

Although more accuracy can be established when the data are collected at the time of the events than in retrospective studies, it would be mistaken to assume that information is necessarily valid. To use Newson and Newson (1963) as an example, these authors found that data collected by the university research worker were not in close agreement with those obtained by the health visitor whose results appeared to be distorted by social desirability: mothers were telling her what they thought they *ought* to do.

The actual method of obtaining weaning and toilet-training information is also important – as stressed by Caldwell (1964). A superficial questionnaire, a structured interview and a long series of depth-interviews are likely, for example, to yield different results depending on the degree of rapport that can be achieved with the parent. The interviews, if well conducted, ought to be able to avoid obvious distortion from social desirability. On the other hand, if the interviewer is also conducting the research, he may unwittingly reinforce the responses he would like to hear (the Greenspoon effect). Again, observation in the home may well produce distortion – e.g. inhibition of paternal aggression (see Lytton, 1969). Nevertheless the high reliability of the rating scales used in the study by Sears, Maccoby and Levin (1957) does suggest that with care reasonable validity of data can be attained. What must be stressed, however, is that current data are not *necessarily* more valid than retrospective.

AGE OF SUBJECTS

This constitutes the most important objection to this approach to the study of Freudian psychosexual theory. The oral, anal and phallic characters (see p. 8) are *adult* personality patterns considered to be derived from infant-training experiences. Thus to attempt to observe these characteristics in children or even adolescents is not an adequate test of psychoanalytic theory. This is especially true in the case of pre-pubertal children. Thus in Freudian theory, after the Oedipus complex has been repressed and the super-ego comes into being around the age of five, the child enters the latency period. Until puberty repression is relatively successful and there are few signs of conflict. Since the personality traits, subsumed under the various psychosexual syndromes, are in fact defences against repressed pregenital erotism – sublimations and reaction-formations (see p. 6) – it is not to be expected that such configurations would show up in childhood. This means, therefore, that only studies of infant-training procedures which are followed up to adulthood constitute proper tests of Freudian theory. Investigations of childhood disturbances in behaviour are not relevant.

MEASURES

Even if we were to admit into the discussion studies of the effects of weaning or pot training on children's behaviour, we run into the further problem of adequate measures for children of this age. Projective techniques such as the Rorschach and the TAT are not considered suitable (see p. 4) for reasons of validity and reliability and Eysenck and Eysenck (1969) have clearly demonstrated that personality questionnaires for children younger than nine are of dubious validity.

Finally a problem will be discussed which, though relevant to other approaches (adult and cross-cultural studies), is of particular importance in investigations of children. For obvious reasons it is usually ignored in the other approaches.

THE TERMINOLOGY

Caldwell (1964) makes the point that even in an area of study as apparently simple as child rearing, the concepts (if that is not too grand a term) are not clear.

For example, weaning can mean the withdrawal of the breast but the continuation of the bottle, the introduction of solid food into the diet, or the abrupt transition to solid food followed by milk, sufficient only for thirst and fed by cup. In tropical countries, indeed, weaning may mean an abrupt change to solid food only. Again the terms early or late, applied to weaning or toilet training, are purely subjective judgements in the absence of accurate up-to-date normative data (which still do not exist). Indeed the meaningfulness of 'weaned' or 'toilet trained' can be questioned. Most children, for dietary reasons, continue to drink milk long after weaning (even if from a cup) and many children who are considered to be toilet trained continue occasionally to soil or wet the bed. The vagueness of the terms means that precise investigation is difficult and that investigations may not be strictly comparable.

One further point remains to be noted about researches of this type. Some studies of children still use retrospective data about infant-training procedures. This means, in this writer's opinion, that they have the faults of retrospective as well as current and longitudinal studies with the merits of none.

SUMMARY OF POINTS

Current and longitudinal studies overcome the inadequacy of recollected data about infant training although such data are still often imprecise. In addition they pose their own problems of measurement and are often irrelevant to psychoanalytic theory. Some studies indeed are retrospective.

In the discussion below, only those investigations which have successfully overcome the problems inherent in the method will be examined.

THE ORAL CHARACTER

Most of the investigations are seriously deficient as tests of psychoanalytic hypotheses mainly because the personality measures are of unproven validity and the children too young. Thus Rogerson and Rogerson (1939) might be held to support Freudian theory in that, compared with breast-fed children, bottle-fed children suffered more from enuresis and sibling jealousy and were considered to be more nervous. However the data consisted of observations made in visits to the home and school. In addition, the children were but seven years old. This study cannot constitute objective evidence for Freudian theory. Peterson and Spano (1941) investigated a large sample of normal children in a research that is often seized on by opponents of psychoanalytic theory as disproving Freud (e.g. O'Connor and Franks, 1961). Certainly the result that there were no correlations between length of breast feeding and indices of personality development does appear to refute Freudian theory. However the measures used – Fels rating scales, the Joel Behaviour Maturity scale and the Vineland Maturity scale together with the Brown Personality Inventory – are not of proven validity. This study, therefore, cannot refute the theory. These two investigations have been

mentioned because they highlight the problems, discussed above, in the verification of this part of psychosexual theory and because they suffer from being
too general. Neither of these researches set out to investigate specifically the
psychoanalytic hypotheses concerning breast feeding and its effects on personality. These were empirical studies of the broad effects in terms of personality
development and disturbance. What is needed to test the Freudian theory are
investigations aimed at the *oral traits* – dependency, optimism and typical oral
euphoria.

In fact only one study (Hernstein, 1963) follows up the sample until subjects
are old enough to put the psychoanalytic hypotheses to the test. Of the studies
with children, only that of Sewell and Mussen (1952) used measures with known
validity, although the work of Sears, Maccoby and Levin (1957) did use carefully
developed and reliable rating scales. It is to be noted, however, that both these
last two investigations based their feeding data on maternal recollection. The
results of these three studies will now be considered, together with an earlier
study by Sears *et al.* (1953).

The work of Sewell and Mussen (1952) and Sewell (1952)

Sample. 162 farm children of 'old American stock'. They were aged 5-6 years
and from unbroken homes.

Child-training data. Obtained from interviews with mother – and, therefore,
retrospective.

Personality data. Interviews and tests were used. The California Test of
Personality, the Haggerty-Olson-Wick Behaviour Rating Scale and the Wisconsin
Test of Personality (a projective technique) were administered to the sample.
From the interview ratings an adjustment index for each child was calculated.

Statistical analysis. X^2 was used to test associations between various infant-
training practices and scores.

Results. There was no association between personality test scores and breast or
bottle feeding, demand or schedule feeding, gradual or sudden weaning, or finally,
favourable (as judged by the authors) feeding practices. In addition oral
symptoms, as rated by observers, were not associated with any of the feeding
variables.

Conclusions and comments

Sewell (1952) and Sewell and Mussen (1952) concluded from these results that
there was no support for the psychoanalytic claim that infant-feeding practices
affected personality development.

This conclusion cannot, of course, be disputed. Nevertheless the findings
cannot be regarded as a refutation of Freudian theory because of the methodological imperfections in the study, although it is undoubtedly one of the better
investigations into this problem. These imperfections will be briefly discussed.

(a) *The statistical analysis.* To dichotomise the scores for analysis by Chi-square is inevitably to lose an immense amount of information – a twenty-point scale is far more discriminating than a two-point scale. Furthermore the dichotomies imposed on the weaning data may well have been artificial – some children are *both* breast- and bottle-fed.

(b) *The weaning data.* The retrospective data may have been of dubious accuracy.

(c) *The personality data.* Personality scales such as the California test are notoriously unreliable and thus invalid with such very young children. Similarly the validity of the other scales is not fully established.

Thus then these data are so likely to be compounded with error that failure to demonstrate any significant associations is not unexpected.

The work of Sears *et al.* (1953)

This study examined the childhood antecedents of aggression in 40 pre-school children. Although a less popular study than their later work on patterns of child rearing, probably because it was written up with greater emphasis on the technicalities of the research, it is in some ways superior to the later work.

Sample. 20 boys and 20 girls.

Feeding data. Obtained from interviews with the mother – retrospective.

Personality data. Observations of dependent and aggressive behaviour in the nursery school.

Results. Dependency was positively correlated with severity of weaning and rigid schedule feeding.

Comments and conclusions

Dependency is, of course, one aspect of the oral character, so that this result appears to give some support to Freudian theory. However the sample size is small, probably too small, to accept conclusions opposed to the results of most of the other studies. Furthermore, the feeding data were retrospective – although the age of the children was such as to minimise errors due to loss of memory. The personality data, based on observations of specific behaviours at specific times in the nursery school, are probably about as good of their kind as is possible. Certainly they are far superior to teachers' ratings, maternal reports or Rorschach protocols. Although this study supports the theory, Sears *et al.* (1957), discussed below, with a far larger sample but with inferior data based on maternal interviews, were not able to confirm the findings.

This investigation does support psychoanalytic theory. However the sample size was small so that the results must be accepted with caution.

The work of Sears, Maccoby and Levin (1957)

Their investigations into the effects of child-rearing procedures on the personality development of children described in *Patterns of Child Rearing* are monumental in size and effort. Nevertheless their conclusions must be cautiously considered because the original data are by no means ideal.

Sample. 379 mothers in the Boston area. Their children were 5 years old.

Data. The data were obtained by interviews with the mother. These data were concerned with child-rearing procedures and child variables – aggression, dependency and conscience developments were among those studied. Again, therefore, the feeding procedures had to be recollected by the mother.

Statistical analysis. Correlation between rating scales.

Results. Bottle and breast feeding had no effects on aggression dependency or conscience development. Indeed the only relationship found significant was that late weaned children were more upset when weaning did occur.

Comments and conclusions

As with the Sewell (1952) study, no effects on personality from either breast-feeding or bottle-feeding have been noted. Nevertheless the nature of the data, especially the retrospective feeding data, does not inspire confidence in the results. Nor indeed do the high reliabilities of the rating scales necessarily mean high validity. If a mother incorrectly recalls her methods on one occasion, on the second occasion she is likely to repeat what she said. Thus unless it were maintained that the error of recall was due to *deliberate* distortion, these high reliabilities are not altogether convincing. The most that can be said for them is that they are better than low reliabilities.

Although *Patterns of Child Rearing* is a well-known work on the effects of training procedures, its results cannot be regarded as serious refutation of Freudian theory. The fact is that the data cannot stand careful scrutiny.

The work of Hernstein (1963)

This study will be briefly discussed because it is the only longitudinal study which follows up the sample into adulthood. It is also of interest because the work has been described by Caldwell (1964) as the 'best designed' study of those that she reviewed and as an 'excellent' investigation.

Sample. 47 boys and 47 girls, followed up to age 18.

Infant-training data. Taken from records made at the time: type of feeding and duration of sucking were recorded.

Personality data. TAT (age 12), Rorschach (age 18), also incidence of personality problems.

Results. Bottle or breast feeding had no effect on the personality scores.

Comments and conclusions

As we have made clear throughout this book, projective tests are not regarded, in general, as valid measures of personality. The Rorschach especially is under suspicion in view of Eysenck's powerful indictment (Eysenck, 1959) where he points out that validity studies of the Rorschach are positive in outcome in inverse relation to the statistical rigour with which they are conducted. Similar gloomy findings apply to the TAT. Thus this study cannot be regarded as either well designed or excellent by this writer.

These studies have been singled out for examination because, despite their shortcomings, they are the best of their kind. Nevertheless, as has been shown they are not sufficient to support or refute the theory.

Other longitudinal studies of orality

Caldwell (1964) lists a large number of studies of the effects of breast feeding which we have not discussed on account of their methodological imperfections. These are listed below followed by the reason for omission:

Hoefer and Hardy (1929)	No measures of personality.
Childers and Hamil (1932)	Data reported symptoms of disturbance: feeding data retrospective.
Holway (1949)	Personality data based on doll-play sessions: sample very small.
Newton (1951)	Teacher's rating of personality data.
Hytten *et al.* (1958)	Sample only three months old.
Durrett (1959)	Retrospective feeding data: personality data based on doll play.
Murphy (1962)	Personality measures not reliable.
Bernstein (1955)	Oral behaviour not personality data examined.

THE ANAL CHARACTER

Needless to say, the problems discussed in connection with studies of the oral character are all pertinent to investigations of the anal character. Many of the studies are not truly relevant to the psychoanalytic theory of the anal character in that they have been concerned with aggression or disturbance rather than the postulated anal traits of parsimony, orderliness and obstinacy.

Thus Huschka (1942) studied, from case records, the effects of coercive bowel training on emotional disturbances as noted in the clinic among a large sample of children who were aged from 1-13 years. Over half of this sample of emotionally disturbed children had been severely trained and most of these had reacted against the training. However, without a normal control group the results cannot be interpreted (it could be that the greater proportion of normal children receive a severe pot training). In addition emotional disturbances are not predicted only by Freudian theory as the result of harsh training. This much quoted investigation, therefore, cannot be held to refute or confirm psychosexual theory. Nevertheless some studies are relevant to psychosexual theory and use measures which are acceptable, to some extent, as objective evidence. These will be considered in more detail after the three studies discussed in relation to the oral character have been briefly examined. These studies investigated pot training but did not attempt to test the Freudian theory with any precision.

The work of Sewell (1952)

Sample, methods and analysis. These have all been fully described in the section on the oral character (see p. 63) and will not be repeated here.

Results. Sewell argued that, since only a small percentage of the chi-squares was significant, there was really no evidence for a link between toilet training and later personality in the child.

Comments and conclusions

Caldwell (1964) points out that most of the significant chi-squares were those related to toilet training. This suggested to her that there was a link and that better adjustment as measured by the California Personality Test was related to late training.

This study is cited because the dependent variables were measures with some kind of validity. Nevertheless to link late training to good adjustment (albeit tentatively) is a far cry from confirmation of the psychosexual aetiology of the anal character.

The work of Sears *et al.* (1953) and (1957)

These two investigations have been described in the previous section on the oral character. In addition, the effects of toilet training on dependency and aggression (Sears *et al.*, 1953) and the emotional reactions to training (Sears *et al.*, 1957) were studied. Again, as was the case with Sewell (1952), this work is not relevant to the psychoanalytic theory of the anal character. It has been mentioned here only because it has been previously discussed.

The work of Alper, Blane and Abrams (1955)

Samples. Two small samples of middle-class children and two small samples of lower-class children in a nursery school.

Pot-training data. No data. It was assumed that middle-class children had a more severe pot training.

Personality tests. Finger-painting and crayoning tasks, under observation.

Results. The middle-class children, compared with the working-class sample, appeared more concerned about the messiness of finger-painting and with cleanliness generally. There were no such differences on the crayon drawings.

Comments and conclusions

This study is entirely vitiated by the assumption that middle-class children have a more severe bowel training than do their working-class contemporaries. Even if this were generally true, two small samples (18 and 20) would be insufficient for the purposes of generalisation. Thus the differences cannot be attributed to differences in pot training (and hardly to social class differences). However, the personality measure – finger-painting – is, in psychoanalytic theory, a good index of anal erotism. Thus Jones (1923) says that painting is a sublimation of smearing faeces. This means that those receiving a severe training should be less likely to sublimate than those who are gently trained, since sublimation, although a defence, is not as effective as reaction-formation, in this case being too like the original, unacceptable activity.

Thus the interpretation of the results can only be that middle-class children dislike finger-painting more than do working-class children. The reasons for this may be simply in terms of domestic habits. Bowel training *cannot* be implicated in these findings.

The work of Bernstein (1955)

Sample. 47 pre-school children.

Pot-training data. Based on maternal interview.

Personality data. Observations of child in test situation. Collecting and smearing tasks.

Results. Severity of training was not related to collecting objects or to playing with paint or cold-cream.

Comments and conclusions

The pot-training data were retrospective but the age of the children was such that the length of time was not excessive. The collecting and smearing tasks are relevant to Freudian theory. Nevertheless, the study needs to show whether tasks in an experimental situation are related to similar activities in real life. Do children who collect stamps, for example, collect more in the test situation than non-stamp collectors? A more serious objection to the study lies in the age of the children. Repression of anal erotism is cultural as well as domestic. Modesty training for example plays its part. In these children the full fruits of repression may not have emerged. Finally the subjective nature of the pot-training data based on interviews must be remembered.

This study clearly fails to confirm the psychosexual theory of the anal character. It cannot be held to refute it, however, without more evidence concerning the validity of the measures of personality and the accuracy of the pot-training data. In addition, the age of the children throws some doubt on the negative interpretation of the results with regard to psychoanalytic theory.

The work of Hetherington and Brackbill (1963)

This study of nursery school children is certainly the best conducted of those investigations which use children as subjects.

Subjects. 35 pre-school children – 20 boys and 15 girls.

Pot-training data. Questionnaires were sent to the mothers.

Personality data. Obstinacy, parsimony and orderliness were assessed by several different behavioural indices for each of the three traits.

Analysis. Correlations for each sex separately.

Results. Obstinacy and orderliness were not, in these samples, found to be unitary traits, i.e. there were no correlations between the different observations of orderliness or of obstinacy. For girls the total scores for the three traits were correlated together, i.e. they formed a syndrome, but this was not the case for boys. None of these three total scores was related to severity of pot training, but the scores were related to measures of the trait (by attitude questionnaire) in the dominant parent in the household.

The authors conclude from these results, as did Beloff (1957) (see p. 22), that the term 'anal character' should be dropped. If there is an anal character it is clearly unrelated to pot training.

Comments and conclusions

The power of this study resides in the fact that more than one observational measure of each of the triad of anal traits was made. If, as it turned out, obstinacy and orderliness are not unitary traits it is impossible to say they originate in any kind of family attitude or child-rearing procedure. Nevertheless the fact that in girls the three traits cluster together to form a syndrome supports one part of Freudian theory. The derivation of the anal character from the attitudes of the dominant parent supports the concepts of Fromm and Horney (see p. 333) who regard the anal character as originating from family attitudes, not repressed anal erotism.

However, against the good points it must be remembered that the sample size is very small: correlations on samples of 20 and 15 have a large standard error. Thus failure to correlate together could easily be due to the small size of the sample. In personality studies correlations of beyond ·5 are rare and thus would not be significant with this sample. Furthermore the scales given to the parents to assess anal traits and pot training are of unknown validity. This failure to establish correlations between pot training and personality may again be due to the small size of the sample.

Finally we come to the question of the age of the sample. The anal character is an adult personality pattern and it is possible that in childhood repression of anal erotism produces different symptoms.

This study deserves replication on a larger sample. As it stands, it cannot be considered as refuting the Freudian theory of the anal character, although it is a powerful piece of evidence against it.

CONCLUSIONS FROM ALL THE STUDIES OF THE ANAL CHARACTER

As was the case with the oral character, these studies provide no support for the Freudian theory of the aetiology of the anal character. On the other hand none of these investigations fulfils adequately the criteria of a good study. The best

of them, that of Hetherington and Brackbill (1963), suffers from having far too
mall a sample.

THE PHALLIC CHARACTER

There appear to be no studies in the literature examining the origins of the
phallic character. In the previous chapter, it will be remembered, there was no
objective evidence for the phallic character as a syndrome (see p. 44). It might
be thought that studies of bladder training were related to phallic characteristics.
However the studies of bladder training, e.g. Despert (1944), have not attempted
to relate this to personality development. One further point remains to be noted
about the possible antecedents of the phallic character according to psychoanalytic theory. Weaning is important in the development of personality because
it contributes to the repression of oral erotism at a time when the child is in the
oral phase, when the mouth is the centre of excitation – the most important of
the erotogenic zones. Similarly, in Western society at least, anal training takes
place when the anus has become the centre of excitation. Bladder training on
the other hand characteristically takes place *before* the phallic stage has been
reached. Thus it may not be the crucial variable, even theoretically, in the
development of the phallic character. Rather it may be the treatment of
infantile masturbation. However the fact remains that no studies have been
conducted.

THE CORRELATIONAL APPROACH

Dissatisfaction with the results of studies such as those reported above has led
some investigators to approach the problem in a different way. Thus Triandis
and Lambert (1961), for example, subjected interview data on child-rearing
practices in six cultures to factor analysis in an attempt to discover what were
the basic variables in maternal behaviour. In the American sample, factors of
maternal warmth and the control of aggression were shown to be important.
In the less technological societies, a factor concerned with putting responsibility
on to the child emerged. Finney (1961a and 1963) has used this method in an
attempt to discover what child-rearing practices were related to personality
development.

The work of Finney (1961a, 1963)

Since both these papers report different aspects of the same investigation they
will be considered together. Finney (1961a) deals with the oral character, while
the 1963 paper examines the anal syndrome.

1961a

Sample. 31 male children and mothers. The children were all seen at a child-
guidance clinic.

Child variables. Ratings by teachers and clinicians for the following variables:

dependency, anxiety, pessimism, conscience, hostility – both overt and covert, repression.

Maternal variables. Clinical ratings and ratings at interview of the following variables: nurturance, hostility, selective reinforcement of dependency, failure to be firm, rigidity and need achievement. In addition, the MMPI hysterical character scale was used.

Analysis. Correlations were computed between all variables.

Results

(a) A syndrome of oral traits was shown to occur in this sample of children.

(b) This oral character in children was related to lack of nurturance in mothers, though only the correlation with pessimism reached the ·05 level of significance. An interesting finding was that the correlations with nurturance rose when selective reinforcement of dependency was partialled out.

Conclusions. Finney (1961) concluded from this study that these results supported the work of Goldman-Eisler (1950, 1951), discussed earlier in this section and in Chapter 3 (see pp. 47 and 13), who had argued that the oral character in adults was related not to feeding but to the general nurturance of the mother (of which feeding is a measure).

1963

Child variables

(a) General anal character
(b) stubbornness
(c) submissiveness as rated by teachers and clinicians.

Maternal variables. Rigidity – as rated in previous study. All the other variables of the previous study were available for analysis.

Hypotheses. Rigid mothers would have children above average in

1. stubbornness
2. submissiveness
3. anal character.
4. This maternal rigidity would be related more closely to the general concept – the anal character – than to either of its components.

These four hypotheses were derived from the results of Sears *et al.* (1957) who tentatively suggested that anal characteristics might be caused by direct training for orderliness – and that the relationship to toilet training was therefore coincidental in that these mothers (who tend to be rigid in everything) are the ones who give strict training. In addition, it will be remembered (see p. 49), that Beloff (1957) found that her anal students had anal parents. This attempt to link

the anal character not to repressed anal erotism but rather to more genera
parental antecedent behaviour is reminiscent of Horney and Fromm (especially
the necrophilous character, Fromm, 1965), whose ideas are briefly discussed in
the light of the evidence in Chapter 12, see especially p. 334.

Results

(a) *Within-children correlations.* Stubbornness was correlated with submissiveness ·60. The anal character correlated ·25 with stubbornness and ·44 with
submissiveness.

(b) *Correlations between mothers and children.* Maternal rigidity correlated ·59
with anal character, but only ·23 and ·18 (NS) with submissiveness and
stubbornness. Maternal need achievement correlated ·34, and over-pro-
tection (nurturance held constant) ·46 with anal character.

(c) *Further correlations in the child.* In the child, further correlates of the anal
character were: orderliness, rigidity, reaction-formation, obsessiveness and
feelings of guilt.

Conclusions. Finney (1963) argued that these results demonstrated the utility
of the Freudian concept of the anal character. Thus the anal character may be
regarded as a source trait for two reasons:

(a) It has a high correlation with its antecedents while the surface traits of
stubbornness and submission have a smaller one.

(b) It is less related to other source traits than its components. In fact anal
character was not related to aggression dependency or repression whereas
submission was related to all of these.

Thus Finney (1963) concludes that anal character is a source trait related to
rigidity in the mother.

Comments on both studies

Both these studies support the existence of an oral and an anal syndrome in
children and relate them to maternal variables. The argument, that perhaps the
oral character is related to nurturance in general (of which feeding is a measure),
is not supported by this data. If breast feeding is itself related to nurturance the
correlation with nurturance may be equally due to the relation between nurturance and breast feeding. The observed correlation, therefore, may be an artefact
of the relation between nurturance and breast feeding, just as much as the
opposite suggested by Finney – that the Freudian claim was an artefact. Similarly
with the anal character. It *may* be related to rigidity through pot training or to
pot training through rigidity. Correlational studies cannot answer this problem
unless feeding and toilet-training data are also inserted into the investigation.

Without these data, these results are predicted from Freudian theory if indeed rigid mothers do pot train severely and nurturant ones indulge their hungry infants.

The sample of 31 mothers and children is not large and, in that the children were attending child-guidance clinic, cannot be regarded as representative of the general population. The data too – ratings by teachers and clinic staff – are of questionable validity. However the neat and psychologically meaningful pattern of the results suggests that the data are in fact valid.

Conclusions

These studies confirm the existence, even in children, of oral and anal personality syndromes. They link these to maternal attitudes which are associated with different kinds of child-rearing procedures. In that there are no measures of breast feeding or pot training, Freudian theory would have predicted these results along with Fromm and Horney. Without these extra data there is no way of deciding which hypotheses the results support.

PRE-GENITAL EROTISM

So far the work discussed in this section has been concerned with the effects of child-rearing procedures on psychosexual personality syndromes. As was made clear in the outline of psychoanalytic psychosexual theory, the hypothesis is that these procedures cause repression of pregenital erotism. It is clearly important to establish whether the concepts of oral and anal erotism can be demonstrated to be useful in understanding infant behaviour. Thus the work already examined has tended to the conclusion that these psychosexual syndromes are useful dimensions of personality but are related to child-rearing practices only in so far as these practices themselves reflect the personalities of the mothers (Goldman-Eisler, 1951, Beloff, 1957, Hetherington and Brackbill, 1963, and Finney, 1963). However this evidence is far from decisive. If the existence of pregenital erotism could be unequivocally demonstrated or refuted, a far better evaluation of Freudian psychosexual theory would be possible than from studies of the effects of infant training alone.

Oral erotism

In his 'Three Essays on Sexuality' Freud makes it clear that the mouth becomes a focus of excitation partly because in feeding the warm flow of milk has caused pleasurable sensation there and partly because of a 'constitutional intensification of the erotogenic sensation of the labial region' (Freud, 1905, p. 182). Such children, oral children, become epicures of kissing and inclined to smoking and drinking. What is the empirical evidence for oral erotism – the erotogenicity of the mouth and lips of the infant? Sears (1943), in his review of the early work on this problem, argues that generally the evidence supports the Freudian claim implicit in the concept of oral erotism, that thumbsucking is the result of oral deprivation.

Levy (1928), in an early study which is still extensively quoted, showed that finger sucking was related to inadequate sucking while feeding. Sears (1943) elegantly summarises his findings in a table which indicates that of 94 children who did not suck their fingers only one had experienced inadequate sucking while feeding, defined by withdrawal from feeding too quickly due to excess of milk or lack (as in breast feeding), forced withdrawal due to time-regulated feeding, or feeding without sucking. Of the 28 finger suckers, 20 came from these 'unsatisfactory categories'. Furthermore children who used dummies did not suck their thumb. This category of dummy suckers were included as non-finger suckers, thus confusing the results. Nevertheless the main conclusion still holds – finger or dummy sucking seems to be a compensation for insufficient sucking during infancy. The Freudian concept of oral erotism is, therefore, supported. It must be pointed out, however, that the data were parents' recollections of infant behaviour. The dubious nature of such data has already been fully discussed earlier in this chapter.

Levy (1934) conducted a brilliant *experimental* investigation into sucking with puppies. The use of dogs enabled Levy to vary feeding conditions experimentally and thus provide a rigorous test of the hypothesis that insufficient sucking during feeding caused increased non-nutritive sucking – as the Freudian concept of oral erotism suggests. From a litter of six, two puppies were fed with a nipple with a small hole; in addition, after feeding they were allowed to suck a nipple to satiety. These *long feeders* averaged around one hour's sucking per day. Two puppies were *short feeders* – a large-holed nipple and no extra sucking. These averaged around 20 minutes sucking per day. The *breast feeders* were left with the bitch. The breast feeders did no body sucking and were uninterested if a finger was offered to them. The long feeders responded to the finger only before meals. The short feeders chewed and sucked each other's bodies between meals. This is impressive support for the claim that sucking is related to the amount of sucking during feeding. In this book we have eschewed experiments and studies with animals on the grounds that they were unlikely to be relevant to Freudian theory which is distinctively concerned with human motivation. However this study by Levy has been included because it was done to provide experimental support for his previous finding with infants. The results may well only apply to dogs but they support his previous findings. Sears (1943) argues that the studies by Levy confirm Freudian views in that sucking appears to be, to some extent at least, independent of hunger.

However as Caldwell (1964) points out, further studies of the effects of different lengths of feeding on oral behaviour have not all supported the work of Levy (1928) and thus have run counter to Freudian theory. Roberts (1944) found, among two small groups of thumb suckers and non-thumb suckers, that thumbsucking was related to length of feeding time. Klackenberg (1949) found that more sucking occurred after short feeds and did not occur at all in a group which used pacifiers. Levine and Bell (1950) also supported the findings of Levy (1928) in that a small group of children who were given dummies did not develop thumbsucking, with the exception of two subjects who preferred their fingers. These three studies may be held to confirm the link between the amount of non-nutritive and nutritive sucking. These investigations support therefore, the concept of oral erotism. Simsarian (1947), however, made a careful investigation of five children breastfed on demand. All these sucked their thumbs and Simsarian concluded from this that unlimited sucking opportunities did not necessarily preclude thumbsucking. This of course implied that there were other reasons, as yet unknown, for the habit. This study appears to be the first to cast doubt on the work of Levy; although in fact Simsarian generally supported the findings while emphasising that there were exceptions to the rule.

Davis et al. (1948) were the first investigators to challenge seriously the findings briefly reported in the previous paragraph. Sixty infants were studied from birth for 10 days. There were three groups – breast-, bottle- and cup-fed. The measure of oral drive or oral erotism was the length of time the babies sucked a finger offered to them. Contrary to previous findings, over the 10 days the breast-fed children increased their sucking time; there was no change in the others. Thus the very group which would have been expected to have shown the least deprivation and the least amount, therefore, of non-nutritive sucking, showed the most. However these children were very young. What would have been more interesting would have been the amount of sucking after three months. Furthermore, there was no check on the length of feeding time and if the breast feeders were quick compared with the bottle-fed, this might have accounted for the difference. That the cup-fed showed no increase in sucking is not as opposed to Freudian theory as might appear. For Freud claimed that the erotogeneity of the mouth was due in part to the pleasurable experience of sucking during feeding which was denied this sample. Clearly, however, the whole study is contrary to previous results and since the sample was so young it was clear that further research was necessary.

Sears and Wise (1950) did this in a well-known investigation in which they studied the children from 80 families. These children, from 5-8 years, were divided into groups – breast feeding, bottle feeding and cup feeding. This data was, as can be seen from the ages of the children, retrospective. Age of weaning was also studied to investigate the amount of nutritive sucking.

The results of this investigation were:

(*a*) The later the weaning, the greater the reaction to it. This result is contrary to the work of Levy and psychosexual hypotheses, in that these are the children who have had the most sucking, and who should, therefore, be less disturbed than early-weaned infants.

(b) More thumbsucking among the late-weaned infants (difference not sig.). Again this is contrary to Freudian theory.

These results support a learning-theory (Skinnerian) model for thumbsucking. Those children who have had the most experience of sucking and the most reinforcement will have the greater difficulty in renouncing the habit. Thumbsucking by stimulus generalisation from the breast or teat will be equally hard to extinguish in satisfied infants. This interpretation would account, of course, for the finding of Davis *et al.* (1948) that cup-fed children whose sucking had minimal reinforcement did not suck their thumbs. Before the results are accepted as disproving Freud and supporting Skinner, it is necessary to explain the earlier findings and to scrutinise the data on which this study is based.

First the data are retrospective: the smallest gap between weaning and recollection was four years. As we stressed earlier in this section, such data are unreliable. Robbins (1963), who asked mothers who had taken part in a longitudinal study to recollect the same data a few years later, found differences between the two sources of data as great as the differences in child-rearing procedures between the social classes! Furthermore, the amount of nutritive sucking was estimated from the age of weaning. This takes no account of the speed or duration of individual feeding so that, in fact, early-weaned infants *could* have had more sucking than late-weaned infants. Furthermore, all weaning was completed by seven months – relatively early.

Caldwell (1964) attempts to reconcile the work of Levy (1928) and Sears and Wise (1950) on just this point by claiming that the two studies do not present data on the same issue (Sears and Wise being concerned with the effects of *the age of weaning*, Levy with the effects of *duration of feeds*). This rather facile explanation will not do however because Traisman and Traisman (1958), who studied over 2,000 subjects, found that length of feeding was positively correlated with thumbsucking although very long feeders (+ one hour) had the lowest incidence. This non-linearity of relationship may indicate that the relationship between feeding and thumbsucking is very complex or, as Caldwell (1964) suggests, that the long feeding infants drifted off to sleep and thus did not receive constant oral stimulation. This last explanation is most unconvincing in view of the commonplace of reinforcement learning that random schedules of reinforcement lead to responses more difficult to extinguish than those constantly reinforced. Thus this group, if the learning theory model were correct, would be expected to show the greatest amount of thumbsucking. This study cannot really be held to support the findings of Sears and Wise (1950). Bernstein (1955), in a research that has already been discussed (see p. 68), found that feeding gratification, as estimated from time of weaning and length and number of feeds per day, was positively correlated (although not significantly) with the choice of lollipops rather than chocolate. Thus if such a food choice is related to sucking, as Bernstein assumes, it supports Sears and Wise (1950) rather than Levy (1928).

Caldwell (1964) considers that the study by Yarrow (1954) solves the apparent contradiction in these two sets of findings – the one supporting Freudian theory, the other a reinforcement model.

Yarrow (1954) investigated the relationship in 66 children between thumb-sucking and length of breast feeding, duration of individual feeds and the time during which breast feeding lasted.

The results of this investigation were:

(*a*) Children who had no breast feeding did no more thumbsucking than children who had three months of such feeding, although the non-significant difference was in the direction that longer breast feeding produced less thumbsucking. This result therefore favours Levy and the Freudian hypothesis.

(*b*) Age of weaning from breast or bottle produced no significant difference in thumbsucking. Here the non-significant difference was that late-weaned children showed more thumbsucking and emotional disturbance. This result supports Sears and Wise and the reinforcement model.

(*c*) There was a significant relationship between short feeding in the first six months and thumbsucking. This finding confirms Freudian theory.

Yarrow argues that reinforcement theory cannot account for the findings of his own research (or of the researches discussed here): that thumbsucking is re-lated to brief feeding during infancy *and* late weaning (i.e. long overall sucking time). He hypothesises that in early infancy (the oral period) the oral drive is strongest. Then fast feeding can lead to deprivation of sucking, hence fixation and thumbsucking. Prolonged satisfaction of this drive when it has begun to wane (the oral-sadistic stage when biting is more important) can lead to fixation and hence thumbsucking. This, therefore, is a critical period hypothesis but so, too, is Freudian psychosexual theory.

Conclusions from studies of oral erotism

Yarrow (1954) has certainly offered a plausible explanation of the empirical findings discussed in this section and his explanation closely fits Freudian theory in that the oral stage is precisely that period when the mouth is the centre of excitation; also, sucking would be expected to become less important as the oral-sadistic stage was begun. In addition, as Fenichel (1945) emphasises, fixation in psychoanalytic theory can be thus derived from deprivation or excessive satis-faction. These studies have indicated that at the oral phase early in infancy, failure to get enough nutritive sucking leads to other forms of oral activity. This is powerful support for the concept of oral erotism as it is described in Freud (1905). It thus appears from these studies that it is a useful and meaningful concept.

Anal erotism

Freud (1908) claimed that the repression of anal erotism in infancy produced the anal character. We have already reviewed studies demonstrating that there is a syndrome of traits or a dimension of personality that fits the Freudian description – obstinate, parsimonious and orderly. Studies relating this to pot training and anal erotism have not been generally successful and both Beloff (1957), Hetherington and Brackbill (1963) and Finney (1963) all considered that the term 'anal' was a misnomer and should therefore be abandoned. The inference to be drawn from these findings is, perhaps, that there is no such thing as anal erotism.

We shall now turn, therefore, to an examination of those investigations which throw light on the concept of anal erotism. In psychosexual theory, anal erotism refers to the highly pleasurable sensations arising from stimulation of the anal canal (Freud, 1905, p. 186).

Unfortunately the studies involving anal behaviour involve disorders of bowel function. Prugh (1954) found that colonic disorders were related to severe training. Anthony (1957) related various kinds of encopresis to types of toilet training, while Woodmansey (1967), using careful clinical studies of 60 children and reviewing a large number of clinical studies, concludes that bowel training is the most important circumstance leading to dyschezia and that 'the prevention and treatment of functional disorders of defaecation (including constipation, diarrhoea and incontinence) generally depends on avoiding toilet training . . .' (p. 221).

The reason for the lack of investigations relevant to the Freudian concept of anal erotism, compared to oral erotism, is, of course, relatively simple. In the case of the oral zone, evidence of oral stimulation, independent of hunger, is to be seen in sucking behaviour. In the case of anal erotism no such obvious evidence of stimulation is forthcoming: what perhaps might be regarded as relevant evidence would be anal masturbation or passive sodomy. No studies of these behaviours in fact exist, partly because in Western cultures at least, these responses are heavily discouraged. Anal erotism tends to be repressed. Furthermore, unless the concept of anal erotism be accepted, functional disorders of the bowel cannot be accepted as evidence for the concept. Indeed Woodmansey regards the effects of bowel training on defaecation as evidence for the inhibition of the defaecatory reflex – hence the constipation.

From this it must be admitted, therefore, that in the investigations of the consequences of toilet training on infant behaviour there exists no evidence relevant to the concept of anal erotism. One investigation of an entirely different type does deserve mention. Duthie and Gairns (1960) showed that the anal canal in man was exquisitely sensitive to pain, heat and cold. This study is evidence that the anus *could* be a centre of excitation unlike areas of the body not well endowed with sensory nerves.

Conclusions

There is no experimental evidence relevant to the concept of anal erotism.

CONCLUSIONS FROM ALL CURRENT STUDIES OF CHILDREN

The conclusions from these studies may be briefly stated. There is no strong evidence relating oral or anal characteristics in children to either weaning or pot training. However, severe problems of methodology mean that this failure to support Freudian theory cannot be regarded as a refutation of the theory. There is some evidence, however, in respect of the anal character (Hetherington and Brackbill, 1963 and Finney, 1963) that it is associated perhaps not with pot training but maternal rigidity.

The concept of oral erotism in psychosexual theory does seem to be confirmed by the experimental studies of Levy (1928), if the interpretation of results which fit the reinforcement model of sucking behaviour (Yarrow, 1954) is accepted. Anal erotism however, which is, in essence, far harder to demonstrate, has no relevant experimental work.

From this summary of the conclusions it is clear that we have not advanced far since Orlansky (1949) wrote that there was no firm evidence showing that early infantile experiences had any effects on personality development.

4. THE BLACKY PICTURES

Because of the problems of measuring child-rearing procedures and parental attitudes to them, both with adults and children, indirect testing techniques such as are provided by projective tests are of great interest. Blum (1949) has developed a projective technique – the Blacky Pictures – for precisely the purpose of testing psychoanalytic hypotheses concerning personality development.

The Blacky Pictures are a set of twelve cartoons portraying a family of dogs in situations which are peculiarly relevant to psychoanalytic theory. There are four dogs in this family – two parents, Blacky who can be of either sex (always the same as the subject taking the test) and Tippy, a sibling of Blacky. Subjects have to tell a little story about what they think is going on in each picture and how each of the characters is feeling. This spontaneous story is then scored for presence or absence of disturbance in the area concerned. In addition, after each story the subject is asked several multiple-choice questions about the cartoon. A further source of scoring is a spontaneous mention of a cartoon other than the one to which they are responding. A final task in this test is to sort the pictures into liked and disliked and choose the most liked and the most disliked. These two choices, according to the manual to the test, are symptomatic of disturbance in the relevant areas.

Variables measured and relevant cartoon

1. Oral erotism:	Blacky being suckled.
2. Oral sadism:	Blacky tearing his mother's collar.
3. Anal expulsiveness:	Blacky defaecating between his parents' kennels.
4. Anal retentiveness:	As above, with different scoring.
5. Oedipal intensity:	Blacky watching his parents making love.
6. Masturbation guilt:	Blacky licking his genitals.
7. Castration anxiety (males) or penis envy (females):	Blacky watching Tippy, apparently about to have her tail cut off.
8. Positive identification:	Blacky playing with a toy dog.
9. Sibling rivalry:	Blacky watching parents fondle Tippy.
10. Guilt feelings:	Blacky having a vision of an angelic figure.
11. Positive ego ideal and	
12. Love object:	Variables 11 and 12 use two pictures differently scored for each sex.
	(a) vision of an ideal female dog
	(b) vision of an ideal male dog.

This description of the variables makes it clear that if these measures were valid the Blacky Pictures is an ideal technique for examining the postulated relationship between child-rearing procedures and adult personality syndromes – the oral, anal and phallic characters. Variables 1, 2, 3, 4, and 7 are clearly of especial interest.

The reliability of the Blacky Pictures

Since low reliability is a general fault with projective techniques as a whole (e.g. Jensen, 1958) – a fact which virtually precludes high validity – it is essential to ensure that the Blacky Pictures are not deficient in this respect. In considering the reliability of these pictures we must not ignore the point raised by Beck (1958), who claims that results with this test are not comparable from administration to administration except between examiners who have worked together, or for the same tester. Even if this view is too extreme we must realise that the fact that highly skilled testers can achieve reliable results does not mean that all testers will be able to do this.

Test-retest reliability

Charen (1956a, b) calculated test-retest reliabilities for the Blacky dimensions among a group of tuberculosis patients. All except for the castration complex score were low or negative. These poor reliabilities could not have been due to actual personality changes, it was argued by Charen, since other personality tests revealed no such differences. Blum (1956) however has objected to this study on a number of counts, the main one being that Charen had not administered the test in full but had based his findings on the multiple-choice items alone. Actually this restriction to the multiple-choice items should have led to increased reliability since the rating of the stories is subjective and far more likely to differ from occasion to occasion as well as from marker to marker.

A further study of test-retest reliability by Berger and Everstine (1962) on a sample of college students was more promising. All the dimensions revealed significant reliabilities ranging from ·2 to ·54. It must be noted that these are scarcely high enough to justify the use of the Blacky Pictures with any confidence in an individual case. Thus as far as test-retest reliability goes, it may be concluded that although low it is high enough to support the use of the test with groups, as in most research.

Internal consistency reliability and inter-marker reliability

Granick and Scheflin (1958) using a sample of 40 children carried out a detailed study of the inter-marker reliability of the Blacky Pictures. On all but two dimensions there was 68-95% agreement in scoring the spontaneous stories among ten judges. Five judges were able to match test-retest protocols with between 72% and 100% accuracy. It is to be noted that this finding supports the contention made above concerning the importance of the marker's skill in projective tests. The internal consistency of response was high, as judged by the correlation (·92) between structured and unstructured stories. It was discovered however that there was little consistency in thematic production in response to cartoons among this sample. From this study it is probably fair to conclude that considerable consensus of opinion regarding the marking of the stories can be reached and that an individual's test-retest protocols can be satisfactorily matched. This, of course, implies that the reliability of the test is not too low.

Conclusions from the studies of reliability

The general conclusion to be reached from these investigations is that there is some agreement between markers, between occasions and between different parts of the test. It is also fair to emphasise the fact that the multiple-choice items in the test, a very unusual feature for a projective technique, do not yield any inter-marker variance – a considerable advantage. Nevertheless the reliability is not as high as is desirable and it must be admitted, along with Sappenfield (1965), that the Blacky Pictures are best used with groups rather than individuals. However it is clear that the Blacky Pictures are reliable enough to be valid. The evidence for their validity must now be examined.

The validity of the Blacky Pictures

A basic problem in the validation of the Blacky Pictures lies in the difficulty of establishing a firm criterion. This is because the criterion, psychoanalytic theory, is itself being examined by the test. Thus failure of prediction, e.g. that ulcer patients will be oral, can be due to faults in the theory, the test or both. However some evidence for the validity of the Blacky Pictures has been adduced.

Thus Sappenfield (1965), reviewing the relevant evidence, argued that their validity was supported in that generally some theoretical predictions have been confirmed in each study and only rarely have results contradicted hypotheses. However, since precise prediction is difficult from psychoanalytic theory, such an argument does not carry much weight.

Blum (1949), in the first reported study with the Blacky Pictures, argued that sex differences and intercorrelations between the psychosexual dimensions strongly supported Freudian theory and hence the validity of the test. Seward (1950), however, and Zubin, Eron and Schumer (1965) have attacked this study on the grounds that Blum only studied the significant correlations, thus capitalising on chance, and only looked for theories to test after he had obtained the results: a procedure involving the danger of fitting the data to theory and in the case of psychoanalysis, theory to data.

Blum and Hunt (1952) reviewed a number of studies which had used the Blacky Pictures on the grounds that confirmation of Freudian theory clearly implied the validity of the technique. Thus Lindner (1953) found sexual offenders more disturbed than a control group of other prisoners on nine of the Blacky dimensions. Blum and Miller (1952) found that a nine-year-old girl who was extremely high on the Blacky oral erotism dimensions was very high on other oral variables, for example, rate of ice-cream eating. Aronson (1953) was able to differentiate paranoid schizophrenics from non-paranoid cases on the two oral scales and the anal retention dimension. From studies such as these it does appear that the Blacky Pictures have some sort of construct validity.

A factor-analytic approach to the problem has also been tried. Neuman and Salvatore (1958) factored the responses and found that the internal structure of the scores generally supported the validity of the pictures in that the factors emerging were in accord with psychoanalytic theory. However, this was true only for the male sample and they concluded that the Blacky Test was best used with males alone. Apropos of this point Rossi and Solomon (1961) found that among a group of college females the words 'Blacky' and 'Dog' were regarded as significantly more masculine than the term 'Cat'. It must be pointed out here that this is scarcely surprising in that 'dog' has a specifically masculine meaning. Nevertheless this may account for the fact that the technique appears to be more effective with male samples.

Blum (1962) also factored the responses of 210 male students to the pictures. Thirty factors emerged which, in effect, replace the old scoring manual to the test. Many of these were in accord with psychoanalytic theory although the study was based on data obtained from group administration. Great weight appears to be attached to the multiple-choice items in this marking scheme.

Conclusions concerning the validity of the Blacky Pictures

The general conclusion to be drawn from these studies of the validity of the Blacky Pictures is that they do have some kind of validity. The fact that in some cases the theory is supported in studies using these pictures must be adduced as evidence for their validity. After all, it is difficult to construct *ad hoc* hypotheses to relate, for example, the responses to a picture of a dog tearing its mother's collar to the possession of gastric ulcers. This means that it is possible to use the Blacky Pictures as a test of psychoanalytic theory. Where the results agree with theory, the theory may be regarded as supported – at least to some extent. Where the theory is refuted it will not be acceptable to impugn the validity of the Blacky Pictures. The only caveat concerns the sex of the sample. Clearly failure with female samples may be due to failure of the technique.

Since it appears that the reliability and validity of the Blacky Pictures is such that they may be used to test psychoanalytic theory (although the results must be interpreted with caution), in the next section the relevant investigations will be examined. Studies will be reviewed which examine the postulated relationship between adult personality traits and the child-rearing procedures which are regarded as bringing about the repression of pregenital erotism.

A. THE ORAL CHARACTER

The work of Blum and Miller (1952)

This first study may be briefly considered because its sample consisted of nine-year-old children and it by no means follows, from psychosexual theory, that the adult character traits representative of fixation at various levels will, in fact, manifest themselves in childhood.

Tests. Measures used apart from the oral dimensions of the Blacky Pictures included teachers' ratings for oral behaviour and oral personality traits, sociometric studies and actual observations in the class-room.

Results. Rank-order correlations indicated that extreme interest in food was strongly related to oral erotism as measured on the Blacky Pictures: the need for approval and concern over giving and receiving were also significantly related.

Comments and conclusions

This study cannot be regarded as impressive support for the relationship between oral traits and oral erotism because the validity of the teachers' ratings is not known. Some of the observational data are better, e.g. the number of ice-creams consumed. However the interesting part of psychosexual character development does not lie in the 'unchanged perpetuation of oral erotism', as in eating, but in the sublimations and reaction-formations against it, as in the oral traits. The fact that the sample consists of children also weakens this investigation.

The conclusion to be drawn from this study is that the oral dimensions of the Blacky Pictures are related to eating behaviour in children. This is good evidence for the validity of the Blacky Pictures. This study, however, does not provide good support for the relationship between oral character traits and oral erotism.

The work of Kline (1970)

Kline, in an investigation of the relationship between oral erotism and oral character traits, administered the oral dimensions of the Blacky Pictures and the oral scales of the Dynamic Personality Inventory to a sample of students.

Sample. 42 female students in a College of Education.

Tests. DPI (see p. 20 for a discussion of its validity) and the Blacky Pictures.

Results. None of the oral scales of the DPI correlated significantly with the oral scales of the Blacky Pictures. Freudian theory, therefore, was not supported. However none of the oral scales of the DPI correlated with each other to any significant extent – a fact which suggests that there is nothing in common among them and which itself belies Freudian theory. Examination of the item content of the DPI oral scales certainly suggests that they are measuring oral traits as they are conceived in psychosexual theory. Item analysis reveals that they are indeed measuring common factors.

Conclusions

If the oral scales of the DPI are not valid, it is difficult to account for this invalidity. As has been discussed in Chapters 3 and 4 (pp. 13-44), there is some objective evidence for the existence of the oral character. This study, therefore, does not support the Freudian psychosexual aetiology.

B. THE ANAL CHARACTER

The work of Adelson and Redmond (1958)

Adelson and Redmond investigated personality differences in the capacity for verbal recall in a study which is of some relevance to the aetiology of the anal character.

Sample. 61 female college students.

Tests. The anal retentive and anal expulsive dimensions of the Blacky Pictures.

Method. 32 anal expulsives, 18 anal retentives and 11 neutrals were selected by their Blacky Pictures scores. One disturbing passage of prose and one neutral passage was then given for the students to learn. It was hypothesised that retentives would recall verbal passages significantly better than expulsives.

Results. Retentives did recall both passages better than expulsives: the neutral group fell between them and there were no differences in non-verbal material.

Comments and conclusions

Adelson and Redmond are not clear as to how they derive their hypothesis from psychoanalytic theory. They quote Fenichel (1945) as a support but give no more detailed reference. It seems to the present writer that the hypothesis is based on little more than a generalisation of the term 'retentive'. Clearly the non-verbal material in the experiment did not cover all the possibilities of what could constitute such material so that the comparison with verbal material must be limited.

The interest of the experiment as regards this chapter is that character traits related, even if tenuously, by psychoanalytic theory to the anal phase (thus supporting the anal aetiology of the anal character) are shown to be so related. In short this investigation may be regarded as slight support for psychosexual theory.

The work of Pedersen and Marlowe (1960)

These investigators attempted to replicate the findings of Adelson and Redmond (1958) which have been discussed above.

Sample. 70 college students.

Results. In this study expulsives recalled more disturbing material than did the retentives, whereas the retentives recalled more neutral material.

Comments and conclusions

Pedersen and Marlowe have clearly failed to replicate the findings of Adelson and Redmond. As was pointed out in the discussion of the first study, the basic psychoanalytic hypothesis under investigation was not easily derived. The conclusion to be drawn from these two studies therefore is that despite appearances they have little relevance for classical psychoanalytic theory. They cannot support it on any grounds but they can hardly refute it either.

The work of Kline (1968)

Kline (1968) investigated the relationship between obsessional traits and symptoms and anal erotism by administering to a small sample the anal dimensions of the Blacky Pictures and a number of personality tests.

Sample. 46 university students.

Measures. Hazari obsessional trait scale, Hazari obsessional symptom scale, the Beloff scale and Ai3 (anal character) were the personality questionnaires used in this study. All have been fully discussed in a previous chapter (p. 26). The anal dimensions of the Blacky Pictures were also given.

Results. All the personality scales except the Hazari traits had correlations significant at the 1% level with the anality score from the Blacky Pictures. This anality score was the total score on the two dimensions. The rationale for this addition comes from the factor-analytic study of the Blacky Pictures by Blum (1962), where a common anal factor seems to emerge. The highest of these correlations was ·6 – with Ai3. The Beloff scale and Ai3 correlated significantly (1% level) with the retentive score while only the Hazari symptom scale correlated with the expulsive score (·05 level).

Comments and conclusions

The fact that two anal scales, the Beloff scale (Beloff, 1957) and Ai3 (Kline, 1967), had positive correlations with the anal retentive dimension of the Blacky Pictures and the anality score must be regarded as positive evidence for Freudian psychosexual theory. This is particularly the case when the concept of the anal constitution (Freud, 1905), the anal stamp, is also brought into consideration. This would account for the failure of studies attempting to find positive correlations between pot-training procedures and adult personality when this factor is ignored. A given type of pot training would be of different severity for children whose anal erotism was of different strength.

The factor analysis of Blum (1962) also suggests that it is best to ignore the expulsive-retentive distinction in the Blacky Pictures and regard both scores as measures of anal erotism. This means that the fact that the symptom scale correlated significantly with the expulsive dimension and not the retentive should not be stressed. However this correlation is again support for psychosexual theory since obsessional symptoms are regarded as intrusions of repressed material into consciousness – the result of unsuccessful defence against anal erotism.

Even if the validity of the Blacky Pictures is considered suspect it is still striking that responses to an anal situation, a picture of a defaecating dog, should be linked to the possession of anal traits and symptoms.

It must be concluded that this study offers support for the Freudian aetiology of the anal character, especially when the full theory including the anal constitution is taken into account.

C. COMBINED STUDIES OF THE ANAL AND ORAL CHARACTERS

Some studies have concerned themselves with differences between the oral and the anal personality as defined by the criterion of the Blacky Pictures. These investigations will now be examined. In fact all these studies have been done by Noblin, Timmons and associates.

The work of Noblin (1962)

In his doctoral dissertation Noblin investigated operant conditioning among oral and anal psychiatric patients. However, it would be incorrect to cite this work as evidence for the psychosexual aetiology of these character types because they were selected not only on the criterion of the Blacky Pictures (measure of pregenital erotism) but also on the criteria of specific behaviours, related in psychoanalytic theory to fixation at these levels, and of the neurotic disorder from which they were suffering. These last two criteria confound the experiment since this section is devoted to the evidence for the relationship between the first criterion and these last.

The work of Noblin, Timmons and Kael (1963)

In this study Noblin *et al.* (1963) investigated the differential effect of positive and negative verbal reinforcement on anal and oral characters, as defined by the Blacky Pictures alone, so that the results become relevant to the aetiological problem.

Sample. Undergraduates classified as oral or anal by the Blacky Pictures.

Hypotheses. Orals would show conditioning to positive reinforcement and worsening of performance with negative reinforcement whereas anals should show the opposite effect.

Basic psychoanalytic hypothesis. In psychoanalytic theory the oral character is depicted as dependent and compliant, the anal character negative, hostile and resistant.

Results. All hypotheses were supported.

Comments and conclusions

Although the experimental hypotheses were supported, it is difficult to estimate how closely these results bear on psychosexual theory. It is surely arguable that ease of conditioning by positive reinforcement is evidence for dependence and submissiveness and that the opposite result is evidence for hostility and obstinacy. Thus, although these findings do not run contrary to psychoanalytic theory they may not be regarded as very positive support.

The work of Timmons and Noblin (1963)

In this investigation the same hypothesis as above was put to the test – that orals would condition more easily than anals in a verbal conditioning association. The hypothesis was supported.

Comments and conclusions

As with the previous study it is hard to be certain to what extent these findings are relevant to psychoanalytic theory. Indeed, Beloff (1957) predicted that anals would be easy rather than difficult to condition, if psychosexual theory were correct, on the grounds that anal traits are evidence of overlearning and stimulus generalisation of toilet training. Thus again it must be concluded that this study cannot with justification be used to support Freudian psychosexual theory.

D

Conclusions from all the joint studies of the oral and anal character

For the reasons discussed above, it does not seem that any of these three conditioning studies of the oral and anal character are closely relevant to the Freudian theory of psychosexuality and character development.

D. THE PHALLIC CHARACTER AND OTHER PERSONALITY SYNDROMES

No studies of these have been carried out with the Blacky Pictures.

CONCLUSIONS FROM ALL THE BLACKY STUDIES
OF THE AETIOLOGICAL HYPOTHESES

The only studies which bear specifically on this problem are those of Kline (1968, 1970). In the case of the oral character Freudian theory was not supported, while in the case of the anal character it was. However even optimistic Freudians could not regard correlations with the Blacky Pictures as definitive evidence. At best such studies offer positive evidence which must be considered alongside evidence from other sources.

The other studies of the oral and anal character discussed above are hard to interpret. In fact, despite their promising appearance they add very little relevant evidence to the problem. At least they do not run counter to psychosexual theory.

To sum up: one study contradicts the theory of the oral character (Kline, 1970); one study supports the theory of the anal character (Kline, 1968); other studies are not relevant.

FURTHER POINTS ABOUT THE BLACKY PICTURES

Since the Blacky Pictures appear to offer such good opportunities to examine the Freudian psychosexual aetiological hypotheses the paucity and the general irrelevance of the studies may, perhaps, have struck the reader as curious. However, the reasons for this are clear. Most of the investigations with the Blacky Pictures assume the validity of the Pictures and much of psychoanalytic theory and hence use them to test different hypotheses. These researches are, of course, extremely important in a study of Freudian theory and will be examined in the relevant chapters.

SUMMARY

Studies of the relationship between repressed pregenital erotism and personality traits in which the Blacky Pictures were used have been reviewed. Most of the studies were found not to relate with any precision to the theory. Only two studies seemed to be truly relevant – those of Kline (1968, 1970). One of these supported the theory (the anal character) the other failed to do so (the oral character). However it was stressed that, inherently, the Blacky Pictures can only provide interesting supportive, rather than definitive, evidence.

5. OTHER TECHNIQUES

The work of Gottheil and Stone (1968)

Gottheil and Stone carried out a most important study relevant to the libidinal theory of the oral and anal characters, in which they used the oral and anal scales developed by Gottheil (1965) (see p. 24 for a discussion of these tests).

Sample. 179 subjects. The age range was 17 to 26 years and their mean intelligence was 112. They can be considered to be of normal personality in that none was receiving psychiatric treatment.

Measures. The Gottheil (1966) 40 item oral and anal scales. In addition items were written enquiring into the mouth and bowel habits of the subjects. In all there were 186 items.

Method and analysis. The 186 items were treated each as a separate variable. Scale scores were also used as variables. The inter-correlations were subjected to an oblique (Quartimax) factor analysis. In addition an inverse factor analysis was carried out – of subjects not items. Inter-correlations between subjects were also given a cluster analysis.

Rationale. If the oral and anal characters are related to pregenital erotism, then mouth and bowel habits should also be related to these personality syndromes.

Results

A. *The first oblique factor analysis* of items yielded five factors:

1. denial of difficulty of bowel function,
2. oral traits, anal traits and one mouth habit,
3. dullness and indifference,
4. denial of anal trait items, and
5. oral optimism.

These last two factors accounted for but 5% of the variance.

This first analysis, therefore, does not suggest that oral and anal character are important features of personality (their factors account for little variance). Furthermore neither is related to mouth or bowel habits.

B. *The sub-scale analysis* yielded three oral factors – dependency, passivity and pessimism, and a demanding factor, five anal factors – non-resilience, obsessive rumination, perfectionism, parsimony, and a practical factor. However all the loadings were low. Factor scores were calculated and the inter-correlations between factors were examined. There were no correlations between oral character and mouth habits, or anal character and bowel habits.

C. *The inverse factor analysis.* This should show types of people. In fact three such types (factors) emerged:

1. weak, worrying and complaining,
2. shy, timid and constricted.
3. This factor was not meaningful.

D. *The cluster analysis* or correlations between persons revealed similar factors to the inverse factor analysis.

Gottheil and Stone concluded from these results that the existence of the oral and anal characters as syndromes of personality was supported but that they were relatively unimportant in the description of personality. The sub-scale analysis, too, reflected to some extent the psychoanalytic description and was thus a further confirmation. However there seemed to be no relationship between these syndromes and mouth or bowel habits and there was no evidence of types of people resembling the anal or oral character.

Comments and conclusions

As has been already pointed out, these oral and anal scales have no demonstrated validity other than the fact that, to experienced clinicians, the items appear pertinent to the personality syndromes, i.e. face validity. The fact that items are discriminating and measure common factors in no way shows what those factors are. Thus the failure to relate mouth and bowel habits could be due to the invalidity of the scales. Social desirability and behaviour mediated by class – e.g. 'When you meet people do you notice whether their fingernails are clean?' (item 30, anal scale) – might be confounding factors.

These same objections can apply to the mouth and bowel habits items. Social desirability, to appear in a good light, could well be expected to apply to items relating to such personal behaviour. Thus the failure to relate such habits to these personality syndromes cannot be imputed to the fact that no such relationship exists.

A more serious objection lies in the size of the correlation matrix. It is generally accepted (e.g. Harman, 1964) that there should be far more subjects than variables to achieve a stable analysis. In this case it must be noted that there are almost equal numbers. This may well account for the meaningless factor three in the inverse analysis. Thus the large number of variables (or the small number of subjects) makes the factor analysis of doubtful worth. Great caution must be shown in interpreting the loadings. The small amount of variance, therefore, accounted for by oral and anal factors may be a statistical artefact.

A further point related to the sample size should be considered in assessing the results of the inverse factor analysis. If, for example, a person scoring one SD above the mean on the anal test were regarded as an anal character, we should expect about thirty anal characters in this sample, by definition. This we might expect to find using inverse factor analysis. If, however, our criterion is more stringent this number rapidly drops, and with the imperfections of any testing devices inverse factor analysis would be hard put to isolate so small a number. Clearly, as the authors point out, inverse analysis needs a far more heterogeneous sample including non-normal subjects.

From this study therefore, we cannot conclude that the oral and anal personalities are unimportant in the description of personality and unrelated to mouth or bowel habits. The technical problems discussed above and the limitations of the sample make this far too general. Nevertheless Gottheil and Stone (1968) do not provide any support for the Freudian aetiological theory. There is some confirmation of the personality syndromes.

The work of Pettit (1969)

This investigation sought to test the psychoanalytic claim that the anal character over-values time.

Sample. 37 male and 54 female undergraduates.

Tests. A 40 item time scale, the DPI anal scales (see p. 19) and Schlesinger's (1964) anal scale.

Results. The time scale correlated significantly and positively with the Schlesinger scale (·643) and the DPI scales (·507). Pettit concluded that the psychoanalytic theory was supported.

Comments and conclusions

Although this result supports Freudian theory it does not constitute impressive evidence because of the contamination of anal and time scales. This is because the psychoanalytic writers stress the importance of time to the anal character and thus measures of the anal character tend to have time references in them. For example, item 1 of the Beloff (1957) scale is concerned with unpunctuality, as is item 15. The other items in the scale are by definition and method of scale construction related to these. Thus a correlation with a time scale is inevitable. Similarly the time scale itself is concerned with more than time. For example, this item: 'I feel I am *more conscientious* about being on time than most people.' This conscientiousness is also part of the anal character. In addition the social desirability of time scale and anal items is often high for middle-class samples – a fact which could account for the correlations.

This positive correlation between time scale scores and anal character scores means little other than that the anal measures contained, as they ought, references to punctuality. Presumably it does support the validity of the anal scales in that the correlation would be predicted.

Scodel (1957) and Wiggins *et al.* (1968)

Finally, two studies which produced results which confirmed Freudians would certainly regard as relevant to the aetiology of the oral and anal characters, deserve a brief mention. Scodel (1957), in a study of the determinants of heterosexual preference in males, found that men who liked small breasts gave more dependent responses on the TAT. Dependency, of course, is a trait claimed to be part of the oral character, who, according to psychoanalytic theory, should be concerned with breasts. The fact that small rather than large breasts were preferred would have to be attributed to reaction-formation. If we ignore the question of the validity of the TAT we must admit that only psychoanalytic theory could have explained this observed relationship. This, then, could be regarded as support for the Freudian aetiology of the oral character.

Wiggins *et al*. (1968) carried out a further investigation of this same question. Their aim was to attempt to establish whether there was any truth in the popular belief, often held by men themselves, that there are leg men, breast men and buttock men (to formalise the linguistic terms). The result relevant to Freudian theory was that preference for large buttocks was associated with a need for order, as measured by the Edwards Personal Preference scale. Need for order is one of the anal triad of characteristics. The anal character prefers large buttocks. Certainly no other theory than Freudian psychosexual theory could have predicted this finding.

Clearly these two findings could not support Freudian psychosexual theory. Nevertheless it must be admitted, even by the most convinced Eysenckian, that these results are highly interesting in the light of the theory.

CONCLUSIONS FROM THE FIVE METHODS

The number of investigations examined in this chapter is good evidence for the immense amount of research effort that has been expended in the study of the aetiology of psychosexual personality syndromes. Nevertheless Freudian theory is supported by only a few studies. Goldman-Eisler (1950, 1951) found some relationship between weaning and oral characteristics, and Kline (1968), using the Blacky Pictures, linked anal characteristics to anal erotism. The concept of oral erotism does seem to be supported (Yarrow, 1954 and Whiting and Child, 1953). Apart from this, all the other studies failed to confirm the Freudian hypotheses.

Should the weight of this negative evidence, therefore, compel us to reject the aetiology of these personality syndromes? Certainly the work of Beloff (1957), Finney (1963) and Hetherington and Brackbill (1963) on the anal character supplies a more commonsense developmental background – that orderly parents tend to produce orderly children – than does psychoanalytic theory. These findings, indeed, support the neo-Freudian views of Fromm and Horney (see p. 342).

It seems to us, however, that this heavy weight of negative evidence cannot be used to refute the theory. Rather it is a sign of the profound problems involved in testing psychological hypotheses involving infant behaviour and experience. As has been amply demonstrated, few of these studies are free from methodological difficulties. Certainly the few supporting studies cannot be used to demonstrate the truth of the Freudian theory. These too are beset with problems and the results, while reaching statistical significance, are not decisive enough to confirm the theory.

In brief, therefore, it must be concluded that Freudian psychosexual theory, as it relates personality syndromes to infantile experiences and repressed pregenital erotism, receives almost no support. On the other hand, methodological problems are more than sufficient to account for such failures.

As was shown in Chapter 2, devoted to the outline of Freudian psychosexual theory, there are implicit in the theory three distinct propositions.

(*a*) That certain constellations of personality traits may be seen in adults.
(*b*) That these syndromes are related to infant-rearing procedures.
(*c*) That pregenital erotism is a feature of childhood. It is, of course, the repression of this pregenital erotism (*c*) by the infant-rearing procedures (*b*) that gives rise to the psychosexual personality syndromes (*a*).

Chapters 3 and 4 have examined the evidence for the first of these propositions while the evidence for the last two hypotheses has been scrutinised in Chapter 5. The studies of psychosexual theory as a whole, therefore, depend upon the conclusions reached in all these chapters. In the final part, which will be of necessity extremely brief, all the evidence so far adduced will be brought together, so that the theory may be properly evaluated. All that will be presented will be the bare conclusions. Thus stated, they may appear as somewhat dogmatic assertions. The evidence, however, has been fully discussed in previous chapters and for corroborative details readers must look there.

SUMMARY OF FINDINGS

1. There is good evidence to support the existence of an *anal syndrome*. (Cattell, 1946; Beloff, 1957; Finney, 1961; Grygier, 1961; Lazare *et al.*, 1966; Pichot and Perse, 1967. Kline, 1969;)

2. There is some evidence (not so strong as above) to support the existence of an *oral syndrome*. (Goldman-Eisler, 1948, 1950, 1951; Lazare *et al.*, 1966.)

3. There is no evidence for any other hypothesised psychosexual dimensions.

4. From the considerable number of studies attempting to relate infant-rearing procedures to personality development only two studies give even slight support to the Freudian theory:

(*a*) The oral character (Goldman-Eisler, 1950, 1951)
(*b*) The anal character (Kline, 1968).

5. There is evidence for the concept of oral erotism (Whiting and Child, 1953; Yarrow, 1954).

6. Grave methodological problems have made it difficult to accept the weight of evidence, thus failing to show the effects of infant-rearing procedures on personality as refutation of Freudian theory.

CONCLUSIONS

The obvious implication of these results, and one that would be eagerly seized on by opponents of psychoanalytic theory, is that psychosexual theory has not stood up to objective empirical testing and should therefore be abandoned. Freud, the argument would run, successfully observed two personality constellations but his aetiological hypotheses to account for them were totally wrong. Furthermore the great importance attached to weaning and toilet training by psychoanalysts on account of this theory is unjustified, as is the nomenclature of these personality syndromes. If all this is abandoned the clinical observations of these oral and anal characters become less impressive. The anal character becomes the obsessional personality, a well-established syndrome in psychiatry (Mayer-Gross *et al.*, 1961), or the anancastic psychopath of Schneider (1958). The oral character, which is not as clear-cut, could doubtless be accommodated somewhere in the concept of social extraversion.

This view is not entirely acceptable however. In the first place, the studies attempting to relate these personality syndromes to infant-training procedures are methodologically deficient. This does not mean, however, that the theory should again be abandoned because it is untestable. Testability as a criterion for scientific theories applies to *logical* testability. The abundance of evidence cited already points to the fact that psychosexual theory meets this criterion. At present the theory is untestable for *technical* reasons – the difficulty of obtaining adequate training data for adults or personality data from children. Clearly we must await longitudinal studies.

A second reason for not abandoning psychosexual theory lies in the fact that it is relevant to other branches of psychology, notably in the understanding of sexual disturbances and neuroses. This side of the theory is discussed and the evidence examined in Chapter 10 (see pp. 282-306). If psychosexual theory is also found to be disconfirmed by this evidence, then there may well be good reason to reject it.

The conclusions that we draw from the evidence on psychosexual theory may be briefly stated. There is good evidence for the existence of personality dimensions resembling the anal and oral characters but these have not been linked to repressed pre-genital erotism nor to infant-rearing procedures. The aetiological hypotheses may not, however, be rejected until better techniques of investigation have been devised.

6

The Oedipus and castration complexes

OUTLINE OF THE THEORY

In the boy

The Oedipus complex is described by Freud as a situation which every child is fated to pass through and which is the inevitable result of the length of his dependence in childhood and his life with his parents. At the phallic phase, the boy 'becomes his mother's lover'.

> He desires to possess her physically in the ways in which he has divined from his observations and intuitive surmises of sexual life . . . his early awakened masculinity makes him seek to assume, in relation to her, the place belonging to his father. . . . His father now becomes a rival who stands in his way and whom he would like to push aside. (Freud, 1940, p. 189).

This is Freud's description of the Oedipus complex. However in our civilisation it is 'doomed to a terrible end' (Freud, 1940).

→According to Freudian theory, the Oedipus complex is repressed into oblivion by fear of castration – the castration complex. The mother, in an effort to stop infantile masturbation, threatens that his father will cut his penis off.

> But if, when he is threatened, he is able to recall the appearance of female genitals or if, shortly afterwards, he has a glimpse of them – of genitals, that is to say, which really lack this valued part – then he takes what he has heard seriously and coming under the influence of the castration complex experiences the severest trauma of his youthful life. (*Ibid.*, p. 190).

> From this description of the theory so far, it is clear that two brief definitions are possible:

> *Oedipus complex*. Love of mother by boy, and jealous hatred of father.
> *Castration complex*. Fear of castration by father.

> In 'The dissolution of the Oedipus complex' Freud (1924) claimed that the complex is 'smashed to pieces by the shock of threatened castration.' At the same time as this, the super-ego – the heir of the Oedipus complex – is developing by introjection or identification with the father (through this castration fear). This therefore brings about the end of the Oedipus complex and introduces the latency period.

In boys, therefore, the castration complex effectively destroys the Oedipus complex and brings about the development of the super-ego.

In the girl

With girls, the situation is clearly different. The castration complex for them consists in feelings about not having a penis; this is referred to by Freud (1927) as penis envy. At the phallic phase the girl, finding her clitoris inferior to the penis as a source of pleasure, turns against her first object of love, the mother – whom she holds responsible for her lack of penis (Freud, 1933). Thus she turns towards her father and the Oedipus complex (called in the case of girls the Electra complex) has begun. In psychoanalytic theory the girl turns towards the father, first to have a penis at her command but later to have a baby (a baby being a symbolic penis). As Fenichel (1945) points out, once the object change has been accomplished the girl's Oedipus complex is analogous to that of the boy. She loves the father and hates the mother. In girls, therefore, the castration complex effectively creates the Oedipus complex.

One further problem remains: in boys the castration complex brings about the end of the Oedipus complex and the development of the super-ego – identification through fear. What brings about the end of the Oedipus complex in girls and the development of the super-ego ? In girls the identification is anaclitic, i.e. through fear of loss of love. This means that the super-ego is not so strongly developed in women (Freud, 1927). In addition Oedipal attitudes are more likely to remain with women – they are not so strongly repressed – which (Freud, 1940) is not altogether harmful.

Thus because the Oedipus complex is the result of the castration complex in girls the development of the super-ego is different.

IMPORTANCE OF THE THEORY

Apart from the fact that the Oedipus and castration complexes are involved in the development of the super-ego and account for sex differences in that development, the Oedipus complex is crucial to an understanding of later behaviour. Thus at puberty when the repressed Oedipal feelings are reawakened the individual must 'Devote himself to the *great task of freeing himself from the parents*' (Freud, 1916-17). For the son it means freeing himself from his love of his mother and for his hatred of, or domination by, his father. Few achieve an ideal solution. 'In neurotics . . . this detachment is not accomplished at all. . . . In this sense the Oedipus complex is justifiably regarded as the kernel of the neuroses' (Freud, 1916-17).

Indeed, in his last work (1940) Freud said: '. . . if psychoanalysis could boast of no other achievement than the discovery of the repressed Oedipus complex, that alone would give it a claim to be counted among the precious new acquisitions of mankind.'

THE EMPIRICAL HYPOTHESES ARISING FROM THE THEORY

The outline of the Freudian concepts of the Oedipus and castration complexes ought to make it clear that this part of psychoanalytic theory contains propositions that can be put to empirical test. In fact the following hypotheses have been constructed from the theory:

1. Boys at the phallic stage have an overt love for their mothers: later this is repressed.
2. Girls at the phallic stage have an overt love for their fathers: later this is repressed (not perhaps as entirely as with boys).
3. Boys at the phallic stage are afraid of castration.
4. Girls at the phallic stage greatly desire a penis and regret their lack of one.
5. Boys at the phallic stage are hostile towards their fathers.
6. Girls at the phallic stage are hostile towards their mothers.
7. In adults there should be sex differences in moral behaviour – justice, guilt, duty. This hypothesis is derived from the fact that the Oedipus complex is not so surely resolved in women thus producing a less powerful super-ego.
8. Cultural factors should affect these findings, e.g. in cultures where the father does not live with the mother.
9. Different results would be expected in orphan children.

N.B. We have not considered the *genetic* hypothesis concerning the Oedipus complex stated in 'Totem and taboo' (Freud, 1913). Here Freud suggested that in some unstated (presumably Lamarckian) fashion the Oedipus complex was inherited. Since this is entirely contrary to the findings of modern genetics, we have followed Fenichel (1945) in regarding it as a cultural phenomenon depending upon the family environment. This and similar apparently unacceptable notions in psychonanalytic theory are discussed in the final chapter of this book.

EMPIRICAL STUDIES OF THE OEDIPUS AND CASTRATION COMPLEXES

THE WORK OF KUPPUSWAMY (1949)

Kuppuswamy attempted to investigate the incidence of the Oedipus complex by sending questionnaires asking which child parents preferred and which parent children preferred. This study merits only the briefest consideration since it is highly unlikely that a questionnaire could tap the Oedipus complex which was only discovered or inferred from lengthy free associations. In summary, Kuppuswamy found that fathers and mothers prefer sons and that boys and girls prefer mothers. This result was regarded as partial confirmation of the Oedipus complex.

Conclusions and comments

First of all, simple questions of preference are not relevant to the Oedipus complex. They ignore defence mechanisms such as reaction-formation and sublimation – also part of Freudian theory and not to be ignored since, according to the theory, the Oedipus complex in boys is 'broken upon the rocks' of the castration complex – that is it is repressed and unconscious. In addition problems of social desirability of responses are inherent in the questionnaire method. This study, therefore, may be dismissed as of little value. It is a good example of one of the reasons psychoanalysts ignore psychological research into psychoanalytic theory: the research concerns itself with psychoanalytic concepts so grossly distorted as to be unrecognisable.

THE WORK OF MCELROY (1950)

McElroy discussed three methods of testing the Oedipus complex. Unfortunately he gives no report of the results thus obtained but the paper is worth brief examination because it provides a useful background to the methodology of empirical investigations. It indicates immediately, for example, the shortcomings of the work of Kuppuswamy (1949). A short description of the methods is set out below.

1. A questionnaire is constructed to deal with all possible aspects of the physical appearance of women and this includes the use of drawings. Half a sample of young married men complete this questionnaire first concerning their mothers and then their wives. The other half reverse this order. The intensity of the Oedipus complex (or its presence) is measured by the correlation between the two profiles.

2. Photographs of mothers and wives are used. Three copies of the photograph of each wife are necessary. Then cards are constructed with four photographs. The mother of subject X is in the left hand corner. One of the other three pictures is the wife of subject X, the other two photographs are the wives of two other subjects selected at random. Subjects in the experiment are told the aim of this is to assess the likeness in appearance of mothers and daughters. Since selection of wife and mother will occur by chance in the proportion of one in three, an index of Oedipal strength may easily be estimated.

3. Parent preference in children. Children use pastel colours on grey paper. Then they draw their parents in pastel. Finally they are asked to name their favourite colour. The colour of each parent is then noted.

Comments

These methods may be easily elaborated. For example, a more accurate way to find the child's favourite colour would be by the psychophysical method of paired comparisons (see Woodworth and Schlosberg, 1955) where every colour is compared with each other. Again, in method two, care would have to be taken that the photographs were of a similar quality. Nevertheless it is clear that these three methods are all viable ways of attempting to assess both the strength and the existence of the Oedipus complex as it is conceived in Freudian theory.

THE WORK OF FRIEDMAN

Friedman (1950) summarised some results of his study of the Oedipus complex in the *American Psychologist*. This report was, in fact, part of his doctoral dissertation (Friedman, 1950a) and it was more comprehensively written up in a later paper (Friedman, 1952). These three reports will therefore not receive separate treatment.

For his sample he used 305 normal children, 5-16 years old. Age groups were formed of two years span. In each group there were 26 male and 26 female children.

Hypothesis

A. *Castration complex*

At the age of 5 years fears of castration will be great. During latency these fears will subside but by puberty they will be great again.

Method. Three unfinished 'castration fables' were presented to the children to complete. It was hypothesised that there would be *fewer* mentions of loss of tails, etc. at 5 years and 13 years than at other ages. Fewer castration stories were expected when castration anxiety was high because it had previously been shown that reaction-time to stories with no cutting in them was longer.

The fables used by Friedman (1952) were those originally used by Duss (1940) and translated by Despert (1946). The castration-complex fable is known as 'The Elephant'. In this a child comes into a playroom and finds his favourite toy, an elephant, broken. The subject is asked to say what he thinks is wrong with it.

Results

Boys. Significantly more had stories without cutting at ages of 5 and 13 years than at other ages. Freudian theory was, therefore, supported.

Girls. There was no difference between Oedipal ages and latency. Overall 75% of children had castration fears. This is interesting in the light of Sears' (1943) claim that Freud grossly over-estimated the incidence of castration fears.

B. *The Oedipus complex*

Friedman reviewed the earlier studies of the Oedipus complex, many of which have been discussed by Sears (1943) who concluded that Freud's notion of the Oedipus complex was a grotesquerie. Most of these studies simply asked the children which parent they preferred. As has already been pointed out, these questions are irrelevant to the Freudian concept of the Oedipus complex which is repressed and therefore unconscious. The fact that the majority of these investigations failed to support the theory is, therefore, irrelevant.

Method

(1) There were two fables for the children to complete: a child enjoys himself with one parent then meets the other. Why does the face of 'at home' parent look different? Then the same fable, with parental roles reversed, has to be completed by the children.

(2) Three TAT-like pictures were shown:

   (*a*) *Boys:* father and son are standing by the stairs and near them is a toy waggon. *Girls:* father and daughter by stairs, with a toy doll.
   (*b*) Mother and child.
   (*c*) Father and mother.

Data

1. Direct questions as to parental preference, as in other investigations.
2. Analysis of themes to pictures.
3. Analysis of movement tendencies and reactions to common psychoanalytic symbols.

Results

1. *Direct questions.* There were no significant differences between the sexes. Each sex liked each parent equally. This, therefore, follows the results of other similar investigations and fails to 'support' Freudian theory.

2. *Incomplete fables.* There were more negative endings to the fable where a child met the parent of his own sex than to the other fable. This fits Freudian theory in that the child would be expected to project his own feelings on to the parent. The difference was significant at the ·05 level. Method 2 therefore supports Freudian theory.

3. *Themes*

   (*a*) Boys had more conflict themes to father figures as did girls to mother figures. The difference was significant at the ·001 level. Freudian theory is again supported.
   (*b*) More girls fantasised that father-figure takes some positive action to toy than boys. The difference was significant at the ·001 level and confirms Freudian theory.
   (*c*) More girls than boys (sig. ·001 level) fantasised that the male figure mounts the stairs and enters the room. Again this strongly supports Freudian theory in that mounting stairs in psychoanalytic theory symbolises sexual intercourse and entering a room symbolises inserting the penis into the vagina. (See Chapter 9 for the evidence concerning symbolism and dream theory.)

As Friedman (1952) points out, all methods other than the one most commonly used, which has been shown to be faulty, support the Freudian theory of the Oedipus complex.

Comments and conclusions

These results are so clear-cut and the hypotheses tested are so clearly derivable from the psychoanalytic theory that little comment is necessary. The large sample, 307, means that the investigation cannot be attacked on grounds of sample size. The fact that the pictures and fables constitute a projective technique does not mean that the results must be regarded as untrustworthy. Certainly, throughout this book, the Rorschach and similar tests have been eschewed. But the projective techniques used here, as is the case with the Blacky Pictures, have a clear rationale rooted in psychoanalytic theory. The results hypothesised depend upon this theory, not on the theory of the test itself as is the case with the Rorschach and the Szondi. The last finding concerning the mounting of the staircase is the most extraordinary. Only on Freudian Oedipal theory could such a finding have been predicted. This result supports, also, Freudian claims about symbolisation.

It must be concluded therefore that this study by Friedman (1952) has made three main points:

1. It has empirically demonstrated the inadequacy of the questionnaire approach to investigations of the Oedipus and castration complexes.
2. It has provided good evidence for the existence of a castration complex in boys.
3. It has provided good evidence for the existence of the Oedipus complex in boys and girls.

THE WORK OF MICHAL-SMITH, HAMMER AND SPITZ (1951)

This was a case study of a Negro boy whose Oedipal desires were very close to consciousness. The Oedipal dimension of the Blacky Pictures (see p. 79) agreed with the psychiatric diagnosis and showed him to be highly disturbed about such conflicts. This is, at least, an objective verification of clinical data and as such supports the existence of the Oedipus complex.

SURVEY BY ROHEIM (1952)

Roheim reviewed some anthropological evidence concerning the Oedipus complex, in an attempt to show that the Oedipus complex occurs even in those societies where free sexual play is allowed for children. Although the evidence quoted is not objective in that no standardised measurements were used, the data are pertinent to the Oedipus complex, being myths, dreams and characteristic doll-play. Thus, according to Berndt and Berndt (1951) there is a myth among the Alaiva in Arnhem Land about Kadjari, who killed his son because the boy wanted to lie with his mother. Both now live on in a heavenly constellation. Yet among this tribe children are given complete sexual freedom. Among the Lesu in New Ireland (Powdermaker, 1933) Oedipal dreams, of which the men are much ashamed, are common. Henry and Henry (1944), in their study oı the Pilaga Indians, claimed that the doll-play of the children showed clear indications of the Oedipus complex. Finally the Fan of West Africa (Trilles, 1912) have a myth of Crocodile, son of Crocodile, who kills his crocodile father. Yet in these three societies there is freedom of sexual play for the children.

Now it is not argued that these anthropological findings are objective evidence for the existence of an Oedipus complex. However, it would be wrong to ignore them totally, because the power of a theory depends upon its ability to comprehend a wide variety of evidence and it is in this that psychoanalytic theory is outstanding. These anthropological findings are examples of such a comprehensive power.

THE WORK OF SCHWARTZ

Schwartz (1955) developed from the TAT and validated a measure of castration anxiety. Using this measure, Schwartz (1956) then carried out an empirical study of two Freudian hypotheses concerning castration anxiety.

The measure of castration anxiety (Schwartz, 1955)

Method and sample. Three groups of students, 18 in each group. There were three treatments – different films were shown. *The castration group* were shown a film of sub-incision rites. *The anxiety group* were shown a film about Negro deprivation. *The control group* saw a Chaplin comedy film.

The TAT variables. The TAT cards were subjected to a content analysis. Interrater correlation was high, ·80. Ten variables were extracted and examined. Validation was demonstrated if the castration group was discriminated from the other two groups. A list of the variables is set out below: whether they were valid or not is also indicated.

List of variables and results	*Valid*
1. Genital injury or loss	No
2. Loss or damage to other parts of the body	No
3. Damage to body image or symbols (e.g. guns)	Yes
4. Sexual inadequacy	No
5. Personal inadequacy	Yes
6. Repetitive attempts at mastery (e.g. risk-taking)	Yes
7. Intrapsychic threat: guilt, expectation of punishment	Yes
8. Extrapsychic threat: retaliation from external sources	Yes
9. Loss of cathected objects	Yes
10. Total score 1-9	Yes

As was pointed out by Schwartz (1955), Variables 1, 2, and 4 probably failed because they were simply too obvious for normal subjects.

Comments and conclusions

The fact that these variables, derived from the TAT, can discriminate the castration group from the other two groups is good evidence for their validity as measures of castration anxiety. Since one of the groups was an anxiety group, this discriminative ability cannot be due to their being made anxious by pictures of sub-incision. This validity is, on its own, support for the Freudian concept of castration anxiety. If no such anxiety existed the first two groups would not score differently.

Schwartz (1956)

With this TAT measure of castration anxiety, Schwartz (1956) made further investigations of the castration complex.

Sample. 20 homosexual male students compared with a control group of 20 normal students, matched for age, education and socio-economic status.

Tests. Variables as in the previous study.

Results. Variables: 4 – sexual inadequacy, 7 – intrapsychic threat, 8 – extra-psychic threat and 11 – a new variable based on the formal characteristics of the story (mis-spelling and discontinuity for example) discriminated the groups in the predicted direction at the 1% level by Chi-square – as did the total score. Variable 5, personal inadequacy, discriminated at the 5% level by Chi-square. Similar but less significant results were obtained using the Link-Wallace statistic (Lindzey, 1954). Variables 6, 2, 3 and 9 failed to discriminate. Schwartz (1956) argues that these results support the psychoanalytic claim that castration anxiety can create homosexuality.

Comments and conclusions

Four of the variables fail to support the Freudian theory. Furthermore variables 4 and 11, which discriminate the homosexuals, were not, in the previous study (Schwartz, 1955), related to castration anxiety. Thus only three of the original scores discriminate the groups. This cannot be regarded as good support for Freudian theory. Clearly a replication of this study is needed with more substantial samples. Nevertheless it is slight evidence for the psychoanalytic hypothesis that homosexuality is linked with castration anxiety. It is to be noted that such evidence as this inherently cannot demonstrate a *causal* link.

Schwartz (1956) also investigated sex differences in castration anxiety.

Hypothesis. Men have greater castration anxiety than women.

Sample. 20 matched pairs of males and females.

Results. Variables 5 and 6 – personal inadequacy and repetitive attempts at mastery – discriminated the groups at the 5% level, as did the total score. The other differences were non-significant.

Comments and conclusions

The Freudian hypothesis receives some support although it is clear that there is a considerable over-lap of distributions. It is interesting that variable 5, which failed to discriminate before, was this time successful. From this study the Freudian theory that men have greater castration anxiety than women is supported to a limited extent.

Conclusions from the studies by Schwartz (1955, 1956)

These studies provide good evidence for the existence of castration anxiety and a useful measure of it. However the investigations with this TAT device give only limited support to the notion that homosexuality is linked with castration anxiety and that men have greater castration anxiety than women. Clearly more studies are needed with these variables and a factor analysis of them would enable weighted scores from each to be used, perhaps allowing for greater discriminative power. In brief the results may be thus summarised:

1. The existence of castration anxiety: good support.
2. The link between homosexuality and castration anxiety: limited support.
3. Greater castration anxiety among men than women: limited support.

Findings 2 and 3 will be discussed again in a later chapter (p. 279).

WORK OF BIDDLE (1957)

Biddle regressed 100 subjects back to three years old under hypnosis and then investigated their Oedipal fantasies. The major finding was that all children strive for union with both parents. The conclusion, therefore, was that the Oedipus complex was not supported.

Comments and conclusions

This is an interesting study in that hypnosis was the original technique by which unconscious mental activity was uncovered in the beginnings of psychoanalysis. Only later was free association preferred, partly because Freud found difficulty in hypnotising patients. However the assumption that hypnotic regression to any age gives a true representation of what in fact occurred at that age is by no means proven. Furthermore the choice of three years of age to investigate the Oedipus complex is curious. Yet another objection to the study involves the lack of quantification of the data and their interpretative nature. Thus the assertion that the concept of the Oedipus complex was not confirmed by this study is not considered of great importance in the empirical study of the problem. This investigation is best ignored.

THE WORK OF RABIN (1958)

Rabin investigated some psychosexual differences between Kibbutz and non-Kibbutz Israeli boys.

Sample. 27 boys reared in a Kibbutz. Mean age, 10 years 2 months. 27 boys reared in their families. Mean age, 10 years 2 months.

Test. The Blacky Pictures (Blum, 1949).

Hypotheses
1. Fewer Kibbutz-reared children will exhibit Oedipal intensity compared with the family children.
2. Less identification with the father will be noted among the Kibbutz children compared with the family children.

Results. These hypotheses were supported. Among the Kibbutz boys there was less Oedipal intensity and less identification with the father.

Comments and conclusions

In the Kibbutz children are reared by a nurse, live communally, and see their parents only for a short time during the day (usually in the evening). Thus these hypotheses follow naturally from such a regime. The fact that they were supported fits psychoanalytic theory but can hardly be regarded as very powerful evidence. It means little other than that the less you see your parents, the smaller will be the emotional attachments to them. This study is useful only in the context of other studies of the Oedipus complex, where it may be used as one small piece of evidence.

THE WORK OF LASKY AND BERGER (1959)

Lasky and Berger administered the Blacky Pictures to patients before and after genito-urinary surgery in a study relevant to the castration complex.
Sample. 30 adult male patients. Age range 20-67 years, median 48.
Tests. The Blacky Pictures were given seven days before the operation and six days after it.
Results. Phi-correlations were worked out for all the dimensions of the Blacky Pictures (see pp. 79-83 for description of this projective test). The most affected dimensions (the smallest correlations) were: *masturbation guilt, castration anxiety* and *narcissistic love object*. These findings certainly support the hypothesis that genito-urinary surgery would produce castration anxiety.

Comments and conclusions

Although these results support Freudian theory, it must be remembered that the test-retest reliability of the Blacky Pictures is not high (Charen, 1956). This investigation by Charen has been discussed (p. 81) where it was pointed out that he only used the multiple-choice questions. Nevertheless the fact that the two dimensions most affected were those related to castration discounts to some extent the effects of low test reliability. It must be concluded, therefore, that this study supports the concept of castration anxiety.

WORK OF HAMMER (1953)

Relevant to the study by Lasky and Berger (1959) is the study of symbolism among a sample of prisoners who had been eugenically sterilised (for sexual offences). This investigation by Hammer has been fully described in the chapter on symbolism (p. 209). Suffice it to say here, therefore, that these sterilised prisoners showed evidence of castration fear in their drawings on the House, Tree, Person Test. Chimneys were affected as were the branches of trees. Similar changes were not noted among a control group of surgical patients. Thus, in a manner similar to that of Lasky and Berger, although only incidental to the study of symbolism, Hammer also provides evidence for the existence of the castration complex.

THE WORK OF SARNOFF AND CORWIN (1959)

This was an experimental study of castration anxiety and the fear of death.

Rationale. Repressed castration anxiety is likely to be manifested as a fear of death. It therefore follows that individuals with severe castration anxiety should have a very considerable fear of death. Subjects with severe castration anxiety should show a greater fear of death than subjects with low castration anxiety after this castration anxiety has been aroused.

The following abbreviations will be used to describe this experiment since otherwise, as can be seen from the rationale, the repetitious language becomes too cumbersome:

HCA	High castration anxiety	MS	Morality scale
LCA	Low castration anxiety	HSA	High sexual arousal
FDS	Fear of death scale	LSA	Low sexual arousal

Hypothesis. HCA subjects will show greater fear of death than LCA subjects after being exposed to sexually arousing stimuli.

Design. A before and after design was used. There were two treatments (levels of sexual arousal) and two levels of castration anxiety which was measured in a pre-experimental session.

Subjects. 56 male undergraduates.

Method

A. *The pre-tests*
   1. 5 item FDS
   2. 5 item MS
   3. Blacky Castration Picture used to test for castration anxiety. On this variable, *36 LCA* and *20 HCA* subjects were selected.

B. A four week time-gap was allowed.

C. *The experimental sessions.* Two experimental conditions to which half of each group went. HSA: 4 pictures of nude women to which subjects wrote aesthetic responses. LSA: 4 pictures of fully-clothed models. Again aesthetic responses were recorded.

D. *The post-tests.* MS scale and FDS scale were again completed. In addition a questionnaire to assess degree of sexual stimulation was filled in.

Results

1. The HSA group were, in fact, more sexually aroused by the nude women than were the other group by the models.
2. HCA group showed a significantly greater increase in score on the FDS in the HSA condition than did the LCA group.
3. In the LSA condition there were no significant differences.
4. To test whether it was guilt causing the shift of scores, high and low subjects on the morality scale were compared on the FDS under both conditions. The difference was not significant.

Finding 2, that under conditions of high sexual arousal the fear of death score of those with great castration anxiety increased, while under low conditions it did not, is very strong support for the Freudian concept of the castration complex.

Comments and conclusions

As should be clear, this is an elegant and clever design. Any failures in the tests used would spoil the results so that it can hardly be argued that the tests were invalid. If they were, these results are even more remarkable. The fact that those with strong castration anxiety should, when sexually aroused, show a greater fear of death than those low on castration anxiety, can only be understood in terms of the whole Freudian concept of the castration complex. Finding 4 makes it clear that the results were not due to feelings of guilt.

Unlike correlational studies where the correlations can be due to errors common to both tests, e.g. response sets, and where the validity of the test must be proven beyond doubt, experimental studies, where conditions are manipulated according to a rationale and mean scores predicted, are more difficult to fault. They provide a far more rigorous test of any theory than do non-experimental studies, provided that, as in this case, the experimental rationale is relevant to the theory.

It must be noted that the castration complex is different from castration anxiety. It embraces much more: for example it is related to fear of death and other symbolic injuries. Castration anxiety on the other hand is more specific, as in the study by Lasky and Berger (1959), where it refers simply to fear of genital injury. The complex refers to all the associated repressed material. This study by Sarnoff and Corwin provides strong support for the Freudian concept of the castration complex.

THE WORK OF STEPHENS

Stephens (1961) carried out a cross-cultural study of menstrual taboo using the method of Whiting and Child (1953) which has been fully described and discussed on p. 52. This study is also to be found in Stephens (1962).

Rationale. In 'Totem and taboo' Freud (1913) argued that in the taboos, myths, superstitions and ceremonies of primitive societies could be seen phenomena which in our society are usually deeply hidden. For example totemism was considered to be an institutionalised neurotic symptom caused by the Oedipus complex.

Hypothesis of the present study. The extensiveness of menstrual taboos in any society is determined by the intensity of castration anxiety felt by the men of that society.

Measures. Stephens (1961) argued that because there was no measure of castration anxiety *per se*, it would be necessary to measure the *antecedents* of castration anxiety. These are, according to Freudian theory, child-rearing procedures, especially those connected with the Oedipal situation. In addition he used three measures of the hypothesised *consequences* of castration anxiety – in this case, castration-like incidents in folk lore. Finally a menstrual taboo scale was used. Thus 15 measures were used in all:

10 measures of antecedent child-rearing procedures
The total scores derived from these measures
3 measures of the consequences of castration-like anxiety
1 menstrual taboo scale.

Data on which measures were based. The anthropological reports of 72 primitive societies, as used by Whiting and Child (1953). Ratings were made for each of the variables.

Results. These are best set out in a table.

Child-rearing antecedent	Relation to taboo scale in expected direction	Probability of chance occurrence
1. Diffusion of nurturance	Yes	·27
2. Post-partum sex taboo	Yes	·01
3. Severity of masturbation punishment	Yes	·01
4. Overall severity of sex training	Yes	·05
5. Severity of aggression training	Yes	·18
6. General pressure for obedience	No	·65
7. Severity of punishment for disobedience	Yes	·19
8. Strictness of father's obedience commands	Yes	·20
9. Whether or not father is main disciplinarian	Yes	·02
10. Importance of physical punishment as discipline	Yes	·07
11. Total of variables 1 to 10	Yes	·000001

The folk-lore incidents were not related to the menstrual taboo scale.

Comments and conclusions

It is clear from the results that the hypothesis is very strongly confirmed. This means, as Stephens (1961) points out, that menstrual taboos are affected by the castration complex, that there is a widespread phenomenon (72 societies) of castration anxiety and that it does originate in the Oedipal situation. It also implies that there is a widespread phenomenon of the Oedipus complex. All this is powerful evidence for the Freudian theory.

Careful scrutiny of the table of results, from the viewpoint of psychoanalytic theory, makes the evidence even more impressive. Thus the antecedent child-rearing procedures which would appear to be less relevant to castration anxiety are supportive of the hypothesis but to a less degree (e.g. variables 1 and 8) than those which are clearly most pertinent (e.g. variables 3 and 10). The enormously high statistical significance of the total score with the menstrual taboo scale is remarkable.

The fact that the folk-lore incidents did not also confirm psychoanalytic theory is curious but may only be due to the fact that other influences than castration anxiety affect the incidence of genital injury, severing and other kinds of physical injury in folk-tales. There must, for example, as in Homer, be historical antecedents as well as psychological ones.

This study by Stephens (1961) seems to us to constitute most impressive and powerful evidence for the Freudian concept of the castration complex.

THE WORK OF WHITING, KLUCKHOHN AND ANTHONY (1958)

Whiting *et al.*, using the technique of rating societies, studied the function of male initiation ceremonies at puberty. In so doing they examined certain hypotheses concerning the Oedipus complex.

Rationale and hypothesis. The rationale for this study was derived from the anthropological speculations in 'Totem and taboo'. It was assumed that the ideal antecedent for the development of the Oedipus complex was a long *post-partum sexual taboo*. This, of course, enables the child to sleep with its mother. Similarly a short post-partum sexual taboo will tend to inhibit development of the Oedipus complex. Thus, by selecting societies with long post-partum sexual taboos and those with short taboos, the effects of the Oedipus complex should become apparent. The following hypothesis was formulated:

> Societies with a long post-partum sexual taboo (high on the Oedipus complex) will be more likely to have initiation rites (which are symptomatic of the Oedipus complex in psychoanalytic theory (Fenichel, 1945)) than will societies with a short taboo.

Sample. 56 societies, representing 45 of the 60 culture areas designated by Murdock (1957).

Measures. The ethnographic literature relevant to these 56 societies was searched and ratings made.

Results. 80% of the tribes with long taboos had initiation ceremonies. The chi-square (sig. at ·001 level) is hard to interpret in that through known historical connections the societies may not have been entirely independent cases.

Comments and conclusions

In this paper Whiting *et al.* concentrate on a careful examination of the background of various tribes in the sample, whose child-rearing procedures do not accord with their initiation rites, so that they are less interested than Stephens (1961) in testing the psychoanalytic theory. Nevertheless these results do support psychoanalytic theory concerning the Oedipus complex and its acting out in ceremony.

THE WORK OF BLOCK AND VENTUR (1963)

This was an investigation of castration anxiety in a sample of amputees (symbolic castrates).

Test. The Blacky Pictures – the castration dimension.

Sample. 20 amputees were compared with 20 surgical controls.

Results. The amputees were more disturbed on the castration dimension than the controls. Block and Ventur argue that this is support for the psychoanalytic theory of the castration complex and *ipso facto* for the validity of the Blacky Pictures.

Comments and conclusions

Although it is true that Freudian theory would predict an increase in castration anxiety among amputees, this study cannot be regarded as powerful support for the theory. This is because a simpler explanation of the findings is available. The castration card of the Blacky Pictures shows Blacky, blindfolded, with a knife suspended over his extended tail. It is not surprising that patients whose limbs have recently been cut off should be more upset at this picture than other surgical patients. This is not to impugn the Blacky Pictures. If, for example, homosexuals were higher scorers on this picture than normals, as Freudian theory predicts, a simple explanation would not be available.

This study, therefore, cannot rank high as supporting evidence for the Freudian theory of the castration complex.

THE WORK OF LEVIN (1966)

Levin investigated the Freudian concept of the female castration complex.

Sample. 26 career women (mean IQ 129) and 25 homemakers (mean IQ 122).

Tests. 8 independent scores from the Rorschach test and the total of these scores.

Results. The unmarried, career women scored significantly more highly on the total measure of the castration complex than did the homemakers. This difference was not attributable to a general neurotic disturbance. However since 5 of these 8 scores failed to discriminate the groups (Chi-square test), Levin questions the use of the word 'complex'. It appears from this evidence that it is not a unitary variable (not all scores discriminated) and that the construct of the castration complex is unnecessary.

Comments and conclusions

The dubious validity of the Rorschach test makes these results of doubtful value. Until the study is replicated, using different measures of castration anxiety or the castration complex, or using an experimental procedure as did Sarnoff and Corwin (1959), little weight can be placed on these results.

THE WORK OF KREITLER AND KREITLER (1966)

Kreitler and Kreitler investigated children's concepts of sexuality and birth.
Method. 25 kindergarten workers interviewed the children. They were trained to do this during a course at university.
Sample. 60 Western boys, 60 Western girls, 35 Oriental boys and 35 Oriental girls. Age range 4-5$\frac{1}{2}$ years.

Freudian hypotheses tested

1. Boys believe in the universality of the penis.
2. The sexual act is considered to be aggressive.
3. Children are believed to be born through the anus.

Results

1. There was no hint of castration of girls in any of the sample. The majority of the Western and over half of the Eastern sample knew that boys were different from girls. Therefore Freudian theory must be rejected, according to the authors.
2. 95% of the sample said anal birth was an impossibility. Again Freudian theory is rejected.
3. Father's role in the production of children was not grasped and only 30% of the children thought that their parents were different from other parents.

According to Kreitler and Kreitler the universality of the penis, a view according to Freudian theory held by children, is refuted by these results. As a result a new basis for the castration complex is required.

Comments and conclusions

There are several points about this study which merit attention before the conclusions of the Kreitlers can be assessed. The first of these concerns the interviewers, who were not fully trained social scientists but kindergarten teachers. Their level of skill remains therefore an important yet unknown factor. The next point concerns the validity of the children's responses. It has long been, for example, a criticism of Piaget's work on animism among children that the very form of the questions may have suggested answers to the child, a view which receives some support from similar work carried out in non-European languages where the structure of the language is very different (Munn, 1961). In the present investigation, children who had been formally acquainted with the anatomical differences between the sexes might well be unwilling to tell an interviewer what they really thought in case it seemed silly. This is a similar response set to that of social desirability. Only very sensitive and skilful interviewing can overcome this. As Newson and Newson (1963) found even among adults, telling the interviewer what he seems to want is also an extraneous variable affecting the veracity of interview data. Thus the skill of the interviewers and the accuracy of the data are not unquestionable.

However, even if we accept the results, the basis of the castration complex is not swept away as is claimed by Kreitler and Kreitler (1966). Thus Fenichel (1945) argues that 'Only the high narcissistic cathexis of the penis at this period (around 5 years) explains the efficacy of castration anxiety. . . .' This high narcissistic evaluation is due to the fact that at the phallic stage the penis becomes rich in sensation. Freud (1909), in the case of Little Hans, also points out that castration fear can be induced by the sight of the female genitalia which cause the boy to take a joking castration threat seriously. Thus the part of the psycho-analytic theory which the Kreitlers claim to be the cause of the castration complex and which their findings refute, namely the belief that women once had a penis, is merely *one* of the causes, not the *sole* cause.

Thus their results by no means cast doubt on the concept of the castration complex even if they are accepted. Nevertheless the difficulties of interview data, and the fact that the interviewers were not highly trained, makes the results questionable. Rational knowledge does not so easily move fantasy. Since, too, the castration complex depends in psychoanalytic theory on factors other than a belief in the universal penis, indeed it is partly due to Oedipal guilt, this study does not appear to us, as it does to Kreitler and Kreitler, to undermine Freudian theory.

STUDIES OF THE OEDIPUS AND CASTRATION COMPLEXES THROUGH THE COLLECTION OF DREAM MATERIAL

Hall and his associates at the Institute of Dream Research have conducted some large-scale studies of dream content. These investigations have been fully described and discussed in the chapter on dreams (p. 229 et seq.). However a very short summary of the findings will be given here because many of these studies were concerned with the Oedipus and castration complexes.

Hall (1955) studied the dream of being attacked (see p. 229). He concluded that it was symbolic of being castrated rather than of castration anxiety. One of his reasons for this conclusion was that it was usually associated with feelings of weakness and impotence. Despite the ingenuity of the arguments this particular study, on its own, cannot be regarded as very convincing evidence for the castration complex.

Hall and Van de Castle (1963) formed the hypothesis, from psychoanalytic theory, that males would have more dreams of castration anxiety than would females who, in their turn, would dream more of castration wish and penis envy (see p. 233). Examples of dream material regarded as symbolic of castration anxiety were the inability of the dreamer to use his penis or a penis-symbol such as a gun or spear. If this happened to another person, the dream was classified as symbolic of castration-wish. Finally, if a dreamer acquired a penis or symbol in the dream or changed into a man, this was regarded as a penis-envy dream. With such criteria as these the content of the dreams of 120 college students was examined. The hypothesis was strongly supported. This study by Hall and Van De Castle is impressive support for the Freudian concept of the castration complex, as indeed it is for psychoanalytic dream theory.

Hall and Domhoff (1963) investigated some sex differences in dreams (see p. 231). They found that in the dreams of males there were significantly more encounters with males than there were in the dreams of females. These authors interpreted this sex difference as positive evidence for the Oedipus complex. Certainly such a difference would be predicted from Freudian Oedipal theory, but clearly on its own it is not very strong support.

Hall and Domhoff (1962a, b) studied aggression in dreams (see p. 231). In the dreams of men there were significantly more aggressive encounters with males than with females. In the dreams of women, however, aggressive encounters were evenly split between men and women. As with the previous study these findings are in accord with Freudian theory since hostility to males is a reflection of the old Oedipal hatred of the father. Nevertheless the findings are only corroborative evidence, not definitive proof.

Hall (1963) carried out a further investigation of the Oedipus complex in dreams (see p. 231). There were four hypotheses:

1. that in all dreams there would be more male than female strangers,
2. that there would be more male strangers in male than in female dreams,
3. that there would be more aggressive encounters in dreams with male strangers, and
4. that such encounters would be more common in male than in female dreams.

The basic assumption of these hypotheses is, of course, that a male stranger represents the father. Even for a girl this is true since the castration complex for girls does not entirely wipe out the fantasy of the good mother.

All these hypotheses were supported, a finding which strongly confirms

Freudian Oedipal theory, in that other hypotheses to account for the results, even of the *ad hoc* variety, are not easy to develop.

Conclusions from the dream studies

If the results of all these dream studies are considered together, they constitute impressive support for the concepts of the Oedipus and castration complexes. To account for all these results, a large number of *ad hoc* hypotheses would have to be pressed into service – a less parsimonious procedure than the invocation of Freudian theory by which they were predicted.

THE WORK OF ALLEN (A STUDY OF EGO STRENGTH)

Allen (1957) investigated the effects of childhood experience on adult personality, using the cross-cultural methods of Whiting and Child (1953). However, this research differs from the others discussed in this chapter in that it is concerned with the more general psychoanalytic proposition that such experiences affect ego strength. It is not concerned with the effects of specific experiences on specific personality patterns.

Rationale. In Freudian theory indulgence or deprivation should result in low ego strength. Psychoanalysis thus produces a curvilinear prediction.

Measures. As developed by Whiting and Child, a rating of *initial satisfaction* for a society was based on such variables as the amount of freedom for a child to perform an initial habit, encouragement of such habits and the amount of concurrent anxiety aroused by the habit.

Similarly a seven point rating scale of societies for *ego strength* was developed. At one extreme were societies characterised by passive acceptance of, and rigid approaches to, problems where defensive processes seemed visible, at the other were those societies where there was evident a flexible approach to difficulties and a tolerance of frustration. The reliability of this measure (independent markers) was ·74.

Finally a measure of the environment was taken where climatic factors, food supplies and soil fertility were taken into account along with other similar variables.

Sample. 58 societies which had been rated by Whiting and Child for initial satisfaction.

Results. Correlations with ego strength were:

		Sig
Average satisfaction (oral, anal, sexual, dependent, aggression)	+ ·34	·05
Average anxiety	− ·54	·001
Erogenous satisfaction (oral, anal, sexual)	+ ·32	·02
Erogenous anxiety	− ·44	·001

Of the individual variables, sexual satisfaction and sexual anxiety had the highest correlations with ego strength, being + ·4 and − ·44 respectively. Severity of the environment had no significant correlations with any of these scores. All these regressions were linear, *not* curvilinear as predicted from psychoanalytic theory.

Comments and conclusions

The psychoanalytic claim that excessive satisfaction is as fixating as deprivation is not supported by the linearity of these results. However, although it could be argued from these findings that psychoanalytic theory is wrong on this point, Allen (1967) suggests that there may not have been sufficient numbers in the sample with very high or very low scores on indulgence or deprivation of satisfactions. This is, of course, because societies as a whole are not as extreme as individuals within a society with whom psychoanalytic theory is concerned.

Nevertheless, the general finding that these childhood experiences of satisfaction and frustration were related to ego strength is support for Freudian theory. Objections to the validity of these societal measures will not be considered here (see p. 54 for a full discussion of this cross-cultural method), but in view of the positive correlations reported which would be lowered by metric error it must be concluded that this study of Allen supports in general rather than in detail the Freudian claim that child-rearing experiences affect the balance of the adult personality.

TWO LIGHT-HEARTED STUDIES

The work of Johnson (1966)

Johnson, in a report which perhaps should not be taken wholly seriously, found that significantly more men than women in a sample of 300 undergraduates taking an exam returned their pencils. This, he claimed, *could* be taken as evidence of penis envy. It could, of course, also indicate that women need pencils more than men or are more dishonest than men or more flustered by the rigours of examination. Readers can put their own value on this study.

The work of Landy (1967)

Landy also investigated the Freudian theory of penis envy and castration anxiety in a study which the present writer considers to be a satire of experimental studies of psychoanalytic theory. He hypothesised that women would open an American cigarette pack by raising the top flaps to form a cavity and would get the cigarette by pushing it up from the bottom. Men, due to castration anxiety, would tend to castrate the pack and get the cigarette by thumping the bottom so that, like an ejaculation, it leaps out. 65 men and 61 women were observed through a one-way mirror when a heavily bandaged experimenter asked them to get him a cigarette from a new pack. A chi-square analysis of the methods of opening the pack supported the hypotheses derived somewhat tenuously from Freudian theory. Neither of these two studies can be considered as powerful support for psychoanalytic theory.

CONCLUSIONS FROM ALL THE STUDIES OF THE CASTRATION AND OEDIPUS
COMPLEXES

The conclusions to be drawn from these studies may be briefly summarised:

1. Direct questions of parental preference are not relevant to the Oedipus complex (Kuppuswamy, 1949; Friedman, 1952).
2. There is good evidence for the Oedipus complex (Friedman, 1950; Hall, 1963).
3. There is good evidence for the castration complex (Friedman, 1950; Schwartz, 1956; Sarnoff and Corwin, 1959; Stephens, 1961; Hall and Van De Castle, 1963).

Summary of findings on the castration complex and Oedipus complex

Investigation	Result	Comments
Kuppuswamy (1949)	No support	Inadequate methodology
Friedman (1952)	Support for O. and C.	Large sample, projective measures
Michal-Smith *et al.* (1951)	Some support for O.	Case study with Blacky pictures
Schwartz (1955, 1956)	Support for C.	Projective measures
Biddle (1957)	No support for O.	Hypnotic regression used of questionable validity
Lasky and Berger (1959)	Some support for C.	Blacky pictures with surgical patients
Hammer (1953)	Some support for C.	HTP projective test
Sarnoff and Corwin (1959)	Support for C.	Experimental technique used. Very powerful evidence
Stephens (1961)	Support for C.	Cross-cultural study. Very powerful evidence
Whiting *et al.* (1958)	Some support for O.	Cross-cultural study
Block and Ventur	Some support for C.	Blacky pictures used with amputees
Levin (1966)	No support for C.	Rorschach used, of dubious validity
Kreitler and Kreitler (1966)	No support for C.	Interview data, of unknown validity
Dream studies by Hall and associates (1955-63)	Support for O. and C.	Based on analysis of dream content

PSYCHOANALYTIC THEORY AND STUDIES OF MATERNAL DEPRIVATION

Since psychoanalytic developmental theory stresses the importance of early infantile experience on later adult personality and since the mother is, clearly, in Western child-rearing procedures at least, a key figure in such experiences, it is generally assumed that studies of maternal deprivation are of great relevance to psychoanalytic theory. This view is reinforced by the fact that many of the investigations of the effects of maternal deprivation have been carried out by researchers with psychoanalytic orientations, for example Bowlby (1944) and Anna Freud and Burlingham (1944).

Before it is possible to interpret the results of these studies, a number of points need clarification and certain methodological problems need to be understood.

THE MEANING OF MATERNAL DEPRIVATION

Yarrow (1961) points out that 'the concept of maternal deprivation is a rather muddled one'. Thus in the literature the term has been used to encompass such different events as institutionalisation, separation from the mother or mother substitute, multiple mothering and distortions in the quality of maternal care. A major problem of research in this area is that, for obvious reasons, it is often difficult to find samples where only one of these events has occurred. Institutionalisation often takes place just because there are severe distortions in the quality of maternal care or because the child has perforce been separated from his mother. Where separation is due to death the traumatic nature of death itself may produce effects independent of the separation.

THE RELEVANCE OF STUDIES OF MATERNAL DEPRIVATION TO PSYCHO-ANALYTIC THEORY

Of course it must be pointed out before discussing the consequences of maternal deprivation in the light of Freudian theory, that Bowlby himself is in the English rather than the classical tradition of psychoanalysis. This means his interest in maternal deprivation is not the same as that of an orthodox Freudian. Thus he explicitly states (1969) that he has abandoned the psychical energy model of Freudian theory which only a few psychoanalysts have done. He has done this for a number of reasons, chief of which is his claim that the model is unrelated to the concepts that 'Freud, and everyone since, regards as truly central to psychoanalysis – the role of unconscious mental processes, repression as a process actually keeping them unconscious, transference as a main determinant of behaviour, the origin of neurosis in childhood trauma.'

The psychical energy model

In 'The neuro-psychoses of defence' Freud (1894) drew up the model, arguing that in mental activity a quota of affect or a sum of excitation can be distinguished. This is capable of increase, diminution, displacement and discharge and is analogous to an electric current. Furthermore he claimed that two principles, inertia and constancy, govern the mental apparatus. The principle of inertia tends to keep the quantity of excitation within the system as low as possible, whereas the principle of constancy attempts to keep it constant. These last properties are more elaborately described in *A Project for Scientific Psychology* (1895).

The object-relations model

In place of this Bowlby (1969) has used the *object-relations model*. He states that unlike the psychical energy model that was taken from current scientific thought and was not implicit in the clinical data gathered by Freud, the object-relations model is derived from clinical experience and from the data obtained during analysis of patients. From the viewpoint adopted in this book this is, of course, no recommendation! For the whole point of this book is to attempt to underpin Freudian theory with observations and data more satisfactory by the criteria of science than clinical experience and analysis of patients, on which most of Freudian theory is based.

Since this model is a product of clinical data, cannot be regarded as scientific and is a long way removed from orthodox theory, a brief description must suffice. Bowlby uses his own version of the model although he admits to being strongly influenced by the work of Melanie Klein, Balint, Winnicott and Fairbairn. His model employs a view of instinctive behaviour similar to that of ethology. The central concepts are 'those of behavioural systems and their control, of information, negative feedback and a behavioural form of homeostasis'. Complex behaviour is supposed to depend on the execution of plans initiated on the receipt of certain information and guided and terminated by the continuous reception of more information originating from the results of the actions already taken (feedback). The use of this model means that Freudian instinct theory, the pleasure principle and defence mechanisms are no longer employed.

This means that Bowlby cannot be considered a traditional psychoanalyst. His work, therefore, is not strictly relevant to Freudian theory. Furthermore his theory is based on data no more sound, except that it involves the observation of children, than that of psychoanalysis. However, since his work concerns a field that is obviously important in orthodox, psychoanalytic theory – maternal deprivation – his studies will be evaluated for the light they throw on the theory. They will not be considered with reference to object-relation theory.

Even if we accept the fact that Freudian theory lays such emphasis on the importance of early experience, it is still pertinent to ask exactly what hypotheses would be adduced from psychoanalytic theory concerning the effects of maternal deprivation, at least in perhaps its most important meaning of maternal separation. As our descriptions of psychoanalytic developmental theory have made clear, by around the age of five years the Oedipus complex has developed. This is repressed by the castration complex and this in turn becomes quiescent through the development of the super-ego. While this applies to boys, in girls the castration complex (penis envy) comes first and brings about the Electra complex which in turn is gradually superseded as the super-ego develops. (See pp. 95 and 127 for the Freudian theories.) From this outline of developmental theory it is clear that for boys, maternal deprivation in all its forms, but especially maternal separation, should produce disturbances in the Oedipus complex, the castration complex and super-ego development. The Freudian concept of identification may also be invoked (see p. 138 for the theory). Since identification with the mother can normally be expected, disturbances in this area would also be hypothesised. In addition the age at time of separation could be expected to be important. Thus children who were separated from their mother at the oral phase might develop symptoms typical of oral fixation whereas those separated later, at the anal stage, might develop correspondingly different symptoms.

The effects of maternal deprivation according to psychoanalytic theory may be summarised as follows:

1. Disturbance in super-ego development due to prior disturbances of the Oedipal and castration complexes.
2. Disturbances of identification.
3. Psychosexual fixations depending upon the age of the child at separation.

PROBLEMS OF EMPIRICAL RESEARCH

As should now be clear to readers of the previous chapters, the empirical validation of these hypotheses is beset by grievous problems.

1. There are no fully adequate, well validated measures of the Oedipal or castration complexes. The Dynamic Personality Inventory (Grygier, 1961) does not appear to be valid (see p. 19) though the Blacky Pictures (Blum, 1949) are at least worth using in an exploratory manner (see p. 79).

2. Super-ego functions might be equated, for the purposes of testing, with moral behaviour. This means, for example, that murderers may be regarded as a group with faulty super-ego development.

3. Measures of identification are difficult to develop – but see the section on identification (p. 138).

4. Measures of psychosexual fixation are to some extent validated, e.g. the Blacky Pictures (which incidentally contain measures of super-ego and identification), the DPI anal scales (Grygier, 1961) and the Goldman-Eisler (1951) oral scale.

These last two psychometric measures are, of course, only suitable for use with adults.

There are thus very considerable problems of measurement in the validation of psychoanalytic hypotheses concerning maternal deprivation. In addition there are further difficulties in research into this area.

5. The meaning of maternal deprivation has already been mentioned and four meanings were distinguished (Yarrow, 1961). However from the viewpoint of the empirical validation of psychoanalytic theory all four categories are still likely to have deleterious effects, in that they all represent disturbances of the mother-child relationship. However the institutionalised child lives in an institution and here differences in institutional regimes are likely to confound results.

E

Furthermore normal control groups, by definition, do not live in institutions. This means that an analysis of variance design using types of institution as a factor has to be drawn up. Again the traumatic experience of parental death can confound results.

6. Immediate or retrospective studies. Retrospective studies of delinquents or neurotics suffer from the difficulty of accurately assessing the infantile history. This is particularly important in the case of maternal separation. This maternal separation may be complete or partial, it may vary in length and it may have occurred once, or on many occasions, as with the unfortunate foster-child shifted from home to home or the child whose parent suffers a succession of serious operations or is himself subjected to intermittent hospitalisation. If maternal separation has any effects whatever, it is apparent that such variations in maternal separation are important. It is also essential to the third hypothesis (psychosexual fixations result from maternal separation) that the age at which separations occurred must be known.

Immediate studies, on the other hand, of infants who have been maternally deprived in any of the senses distinguished above, are not of so great a relevance to psychoanalytic theory. Thus we do not need psychoanalytic theory to understand the anxiety of the infant who has just come to hospital and left his mother. What is distinctive about psychoanalytic theory is that it postulates long-term effects on personality of such experiences. Here, then, longitudinal studies appear the best answer to this problem.

In summary, the problems of validating psychoanalytic developmental theory by studying the effects of maternal deprivation are manifold. The main ones are:

1. Problems of measurement.
2. Problems arising from the fact that the inevitable concomitants of maternal deprivation may have confounding effects.
3. Problems of obtaining the deprivation data.

DESIGN OF INVESTIGATIONS

1. Control groups

Control groups appear to be an essential ingredient of any research into the effects of maternal deprivation and they constitute a great difficulty in this type of research. Thus institutionalised children have no equivalents – i.e. there are no children in institutions who are not separated from their mothers. In many cases (e.g. Bowlby, 1944) there is the added complication of mental disease in the family. This may even have been the cause of the child's separation. Thus it may be difficult to find control children with schizophrenic mothers who are not separated from them. Again if hospitalised children are the object of study, then to find controls without hospitalisation but the same disease is hard. Yet without a control group the finding that a high percentage of neurotics suffered

maternal deprivation is of no value as evidence for a causal link between deprivation and neurosis.

2. Longitudinal studies

Longitudinal studies of infants with known histories of maternal deprivation up
to adulthood are clearly best. Retrospective studies can at least deal with adult
personality but are weak as regards their deprivation data. The reverse is true of
direct studies of infants but such studies are not very relevant to psychoanalytic
theory.

3. Measures

Replicable, reliable and valid measures are essential. This means that tests must
be used. Psychiatric diagnoses, even if made by more than one psychiatrist based
on a clinical interview, cannot be regarded as scientific data.

Beck (1962) and Beck *et al.* (1962) have summarised the case against psychiatric
diagnosis as a useful research method. In the first paper Beck reviews a number of
studies of the reliability of psychiatric diagnosis among different psychiatrists.
A few examples of the results of the best designed studies make the point quite
clear. Thus Masserman and Carmichael (1938) followed up 100 patients. In 40%
of these subjects diagnosis required a major revision one year after discharge
from hospital. In fact it is clear that these patients had changed so that the low
degree of agreement is, rather, a comment on the instability of the nomenclature.
But, if these psychiatric classifications have so little temporal stability, it is
pertinent to question their value.

Mehlman (1952), in a most convincing investigation, studied the frequency
distribution of diagnosis among a number of psychiatrists to whom a total of
4,036 patients had been assigned in the course of their work. There was a
statistically significant difference in the frequencies with which each psychiatrist
used the various diagnostic labels in categorising their patients. This is very
powerful evidence that psychiatrist rather than patient variance is important in
psychiatric diagnosis. Schmidt and Fonda (1956) studied agreement between
two psychiatrists in the diagnostic classification of 426 patients. Excluding organic
cases the percentage agreement was only 42. Finally Pasamanick *et al.* (1959)
conducted an investigation similar to that of Mehlman (1952). As previously,
they found that individual psychiatrists significantly favoured certain diagnostic
classifications. They were forced to conclude that 'psychiatric diagnosis is at
present so unreliable as to merit very serious question when classifying, studying
and treating patients' behaviour and outcomes'.

Beck *et al.* (1962), in a further study of the reliability of clinical judgements
and ratings, studied the agreement in diagnostic classification of four psychiatrists
with a total of 153 patients. These psychiatrists, although their classifications
were quite independent, had previously discussed beforehand and reached concensus concerning the specific criteria for each category. In this study the overall
agreement was higher than that in most others – 54%. However this agreement

varied for the different nosological categories, ranging from 63% for neurotic depressive down to only 38% for personality trait disturbance. This last figure is of particular interest as regards the study of the effects of maternal deprivation, since it is likely that many of the psychiatric assessments will fall under this head. In any case Beck *et al.* conclude that, although this overall rate of agreement – 54% – was higher than in other investigations, it is still *not adequate for research purposes.*

From the evidence discussed above it must, therefore, be concluded that psychiatric ratings and diagnoses cannot be regarded as objective evidence for the scientific study of our psychoanalytic hypotheses.

The validity of measures of the Oedipus and castration complexes is not high. Thus it might be better to use more generally acceptable tests of neurosis, e.g. the 16 PF or MMPI than the rather more risky Dynamic Personality Inventory.

4. Statistical analysis

If defined groups are compared with control groups an analysis of variance design would appear to be the most suitable. In this way the effects of different types of institutional regime might be taken into account.

In the light of this discussion of the problems involved in the testing of hypotheses concerning the effects of maternal deprivation, of the empirical propositions derivable from psychoanalytic theory and of possible research designs, it is now fitting to examine the objective investigations. For convenience, the categorisation of researches used by Yarrow (1961) will be followed: investigations of institutionalised children and maternal separation will be examined separately. Where appropriate a sub-division of retrospective and immediate studies will be made. Finally studies of other aspects of maternal deprivation will be reviewed.

STUDIES OF MATERNAL SEPARATION

As has been indicated, studies of maternal separation represent, perhaps, the best method of studying the hypotheses derived from Freudian theory because there is likely to be less confounding effect from the regimes of the foster home or institution than in the case of institutionalised children.

A. Retrospective or longitudinal studies

These are the studies most relevant to Freudian developmental theory which predicts long-term effects on personality from maternal separation. Studies at the time of separation are not of such great importance (from the viewpoint of psychoanalytic validation).

Bowlby (1944) in his study of 44 juvenile thieves and controls, Lewis (1954) who examined 500 children in a reception centre, Bowlby *et al.* (1956) who studied 60 children in a tuberculosis sanatorium and controls, and Berg and Cohen (1959) who investigated 40 schizophrenic and 40 neurotic women are the only studies where *long-term effects* of maternal separation are investigated. All these are retrospective.

Method of obtaining separation data

In all these studies the separation data was obtained by interviews with subjects and their parents and guardians and by details recorded from case histories and files. Thus for each subject in each study it clearly varied in accuracy.

Measurement techniques

Bowlby (1944) used psychiatric diagnoses. He classified subjects into types, e.g. affectionless character, schizoid character. Since he also carried out the rest of the examination, there is a risk of contamination of the diagnosis. Lewis (1954) followed up a number of his sample: the data consisted of case reports by psychiatrists and social workers. Bowlby *et al.* (1956) used intelligence tests (which are irrelevant to Freudian theory) and clinical evaluations from a number of sources. Berg and Cohen (1959) examined the case histories of their samples.

From this it is clear that none of these studies contains basic data from which it is possible to draw any objective conclusions. None of the studies is replicable except by the investigators making the original judgements, the validity and reliability of which are quite unknown. These deficiencies are so serious that the fact that control groups were used by Bowlby (1944) and Bowlby *et al.* (1956) makes them no more admissible.

Conclusions

Clearly, therefore, no conclusions can be based on such inadequate data and it is not surprising that the outcome of these studies was so diverse. Bowlby (1944) found maternal deprivation was linked to the affectionless character but Bowlby *et al.* (1956) were forced to admit that such a link was an overstatement of the case. Lewis (1954) found a great variety of effects and Berg and Cohen (1959) found separation important in schizophrenia. The only firm conclusion we can draw from these studies is that they were inadequate to give objective validation to the psychoanalytic hypotheses.

B. Direct or immediate studies

These are not so relevant to psychoanalytic theory. In all cases the data, apart from intelligence (e.g. Schaffer, 1958), are from clinical observation. Thus studies of maternal separation have not been sufficiently rigorous to support or refute psychoanalytic theory.

STUDIES OF INSTITUTIONALISED CHILDREN

With studies of institutionalised children, whether retrospective or current, a major problem lies in the variance of child-rearing regimes among different institutions and the fact that institution life differs from family life in more ways than just mother separation.

A. Retrospective studies

Goldfarb (1943, 1944, 1945, 1947, 1949) carried out a series of famous studies of institutionalised children. Although most of the children in these studies were pre-pubertal and therefore, perhaps, too young to test adequately the Freudian hypotheses, Goldfarb (1947) did test two samples of adolescent boys. However in none of the studies were there valid or reliable measures of personality. Examples of the instruments used make this clear – the Newell Checklist (1943) and the Rorschach (1949). In other instances, except in his measures of intellectual capacity which are not relevant to psychoanalytic theory, clinical assessments only were used. Thus these investigations by Goldfarb cannot be used to provide objective evidence for psychoanalytic theory.

Beres and Obers (1950), in another well-known study, examined 37 clinical cases who had been in institutions when children. These authors questioned the long-term effects of such institutionalisation on overt adjustment. Again, however, little weight can be put on their conclusions since psychiatric diagnoses were the source of their data.

The present writer can find in the literature no retrospective study of institutionalised children in which any acceptable personality measures have been used. Thus, despite the fact that Goldfarb's work is much quoted, it must be concluded that no objective validation or refutation of psychoanalytic theory can be obtained from such studies.

B. Current studies

These are of far less interest to psychoanalytic theory unless they contain specific measures of Oedipal or castration conflict or problems of identification and psychosexual fixation. In fact no such studies have been conducted.

As was the case with the investigations of separation from the mother, it must be concluded that no objective evidence relevant to psychoanalytic theory has come from studies of institutionalised children. This is partly because the investigators have not been, in the main, concerned with hypotheses drawn from classical psychoanalytic theory and, perhaps more importantly, because they have relied on clinical assessments and psychiatric classifications when dealing with personality variables.

RESEARCH ON MULTIPLE MOTHERING

Rabin (1957, 1958a and 1958b) has studied Kibbutz children and controls in a number of studies using a variety of tests. Since the personality assessment in the first two investigations was by means of the Rorschach which is not regarded by the present writer as being capable of providing objective evidence, these studies may be ignored. In the final investigation, however, he used the Blacky Pictures in order to assess differences in Oedipal strength. This study has been fully discussed on p. 105 in the section on the Oedipus and castration complexes.

His main finding was that, as expected, Kibbutz children had less Oedipal intensity and a more diffuse identification than their controls. This provided, therefore, some support for Freudian theory.

CONCLUSIONS FROM ALL STUDIES OF MATERNAL DEPRIVATION

1. Current studies of infants, unless they concentrate on specific Freudian concepts such as the Oedipus complex, are not really relevant to psychoanalytic theory.

2. The retrospective studies carried out so far are vitiated by their measurement techniques. Psychiatric classifications, clinical assessments and case-study reports cannot be regarded as objective data.

3. Only one study, that by Rabin (1958b), is therefore relevant to the scientific validation of psychoanalytic theory. This has been previously discussed in the section on the Oedipus complex which it supports to some extent.

7

The structure of the mind

or the brief summary of the theory that follows three main papers were used:

(*a*) The question of lay analysis (Freud, 1926).
(*b*) New introductory lectures in psychoanalysis (Freud, 1933).
(*c*) An outline of psychoanalysis (Freud, 1940).

SUMMARY OF THE THEORY

According to Freud the mental apparatus is divided into three parts; id, ego and super-ego.

The id

'To the oldest of these mental provinces or agencies we give the name of id. It contains everything that is inherited, that is present at birth, that is fixed in the constitution – above all therefore the instincts . . .' (Freud, 1940). Freud likens it to a cauldron of seething excitement. It is the core of our being within which the instincts operate and their sole endeavour is to seek satisfaction regardless of consequences, situation or logic.

Thus the id obeys *the pleasure principle*. Its mental processes, subject to no laws of logic, are regarded as *primary processes* and are *unconscious*.

The ego

'The ego was developed out of the cortical layer of the id, which, being adapted for the reception and exclusion of stimuli, is in direct contact with the external world.' (Freud, 1940). Its function consists of interposing, between id demands and satisfying actions, intellectual activity aimed at calculating the consequences of any proposed behaviour. Thus the ego must decide whether the satisfaction may be carried out or postponed or whether the demand of the instinct should be altogether suppressed. *This is the reality principle.* If the main aim of the id is pleasure the main aim of the ego is safety. Some ego activities are *conscious*, some *preconscious* (defined as capable of becoming conscious), and others unconscious.

An example of conscious ego activity obeying the reality principle is the idea that there is a suitable time and place for everything. Preconscious ego activity is only too obvious in the examination hall when the vital facts refuse to come to mind often until the very moment the exam is over. Unconscious ego activity, on the other hand, is best exemplified in the defence mechanisms, e.g. rationalisation

– the finding of good reasons for what we want to do. The processes of the ego and the preconscious are referred to as *secondary processes*.

The super-ego

'The long period of childhood . . . leaves behind it a precipitate which forms within the ego a special agency in which the parental influence is prolonged. It has received the name of super-ego.' This super-ego is regarded in Freudian theory as the heir of the Oedipus complex. It internalises what had been part of the external world (the parents) and continues to carry on their functions: 'it observes the ego, gives it orders, corrects it and threatens it with punishments exactly like the parents whose place it has taken' (Freud, 1940). We are, of course, aware of it as our conscience. Often it is more severe than the parents ever were.

From this outline of the mental structure, as hypothesised in psychoanalytic theory, it is clear that mental activity has a dynamic quality. The ego has to satisfy the instinctual demands of the id and the moral dictates of the super-ego. Indeed this is the aim of psychoanalytic therapy – to strengthen the ego and to make it more independent of the super-ego. Where id was there shall ego be (Freud, 1933).

Finally, since id activity is wholly unconscious, as is part of ego and super-ego activity, it may be justly asked how psychoanalysis can make any claims about it. The evidence for this mental structure comes from free associations and dream material. In dreams, for example – 'the royal road to the unconscious', it is hypothesised that the ego is relaxed and that id material, although distorted by the censor, is nearer the surface. By dream analysis it is possible to learn and understand the workings of the unconscious mind. The objective evidence for this part of Freudian theory will be examined in a later chapter in this book.

IMPORTANCE OF THEORY

It should be clear from the outline description of the theory that the concepts of id, super-ego and ego are crucial to psychoanalytic theory as a whole. These structures are basic to one of the most important findings of psychoanalysis – that behaviour has unconscious motivation. They are also vital in the Freudian theory of neurosis and psychosis. Indeed it is their dynamic balance that accounts for all behaviour.

PROBLEMS IN THE OBJECTIVE VERIFICATION OF THE THEORY

Any attempt to provide objective, scientifically acceptable evidence for these structures is beset with difficulties. Perhaps the most profound problem is that scientific methods, as traditionally conceived, eschew the study of mental processes on the justifiable grounds that they are not public events open to precise observation. This view finds reinforcement in the behaviouristic claim that in the study of behaviour the concept of mind is irrelevant as stressed by Miles

(1965). Nevertheless since Freudian theory *is* concerned with mental processes objective study of it demands that they be investigated.

The scientific investigation of the Freudian theory of mental structure necessitates a clear statement of just what empirical hypotheses and statements are implicit in the theory. One hypothesis is plain: there are three kinds of mental activity – conscious, preconscious and unconscious.

The empirical consequences of the actual tripartite division of the mind are, however, far more difficult to state. Nevertheless they may be discussed under two heads – physiological and behavioural.

A. Physiological hypothesis

If three physiological systems in the brain could be isolated with functions similar to those required by the Freudian structures this would provide good evidence for the theory. Nevertheless, as Alexander (1950) points out, this would mean stricter localisation of brain function than is justified by evidence. A possible hypothesis, therefore, is that there are brain structures corresponding in function to the ego, super-ego and id.

B. Functional hypothesis

This hypothesis would stress the essentially *functional* nature of the structural theory. That is these divisions are divisions of function. Consequently the hypothesis would be that in certain behaviours three strands can be distinguished – rational (ego), moral (super-ego) and wishing (id). This would have to be the case in that behaviour is mediated by the dynamic balance of ego, super-ego and id. In essence it is a three-factor theory of motivation.

In summary three empirical hypotheses have been extracted from the structural theory:

1. That there are conscious, preconscious and unconscious mental events.
2. That there are brain structures corresponding in function to the ego, super-ego and id.
3. That behaviour may be defined in terms of these three factors.

It is to be noted that hypothesis 2, the physiological hypothesis, is not implicit in Freudian theory but would provide very strong support for it if shown to be true.

Before examining the evidence for these three hypotheses it must be stated that there are other empirical statements implicit in the structural theory which will not be considered in this chapter. Thus, for example, the ego defences or defence mechanisms – one of the major functions of the ego – will be discussed in a separate chapter. So too will the nature of the id processes. These are claimed to be revealed in dreams and the objective evidence relevant to them will be examined in a further chapter. Indeed most of the theory of psychoanalysis consists of a detailed study of the functions of these three divisions of the mind so that in a sense the whole book is relevant to this problem.

There are, too, what may be regarded as quasi-empirical statements, e.g. the super-ego is the heir to the Oedipus complex. However such a statement is very hard to put in precisely testable form other than that moral behaviour is not to be expected in the under fives. Were this found to be true it would not constitute impressive evidence for the super-ego! Readers can easily furnish more parsimonious hypotheses.

Consequently this chapter will be devoted to the evidence for the three hypotheses outlined above. It must be remembered however that many of the later chapters are also relevant to it although in a more indirect way.

EVIDENCE FOR THE HYPOTHESES

1. THAT THERE ARE CONSCIOUS, PRECONSCIOUS AND UNCONSCIOUS MENTAL PROCESSES

As these terms were defined by Freud there can be little doubt that it is indeed the case. Some mental processes and memory content are conscious, i.e. we are aware of them. As was shown in the outline, other material is preconscious in the sense of capable of becoming conscious, e.g. the forgotten telephone number. As for unconscious mental processes, ones of which we are not aware, from the time of James these have been accepted and were demonstrated in the work on suggestibility and hypnosis by Charcot and Janet. Thus the Freudian postulate of an unconscious was not new (see Whyte, 1968). What was new, however, was the emphasis he placed on it and his description of its nature, the primary processes, based on dream analysis and free association. Thus it can be seen that, as defined by Freud, there are indeed three kinds of mental process – conscious, preconscious and unconscious. There is, however, little of psychological interest in this hypothesis and it will not be further discussed.

2. THE PHYSIOLOGICAL HYPOTHESIS: THAT THERE EXIST THREE PHYSIOLOGICAL STRUCTURES IN THE BRAIN CORRESPONDING TO THE EGO, ID AND SUPER-EGO IN FUNCTION

It must be stated that this is not implicit in the Freudian structural theory although Freud (1895) did indicate that ultimately he thought all brain functions would be tied down to brain mechanisms. Nevertheless it is clear that were three such structures or systems discovered, they would constitute very strong, if not irrefutable, evidence for the Freudian theory. It is therefore necessary to consider the physiological evidence.

Studies testing the physiological hypothesis

In a study of the influence of Darwin on the work of Pavlov, Freud and Hughlings Jackson, Magoun (1961) pointed out certain similarities in the concepts of these writers. Thus the three levels of Jackson correspond to the id, ego and super-ego of Freud and to the reflex, conditioned reflex and second signalling system of

Pavlov. This paper, without delineating any of the possible structures involved in the Freudian model, at least suggests that physiological correlates are possible.

It is, of course, tempting, and Grey-Walter (1961) succumbs, to attempt to locate these Freudian structures. Grey-Walter tentatively suggests the mid-brain for the id, and the sensory cortex for the ego. A brief examination of the physiological evidence reveals, however, that it is not possible to postulate structures corresponding to the Freudian provinces with any confidence. Indeed it is probably true to say that the precise function of almost no part of the brain can be stated so that any attempt to relate neurophysiological concepts to the Freudian model is futile in our present state of knowledge. Grossman (1967), discussing the role of the cortex in emotion, is forced to conclude that so far the role of the central nervous system in the regulation of emotional behaviour is poorly understood. Thus the Papez (1937) theory of emotion which suggested that emotional experience was a function of the cingulate gyrus, which has connections with the hypothalamus – itself certainly concerned with the expression (if not the experience) of emotions – does not fully fit the data, nor indeed does Maclean's (1949) revision of this theory in which the hippocampal formation was substituted for the cingulate gyrus. This is particularly unfortunate since both the hippocampus and the cingulate gyrus were tempting sites to locate the id.

Similarly the super-ego, at the height of the popularity for lobotomy, might have been postulated to reside in the frontal lobes – i.e. the frontal lobes were responsible for super-ego control. Moniz (1936), for example, claimed that mental diseases characterised by severe inhibition (super-ego) such as obsessional and anxiety states were considerably improved by lobotomy. However, as Grossman (1967) points out, results with this procedure have not been clear-cut and in some cases intellectual deficits outweigh any other advantages.

Arnold (1950) has proposed that the frontal lobes are concerned with the sympathetic aspects of emotion, which accounts for their regulatory function in anxiety. However, with our present knowledge it would be quite foolhardy to attempt to argue that the function of the super-ego was attributable to the frontal lobes.

Conclusion

There is no firm support from neurophysiological studies of brain function for the Freudian tripartite division of the mind. Brain function is not sufficiently well understood for this to be possible.

3. THE FUNCTIONAL HYPOTHESIS: THAT ID, EGO AND SUPER-EGO FACTORS OCCUR IN CERTAIN BEHAVIOUR

Clearly in some responses, e.g. adding $2 + 2$, ego functions predominate – hence the restriction to 'certain' behaviours.

Work of Cattell (1957)

The researches relevant to this third hypothesis are embodied in Cattell's studies of attitudes and interests, work that is far less known than his personality studies. An attitude is defined as a tendency to act in a particular way to a situation. Cattell is careful to stress that his definition embraces far more than the 'sociologists'' approach embodied in most attitude scales, of being for or against something. It will be seen that this definition of attitude used by Cattell embraces interests, in that interest in particular courses of action strongly affects tendencies to enact them or not. Indeed Cattell considers that these studies of attitude and interest are best subsumed under the label of motivation.

Attitudes and interests studied

   (*a*) A major professional job attitude
   (*b*) A respectable hobby interest
   (*c*) A somewhat disreputable interest
   (*d*) An attitude with relatively strong unconscious roots, and
   (*e*) Another with a marked moral component.

Sample. 374 adult males.

Tests and scoring. The tests used were all objective devices using T data. The principles behind their construction were ingenious as a few examples indicate. Where interest is strong in a field, a high level of information and perceptual skill may be expected. Where new material is presented, memory will be best for topics of greatest interest. Motivation sharpens attention so that in the presentation of competing stimuli there will be selective attention in areas of interest. In addition physiological measures were used, e.g. GSR, muscle tension, blood pressure. These are only a selection of the tests – simply to indicate their nature. Scoring was *ipsative*. Thus the scores did not represent individual differences in level, but changes within each individual. For each person the scores were standard scores from his own mean. This is of great importance in the interpretation of the rotated factors emerging from the intercorrelations of all these variables.

Results. The following factors emerged:

Motivation factor alpha: the id component in interests. Cattell describes this factor as characterised by autism – believing that what one wants is true or practicable – by high emphasis on stated preference, by rapid decisions, by fluency on cues, means and ends to desired goals and by rationalisation. It has almost no cognitive content or physiological loadings.

'Clearly it represents a component in interest most nearly corresponding to the psychoanalytic concept of the id, though we must be definite that we are redefining this as conscious id' (Cattell, 1957). It appears to be an 'I desire' component, of which the individual is partly conscious but which he has not tested against reality.

Although this factor alpha, with its emphasis on desire and lack of reality, is not unconscious, it yet appears to be not unlike the id component as defined by Freud.

Motivation factor beta: the realised ego. This is considered to be the component of realised, integrated interest: an ego component adjusted to super-ego and reality demands. The motivational elements loading on this factor include high informational content relevant to the field of interest, some perceptual skills and good capacity to learn in the interests of the activity together with a regard for remote but realistic rewards. Cattell hypothesises that this factor is interests acquired through habit and duty, fully conscious and well integrated into the daily habits of the self. 'It corresponds pretty closely to the psychoanalytic concept of ego forces – of habits acquired under the constraint of the super-ego and reality testing' (Cattell, 1957). Ipsatising the scores rules out the possibility of the factor being interpreted as one of intelligence.

Again, as Cattell points out, there is a considerable resemblance to the ego functions as defined by Freud. Nevertheless before the identification of this factor could become entirely convincing the negative loadings of the PGR response would have to be studied further.

Factor gamma: component of the ideal, desired self, or unrealised super-ego. This factor, according to Cattell, is the most difficult to fit into existing psychoanalytic concepts because it overlaps with the alpha factor (negatively correlated) and with the beta factor. It shows autism, fantasy, some conscious preference for an activity and a complete absence of information about it.

There is no defensiveness about and no fluency on cues, means and ends. It is identified, albeit very tentatively, as the desired ideal self.

Super-ego is perhaps the nearest existing concept (in any psychology) to this factor, but it is clearly difficult to identify the factor with any confidence.

The other factors contributed much less to the variance and were not so well replicated from matrix to matrix. These will, therefore, receive much briefer treatment:

Factor delta: unconscious symphathetic system and circulatory sensitivity or biological interest. Cattell tentatively suggests that this factor delta is the entirely unconscious id contrasted with the preconscious id, factor alpha, with its wishful cognitive loadings.

Factor epsilon: interest component from repressed complexes. Although there are no preferences or overt verbal interests loading on this factor there are memory effects and PGR effects, such as have long been noted in word association studies, e.g. the Kent-Rosanoff list. From this evidence Cattell hypothesises that this component of interest arises from successful repression.

Cattell concludes by arguing that it is up to further research to find out whether these five factors have opened up methods for accurate quantitative assessment of the parts played by the Freudian mental provinces in motivation.

One final point must be made about this research. Since these five factors are oblique Cattell carried out a factorisation of their inter-correlations. Two second-order factors emerged.

1. *Integrated self-sentiment interests:* beta and gamma, relevant to reality-oriented and morality-recognising habit organisations, load on this.

2. *Unintegrated unconscious interests:* on this load delta, epsilon and alpha, the factors which have in common unintegrated desires and untested wishes and aspirations. Lack of integration with self is preferred to unconscious as the identification because the id factor, at least as measured here, is not unconscious.

Comments on the whole factor analysis

It will be remembered that this study was invoked to investigate the hypothesis derived from the structural theory, that there would be three motivational factors corresponding to ego, super-ego and id. Cattell certainly attempts to identify the primary factors with these Freudian concepts and the second-order analysis supports the dynamic analysis of human behaviour ego and super-ego (reality principle) *v.* id (pleasure principle).

However it must be stated that any such identification of factors, as stated above, is tentative and provisional on further research. This is mainly due to the nature of the objective test variables.

As was discussed in the chapter on personality development, these objective tests have not been fully validated. Since face validity is almost entirely irrelevant to their actual validity, a description of them would hardly be useful. Indeed their complexity and number is such as to make any kind of adequate discussion of them here out of place. For a full description, rationale and survey of the evidence, the reader is referred to Cattell and Warburton's compendium of objective tests (1967).

Conclusion

This study of motivation supports a three-factor theory, as demanded by the Freudian theory. The nature of the factors is not a bad fit to the hypothesis. However, the experimental nature of the variables makes definite identification risky. This study cannot therefore be regarded as strong support for the psycho-analytic theory. It is however possible to consider it as positive support which urgently needs further clarification. In its present state, for example, this factor analysis supports equally well the Platonic tripartite concept of the mind, as propounded in the *Republic* or the *Phaedrus*.

Pawlik and Cattell (1964)

Another similar approach to the three-factor hypothesis of motivation was used by Pawlik and Cattell who subjected a battery of objective personality variables to third-order factor analysis.

Sample. Three samples were used, two consisting each of 86 college undergraduates, the other of 315 Navy Submarine School candidates. These three studies have been described previously (when second-order factors were extracted) by Cattell *et al.* (1961).

Tests. Objective test devices UI16-UI36 were used. For a description of these see p. 34 and, in more detail, Cattell and Warburton (1967).

Method. The correlations between the second-order factors were subjected to two oblique rotated factor analyses – Oblimax and Maxplane. (Pinzka and Saunders, 1954, and Cattell and Muerle, 1960.)

Results. Three main factors emerged:

1. *Immature self-centred temperament.* Its principal loadings were on temperamental ardour, low self-consciousness and narcissistic development.
2. *Restrained acceptance of external norms:* tied socialisation, low self-consciousness and history of restraining environment.
3. *High self-assertion:* this factor loaded most highly on expansive ego and tension to achieve. Here the two rotations gave results which were not identical. This solution, preferred by Cattell, is the Maxplane solution.

Interpretation and comments. This is best left to Pawlik and Cattell (1964). They write 'Although we did not start our studies with any predilections for psychoanalytic theory, it is a striking fact that the psychoanalytic descriptions of ego, id and super-ego would fit very well the three major patterns found in this research.'

Conclusions

Pawlik and Cattell admit that this identification with ego, super-ego and id is tentative and premature and that further replication is needed. Even more important, the validity of the original objective tests on which this study is based remains far from proven. Nevertheless these results may be regarded as tentative support for the functional hypothesis implicit in the Freudian theory of mental provinces.

Warburton (1968) submitted second-order factors from Gorsuch and Cattell (1967) – in this case derived from Cattell's 16 PF questionnaire – to third- and fourth-order factor analysis. Two factors finally emerged, *integration* and *morality*. Integration appears to be related to adaptation to the environment and changing that environment where adaptation is unsuitable. This research does not, therefore, support the three-factor theory. Nevertheless these two factors are again not unlike the ego and super-ego of Freudian theory.

To sum up, it is clear that these two studies illustrate the potential of higher-order factor analysis to illuminate the functional hypothesis of psychoanalytic theory.

The IES test – a direct approach to the measurement of ego, super-ego and id behaviour

As was mentioned at the beginning of the chapter, one approach to the investigation of the Freudian concept of the mental apparatus is to investigate by means of tests the kinds of behaviour hypothesised in psychoanalytic theory to be sub-sumed by ego, id and super-ego. In this method obsessional neurotics would be expected to be dominated by their super-ego in contrast to, for example, psycho-paths who would be dominated by their id. Careful examination of Freudian theory would allow many such hypotheses to be set up and investigated. Dom-brose and Slobin (1958) have adopted this approach and developed what appears to be the only test of this type – the IES test.

The IES is designed to measure the relative strength of impulses (id), ego and super-ego. It consists of a number of sub-tests as described below.

1. *Picture title test*

'This consists of 12 drawings, each showing activities and objects which may be classified into impulse and super-ego categories' (Dombrose and Slobin, 1958). Subjects simply have to give a title to each picture.

Scoring. An impulse score is given to a title referring to an impulse activity or area. Similarly a super-ego score is given if reference is made to a super-ego activity or area. An ego score is made where both these factors are fully integrated by the title. Finally there is a defensive category where the title is claimed to put great psychological distance between subject and picture. There is an appendix to this test to facilitate scoring.

2. *Picture story completion test*

13 sets of cartoons, each set consisting of two or three cartoons, have to be completed by the subject. Each set may be completed by 3 cartoons one of which is chosen by the subject. Thus for each story, depending on his choice, a subject scores on ego, impulses or super-ego. Scoring is, therefore, objec-tive.

3. *Photo-analysis test*

This test consists of the photographs of nine men. Two multiple-choice (3 possibilities) questions are posed to the subject about each of the men. Each multiple-choice response indicates an ego, super-ego or impulse score. The rationale is that by projection the responses indicate how the subject would like to function. Again scoring is objective.

4. *The arrow-dot test*

This is a performance test where the subject has to draw the shortest possible line from an arrow to a dot between which are barriers of solid lines which must not be crossed. In addition dashed lines and bars, not mentioned in the instruc-tions, provide the subject with limitations 'as determined by self-needs' (Dom-brose and Slobin, 1958). There are 23 of these problems. An appendix scores the majority of possible solutions in terms of E, I or S. For example, lines going straight through forbidden barriers are scored I. An E score is obtained by the shortest and therefore most realistic path to the goal. An S score is obtained when subjects create their own barriers out of the dashed lines and refuse to go through the parallel bars.

Such then, is the IES test. The reliability and validity of the test must now be briefly scrutinised. First the evidence presented by Dombrose and Slobin will be considered.

Reliability of the IES test

(*a*) *Test-retest reliability coefficients* for the three scores derived from the four tests were computed for a sample of 30 men under out-patient therapy. These ranged from ·35 to ·83. The median value was ·62.

(*b*) *Internal consistency reliability*. The Kuder-Richardson formula 20 (Richardson and Kuder, 1939) was used to compute these on three different small samples. The median value was ·55, overestimated, since in six scores no figure was quoted because it was below ·2.

(*c*) *Inter-scorer reliability*. Only the Picture-Titles test demands judgements by the scorer. Here there was 91% agreement by raters.

Comments

These reliabilities are too low to allow the test to be used with any confidence for individuals. For purposes of research with groups they are probably sufficiently high.

Validity of the IES test

The studies of the validity of the IES test quoted by Dombrose and Slobin are based on a number of doctoral dissertations presented at Western Reserve University (Dombrose and Slobin, 1951; Charnes, 1953; Alexander, 1954; Golden, 1954 and Ritz, 1954). However, as Katkovsky (1965) points out, the description of these investigations is far too short for the construct validity of the test to be accurately assessed. The basic method in all these validity studies has been to compare small samples of neurotics and psychotics, aged subjects in different environments, or latents and adolescents. Scores on the tests of all these groups are presented. Dombrose and Slobin (1958) claim that these results supported a high proportion of the psychoanalytically derived hypotheses. However they do not say which hypotheses, so that their adequacy is impossible to estimate. In addition, as Crowne (1965) emphasises, there is no evidence as to what the IES does *not* measure (e.g. intelligence or social desirability) – a vital feature of any construct validity study. Thus, although the scores in these doctoral investigations look sensible in the light of psychoanalytic theory, they cannot be considered as good evidence for the validity of the test which still needs to be taken on trust. Equally, however, these results do not *destroy* the test validity.

The norms of this test are clearly inadequate. All the samples used are far too small for normative purposes, e.g. 57 aged subjects in three groups, 30 normals, 15 neurotics, 15 paranoids.

Later studies of the validity of the IES

Verrill and Costanza (1962) found no agreement between ratings for I, E and S by a psychiatric nurse of patients and test scores. It is not, of course, possible to say whether test, rater or both were wrong. Gilbert and Levee (1963) found no differences between young and menopausal women whom they predicted would show weaker ego and greater super-ego and id conflict. On what part of psychoanalytic theory this prediction was based is not clear. These two studies, therefore, do not support the validity of the test. On the other hand they are not rigorously enough designed to refute it.

Of the other published studies of the IES the only one which seems to bear on its validity is that of Herron (1962) who found that children institutionalised for parental neglect had lower ego and higher impulse scores than children reared in a family. To some extent, therefore, this study does support the validity of the I and E scores.

Conclusions concerning validity

This brief summary of the evidence indicates clearly that the validity of the IES test remains unproven. Certainly it has not been disproved. Since this is the only test attempting to measure these variables, clearly what is needed, is a massive study of its construct validity. From the evidence so far, this test appears useful for research into psychoanalytic theory provided the results are treated with caution.

The IES test and Freudian theory

The important question of to what extent studies with the IES test have confirmed or disconfirmed the Freudian concept of ego, super-ego and id, must now be examined.

1. So far work with the IES test has not provided any evidence in support of the Freudian theory. The few reports so far published have done little more than tentatively hint that the test might have some validity.

2. The IES has been carefully examined because it is, at present, the only instrument which could throw light directly on the Freudian theory of ego, super-ego and id. Thus a large-scale study of the validity of the test, using groups specifically designated by Freudian theory, could disprove the validity of the IES test if it showed that theoretical predictions of performance were not confirmed. If they were confirmed, however, the validity of the test *and* the theory would be together proven. This is discussed in the opening chapter of this book (see p. 5): the IES is an example of one of the major problems facing the empirical investigation of Freudian theory. Failure to confirm the theory can always be blamed on the test. Test validity on the other hand automatically implies the validity of the theory.

In conclusion, therefore, the IES test is regarded as a highly interesting test which at the moment is the sole means of investigating the behavioural concomitants of the Freudian concept of the mental apparatus. So far however no firm evidence has been produced by this test.

CONCLUSIONS CONCERNING THE FUNCTIONAL HYPOTHESIS

The studies of motivation by Cattell (1957) and of third-order objective test factors by Pawlik and Cattell (1964) support, in general, the psychoanalytic hypothesis. To a lesser extent the fourth-order factorisation of questionnaire scores by Warburton (1968) confirms the theory. However, as has been pointed out, at the moment all these interpretations must remain speculative because of the question of the validity of the objective tests. Until Cattell has managed to demonstrate that these test devices measure what they purport to do, it is impossible to put much weight on the results.

The IES test has even less demonstrated validity than these objective measures. Again, until such validity is demonstrated little reliance can be placed on any findings achieved with it.

What has clearly emerged from these studies, however, is that factor analysis is a suitable technique for investigating the functional hypothesis and that, contrary to first appearances, it is a formulation capable of scientific verification.

After this examination of the physiological and functional hypotheses implicit in the Freudian theory of ego, super-ego and id, we shall examine the objective evidence for identification – the process by which, according to Freudian theory, the super-ego is acquired.

IDENTIFICATION

As we saw from our description of the development of the super-ego, identification plays an important part in that process. In psychoanalytic theory identification can come about from two causes – fear of loss of love (known as anaclitic identification) and fear of aggression, identification with the aggressor. This last concept is often used as a defence mechanism and has been extensively described by Anna Freud in her *Mechanisms of Defence* (1946).

Since the psychoanalytic concept of identification is clearly a vital process in the socialisation of children it has received considerable attention from psychologists, especially those concerned with learning-theory models of behaviour. This, of course, is hardly surprising since identification is essentially a learning process – learning to be like the particular model.

To review in detail all the research evidence that has accrued from these investigations would be quite inappropriate to the importance of the concept in Freudian theory; it would also take a very long time. So in the section that follows all that will be attempted is a brief summary and discussion of some of the main empirical approaches.

DEFINITION OF IDENTIFICATION AND IMITATION

Kohlberg (1963) points out that in the research literature it is usual to distinguish between identification and imitation on the grounds that the former implies some structural change within the personality. He suggests the following criteria for this distinction (Kohlberg, 1969):

1. In identification, modelling is generalised and trans-situational. A variety of behaviours and roles are reproduced in a variety of situations. In imitation, modelling is of specific behaviours in specific situations.
2. In identification, modelling is persistent and occurs in the absence of the model.
3. In identification, performance of the modelled behaviour appears to be motivated intrinsically. It persists in the absence of any obvious reinforcement to which it is instrumental.
4. In identification, performance of the modelled behaviour is relatively irreversible or non-extinguishable even when it is non-reinforced or punished.

For psychoanalytic theory this distinction between identification and imitation is essential. Bronfenbrenner (1960), in his study of the development of the concept in psychoanalytic theory, claims that there it is regarded as a sweeping and powerful phenomenon in which the entire personality of the parent is taken over *en bloc* with considerable emotional intensity.

If this view of identification – the psychoanalytic view – is adopted, as it must be in the empirical study of psychoanalysis, then as Kohlberg (1969) argues, many of the gibes of the learning theorists at the theory are shown to be irrelevant. Thus Bandura (1969) claims that if psychoanalytic theory were correct a young boy, to imitate a worshipped sportsman, would have to develop incestuous desires towards the hero's wife. This is a confusion between identification and imitation. On the other hand it must be admitted that psychoanalytic theory does not explicitly attempt to explain such everyday imitation (inevitable in view of its neglect of ego psychology) and examples of identification given by Freud (1946) are sometimes, by this definition, imitation. Indeed those researchers who analyse identification in terms of theories of learning do not allow this distinction between identification and imitation but regard them rather as on a continuum, the difference lying in the amount of stimulus generalisation and resistance to extinction (e.g. Bandura, 1969, Aronfreed, 1969 and Gewirtz, 1969). However, it does seem that there is an important qualitative difference, as Bronfenbrenner (1960) argues, between the Freudian concept of identification as it occurs in the development of a child, and the imitation of a model adult whether absent or present, which is frequently the object of empirical study.

RELEVANCE OF EMPIRICAL STUDIES TO FREUDIAN THEORY

From the viewpoint of the validation of psychoanalytic theory the essential questions are whether identification occurs and under what conditions. Thus by Freudian theory we would predict that identification would be likely to occur with aggressive fathers or parents whose love the children were afraid to lose. The most important postulate, however, is the very existence of identification. If it could be shown, for example, that children in no sense imitated their parents the whole aetiology of the super-ego in Freudian theory would have to be abandoned. Actually the interpretation of identification in terms of learning theories, as has been attempted by Bandura and colleagues for example, is by no means inimical to Freudian theory. For as is argued in the last chapter of this book, it seems likely that psychoanalysis has been concerned with the study of the learning processes in human development, examining what events act as reinforcers and conditioned stimuli.

A further point concerning the relevance of empirical studies of identification has already been mentioned. Learning theorists regard imitation and identification as essentially similar so that they set up controlled laboratory experiments using adult models with which children may identify. However, identifying with such a model seems a far cry from identifying with the father through fear of castration. A psychoanalyst would not consider the laboratory experiment a satisfactory analogue except to understand imitation.

THE EMPIRICAL STUDIES OF IDENTIFICATION

A brief discussion of some of the most important empirical studies of this concept appears below. It is not intended to be comprehensive but to illustrate the different approaches and the general concensus of opinion, as was stated earlier.

THE WORK OF SEARS, RAU AND ALPERT (1965)

Sears *et al.* studied, not the process of identification itself, but the hypothesised consequences of identification and their relation to child-rearing procedures. Thus, according to these writers sex-role behaviour, pro-social aggression, adult attitudes and conduct, resistance to deviation and feelings of guilt if transgressions occur, are all consequent upon identification. These variables were therefore studied in a sample of children and linked to child-rearing procedures as ascertained from a structured interview with the parents. The measures of identification were behavioural observations in structured situations, projective tests and questions to parents.

One result, which is important, was that these indices of identification were not positively correlated to any important extent among themselves. This means that it is unlikely that they are all simply the result of one simple process of identification.

However, there are methodological problems in researches of this design which, as claimed by Bandura (1969), make it unlikely that this study by Sears *et al.* is an adequate test of identification. If identification is the taking over of the whole pattern of the parent (see Bronfenbrenner, 1960) then it is essential to know this parental pattern for each individual subject. Thus a child showing little guilt could well have identified with his father if he too showed little guilt. As Bandura succinctly writes, '. . . identificatory behaviour has no intrinsic defining properties and consequently it cannot be measured or identified independently of the behaviour of the persons who have been emulated.' (1969, p. 217).

Of course even similarities between parent and son, for example, especially in the case of behaviour common in the culture, are not necessarily evidence for identification since they could have been learned from some other source. However the fact that identification can only be demonstrated by comparing subject and model means that the work of Sears *et al.* (1965), although yielding information about child behaviour and its child-rearing antecedents, is not really relevant to identification.

PSYCHOMETRIC STUDIES OF IDENTIFICATION

This method is open to a similar objection to that against the previous study. Thus Helper (1955) compared the scores of subjects on a personality questionnaire with the scores of their models for identification. Even had marked similarities been found there would have been no way of assessing whether such similarity was due to identification or to culturally common characteristics. In fact there were no greater similarities to parents than to other figures. In addition to this the common problems of personality questionnaires, especially response sets (which have been fully discussed in the section on psychosexual personality development, see pp. 14-28), are peculiarly important in this type of study since they tend to make scores homogeneous and thus artificially create identification-like similarities. In addition the most valid types of personality questionnaire are those developed by factor analysis (see pp. 31-9) and typically these deal with variables not relevant to studies of identification. The self-descriptive type of questionnaire concerned with attitudes, usually used in the study of identification, has little other than face-validity and thus may be vitiated by inadequacy of self-knowledge and the lack of relation of responses to items and actual behaviour (Cronbach, 1955; Bronfenbrenner, 1958). Thus psychometric studies of identification can carry but little weight.

STUDIES OF MORAL BEHAVIOUR

These, again, are subject to the same objection that the absence of moral behaviour may not mean that identification has not taken place, unless comparable measures of super-ego activity are made of the parental figures. Thus Brown

(1965) is not strictly justified in using the findings of MacKinnon (1938) to relate identification to child-rearing procedures. Similarly the famous studies of moral behaviour by Hartshorne and May (1930) are not really relevant to the Freudian concept of the super-ego. They tell us a good deal about moral behaviour in children of various ages. This behaviour could, however, be mediated by the ego; it fails to show how it came about and is thus not a critical test of the Freudian tripartite division of the mind. As has already been said, for this purpose factor analysis is necessary.

IDENTIFICATION AS OBSERVATIONAL LEARNING – THE WORK OF BANDURA

Bandura (1969) presents a succinct account of his view of identification and the experimental work supporting it. This paper forms the basis of the summary and discussion of his research which is of especial interest in that he has explicitly tested some of the Freudian formulations concerning anaclitic and defensive identification. Furthermore these investigations do not suffer from the defects of the other types of study previously discussed because identification is always related to the behaviour both of subject and model.

Bandura regards identification, imitation, introjection, incorporation, internalisation, copying and role-taking as essentially the same, all referring to behavioural modifications resulting from exposure to models. It must be noted, however, that this view, although parsimonious, means that laboratory studies of the effects of models on behaviour may not be relevant to the psychoanalytic concept of identification.

Observational learning is the basic learning process underlying identification and this involves imaginal and verbal representational systems based on contiguity learning. Bandura, Grusec and Menlove (1966) showed, for example, that children watching a model on film who were allowed to verbalise the model's behaviour acquired more matching responses than children who were not so allowed.

Anaclitic identification

Bandura and Huston (1961), Henker (1964) and Mischel and Grusec (1966) have studied the effects of differential amounts of rewards, given by models, on imitative behaviour. In laboratory studies of this kind, all subjects have equal exposure to the models and the reinforcement of the models' behaviour by children is eliminated – variables which can distort naturalistic studies of child-rearing in that, for example, warm nurturant mothers are likely to see more of their children and thus give greater opportunity for identification than would cold mothers. This would support the Freudian theory of anaclitic identification but merely because the children of nurturant mothers had more time to learn. The results of these laboratory studies support the Freudian claim that there is more identification with warm and nurturant models. However these studies also showed that the warmth of the model did not increase the propensity to produce aversive responses whereas aggressive responses were imitated eagerly from all types of model. In addition a further study by Bandura, Grusec and Menlove (1967) showed that in some conditions nurturance may in fact diminish identification. Bandura (1969) also argues that the generality of these experiments may be impugned on the grounds that they concern dyadic interactions. In a study involving triads, Bandura, Ross and Ross (1963) found that the addition of other social variables affected the relationship between the nurturance of the model and the imitation of the subject.

Bandura (1969) concludes that these studies support in general terms the theory of anaclitic identification proposed in Freudian theory but suggests that it is valid only in certain conditions.

These studies have not been discussed in detail because it seems questionable to us to what extent they are really testing the Freudian theory. Anaclitic identification is said to occur through fear or loss of love. Therefore, it is supposed that warm rather than cold parents should be expected to produce identification in their children. However in these experiments there is no fear of loss of love. The imitation of the model is in no way intended to replace the model, as it is in Freudian theory. Furthermore loving and nurturance cannot be identical: if they were, the problem of substitute mother figures for orphan children (see Bowlby, 1962 and pp. 116-25) would not be so considerable. If, too, as Bandura (1969) suggests, the addition of other social factors affects the relationships, to extrapolate to the natural family situation seems absurd.

On the other hand, the general tenor of the findings supports the Freudian claim that identification is related to affection. It seems to us that the main interest of these studies lies in the fact that the Freudian hypothesis is perfectly acceptable in terms of learning theory which in time may be able to define more precisely the conditions under which anaclitic identification occurs.

Identification with the aggressor

Bandura, Ross and Ross (1963) tested the Freudian theory of defensive identification together with Whiting's status envy theory (Whiting, 1960) and a theory of identification based on social power (Parsons, 1955). From the Parsons theory it would be predicted that the person controlling rewarding resources, not consuming them, would be the model adopted. From the theory of status envy it would be predicted that the person consuming most of the desired resources would be the model. By resources Whiting means such things as food, love, attention and care.

There were two conditions:

(a) One adult was a controller of resources (magnificent toys and food), another adult was the recipient of these while the child watched the events.

(b) One adult controlled the resources of which the child was the recipient while the other adult was neglected.

For half the boys and girls in each condition the male model controlled resources, for the other half the female model.

After the distribution of resources the two adult models performed various actions which later the children had to imitate.

The results showed that children identified with the source of rewarding power rather than the envied competitor for rewards. Furthermore there was cross-sex identification. Thus Whiting was not supported.

Since Bandura (1969) regards Whiting's status envy theory as an extension of Freudian theory, he regards the result of this experiment as evidence against the Freudian theory of defensive identification. However if it is recalled that defensive identification occurs at the threat of castration it is clear that this experiment is an inadequate test of the Freudian theory. Furthermore the imitation of certain dramatic actions of the model does not seem to be a satisfactory measure of identification. This study by Bandura et al. (1963) cannot be considered as evidence against the Freudian theory. Further studies of identification with the aggressor as a defence mechanism can be found in the chapter devoted to them (see p. 187).

Such a study seems to be a clear example of the kind of psychological research that is not relevant to psychoanalytic theory. As Bronfenbrenner (1960) points out, there is a qualitative difference between the Freudian concept of identification, especially as used in the development of the super-ego, and this kind of imitative behaviour. Unfortunately, from the viewpoint of the validation of psychoanalytic theory, most of the research of Bandura has been devoted to a study of imitative behaviour and the conditions influencing its acquisition.

Conclusions to the work of Bandura

Thus because Bandura admits no essential differences between identification and imitation much of his work cannot be considered relevant to the psychoanalytic theory. What is missing from these laboratory analogues is the close relationship between model and subject which is usually present in the family situation. That such factors may be important is evidenced by his admission that result with dyads may not be extrapolated to triads. Indeed he argues (1969) that attentional processes are important to identification, since subjects will not pay equal attention to all models and behaviours. It is easy to argue that it could be the relationship which the child has with its parents which compels it to pay more attention to them as models regardless of the variables which are of importance in a non-emotional situation.

In conclusion there can be little doubt that the work of Bandura has cast much light on the role of imitation in social learning. It does not appear so relevant to the special form of this learning conceptualised in psychoanalytic theory as identification.

THE WORK OF KOHLBERG

Kohlberg (1969) reviews what he calls his cognitive developmental approach to socialisation. Over a number of years Kohlberg (1958, 1963a, 1963b, 1964, 1966a, 1966b, 1967, 1968 and 1969b), to mention only the publications of which he is the single author, has studied the development of moral thought in children. His work was influenced by the work of Piaget (1948) in this field. Kohlberg (1969) considers that the two stages of moral judgement proposed by Piaget, the heteronomous and the autonomous, do not stand the test of logical scrutiny or further empirical study. In their place Kohlberg (1967) proposed three levels of moral judgement each of which embraced two stages of moral development. These levels and stages were based upon the responses to moral dilemmas of children aged between 7 and 17 years. Rest (1968) gives excellent examples of responses characterising the different stages of moral development in the case of a husband who stole a drug to save the life of his wife. At stage 1, for example, the focus is on irrelevant consequences of the act – 'He shouldn't steal the drug . . . he did a lot of damage . . . breaking up the store too.' At stage 6 on the other hand, there is full appreciation of the fact that good motives do not alone justify an act and that moral principles, as legal rules, do not allow exceptions.

Brown (1965) considers that this work of Kohlberg, which indicates that moral judgement continues developing until late adolescence, would surprise Freudians who believe that the super-ego is the heir of the Oedipus complex and consequently that moral development is complete by five. This argument seems to us completely false. The kind of moral development dealt with by Piaget and Kohlberg is a complex intellectual and philosophical activity, and this falls within the realm of the ego, in psychoanalytic terms, not the unconscious super-ego. Consider, for example, the complex chain of arguments by which Plato justifies the existence of The Good as the basis of all morality. These are some of the profoundest products of the ego known to the West and no Freudian would claim that these were the products of super-ego activity. The super-ego governs feeling that this act is good, this one bad, regardless of the intellectual arguments we can adduce against them. Hence, for example, the guilt felt by many adolescents at masturbation despite explanations by enlightened educators (Kinsey *et al.*, 1948).

From this it is argued that the work of Kohlberg and Piaget is not really relevant to the problem of the introjection of the super-ego. This is not, of course, to minimise its importance in the study of the acquisition of morality.

Kohlberg (1969) does not, however, reject the concept of identification. Like Bandura (1969) he regards imitation and identification as essentially similar processes and objects to psychoanalytic theory in that there identification is a special event linked to particular effective family ties. Unlike Bandura however, as was stated earlier, Kohlberg considers there are structural differences between identification and imitation (see p. 139). The cognitive developmental view of identification differs from the Freudian one in the following respects:

1. Identification is viewed as a cognitive structural stage of more general imitative or social sharing processes.
2. Accordingly it is not uniquely dependent upon particular motives and ties only present in the early parent-child relationship.
3. Identifications are not totally fixed, irreversible or 'internalised'.

Identifications are 'solutions' to developmental tasks which may change in object or nature with new developmental tasks (Kohlberg, 1969, p. 426). According to this theory, imitation in the young child occurs because the things imitated are interesting in the sense of arousing (Berlyne, 1961), and only afterwards does imitation come into the control of the kind of social reinforcers discussed by Bandura.

Conclusions to the work of Kohlberg

This summary of the work of Kohlberg has been brief because as has been argued the bulk of his research has concerned an aspect of moral development that is irrelevant to the Freudian theory of the super-ego. Furthermore his view of identification as only one kind of social learning means that he has not concentrated on the Freudian postulate of parental identification at the Oedipal stage. The assumption that there is no difference between identification and imitation, while in Freudian theory there clearly is such a distinction, means, as was the case with Bandura, that much of the evidence cited does not seem truly relevant to the psychoanalytic concept.

OTHER APPROACHES

Mowrer (1950) and Foss (1964)

Mowrer studied the imitation of the human voice in the budgerigar. He argued that the bird only learned to talk when it had grown to like the trainer. In terms of learning theory the sound of the trainer's voice had acquired reinforcement value through pairing with primary reinforcers. Hence imitation through stimulus generalisation could be similarly reinforcing. Mowrer suggested that a similar mechanism could underlie identification. Foss investigated this hypothesis with the myna bird. He found that the myna learned whistles associated with a reinforcer no more quickly than whistles alone. Thus the Mowrer (1950) hypothesis had to be rejected.

The work of Argyle

The studies by Argyle and his colleagues deserve mention if only because they have attempted to put the psychoanalytic theory of anaclitic identification to the test. Argyle (1964) regards introjection as a form of learning with special characteristics:

(*a*) The response tendencies learned are seen to be in conflict with the rest of the personality. As evidence for this he cites the externalised conscience of the authoritarian personality (Adorno *et al.*, 1950): the feeling that one 'ought' rather than one 'wants' to do a certain thing.

(*b*) There is an internalisation of the responses learned so that they occur in all situations not only in the presence of the original source of influence. This is similar to the distinction between imitation and identification, already discussed, which was proposed by Kohlberg (1969).

(*c*) The effects of introjection do not seem to decay with time. However, Argyle mainly uses psychoanalytic evidence to support his argument (and it is precisely this evidence that we are attempting to confirm here).

The work of Argyle and Robinson (1962)

These authors gave measures of need achievement to samples of grammar school boys. They found, using the semantic differential, that high need achievement was related to high reported demands by the parents for such achievement. Argyle and Robinson consider this as evidence for introjection. If this is accepted, however, it is difficult to see how introjection differs from ordinary learning.

The work of Argyle (1964)

Tests. Q. technique: children had to put in rank order 16 cards on which examples of being naughty were printed, e.g. being greedy. There were four rankings:

Things that would make you
1. feel silly
2. feel guilty
3. feel failure
4. be cross with yourself.

Parents had to rank these cards for the antecedents of these feelings – laughs at child, indicates child has failed, withdraws love and uses physical punishment.

Subjects. Twenty 9-10 year old children and their parents.

Results. All rankings by children and parents were correlated for each child separately. The overall hypothesis that self-reactions would be related to the type of discipline (e.g. self-aggression to physical punishment) was slightly supported. But the average correlation for all subjects in all areas with the parent of the same sex was only ·17. The highest figures indeed were only ·22 failure and ·19 guilt, which, though significant, are very small. There is thus little evidence to support introjection from this study. Six children, however, showed a much higher relationship (labelled by Argyle, 1964, as introjectors). To extract subjects in this way seems quite inadmissible, however, since in any sample with any variables some subjects would show such an agreement by chance.

Argyle concludes that 'introjection works on average for these twenty subjects over four areas . . . but it works in particular for six of those subjects . . .'.

These conclusions are quite unacceptable from this data. To single out subjects in this way is simply to capitalise on chance. Even if similarity between self-reaction and mode of discipline is evidence of introjection, this study, on a very small sample, gives only the slightest support for the concept.

Another investigation is reported by Argyle (1964) in which subjects completed semantic differentials to include the sort of person one ought to be and the sort of person one's father thinks one ought to be.

Subjects. 80 students and 500 grammar-school children.

Results. Clearly similarity of scales indicates (or is intended to indicate) the extent to which the super-ego is modelled on the parents and hence the degree of introjection.

For 160 male subjects the super-ego was more similar to the father's than the mother's demands. For the girls there was a non-significant tendency to be nearer the mother's demands than the father's. Factor scores based on these semantic differentials corresponded to the parental demand scores in the range ·35-·70 (Mean ρ ·5). This data, Argyle argues, clearly illustrates the phenomenon of introjection in the formation of the super-ego.

Verbal evidence of this sort based on the semantic differential can hardly be regarded as relevant to the super-ego which is, in part at least, unconscious. This means that the extent to which such verbalisations of behaviour reflect the feelings of guilt and moral obligation which, in psychoanalytic theory, the super-ego is thought to subsume, is likely to be slight. Every schoolboy knows his Ovid: *video meliora proboque, deteriora sequor*. This investigation seems to show only that verbal statements of moral obligation are related to statements about parental ideas on these topics.

Conclusions

Both parts of this study, therefore, despite the claim of Argyle (1964) to be testing and demonstrating anaclitic introjection as described by Freud, seem to be of dubious validity. Neither part, it seems to us, convincingly demonstrates the phenomenon of introjection. Finally it should be noted that whereas we have followed Bandura (1969) and conceived introjection and identification as essentially the same process, Argyle attempts to draw distinctions between the terms. Nevertheless his definition of introjection, based on Freud's description, seems to us essentially similar to identification as it has been used in this discussion. In brief, then, the work of Argyle (1964) and Argyle and Robinson (1962) cannot be held to confirm Freudian theory.

Finally, Gewirtz (1969) takes an operant learning theory approach to identification which he regards as synonymous with imitation and other related terms. He reanalyses the work of Bandura (1962, 1965, 1969), which stresses that identification is learned by observational learning without instrumental reinforcement, and the work of Aronfreed (1969), in terms of orthodox operant learning.

THE RELATION OF THE PSYCHOANALYTIC THEORY TO THESE IDENTIFICATION STUDIES

It is now necessary to examine the status of the psychoanalytic theory of identification in the light of all these findings: in effect to summarise this section.

Most of these theorists consider that identification is essentially no different from other forms of imitation. This has therefore led them to study, often most elegantly, forms of imitation far removed from the Freudian phenomenon. As was pointed out in the discussion of the work of Bandura, it seems improbable that a study of the variables influencing the imitation of a few spectacular gestures is closely relevant to the identification of the Oedipal child with his father. It could well be, and evidence not logic must be adduced to eliminate the possibility, that the close affectional and familial bonds produced in the family situation, and the particular developmental stage reached by the child, mean that to identify with the parent is particularly reinforcing and hence likely to occur even in the absence of the reinforcers found effective in the laboratory situation. In addition, laboratory studies of modelling do not include the threat of loss of love which is, in Freudian theory, the precipitating cause of identification. It must be concluded, therefore, that the studies by Bandura and his colleagues, whether or not the claims of observational learning or operant conditioning are accepted, are not truly relevant to the Freudian concept of identification.

Similarly, the work of Kohlberg (1969) cannot be considered relevant to the Freudian concept of the super-ego. His work is concerned with the part of moral behaviour that is the concern of the ego. The super-ego is concerned with feeling and it is highly unlikely, in view of all that is known about response sets, and the fact that the super-ego is unconscious, that simple questionnaires assessing the degree of guilt following transgression will adequately tap that feeling. In addition, a further problem involved in the study of moral behaviour in relation to the super-ego is the simple one, that if the subject has identified with a parent with weak super-ego, it will appear that he has failed to identify at all. A final objection to studies of moral behaviour lies in the fact that in Freudian theory behaviour is dependent on the dynamic balance between ego, id and super-ego. Unless measures of these other variables are included super-ego strength in terms of identification cannot be assessed.

One clear fact, however, seems to emerge from all these investigations. There seems to be no doubt that, however interpreted, identification does occur. In this respect Freud seems to be supported by the evidence – children do take adults for their models. Furthermore this act of identification can be accommodated by learning theory. Thus Mowrer (1950) fits it into classical conditioning, Gewirtz (1969) into operant conditioning and Bandura (e.g. Bandura and Walters, 1963) into observational learning – a special type of learning.

The disagreement with the psychoanalytic theory lies in the importance attached to this identification. To Bandura, identification can occur with any model depending upon such variables as the reinforcement instrumental on the behaviour or the status of the model. There is relatively little support for the Freudian claim that loss of love or fear of aggression are the important variables. From this it follows that other models than the parent will be important sources of identification whereas in psychoanalytic theory this parental identification is of crucial importance.

In conclusion it appears to us that the Freudian notion of identification has not been adequately tested because of the assumption that all forms of imitation are the same.

SUMMARY

The structural theory of the mind, ego, super-ego and id, was outlined. Three verifiable hypotheses were derived from it:

1. That there are conscious, unconscious and preconscious mental processes. This was shown to be acceptable but of little interest.
2. That there exist three physiological structures similar in function to those of the ego, super-ego and id. This was shown to be, in the present state of physiological knowledge, wholly speculative.
3. That in all behaviour there are three major motivational factors corresponding to ego, super-ego and id. This was shown to have tenuous support in the work of Cattell.

It was concluded that the objective evidence for this structural theory was slight. Finally the empirical studies of identification were examined.

8

The mechanisms of defence

In 'The ego and the id' Freud (1923) states that the neurotic conflict takes place between the ego and the id. The ego seeks to bar the expression of certain instinctual impulses and to do this employs characteristic procedures known in psychoanalytic theory as mechanisms of defence. These defences have been carefully described and a brief description of each will be given below. In psychoanalytic theory (e.g. Fenichel, 1945) it is common to distinguish between successful and unsuccessful defences. Successful defences allow expression for the instinctual drive, unsuccessful ones, on the other hand, fail to do this thus necessitating their continuous repetition.

Sublimation

Strictly this refers to successful defences and is not in itself a defence mechanism. Under sublimation are embraced various defences.

1 *Reversal into opposites* (Freud, 1915). This itself involves two processes of which examples will be given:

    (a) *Change from active to passive*. Sadism becomes masochism.

    (b) *Reversal of content*. Love becomes hate.

2 *Turning round on subject*. Masochism equals sadism directed to the self. Exhibitionism is voyeurism turned towards the self. Freud (1916) summarised the general concept of sublimation:

> It (sublimation) consists in the sexual trend abandoning its aim of obtaining a component or a reproductive pleasure and taking on another which is related genetically to the abandoned one but which is no longer sexual.

Painting is an example of this. Handling paint is regarded in Freudian theory as a sublimation of anal erotism (handling faeces). This concept of sublimation, the deflection of aims, is perhaps the commonest in psychoanalytic theory as the general definition, quoted above, indicates.

Repression

Freud (1915) in his paper on repression said that 'the essence of repression lies simply in the function of rejecting and keeping something out of consciousness.' This makes the impulse inoperative. There are two types of repression:

F   151

(a) *Primal repression.* This is the first phase of repression and refers to 'the denial of entry into consciousness to the mental presentation of the instinct' (1915). This is accompanied by fixation – the mental presentation persists unaltered and the instinct remains attached to it.

(b) *Repression proper.* This concerns the mental derivatives and associations of the repressed presentation. These associations suffer the same fate as the objects of the primal repression. 'Repression proper is, therefore, after-expulsion' (1915). The mental energy which belongs to repressed instincts is transformed into affects – especially anxiety. It is this that makes repression a pathogenic or unsuccessful mechanism of defence.

Use of the term repression in the writing of Freud

To avoid confusion in readers who have read some Freud it is necessary to examine Freud's use of the term repression since its meaning gradually changed over a number of years. What follows is a summary of Appendix A to 'Inhibition, symptoms and anxiety' (Freud, 1925a in the standard edition of his works).

In 'Inhibition, symptoms and anxiety' it is clearly stated that repression is a special kind of defence. It typifies hysteria rather as isolation (see below) typifies obsessional neurosis. As is pointed out in Appendix A, this concept of repression as one kind of defence was not how Freud originally used the word. Repression first appears in 'Preliminary communication' (1893). Defence is first used in 'Neuro-psychoses of defence' (1894) where repression refers to the process and defence to the motive. However, in a second paper entitled 'Further observations on the neuro-psychoses of defence' (1896) both terms are equated. By the time of 'Three essays on sexuality' (1905) repression alone is used.

It is to be noted that the later concept of repression – as one kind of defence mechanism (1925a) – is the one adopted in this book. It clearly represents the mature Freudian view.

Denial

The nature of the defence mechanism denial can, perhaps, be illustrated best by an example. Freud (1925b) in his paper 'Negation' gives a clear instance: 'You ask who the person in this dream can have been. It was *not* my mother. We amend this: so it *was* his mother'. In a description of denial he writes: 'The ego has to ward off some claim from the external world which it feels as painful and . . . this is effected by denying the perceptions that bring to knowledge such a demand on the part of reality' (1940).

Projection

As was the case with denial an example of this defence mechanism is clearer than a definition. Freud (1911) in his paper 'On the mechanism of paranoia' (a neurosis which in psychoanalytic theory is characterised by projection) describes the mechanism of projection thus: the proposition 'I (a man) love him' is contradicted by delusions of persecution: for it loudly asserts 'I do not love him – I hate him'. This proposition 'I hate him' becomes transformed *by projection* into 'He hates (persecutes) me'. Projection, therefore, is the attribution of one's own unacceptable impulses and ideas on to others.

Reaction-formation

In 'Character and anal erotism' (1908) Freud claims that during latency

Reaction-formations such as shame, disgust and morality are formed in the mental economy at the expense of the excitations proceeding from the erotogenic zones and these reaction-formations erect themselves as barriers against the later activity of the sexual instinct.

As can be seen from this example, reaction-formations create attitudes opposite to those being defended against. Thus, to continue the example quoted, disgust is a reaction-formation against pleasure in handling faeces. It is to be noted that this kind of concept gives a bad reputation to psychoanalysis. Thus even if the observed behaviour is quite opposed to prediction it can always be interpreted as a reaction-formation.

Undoing

This is a defence mechanism characteristic of obsessional neurosis and is referred to in Freud's discussion of the Rat-Man (1909). It is there described as negative magic which endeavours by means of motor symbolism to 'blow away' not merely the consequences of some event but the event itself. Undoing may be observed in the diphasic symptoms of obsessional neurosis. Fenichel (1945) describes undoing as a process in which something is done which actually or magically is the opposite of something which again either actually or in the imagination was done. Indeed, according to Fenichel, all acts of expiation are really a form of undoing.

Isolation

This mechanism was defined for the first time in 'Inhibitions, symptoms and anxiety' (Freud, 1925a) and is peculiar to obsessional neurosis. If something unpleasant happens the patient interpolates an interval during which nothing must happen. Experiences are not forgotten but are separated from their associations and emotions. Thus isolation can make psychoanalytic therapy difficult. In 'Contributions to the psychology of love', Freud (1910) described the separation of the tender and the sensual components of sexuality. Thus some men cannot have satisfactory physical relations with women whom they respect but only with women whom they despise. This isolation of sexuality from the rest of life is, according to Fenichel (1945), an outstanding example of the defence mechanism of isolation – it allows such men to express their sexual drives without guilt.

Regression

This has already been described (see pp. 6-7) in the chapter on psychosexual development. However Freud (1925a) has argued that the process can be used as a mechanism of defence, citing as an example of this his case study of the Wolf-Man. In enforcing the regression the ego scores its first success in the defensive struggle. In the obsessional neurosis, typically, the defensive regression is to the anal-sadistic level.

IMPORTANCE OF THE THEORY

These defence mechanisms are of major importance in the understanding of behaviour. The curious rituals of the obsessional neurotic, for example, may be understood in the light of *undoing*. Constant handwashing 'undoes' a previous dirtying action. The concept of sublimation gives insight into the creativity of the artist who in psychoanalytic theory is sublimating anal expulsive tendencies. Thus, then, an understanding of an individual's defence mechanisms gives insight into basic and unconscious attitudes and drives. They are also crucial to the understanding of the symptoms of neurosis and psychosis as is evident from the brief description of the mechanisms given above.

EMPIRICAL HYPOTHESES

As must be plain to the reader, these defence mechanisms are not easy to put to the empirical examination. The main reason for this is that, as yet, no measures exist for unconscious attitudes and processes, whereas essentially all these defence mechanisms postulate that a response (x) is due to or related to unconscious attitude (y). For example, cleanliness is due to unconscious anal erotism. As will be seen in the survey of the experimental evidence relating to defensive processes, most investigators test interferences made from the theory rather than making direct observations. Nevertheless, these descriptions of the defence mechanisms do contain some empirical and testable statements.

1. Highly unpleasant events will be forgotten (repression).
2. Highly unpleasant stimuli will not be perceived (denial).
3. People will impute to others their own undesirable traits (projection).

These three defence mechanisms, repression, denial and projection, seem to be the only ones which can be directly investigated. The obvious problems involved in these hypotheses – for example, what is meant by unpleasant in the statement that unpleasant stimuli will be forgotten – will be discussed when the relevant experimental evidence is examined.

DEFENCES AGAINST AFFECT

The defence mechanisms outlined above were defences against instinctual impulses. Although these are of crucial importance in understanding human behaviour there are other mechanisms of defence – defences against affects. These latter will not be described in so much detail both because they are not so important in psychoanalytic theory and because to a large extent they are identical with those already described. The defence mechanisms are turned against affects rather than impulses.

REPRESSION OF AFFECTS

In his paper 'Repression' Freud (1915) argues that repression of affects is most easily identified from its results: substitute-formations (animals instead of the father in animal phobias), symptoms (the rituals of an obsessional neurosis) and an excessive innervation of spirit and body. The methods of bringing repression about have been described by Freud in various papers and a brief summary of the more important of these is given below.

POSTPONEMENT OF AFFECTS

This may be clearly seen in the study of grief. Freud (1918) in 'From the history of an infantile neurosis' gives a clear example of this mechanism. His patient had felt no grief at his sister's death although he had considerable depth of feeling for her. However a few month's later he had visited the grave of Pushkin and, inexplicably, had been overwhelmed by grief. This grief for the poet was a postponement of affect.

DISPLACEMENT OF AFFECT

The example quoted above is a special instance of displacement of affect. Often there is displacement of object. The example of postponement of affects also exemplifies displacement of object – from sister to poet. In 'Analysis of a phobia in a five-year-old boy' Freud (1909) showed how fear of animals was fear displaced from his father.

Displacement of affect is the main defence mechanism against affect in psychoanalytic theory. The other mechanisms will receive a brief mention. *Affect equivalents* were described in Freud's paper on anxiety, 'On the right to separate from neurasthenia a definite symptom complex as anxiety neurosis' (1894). In this work it was claimed that sexual excitement and anxiety could be experienced as irregularities of breathing and heart rhythm – i.e. sexual excitement was displaced to these areas. In addition there is the defence known as *change of quality of affects*. An example of this would be the Freudian claim that anxiety is in fact transformed sexual energy, an argument put forward in his paper 'My views on the part played by sexuality in the aetiology of the neuroses' (1905b), where he states '. . . the symptoms represent the patient's sexual activity.' Fenichel (1945) points out that this has never been refuted. The other defences against affects are identical with those against instinctual impulses – isolation, projection and reaction-formation. Anna Freud (1946) mentions a form of defence known as *identification with the aggressor*. Although not strictly Freudian, it is brought closely into touch with classical psychoanalytical theory by Fenichel who says it is nothing else than introjection of the object against whom the affect was directed. Identification with the aggressor has been briefly introduced because, as the review of the experimental literature will make clear, it has been subject to empirical testing. An example of this defence mechanism from everyday life is the well known anti-Semitism of certain Jews (Sarnoff, 1962). Identification with the aggressor as a developmental process involved in the formation of the super-ego has been discussed in the previous chapter (p. 143).

SUMMARY OF THE THEORY

The basis of the theory of defence mechanisms is that the ego seeks to avoid pain. Instinctual drives are warded off to avoid anxiety or guilt by certain characteristic processes (defence mechanisms). In addition the ego attempts to avoid feelings of guilt and anxiety – defences against affects.

EMPIRICAL HYPOTHESES IN DEFENCES AGAINST AFFECTS

1. Grief or aggression known to be caused by or directed at one object may be expressed towards another (displacement).
2. Persons suffering from anxiety should have severe sexual problems (change of quality of affects).
3. Subjects who have suffered severe aggression should show considerable approval of the aggressors.

THE EVIDENCE FOR REPRESSION

In his paper 'Repression' Freud (1915) distinguishes two types of repression:

1. *Primal repression.* This refers to the denial of entry into consciousness of unacceptable material, e.g. Oedipal wishes.
2. *After-repression.* This is concerned with the expulsion from consciousness of material associated with repressed impulses.

In addition there is a third manifestation of repression – one attendant upon its failure. This is the return of repressed material into consciousness – characteristic of psychotic behaviour. Studies of this manifestation of repression are concerned with disturbances of thought and behaviour (symptoms of the return) and are not relevant to this chapter. These are included in studies of Freudian theories of neuroses and psychosis. However there is one type of study of the return of the repressed which will receive brief discussion here – work done with word-association tests.

As MacKinnon and Dukes (1962) point out, the concepts of primal and after-repression require different experimental designs for proper investigation.

Primal repression of its nature implies disturbance in perception, after-repression, disturbances of memory. In the first part of this chapter we shall examine the evidence for *after-repression*.

STUDIES OF AFTER-REPRESSION

As Eriksen and Pierce (1968) make clear in their summary of the empirical studies of after-repression, the normal experimental method of investigation involves the study of the *learning rate* for emotional and neutral material. Such studies may be further subdivided into those where the anxiety and repression are experimentally induced and those where it is assumed that the repression has been already learned in the everyday experience of the subjects.

PROBLEMS IN THE EXPERIMENTAL DESIGNS

These basic experimental designs are plagued by a number of problems which are best discussed before any examination of individual studies is made. These problems are set out below.

1. *In the second type of experiment is the assumption of repression justified?* This is a major difficulty in the study of repression. Since, obviously, life experiences vary considerably so, if Freudian theory is correct, must repressions – both in strength and the subject matter repressed. This also affects, perhaps even more, the selection of neutral material. Apparently neutral stimuli may, for individuals, be intimately related to repressed material.

2. *In the first type of experiment, is the experimental induction of repression successful?* One common method of inducing anxiety and hence repression is to make subjects think that they have failed on intelligence tests. In the case of students this is, in all probability, anxiety-provoking but to argue that any consequent decrement in learning is therefore due to repression is not necessarily justified. The disrupting effects of failure could be due to motivation (knowledge of good results is a known reinforcer) differences compared with the control group. In addition Eriksen and Pierce (1968) suggest that subjects in the failing group are probably still thinking about their failure, its consequences and reasons and are simply distracted from the subsequent learning task. In any case the kind of repression thus induced experimentally seems a long way removed from the clinical Freudian concept of repression – normally concentrated on Oedipal desires, castration wishes and other profound and basic impulses.

A further method of inducing anxiety has been to capitalise on the Zeigarnik effect. Zeigarnik (1927), in the course of investigating the Gestalt psychologists' claim that a 'good' gestalt was formed of things completed, found that subjects tended to remember tasks in which they were not ego-involved better if they were interrupted than if they were completed. If, however, subjects became ego-involved, completed tasks were remembered better than incompleted. This Zeigarnik effect has been utilised in the study of repression. However, as Sears

(1950) claims, the Zeigarnik effect is so complex that to attempt to attribute the effects to repression is purely speculative. Again it may be questioned to what extent, if at all, such experimentally produced repression resembles the Freudian concept.

Perhaps the most telling point against studies where the experimental induction of repression has been attempted is that made by Eriksen and Pierce (1968). In fact, they argue, such studies are not even tests of repression because the repressing behaviour (failure to remember failed material) is not anxiety reducing – indeed it may even be anxiety provoking in that it represents another failure.

3. *Both neutral and emotive material must be equally difficult to learn.* This is an obvious point but, clearly, if the emotive material contains rare words little known to the subjects, differences in retention could be expected on those grounds alone.

4. *Repression not suppression.* If the experiment requires subjects to verbalise sexual or taboo words in front of an experimenter, responses may be voluntarily suppressed rather than repressed. Care must be taken in the design of the experiment, therefore, lest suppression confound the results.

5. *Individual differences.* Not all subjects use repression as a defence mechanism to the same extent. This is a variable that could clearly affect experimental results.

STUDIES OF REPRESSION USING THE ZEIGARNIK EFFECT

As mentioned above, the Zeigarnik effect – worse memory for incompleted tasks – has been used in the experimental study of repression. It is not intended to discuss any of these experiments in detail because the view of Sears (1934 and 1950), that such studies were not proper tests of the Freudian concept of repression, seems to us incontrovertibly true. Thus in the typical Zeigarnik experiment, activities are interrupted before subjects can have had the chance to complete them: later they are asked to recall these activities and others not similarly disturbed. Glixman (1949) is a good example of this approach in that he analysed the effects of interruption under three degrees of stress. In the non-stressful situation subjects thought a test was being tried out, in the moderately stressful situation subjects felt their ability was being evaluated, whereas in the highly stressful condition great emphasis was placed on the performance of subjects. After subjecting his results to an extremely sophisticated analysis of co-variance where the number of completions was held constant, Glixman found that as stress increased no-recall of incompleted tasks decreased. There was no significant difference for completed tasks.

If we could regard this study as an analogue of Freudian repression, here indeed would be impressive experimental support for it, as in fact would be the majority of earlier studies of this type (Rosenzweig, 1933, 1934, 1938). However if we examine carefully the paper on repression (Freud, 1915) it becomes obvious that the Zeigarnik effect is a pale adumbration of what Freud intended by the term repression – so pale that it bears but little resemblance. Thus Freud says

> . . . a primal repression, a first phase repression which consists in a denial of entry into consciousness to the mental presentation of the instinct. This is accompanied by fixation: the ideational presentation in question persists unaltered from then onward and the instinct remains attached to it.

Again he writes '. . . repression proper concerns mental derivatives of the repressed instinct – presentation . . .'. A little later we find '. . . the instinct presentation develops in a more unchecked and luxuriant fashion if it is withdrawn by repression fron conscious influence. It ramifies like a fungus . . .'. This description of what Freudian repression truly is, is surely evidence enough that interruption of a task cannot be said to be the same thing. What instinct has to be repressed, or what association of instinct, in the Zeigarnik task? Is it credible that such interruption can produce repressed material that will ramify like a fungus? We are forced to agree with Sears (1943, 1950) who considered the situations and problems created in the Zeigarnik experiments as so trivial as to be useless. It is clear from this Freudian description of repression that it is concerned with basic and essential drives and conflicts.

In conclusion, therefore, it must be stated that studies of repression involving the Zeigarnik effect are irrelevant to the Freudian concept. This is particularly unfortunate, since there is apparent support for the theory in carefully designed experiments.

STUDIES IN WHICH ANXIETY IS EXPERIMENTALLY INDUCED

These experiments, of which the Zeigarnik type really constitute a specific subclass are, of course, open to the same theoretical objection that the experimentally induced anxiety, intended to create the repression, is not similar to the kind of anxiety thought to cause repression in psychoanalytic theory. Unfortunately this type of study is favoured by academic psychologists because it follows so closely the hallowed cannons of scientific method. Eriksen and Pierce (1968) regard it as superior to the type of experiment where the repression is assumed to be created in life '. . . when the experiment contains adequate operations for attaching anxiety to specific cues of stimuli'. With this last proviso, Eriksen and Pierce are undoubtedly correct. However the problem remains as to the best way of inducing a satisfactory measure of anxiety.

As has been mentioned, in this type of experiment a common method of inducing anxiety has been to make subjects feel they have grievously failed in an intelligence test and then have them recall the items in comparison with a control group. A much-quoted experiment of this type, often held to support the Freudian notion of repression, is that of Zeller (1950).

Zeller had two groups of subjects learn nonsense syllables. They then underwent a tapping test. One group were told they had done well, the other that they had failed. On retest the group who had failed the tapping were significantly worse at recalling the nonsense syllables than the control group. However when the purpose of the test was explained (removing the repression) the two groups became equal. It could be objected that this difference was not due to repression but due to motivation in that they lost interest in the whole procedure due to failure. Zeller therefore ran a further experiment which included a group whose failure on tapping was understood to be specific to tapping and a group who were told they had failed on both nonsense syllables and tapping as well as the previous experimental group and a successful control group. On this occasion the experimental group who failed the tapping and the group who were told they had failed both tests were significantly worse at recall than the other groups. Thus specific task anxiety did not worsen performance. Again when repression was removed all groups became equal. From these two experiments Zeller claimed that an experimental analogue of repression had been created.

There are several points that must be made about these two experiments.

1. The fact that anxiety concerning one task (tapping) created repression of another (nonsense syllables) means that the design is not really analogous to the Freudian concept. The test should have been of the tapping.

2. This means that the anxiety itself is far more likely to have disrupted the performance through its effects on motivation or interest or simply by distracting the subjects from the recall task. Certainly there is no evidence that this is *not* the case.

3. Zeller makes the point that no experimental test of repression is complete unless it is demonstrated that removal of repression (revealing to the subjects the purpose of the anxiety creating procedures) restores performance in the recall tests. And Zeller (1950) does demonstrate this. However it can be argued that if the repression can be so easily removed then this in itself is evidence that no true analogue of Freudian repression has been created. Typically, repression is most difficult to remove – hence the length of psychoanalytic treatment.

4. Even if it is admitted that Zeller did create anxiety in his students under conditions of failure it is still doubtful whether such anxiety is similar to that causing repression in Freudian theory. No instinctual impulses are involved, no fixation seems possible. Again, as in the case of the Zeigarnik effect, we must agree with Sears (1943, 1950) that this type of experiment is too trivial to be a proper test of Freudian theory.

All these four criticisms mean that the work of Zeller (1950), although it appear to support the Freudian concept of repression, cannot be regarded as constituting a proper test of the theory. Indeed it is hard to see how, experimentally, a truly repression-causing situation can be created. Ethically the kind of procedures likely to produce it – Oedipal incest, patricide, sexual behaviour involving pre-genital zones – are entirely inadmissible and obviously have not been attempted.

To conclude, therefore, it is argued that experimentally induced anxiety is too trivial to form an analogue of Freudian repression. This means that the only design likely to demonstrate the existence of the defence mechanism is that which is concerned with repressions that have been developed already in the past experience of subjects.

STUDIES USING READY-MADE REPRESSION

As has been mentioned, the main difficulty with this kind of study involves the assumption of repression concerning the emotive material. This is particularly the case where negative results are reported. Here, obviously, it could be due to the fact that the neutral material was emotive or the emotive material had not been subjected to repression. A method of avoiding this pitfall is to select words which have been demonstrated for each subject to be either neutral or emotive on the criterion of a word-association test.

An early study by *Flanagan* (1930) showed that paired associates with a sexual connotation were less well recalled than neutral paired associates. This can hardly be regarded as a demonstration of repression since subjects had to utter sexual taboo words in the presence of the experimenter. The detrimental performance could therefore be attributed to voluntary suppression. A similar study by *Williams* (1951), which is not open to the same objection of suppression, showed that words pertaining to violence were less well recalled than non-violent words. However, to attribute this difference to repression is perhaps speculative although the result is certainly of interest.

The work of Wilkinson and Carghill (1955)

Wilkinson and Carghill, however, carried out a study of recalling stories, one with an Oedipal theme (and likely, therefore, to be subjected to repression) and one with a neutral theme. This deserves careful scrutiny.

Subjects. 50 male and 50 female subjects.

Stories. Two stories of a dream theme: one was an Oedipal dream sequence; the other was a similar sequence but non-Oedipal. Both stories were very similar except in the crucial Oedipal scenes, and used in many places identical vocabulary.

Procedure. 25 men and 25 women read either the Oedipal or the control story. Fifteen minutes afterwards subjects were required to recall the stories.

Results. Recall for the Oedipal theme was significantly worse.

Comments and conclusions

Eriksen and Pierce (1968) argue that this result is likely to be due to the fact that both stories were not equally difficult to learn. They write '. . . one can reasonably question whether the content of the Oedipal stories was equivalent to the neutral stories in interest value, difficulty and other variables determining retention.' First it is to be noted that Eriksen and Pierce refer to Oedipal stories (plural). In the Wilkinson and Carghill study there was only one Oedipal story and one neutral story. As indicated both stories were very similar dream sequences. The Oedipal content was not so overtly sexual as to be likely to arouse voluntary suppression, but was symbolic in nature. Thus interest value was very similar for both themes (many of the sentences were the same) and difficulty of learning appeared to be equal. In the light of the actual dream sequences used these objections appear quite unfounded and unconvincing. If this be the case the only viable hypothesis to account for the results is that of repression. Furthermore this was indeed material where true Freudian repression would be expected to occur.

It must be concluded therefore that this study by Wilkinson and Carghill (1955) is impressive support for the Freudian concept of repression. It shows up clearly the advantages of allowing life experiences to create repression (what Freud was actually concerned with) rather than attempting to create it experimentally, and succeeding in provoking but a trivial anxiety.

The work of Laffal (1952 and 1955)

In an effort to ensure that the emotive stimuli were truly emotive and consequently liable to repression, Laffal (1952) first gave his subjects a 100-word word-association test.

Subjects. 80 college males.

Words used. 10 words with association disturbances (long-reaction time, GSR, etc.), and 10 without, were chosen individually for each subject.

Procedure. Each subject learned to say the word in response to a picture. Then separate groups (N = 20) were brought back at the following time intervals: 15 minutes, 2 days, 4 days, 7 days. The recall task was to remember as many of the learned words as possible in five minutes. Then subjects had to relearn the paired associate task.

Results

1. Emotive words took significantly more trials to learn than neutral words.
2. There were no differences in retention of disturbing and neutral words.

Comments and conclusions

The first finding appears to support the Freudian concept of repression. The second fails to support it. Laffal (1952) argued that this failure could be due either to the fact that the anxiety was reduced by learning or that the original difficulty in learning disturbing words was not caused by anxiety at all but by competing responses. For it was observed that there was a far greater variety of associations to disturbing words. Since this factor of number of associations to neutral and disturbing words was not controlled, it cannot be held that the results of this experiment (finding one) support the Freudian concept of repression. Laffal (1955) suggested that the disturbance indications on word-association tests (particularly long-reaction time) were indicative not so much of disturbance but of the availability to the subject of a large number of (and therefore competing) responses. Hence the selection of such words for testing repression apparently produces a repression effect because these conflicting responses also make learning and recall more difficult.

This problem of conflicting responses (response entropy) means that the work of Laffal (1952) does not constitute evidence in favour of the Freudian theory of repression.

The work of Levinger and Clark (1961)

An impressive study by Levinger and Clark has gone a long way towards solving the problems encountered by Laffal.

Subjects. 34 female undergraduates.

Procedure. Reaction times and GSR's were taken to 30 emotive and 30 neutral words balanced for frequency. Subjects were then asked to repeat their associations.

Results

(*a*) Forgotten associations were those accompanied by a higher GSR. Associations to emotive words were forgotten more than those to neutral words. Associations to words which the subjects had rated high on emotionality were forgotten more than those to words rated low.

(*b*) In the light of the work of Laffal (1952, 1955) reported above, these results were analysed in relation to response competition of which two indices were developed:

1. *Population variability* – number of responses given to each word by sample on first testing.
2. *Retest variability* – number of different responses given to each word on second test.

It was found that forgetting associations was equally related to both indices of response suppression.

Comments. So far this study is no different from those of Laffal. The results equally well support the hypothesis that forgetting is a function of response competition as the Freudian hypothesis that associations to emotive words would be repressed. Levinger and Clark (1961), however, went on to conduct further analyses of the results which discriminate between the two hypotheses.

Further analysis. Correlations and rotated factor analysis of all variables derived from the 60 words.

Results

(*a*) Zero recall of associations correlated with all variables except GSR. Partial correlations (holding the two measures of response competition constant) between zero recall and mean emotionality were ·44 and ·50. Thus failure to recall is related to the emotionality of the words even when response competition is controlled.

(*b*) A rotated factor analysis of the variables showed clearly that there were two factors involved in the forgetting of word associations – *emotionality* and *response variability*.

Comments and conclusions

Factor 1 and the partial correlations show conclusively that forgetting associations is related to the emotionality of the stimuli. This, therefore, is a clear example of

Freudian repression. Factor 2, response variability, also affects forgetting as Laffal (1952, 1955) found. However this in no way refutes Freudian theory. That this factor affects forgetting is equivalent to what Cattell and Warburton (1967) call instrument factors. That is, in this particular experimental procedure there is a factor influencing forgetting – response competition. With another procedure this factor would not occur and is of little importance *once its influence is estimated.*

This study by Levinger and Clark (1961) provides irrefutable evidence for the Freudian concept of repression. Their use of multivariate statistical techniques nicely exemplifies their advantages over the univariate analyses of single variables.

SUMMARY OF STUDIES OF AFTER-REPRESSION

It has been argued in this section that the experimental approach which is most elegant in design – that of experimentally creating repression – cannot really provide a laboratory analogue of the Freudian concept of repression. The anxiety created is too trivial. For this reason only a few typical studies have been described. The second approach on the other hand, where repression based on previous experience is assured, has been shown to yield clear evidence of repression. The studies held to have demonstrated repression were:

1. Wilkinson and Carghill (1955) – poor recall of Oedipal themes.
2. Levinger and Clerk (1961) – poor recall of disturbing words with the confounding variable of response competition controlled.

STUDIES OF THE RETURN OF THE REPRESSED

As was indicated earlier, studies of the return of the repressed are not really relevant to this chapter but are better found in the chapter on Freudian theories of neurosis and psychosis. This is because the return of the repressed is usually symptomised by hallucination and disorders of thought. That is, the return of the repressed material distinguishes, in psychoanalytic theory, the neurotic and the psychotic (Fenichel, 1945).

MacKinnon and Dukes (1962), however, consider that Jung's studies (1918) in word association constitute sound evidence for the theory of repression. Thus Jung noticed that subjects, if asked to repeat a list of word associations, were sometimes unable to associate again to certain words, changed their responses, were reduced to silence or responded only with great effort. These disturbances of association, indeed, may occur on the first occasion of going through the list. In addition GSR for such responses is greater than for normal responses. These observations have been instituted into a type of standardised test – the Kent-Rosanoff word-association list (Kent and Rosanoff, 1910). As will have been already noted by the observant reader these indicants of disturbed response have been used in some of the studies already discussed in this chapter in an effort to choose genuinely emotive stimuli for each subject in the investigation.

However the evidence that such indications of disturbance in word association do in fact indicate areas of disturbance is mainly clinical. Although the fact that words so selected are harder to learn than neutral words supports the claim. Thus these indicators of emotionality may perhaps, as Jung (1918) believed, be regarded as evidence for the return of the repressed.

STUDIES OF PERCEPTUAL DEFENCE

Since 1947 when Bruner and Postman first used the term there has been a vast outpouring of research into perceptual defence, a term defined by Brown (1962) as referring to any systematic relationship found to hold between stimulus emotionality and the ease of recognition of stimuli. There have been some excellent reviews of this literature, especially by Brown (1962), MacKinnon and Dukes (1962) and Eriksen and Pierce (1968). This section owes much to them.

DEFINITION OF PERCEPTUAL DEFENCE

Bruner and Postman (1947) found that words of an emotionally disturbing character were more difficult to recognise than were neutral words. This raising of the perceptual threshold was termed by them 'perceptual defence'. In addition they found that some emotionally disturbing words were less difficult to recognise than other less disturbing words – a process they referred to as 'perceptual sensitisation'. Both concepts are important in the objective study of Freudian defence mechanisms as will be seen below. For the moment, however, we must turn our attention to the first finding – perceptual defence – the raising of the perceptual threshold – although the term is now used to embrace both raising and lowering perceptual thresholds.

RELATION OF PERCEPTUAL DEFENCE TO THE FREUDIAN CONCEPT OF REPRESSION

Since in Freudian theory, as stated in the beginning of this chapter (p. 151), repression is defined as denial of entry into consciousness, it can be seen that perceptual defence as used by Bruner and Postman (1947) is precisely the same. The raising of the perceptual threshold to the emotionally loaded stimulus word is simply an example of repression at work. Thus if it could be demonstrated that perceptual thresholds were in fact raised to stimuli that subjects desired to repress and that results were not an artefact of the experimental design (for example that the emotional words were very rare), there would indeed be experimental and unequivocal evidence for the Freudian concept of repression. That perceptual defence, if shown to occur, is an example of repression is fully supported by Fenichel (1945) who makes it clear that the defence mechanism applies to external perceptions of the real world and not just to mental events.

RESEARCH DESIGN IN EXPERIMENTS IN PERCEPTUAL DEFENCE

MacKinnon and Dukes (1962) conclude their review of studies in perceptual defence thus:

> Those who are concerned that repression serves as a shield in perception (i.e. that perceptual defence experiments are demonstrations of Freudian repression) have discovered ample evidence to justify their belief, while those who reject the notion have found no convincing data to support it.

That such a statement can be made indicates that the research designs used in many of the experiments are not sufficiently tight to allow only one interpretation of the results. However, as will be seen below it is possible to design researches such that explanations other than repression are unconvincing.

Eriksen and Pierce (1968) lay down the following criteria for an adequate experiment in perceptual defence:

1. *Stimuli must be shown to be anxiety provoking for students.* Sears (1936) pointed out that many of the early experiments on repression failed in this respect. These investigated memory for pleasant compared with unpleasant words on the assumption that pleasantness was equated with non-provoking of anxiety. The classic example of this fault is the study of whether quinine is less well remembered than sugar! (Hilgard, 1952.)

2. *Avoidance, inhibition or distortion of the anxiety-provoking covert cue must be effective* – i.e. prevent anxiety. Thus in an experiment where electric shocks are coupled with the responses, if non-recall does not reduce shock there is no point in repression and it cannot therefore logically be expected to occur.

3. *The use of repression must not provoke more anxiety than its non-use.* According to Eriksen and Pierce this is frequently overlooked in otherwise good research designs. For example, if a study requires a subject to utter a taboo word, e.g. whore, not to utter it may provoke more anxiety than to do so. Not to say it may make him anxious about his sanity or his ability, especially if he is a college student fulfilling course requirements.

4. *Individual differences in responses must be taken into account*

(*a*) Some subjects have different defences. A *regressive* response is different from a *projection* response. Thus in Freudian theory the paranoid typically projects his unacceptable impulses on to others (see p. 152), the hysteric represses them.

(*b*) The differential effectiveness of the experiment in arousing anxiety in different subjects. It need hardly be said that, for example, patricide is likely to have a different arousal effect on subjects who have never known their fathers, subjects who hate their fathers and, presumably, those rare individuals who have killed their fathers.

(c) Subjects may differ in the amount of anxiety which is required to trigger their defences. Thus Inglis (1961) has argued that introverts need far less anxiety-provoking stimuli to bring their defences into play than do extroverts. If, however, stress is increased, defence mechanisms may collapse at this point, while on the other hand, extraverts may just begin to show their defensive processes. The work of Byrne (1964), who has studied the relationship between personality and defence behaviour, supports this claim.

These then, according to Eriksen and Pierce (1968), are the four essential factors that must be taken into account in the design of adequate experiments into perceptual defence. As has been suggested previously, many of these experiments have been discounted for a number of reasons. Chief amongst these are the confounding effects of certain stimulus variables which also need to be designed out of the experiment. Eriksen and Pierce do not specifically mention these since they fall under the first heading – the selection of stimuli. However they should be made explicit. Since the essence of perceptual defence experiments lies in the difference in recognition time between emotional and neutral stimuli, it is clear that variables likely to influence recognition differentially are important. Thus it is somewhat surprising to find that Brown (1962) discusses variables that affect the recognition of all stimuli equally. These appear to be irrelevant. The main confounding variables which affect recognition differentially are set out below.

1. *Frequency of previous experience of the words*

Howes and Solomon (1950) argued that taboo words, often used in perceptual defence experiments, had higher recognition thresholds because they were rarer than their neutral controls. The measure of word frequency most commonly used, however, is the Thorndike-Lorge word list (1944). The frequencies there quoted are based on a search of literary evidence and it is highly likely that taboo words such as 'whore' and 'bugger' are more commonly known than would be expected from their literary frequency (unless much modern literature were included). Indeed, Eriksen and Pierce argue that to use the Thorndike-Lorge list to balance taboo and control words is therefore to weight the experiment against getting any perceptual defence effect. Sprague (1959) showed with nonsense syllables that previous experience did affect the threshold – the greater the experience, the lower the threshold, if experience and test were in the same modality.

However, an experiment by Wiener (1955) demonstrates clearly that even if frequency is a confounding variable, as the study by Sprague shows it must be, it does not account for all the threshold variances observed in experiments into perceptual defence. With great ingenuity Wiener inserted four words – e.g. fairy, which had both a neutral and a threatening meaning, into lists of words which stressed either one or the other meaning. The four words in the threat list had lower thresholds than the same words in the neutral list (perceptual sensitisation or vigilance). Thus the emotional connotation affected the thresholds.

From this it is fair to conclude that while every care must be taken to ensure that word frequencies do not vary between groups of words, the perceptual defence effect cannot be imputed to word frequency alone.

2. *Word length*

McGinnies *et al.* (1952) investigated the effects of word length on perceptual thresholds by using words of known frequency (Thorndike-Lorge word count, 1944) but of different length. They concluded that word length was a significant factor in recognition thresholds. Brown (1962), however, in his discussion of this experiment points out that this conclusion ignores the fact that word length and frequency are themselves inter-related. Brown claims that only where frequency is itself an important variable (and this is only when it is rather low) does the length of word affect thresholds. It must be concluded that in any study the word length of the emotional and neutral words should be matched. Slight differences, however, would not appear to be important.

3. *Set*

It could be that the threshold differences noted for emotional and neutral words are due to the effects of set – i.e. if a subject expects a certain type of stimulus, his expectation for such stimuli will increase and his recognition thresholds will, for those words, drop. Conversely, for other words they will rise. Wylie (1957) and Neisser (1954) found this to be the case – words for which a set had been induced did have a lower recognition threshold than control words.

Luchins (1950) has attempted to attribute all the perceptual defence effects to set. However if the experimenter is careful not to induce sets in his subject by his instructions and if the design of the experiment is such that the subject is not likely to form any of his own, the effects of set are probably not important. Ideally, research designs should be used such that no kind of set can be built up. Later in this chapter we shall discuss some work of this kind – that of Dixon (1958 et seq.).

Brown (1962) mentions further variables which might confound results – the reward value of previous experience of the words, familiarity with the words, meaningfulness of the stimuli, recency of the experience of the words, and the organic need-state of the subjects. None of these, however, as his discussion makes clear, is of very great importance.

There is one further confounding factor which, although not a stimulus variable, as were the ones already examined, needs discussion.

Suppression or repression

McGinnies (1949) in his experiment on perceptual defence had used taboo words as the emotional stimuli and had found the recognition threshold raised in their case. As has been discussed in the section on frequency, Howes and Solomon (1950) had objected to the perceptual defence hypothesis as an explanation of the results on the grounds that his taboo words were less frequent and therefore less easily recognised than the control words. In addition, however, Howes and Solomon (1950) invoked the concept of suppression rather than repression. They argued that the raised threshold could have been due to the fact that the subject recognises the words but does not immediately say so to the experimenter. This, of course, is particularly likely to occur in the case of taboo words and where the experimenter is in a position of authority relative to the subject. This conscious suppression is quite different from repression. Repression in Freudian theory is an *unconscious* defence mechanism.

Wiener (1955), in an experiment already discussed for its relevance to the confounding factor of frequency, embedded, it will be remembered, four words in two different lists – one threatening, the other neutral. There was a lower threshold of recognition for these words in the threatening list. This disposed of frequency as the sole cause of different thresholds of recognition. In addition, however, Wiener found that subjects who were aware of the taboo meaning had *lower* not higher thresholds than those who were unaware. This disposes of suppression as the cause of raised thresholds.

Whittaker *et al.* (1952) found that response suppression was admitted by Negroes with a Negro experimenter to stimuli generally regarded as derogatory to Negroes, e.g. 'Darky', although it was not admitted by subjects with a White experimenter. Many studies (e.g. Cowen and Beier, 1954) have attempted to counteract the effects of suppression by telling the subjects to expect taboo words. Fulkerson (1957) found that such a technique only affected the first taboo word. Brown (1962) likens this effect to habituation to taboo words.

The work of Wiener suggests that response suppression is probably not of great importance. Certainly it seems likely to occur only in experiments where taboo responses are used. After all in the particular instance, the stimuli of Whittaker *et al.* were in effect taboo words. A good design, therefore, would make no use of taboo words so that any results could not be impugned on the grounds of conscious suppression. This problem is a specific example of Eriksen and Pierce's (1968) third criterion.

Summary

What are needed, therefore, in studies of perceptual defence, if they are to be relevant to the psychoanalytic concept of repression, are research designs such that threshold differences between neutral and emotive stimuli cannot be imputed to the effects of *differential word frequency* or *familiarity, word length, set* or *response suppression*. The criteria laid down by Eriksen and Pierce (1968) are important for different reasons: these criteria are designed to ensure that negative results can refute the theory. This means that stimuli must be shown to be *anxiety provoking* (so that a psychoanalyst cannot retort that repression did not occur because anxiety was not aroused), *repression must be effective and non-anxiety provoking* and *individual differences in response must be taken into account*.

EMPIRICAL STUDIES OF PERCEPTUAL DEFENCE

Blum (1955) stated that perceptual defence as a subject for experiment had obtained a dizzy popularity. This is undoubtedly true and the result is a huge volume of investigations. It is not proposed to review them all in this section for a number of reasons. First, a complete review would be inordinately long and irritatingly repetitious. In the second place many of the investigations are not strictly relevant to psychoanalysis. Thus many researches have concentrated on the problems which we have already discussed – elucidating the effects of frequency and word length on thresholds. Thirdly, many investigations do not fulfil the criteria of good research design. Thus when experimenters choose their emotional words on *a priori* grounds, a negative result cannot refute the concept of repression. A positive result, on the other hand, can support it. This problem – that positive results can support psychoanalytic theory whereas negative results do not refute it – has already occurred in other chapters in this book. Finally, as was pointed out in the beginning of this chapter, there are already in existence some excellent and lengthy reviews of perceptual defence studies.

Rationale for including studies

Investigations of the following kinds have therefore been examined.

1. All those which bear on the essential basis of perceptual defence and repression and which fulfil the criteria of adequate research design.
2. Those which show results in favour of the theory and which in spite of their inadequate design can be held to support it. Remember experiments of this type with negative results are irrelevant to psychoanalytic theory.
3. Well-known experiments which have been cited in opposition to perceptual defence and which do not fall under category 1.

The work of Dixon

The studies of perceptual defence by Dixon differ in experimental procedure from the majority of studies in this area. Since his method avoids the problems bedevilling the interpretation of results, these investigations deserve careful scrutiny. It is all the more surprising, therefore, that the majority of reviews of perceptual defence pay little or no attention to them.

Study 1. Dixon (1958b)

In this first pilot investigation, Dixon studied the phenomenon of perceptual defence by noting changes in the visual threshold of one eye, while the other was subjected to subliminal stimulation by words of neutral and emotive connotation.

Experimental technique. A continuous recording of the visual threshold for one eye, while the other eye is presented with subliminal stimuli, is made. The method, known as closed loop control, has been fully described by Oldfield

(1955) while the apparatus itself is described by Dixon (1958a). Briefly, subjects look through a stereoscope at a screen apparently divided into two, each half visible to one eye only. On the left-eye screen are two spots of light, one brighter than the other. The brightness of both of these is controlled by the subject who during the experiment has to operate the control continuously so that 'you can just see the brighter of the two spots but never the dimmer one'. Kymograph records of all threshold differences are taken. On the right-eye screen appear subliminally the stimulus words. Thus if the visual threshold of a subject rises on the appearance of a stimulus word he increases the brightness of the spot, if the threshold falls he lowers it.

As Dixon (1958a) points out, this method has the advantage that since the subject is never aware of the stimulus material (presented subliminally) and is not required to make a verbal response, the question of voluntary suppression does not arise. In addition the results cannot be attributed to set.

Subjects. Two groups of 10 males and 10 females. The words were presented in a different order for each group.

Words. Whore and penis were the emotional words. Rider and weave were the neutral.

Results. The results supported the perceptual defence hypothesis:

(a) Significantly more subjects gave higher thresholds for the emotional words.

(b) The direction of threshold change tended to be consistent for any one subject.

(c) For women only, 'whore' resulted in a steep fall in threshold, followed by a rise to that above neutral words.

Comments and conclusions. This experiment certainly appears to support the concept of perceptual defence and *ipso facto* the Freudian concept of repression. As Dixon (1958b) points out, this is a pilot study, and hence there are no controls for word familiarity or frequency of word length. Nevertheless the sex difference in response noted to whore is difficult to explain in terms other than of repression.

Despite its imperfections the ingenuity of the experimental technique makes these results difficult to interpret, if perceptual defence or repression is not accepted. This study by Dixon must therefore be regarded as support for the Freudian concept of repression.

Study 2. Dixon and Haider (1961)

Dixon and Haider studied this same problem again with a more refined methodology. Their results were consistent with those of the previous research and provide even surer confirmation of the phenomenon of perceptual defence.

Experimental technique. As in the previous study, closed loop control was the method chosen.

Aim. They wanted to establish that the threshold changes observed in the previous investigations were not due either to differential familiarity with the stimulus material or to the quantity of light transmitted with the words in the closed loop method, but were in fact due to anxiety engendered by the stimulus material.

Subjects. 6 male and 6 female subjects.

Words. Cancer, breast, recant, stance. These words were equated for brightness, length and letter content (as far as possible).

Procedure. Subjects were divided into two groups with different order of presentation of stimuli. In addition to words, in some trials a rectangle of light of the same size and intensity as the words was subliminally presented.

Results

(a) *Familiarity.* There was no relationship between the familiarity of the words (judged from the Thorndike-Lorge word-count) and the threshold recorded during their presentation. It must be noted that since the emotive words were not taboo words, frequency can probably be accurately measured by the Thorndike-Lorge list.

(b) *Light intensity.* The subliminal verbal stimuli produced a significant rise in threshold. The light stimuli produced an insignificant drop. Thus the previous results (Dixon, 1958b) could not have been due to differential light intensities.

(c) *Differences between verbal stimuli.* In the first run, for eight subjects only the word 'cancer' produced significantly higher thresholds than those recorded in the adjacent no stimulus presentations. In this trial the stimulus 'cancer' was significantly different from the two neutral words. In the second run there were no differences between words.

(d) The words were ranked by 56 subjects for the degree to which they were productive of unpleasant emotion. The mean rank was cancer 1·2, recant 2·5, breast 2·9 and stance 3·4.

Comments and conclusions. These results, especially those with cancer, support the claim for the phenomenon of perceptual defence. The fact that on the second run the results were less marked suggests perhaps a generalisation of anxiety (breast is a common site for cancer), for all the thresholds were increased. Certainly the recognition threshold differences were not due to differential frequency of words or light intensity. It should be pointed out that had Dixon and Haider first investigated the anxiety arousing potential of their stimuli for the subjects, as suggested by Eriksen and Pierce (1968), it is highly likely that a far more striking illustration of repression would have been obtained. Only cancer was rated, afterwards, as anxiety provoking. Again it must be concluded that Dixon and Haider have demonstrated perceptual defence taking place and provided us with an example of Freudian repression.

Study 3. Dixon (1960)

Dixon now turned his attention to investigating whether the changes in visual threshold noted in the two investigations previously discussed were dependent on peripheral or central mechanisms. From the viewpoint of psychoanalytic theory this is most important since repression is an unconscious ego defence mechanism against, in the main, instinctual impulses. Hence if perceptual defence is in fact an illustration of repression it must be mediated centrally not peripherally.

Rationale and experimental technique. Using again the closed loop method, Dixon compared threshold changes for complementary colours during subliminal stimulation, with changes in the ratio of these colours needed to produce an achromatic patch. Dixon argued that if the thresholds changed for either of the colours (red and blue-green) and there were no corresponding changes either in the other colour or in the achromatic ratio, then threshold changes must be central not peripheral in origin.

Stimulus word. Cancer: also an inverted mirror image of cancer.

Subjects. 8 males, 4 females.

Results. When the subliminal stimulus was red the red threshold changed (the threshold fell), when it was green, the green threshold changed (it rose). This anomaly Dixon explains by reference to the work of Krafkov (1941) who found that adrenaline decreased visual sensitivity to red but increased it to green. A further experiment reported in this paper, where cancer and stance were used as stimuli, produced similar anomalous findings.

From these results Dixon (1960) argues that the determinant of threshold change must be a central mechanism. Thus observed changes were greater for the colour with which the subject was subliminally stimulated. If the changes were peripheral in origin then any threshold change should have produced an equal change in the complementary threshold. Dixon concludes that the weight of the evidence suggests the changes are in fact central rather than peripheral, although this is a very tentative conclusion.

Comments and conclusions. This is an extremely interesting experiment with a subtle and complex rationale. Unfortunately the results, as Dixon admits, were not sufficiently clear-cut to allow a firm conclusion. Clearly with more subjects and more words (perhaps previously tested for emotional impact) this method might demonstrate the neural origins of these perceptual defence phenomena. As has been mentioned, if central in origin these threshold changes would indeed be support for Freudian theory.

In conclusion this experiment by Dixon is more impressive in rationale and method than in any firm results.

Study 4. Dixon and Lear (1962)

Dixon and Lear approached the problem of central regulation of perceptual defence effects by comparing perceptual defence in three groups – a normal control group, depressives and schizophrenics.

Rationale and experimental procedure. The closed loop method was used in two separate experiments. In the first the subject had to increase, by holding a lever, the brightness of a dark spot until it disappeared – i.e. was equal in intensity to the background. In the second subjects had to make it disappear then re-appear by increasing its brightness. In both experiments, unknown to the sub-ject, all increases in intensity of the spot were accompanied by increases in the intensity of a subliminal stimulus word to the other eye. Both neutral and emotive stimuli were used. If the subject showed a rise in threshold to anxiety words he would be less able to discriminate a difference between the spot and the back-ground. Thus in experiment 1 he would let go of the lever earlier, and later in the second experiment. If he were responding to the fact that holding the lever in-creased the intensity of the anxiety stimulus, he would let go of the lever earlier in both experiments.

Subjects. 30 normals, 9 depressives, 9 paranoid schizophrenics.

Words. Cancer was the emotive word for normals: for a patient it was a word critical for his psychopathology.

Results. The normals responded in a manner consistent with the hypothesis that they were reacting to the increasing intensity of the stimulus – their behaviour in both parts of the experiment was the same. This was not the case with the patient groups: the depressives showed evidence of a raised threshold, the schizophrenics of a lowered threshold.

Discussion and conclusions. Dixon and Lear argue that the normals seemed to be using a process under voluntary control to avoid or prolong the emotive stimulus. Thus their mode of perceptual regulation differed from that of the patients. These differed among themselves in that with depressives the threshold was raised whereas it was lowered in the case of schizophrenics. It is to be noted, however, that both patient groups were under drug treatment which itself could have influenced the results.

Dixon and Lear believe that these results show that two regulatory mechanisms are present.

(*a*) A system mediated by the voluntary nervous system, e.g. focussing attention, turning the head and in this experiment holding a lever.

(*b*) An automatic feedback mechanism operating entirely below the level of awareness of the subject.

Again, as with the previous study, this is a highly interesting piece of work which must be carefully replicated on larger samples. Again however, in the case of the patients, we can see a clear example of perceptual defence in operation. As Dixon (1960) points out, there is already in existence sufficient information concerning the working of the nervous system to make just such a central mechanism underlying perceptual defence a physiological possibility. Clearly more research needs to be done.

Study 5. Dixon and Lear (1963)

Dixon and Lear made a further attempt to investigate the neurophysiology of perceptual defence by examining the EEG correlates of threshold regulation.

They implicate, by reference to the work of Samuels (1959), the reticular activating system. Their admittedly speculative model of the central regulation of perceptual defence phenomena allows certain hypotheses to be made concerning EEG and perceptual thresholds.

Hypothesis. Raised thresholds to emotive material would follow a lack of desynchronisation in the pre-recognition EEG. Lowered thresholds would follow a typical desynchronous activation pattern.

Sample. 7 normal subjects.

Stimuli. 4 neutral and 4 emotional words – chosen for each subject on the basis of a word-association test.

Method. Stimuli were presented with gradually increasing intensity until the subject signalled recognition. EEG records were obtained during this experimental procedure.

Results

1. Differences in alpha for the two types of stimuli (recorded for first 6 secs of onset of stimulus) are correlated (e = ·857) with the awareness threshold differences for the two types of material.
2. During these first 6 secs there was a fall in alpha for the perceptual defenders and a sharp rise for the perceptual sensitisers.
3. During the next two epochs (12 secs) these trends were reversed.

Discussion. If lack of alpha is taken as an index of activation then perceptual sensitisation for emotional stimuli is preceded and followed by cortical activation, while perceptual defence is preceded and followed by increasing inhibition of the activating response.

Comments and conclusions. As has been the case with the previous experiments by Dixon and his colleagues, this study is not conclusive. Nevertheless the results are at least in accord with the hypotheses that the reticular system is an important component in the neurophysiology of perceptual defence. It does seem clear, however, that if studies 3, 4 and 5 are considered together there is fair evidence that perceptual defence is centrally regulated. Thus although none of these investigations is powerful support on its own, the fact that each of them represents a different approach to the problem and each supports the central theory, makes them in total more impressive.

Conclusions from all studies by Dixon

In all these five studies there has been a clear demonstration of the phenomenon of perceptual defence. Since it has already been shown that perceptual defence is simply an example of Freudian repression it follows that Dixon has produced an experimental demonstration of repression. The beauty of these investigations lies in their experimental technique – the closed loop method. This has ensured from the outset that many of the objections to the interpretation of perceptual defence phenomena as examples of repression have been overcome. Thus the results cannot be attributed to voluntary control or suppression since subjects were unaware of the subliminal stimuli. Neither could the results be attributed to the differential frequency of the emotive and neutral stimuli. The attempts to link the regulations of perceptual thresholds to central rather than peripheral mechanisms are suggestive rather than definitive.

However it must be admitted that all these studies were conducted on small numbers of patients and with few stimuli. Clearly, therefore, it is necessary to replicate and extend them. In brief, despite this limitation these experiments are regarded as firm evidence for the Freudian concept of repression.

The work of Blum and associates

Blum and his research workers have contributed much to the empirical study of Freudian defence mechanisms. In many of their investigations they have used the Defence Preference Inquiry which is a special form of the Blacky Pictures. This test and the results achieved with it have both been discussed and described in a later section of this chapter (see p. 182). Some of their researches, however, have used perceptual defence as their method and these investigations will now be examined. Needless to say, they are of especial interest and relevance to this chapter because they have been explicitly designed to test the Freudian concept of repression and have not been primarily concerned with variables irrelevant to the present study.

Blum (1954)

Blum made the start. He hypothesised from Freudian theory that perceptual vigilance was essentially the *unconscious* striving for expression of underlying repressed impulses and that perceptual defence was the warding off of these threatening impulses as they began to approach *conscious awareness*. In operational terms this meant that at very fast tachistoscopic exposure rates perceptual vigilance would occur but at slower rates, approaching the recognition threshold, perceptual defence would take over.

Subjects. 7 males and 7 female subjects ignorant of the Blacky Pictures (see p. 80 for a description).

Procedure

1. First, to establish a base-line of the subjects' choice based on the physical properties of the pictures, 4 pictures, one in each corner of a card, were exposed fast (·03 secs) for 54 trials in the tachistoscope. Subjects had to select the one which stood out the most. Positions of pictures were randomised.

2. Then subjects were subjected to a *sensitisation procedure*. For males the masturbation card was made traumatic and attention was drawn to the sexual nature of the picture whereas the oral sadism card was made neutral. The opposite procedure was adopted with the females.

3. Subjects were again given 54 trials at ·03 secs. At this speed perceptual vigilance should ensure that each sex picked out the traumatic picture.

4. To emphasise the nearness to conscious awareness, subjects were asked to select the traumatic picture which was shown at a much slower speed. Here perceptual defence should ensure that subjects failed in this task.

Results. The vigilance hypothesis was supported in 11 of the 14 subjects (P ·05). The defence hypothesis was supported in 12 of the subjects (P ·006).

Before discussing this study it will be better to review some similar investigations.

The work of Nelson (1955)

Nelson used these same experimental procedures for activating perceptual vigilance and defence with a sample of 44 male undergraduates. In addition, however, he knew the characteristic modes of defence adopted by these subjects who had been tested on the Defence Preference Inquiry.

Results. The perceptual vigilance hypothesis was confirmed. High conflict subjects were more vigilant than low conflict subjects. The defence hypothesis was also confirmed in that subjects who had been classified as repressors on the Defence Preference Inquiry did show evidence of perceptual defence concerning the pictures relevant to their conflicts. Projectors, on the other hand, still showed vigilance. Subjects who were classified as favouring reaction-formation or regression as their mechanism of defence showed evidence of neither vigilance nor defence.

Comments. These two studies by Blum and Nelson would appear to support most strongly the Freudian concept of repression were it not for a study by Smock (1956) which must now be examined.

The work of Smock (1956)

Smock attempted to replicate the study of Blum (1954) but found that the perceptual defence part of the procedures was spoiled by the fact that the males could not pick out the oral sadism picture because they were distracted by the similarity of the identification stimulus. This was attributed to the fact that although a similar stimulus to the others at the fast speed, ·03 secs, at the slow speed, ·20 secs, its stimulus properties change. Smock then ran a second experiment to study this confounding variable of stimulus similarity. In this experiment a new control card A was used, judged very similar to the oral sadism card. When the subjects were looking for the oral sadism card, card A was called more than the other neutral cards, whereas when the subjects were looking for the masturbation card, the oral erotism card, which had been altered to be like the masturbation card, was also called significantly more than the other neutral stimuli. Thus Smock argued that Blum's results with perceptual defence were confounded by stimulus similarity for which there was no control.

Comments. If the identification picture were so similar to the oral sadism picture that males were distracted by it, this, as Smock found, would reduce the likelihood of any perceptual defence results. Thus the fact that Blum (1954) and

Nelson (1955) both obtained perceptual defence effects despite this unfortunate stimulus similarity makes their evidence even stronger for the defence phenomenon. Smock's second experiment which shows that response similarity can offset results is hardly surprising. That two stimuli are difficult to distinguish when presented subliminally cannot be regarded as a striking result. To impugn the Blum and Nelson studies on the grounds of differential stimulus similarity is in fact impossible since for half the sample a different stimulus is critical and thus must differentially, for each half, be similar to a neutral stimulus. Stimulus similarity can only spoil the results (by distracting half the sample); as Smock found, it cannot improve them. Consequently the conclusions from this study by Smock (1956) must be that the results of Blum (1954) and Nelson (1955) still stand. Their results must now be discussed.

The study by Blum (1954) seems to provide incontrovertible evidence for perceptual defence and hence the Freudian concept of repression. It is to be noted that it does not suffer from any of the confounding variables discussed earlier in this chapter and which mar so many studies of perceptual defence. Thus the results cannot be attributed to differential frequency or knowledge of the stimuli for all cards received the same number of exposures. Nor indeed can the variables of set or suppression be invoked to explain the results. As regards set, the subjects were looking for the pictures but could not find them, and there is no reason to think that suppression should have had any influence. Furthermore the experimental procedure, the sensitisation session, ensured that the stimuli were truly anxiety provoking and the use of repression was not more anxiety provoking than the original stimulus. Thus two of the criteria for adequate perceptual defence studies, as suggested by Eriksen and Pierce (1968), are fulfilled. Perhaps even more important than any of these points is the fact that the anxiety provoked (that concerning psychosexual development) in this experiment is actually that typically repressed in psychoanalytic theory and is a far cry from the use of taboo words such as bitch or belly (Rosenstock, 1951) or the use of nonsense syllables followed by electric shock. In brief, therefore, this experiment by Blum is regarded as impressive support for perceptual vigilance and defence and consequently for the Freudian concept of repression.

The investigation by Nelson (1955), which replicates the Blum (1954) study, has one refinement which fulfils yet another of the criteria of Eriksen and Pierce (1968). This takes into account individual differences among the subjects in defence preference. Thus the finding that repressors (as judged by the Blacky Defence Preference Inquiry) showed perceptual defence, whereas subjects preferring other types of defence mechanism did not do so, is even more impressive evidence than the earlier investigation for perceptual defence as an analogue of repression and for the concept of repression. It also supports the validity of the repression score of the Defence Preference Inquiry.

These two studies, therefore, by Blum (1945) and Nelson (1955) are impressive support for repression.

The work of Blum (1955)

Blum carried out a yet more refined study of perceptual defence. He was very keen to answer the critics of perceptual defence studies who had attempted to argue that the results so far observed were in no way attributable to the effects of inhibition. Postman *et al.* (1956), for example, attributed the experimental results to the effects of differential familiarity with the stimuli and set – the two confounding variables which we have discussed earlier in this section and which do, indeed, spoil many experiments. Postman (1953) in a more theoretical discussion of perceptual defence had argued that in the interests of parsimony results could be better understood in terms of *interference among competing hypotheses*. Thus when subjects have only partial information, as is the case in the perceptual defence experiment, strong hypotheses incompatible with the threatening stimulus may be evoked.

In an attempt to answer these criticisms, Blum (1955) set up an experiment implicitly designed to show that perceptual defence was traceable to the perceptual process. The hypothesis was: subjects predisposed to use the mechanism of repression in conjunction with a given conflict will, when confronted subliminally with a conflict-relevant stimulus, show defensive behaviour directly traceable to the perceptual process itself. If Blum achieves this aim, it will, of course, be a clear example of Freudian repression.

Subjects. 17 graduate clinical psychologists well versed in the Blacky Pictures.

Indices of psychosexual disturbance. Subjects were asked to recall the Blacky Pictures freely and then in a timed session. In addition they were asked to rate the pictures as problems for themselves. This they did twice. Indices of psychosexual disturbance were: errors of recall, slips, over-detailed or very brief description, the wrong order of cards, comments and asides, and differences of placing on the two ranking procedures. Normal Blacky Pictures scoring could not be used with these very sophisticated subjects.

Index of repression. Failure in the recall task.

Experimental procedure. As in the previous perceptual defence experiments with the Blacky Pictures, four Blacky Pictures – oral erotism, oral sadism, masturbation guilt and identification – were simultaneously exposed at a subliminal speed in a tachistoscope. This was repeated for 48 trials during which subjects had to name the pictures. The subjects were unaware that in each trial the four pictures were always the same although their positions were randomly rotated. This procedure yielded four conditions:

>Picture present: conflict + repression in subjects 1
>Picture present: subjects neutral 2
>Picture absent: conflict + repression in subjects 3
>Picture absent: subjects neutral 4

On the perceptual defence hypothesis pictures in condition 1 would be named less than in condition 2. Pictures in conditions 3 and 4 would be equally named.

Blum (1955) singles out three points of great importance in this procedure regarding experimental controls:

(a) The antecedents of the situation are closely tied down in the prior assessment of conflict and repression. Furthermore for all conditions these antecedents are the same.

(b) All stimulus differentials are controlled because they are the same in all conditions.

(c) Selective report cannot be a variable since conditions 1 and 3 as well as conditions 2 and 4 require the same report.

Results. As predicted the mean number of calls for conditions 3 and 4 was not significantly different. On the other hand, there was a significant difference ($P = \cdot 001$) in the mean number of calls for conditions 1 and 2. There were far fewer calls for condition 1. Thus where conflict and repression occurred together, so perceptual defence was noted. It was also noted that 14 subjects who had conflicts about the pictures but no repression did not produce perceptual defence.

Comments and conclusions. In this ingenious experiment, familiarity with the stimulus, set, selective verbal report and individual differences in defence have all been controlled. Furthermore the antecedent conditions (conflict and repression) were known. It seems, therefore, that perceptual defence must be a form of perceptual repression. Postman's (1953) concept of an alternative competing hypothesis is not tenable – what hypothesis could it be? The fact that conflict alone did not create perceptual defence but that repression also was necessary is further evidence for the claim that perceptual defence is an illustration of the Freudian concept of repression in action.

In summary this study by Blum is impressive support for the psychoanalytic concept of repression.

The work of Perloe (1960)

Lastly in this series of studies of perceptual defence by Blum and his associates we come to the investigation by Perloe into the inhibition hypothesis for perceptual defence.

Subjects. 30 males and 31 females.

Materials. The Blacky Pictures.

Experimental procedure. An anxiety score for each picture was computed for each subject, similar to the anxiety index used by Blum (1955) but validated in a factor-analytic study reported in Perloe's (1958) doctoral dissertation. A repression score, based on the recall of the Blacky Pictures, was also computed for each subject on each dimension. The perceptual task consisted of attempting to recognise the Blacky Pictures presented tachistoscopically at such a speed that for each subject 50% recognition was possible.

Hypothesis. If perceptual defence is in fact the result of inhibition, subjects ought to be less accurate with the Blacky Pictures which provoked anxiety and were repressed.

Results. Since only the masturbation card provoked anxiety this was the only card where perceptual defence was to be expected. In fact the 14 repressors had a lower accuracy score to this card than the 16 non-repressors (sig. ·01 level). This result could not be attributed to set since the cards were shown in groups of three and the subjects were told this card was in the group. Nor could the result be due to response suppression because the error score to this card was not different for the two groups (the error score was the number of wrong responses to this card divided by the total number of wrong responses).

Comments and conclusions. This study needs little comment. It is further support for the findings of Blum (1955). Extraneous stimulus variables are controlled, individual differences in defence mechanism are taken into account, and it seems difficult to attribute the perceptual defence effects to anything other than the repression caused by anxiety in those who habitually use repression as a defence. This study by Perloe shows a clear example of Freudian repression.

Conclusions from the work of Dixon, Blum and associates

These investigations by Dixon and Blum and their associates seem to us to demonstrate clearly the phenomenon of perceptual defence as defined by Brown (1962) – changes in perceptual threshold due to the emotional nature of the stimuli. These experiments have been so designed that they are free from the confounding variables of stimulus frequency, response suppression, or set. If they really are examples of perceptual defence, then it follows from our definition of repression that they are examples of repression. These experiments, therefore, are laboratory demonstrations of the Freudian defence mechanism of repression which must be regarded as proven.

Since these experiments adequately demonstrate the mechanism of repression and thus support the Freudian theory it is not proposed to examine further any other experiments in perceptual defence since these are all extremely similar. As has been indicated, long reviews of such studies already exist. From the point of view of this book, the work of Blum and Dixon is sufficient: perceptual defence studies have shown that there is a defence mechanism of repression.

DISPLACEMENT

We do not intend to devote much space to the evidence for this Freudian defence mechanism because it was demonstrated to occur beyond all reasonable doubt more than 30 years ago (Dollard *et al.*, 1939) in the case of aggression. Thus in this study of frustration and aggression, an experiment was reported where subjects were deliberately deprived of sleep, tobacco, food and any way to pass the time by what appeared to be (to the subjects) a series of accidents. Subjects did not express their feelings directly to the psychologists for obvious social reasons. One subject, however, whom the authors clearly regard as using displacement, produced a series of drawings of hideous and mutilated bodies which he labelled psychologists.

Another experiment reported in this book (see also Miller and Bugelski, 1948) describes how the attitude scores towards Japanese and Mexican groups of boys at a summer camp were changed by considerable frustration. In this study the boys had to take examinations rather than enjoy themselves playing. The attitudes of the sample towards both ethnic groups were significantly more unfavourable after the examination than before. Sarnoff (1962) regards this displacement of aggression from examiners (authorities) to minority groups as one of the mechanisms responsible for anti-Semitism, a specific form of scapegoating.

In this book we have for the most part eschewed animal studies, especially conditioning studies, on the grounds that generalisation beyond the species and the experimental conditions is of doubtful validity. However as regards displacement, it is noteworthy that the ethologists have described a similar mechanism, under the name 'redirection activities' – *not* displacement which for them is somewhat different (Hinde, 1966). Redirection activities, according to Hinde, are often seen in winter flocks of birds where an individual, if prevented by a superior from obtaining food, attacks an inferior bird instead of retaliating. Tinbergen (1959) describes herring gulls who displace their aggression against other gulls on to objects in the environment. If we can trust these ethological observations, there seems little doubt that there are here natural examples of Freudian displacement amongst birds.

Miller (1948) has constructed an elaborate model based on Hullian learning theory to account for displacement in terms of stimulus and response generalisation. The adequacy of learning theories to accommodate the validated observations of psychoanalysis is discussed in the final chapter of this book.

CONCLUSIONS

Displacement was one of the first Freudian concepts to receive experimental confirmation. It is now a generally accepted mental mechanism with considerable anecdotal support (the clerk ticked off by his boss is quick to kick the cat at home) in everyday life. It seems also to occur among birds.

STUDIES WITH THE DEFENCE PREFERENCE INQUIRY

A number of empirical studies of defence mechanisms have been carried out with the Defence Preference Inquiry. This, therefore, must be described.

THE TEST

The Defence Preference Inquiry is, in effect, a special form of the Blacky Pictures which have already been fully described (p. 79 et seq.). Subjects have to rank a series of alternative descriptions of thoughts and actions in terms of how well each represents the way Blacky seems to be feeling or acting in a particular picture. Each of the descriptions is, in fact, an operational definition of typical Freudian defence mechanisms such as avoidance, projection, intellectualisation, reaction-formation and regression. Thus at the end of the test a subject's preferred mode of defence may be easily calculated; from the mean ranking it receives over each of the 11 Blacky dimensions. In addition it is possible to see how a subject deals with problems in a particular psychosexual area. For example Oedipal desires may be handled by sublimation, oral longings by reaction-formation.

VALIDITY OF THE DEFENCE PREFERENCE INQUIRY

Unfortunately no studies of the validity of this technique have been carried out. Most researches, where it has been used, are content to report the results (as if they were of proven validity) discussing them as 'facts'. Unfortunately most of these researches are not such that it is possible to draw any inferences concerning the validity of the test or to use them as evidence for construct validity. The only evidence, therefore, that can be said to support the validity of any of the measures of the Defence Preference Inquiry is that from the studies of perceptual defence where it has sometimes been used. In these investigations (e.g. Blum, 1955, 1957; Nelson, 1955) subjects classified as repressors on the test have shown repressing behaviour in the perceptual defence experiments in that they have taken longer to recognise emotional stimuli. Thus, to some extent at least, there is evidence that the Inquiry does measure repression validly.

EMPIRICAL INVESTIGATIONS WITH THE DEFENCE PREFERENCE INQUIRY

As has been mentioned above, the published researches in which this test was used cannot be used to support or refute the Freudian concept of defence mechanisms. This is simply because the authors are content to report the scores of various samples. Thus Blum (1956, 1964) applied the test in altogether eight countries: male students in Italy, England, the Netherlands and the U.S.A. (1956); Denmark, France, Germany and Israel (1964). Since the validity of the test is unknown and the aetiology of defence mechanisms in psychoanalytic theory unclearly defined, it is obviously not possible to draw any firm conclusions concerning Freudian theory from these results. Similarly the study by Cohen (1956) of ego-defence preference on interpersonal relations and the work of Thelen (1965) concerned with similar defence preferences among parents and children has no bearing on the correctness of the Freudian concepts of ego-defences.

G

CONCLUSIONS

Thus nothing relevant to psychoanalytic theory can be deduced from any of the investigations which have used the Defence Preference Inquiry. Nevertheless it remains a useful research tool: for example if paranoids (who are supposed to favour projection) were compared on the test with hysterics (who are held to use repression) this would constitute a real test of psychoanalytic theory.

In summary then the Defence Preference Inquiry is considered to be a test whose real potential for the study of psychoanalytic theory has unfortunately not been realised.

PROJECTION

The work of Sears (1936, 1937) and Wells and Goldstein (1964)

Sears (1936, 1937) carried out what appears to have been the first experimental studies of projection. He got students to rate themselves and each other for the anal traits of stinginess, obstinacy, bashfulness and disorderliness. The 'true' amount of each of these tests was the mean rating (on a seven-point scale) received by each subject. The projection score was the mean of his ratings for others. Sears (1936) argued that if Freudian projection were correct there should be a positive correlation between the two scores. In fact the correlation was small and negative. This finding, therefore, appears to refute Freudian theory.

Sears (1937), however, made a further examination of this data. He attempted to take the factor of insight into account. If a subject's self-rating was congruent with his rating of others, the subject was deemed insightful. Then it was found that non-insightful subjects did tend to attribute their traits to others. This therefore appears to confirm Freudian theory, although desirable traits were also projected.

There is of course a logical problem inherent in this method of investigating projection. If projection occurs there is no reason to think that the ratings given by others have much validity. Rather they must represent the raters as well as the ratees. Hence the mean of assessments for an individual will not necessarily be accurate.

Wells and Goldstein (1964) replicated this study by Sears on two samples of students. As with Sears' (1936 and 1937) studies, each subject rated himself on a seven-point scale for stinginess, obstinacy, disorderliness and bashfulness. According to Wells and Goldstein, the results of Sears (1937) did not prove that projection took place – rather they were an artefact of the definition of insightful. Thus they claim that in the Sears study 'insightful' was attributed to those whose average rating of others was lower than their self-rating, while 'non-insightful' was attributed to those whose average rating of others was *higher* than their self-rating. Hence *by definition* the non-insightful project their traits since projection is defined as seeing in others traits in oneself. However in fact Sears (1937) defined 'non-insightful' by the *incongruence* of ratings. If self-rating and average rating by others were in the same half of the distribution a subject was regarded as insightful. Thus Wells and Goldstein's methodological examination does not seem to be fair.

Wells and Goldstein (1964) analysed their data by a method similar to that of Sears. A subject was insightful if more than half the raters agreed with his self-rating of 123 or 567 on the rating scale. They found no evidence for the projection of traits, contrary to the finding of Sears (1937), either among the insightful or non-insightful.

Comments and conclusions

If we ignore the methodological point raised by Wells and Goldstein we are left with the fact that Sears' study gave slight support for the concept of projection while that of Wells and Goldstein failed to do so. However neither of these investigations has been examined in detail because it seems to us that the design used is incapable of putting the Freudian concept of projection to the test. Stinginess is not repressed into the unconscious. Stinginess itself in Freudian theory is a defence against anal retention. It is nonsense to say that a defence must itself be repressed. It is of course true that stinginess is less socially desirable (in the response-set sense) than say generosity but the defence mechanisms are postulated by Freud to be defences against id material. Thus the attribution of traits to others does not seem an adequate test of projection. Hence neither of these experiments seem relevant to the Freudian notion of projection and cannot therefore be regarded as either confirmation or refutation of the theory.

A more general point applies to the method of comparing self-ratings and ratings by others. If in fact projection does occur the validity of ratings by others cannot be used to compare with self-ratings. Indeed the test of projection might be to compare the *variance* of each individual's ratings of a sample (which should be small if projection occurs) with the variance of the overall ratings of the class.

It must therefore be concluded that neither of these studies is relevant to projection and that the comparison of rating scales is a dubious procedure.

The work of Blumberg and Maher (1965)

Blumberg and Maher attempted to test the Freudian theory of projection in a small sample of psychotic patients.

Sample. 33 psychotic patients.

Test. 40 item adjective check-list (20 desirable and 20 undesirable traits).

Method. Subjects had to

(*a*) check traits describing themselves,
(*b*) check traits describing any 12 people whom they knew, and
(*c*) check traits descriptive of 12 anonymous photographs (faces).

The subjects themselves were rated by nursing aides.

Results. There was no significant association (X^2) between having any kind of trait and perceiving it in others. Nor was there any significant difference between paranoids (believed in Freudian theory to favour the defence mechanism of projection: see p. 264 for the theory and pp. 265-73 for the objective evidence) and the others. There was, therefore, no support for the defence mechanism of projection.

Comments

This failure to support Freudian theory could be due to the defects of the theory or the test. In this case, however, the experiment was clearly defective. The unreliability of ratings by any but highly trained observers is considerable. In this study the ratings were done by nurses' aides and psychotic patients. It would therefore be wise to conclude nothing from this investigation.

The work of Price-Williams (1965)

Price-Williams carried out a highly interesting and imaginative study of projection among the Tiv of Northern Nigeria combining the quantitative methods pioneered by Whiting and Child (1953) (see p. 52 for a description) with actual field data, rather than the colourful but possibly unreliable observations of anthropologists – for example Rattray's (1923) description of the Ashanti – used by these latter authors.

Rationale of the study. Severe or protracted illness is attributed by the Tiv to the fact of akombo, a supernatural agency, being offended or to the sick person being assailed by *mbatsav*, a class of supernatural beings generally malevolent. Spiro (1961) has argued that the postulation of the existence of malevolent supernaturals to account for illness or disaster is an example of a culturally-constituted defence mechanism – to permit the gratification of repressed impulses by projection and displacement. Since Tiv witchcraft, as mentioned above, exhibits this cultural defence mechanism (against aggression), it should be possible, if the theory is correct, to trace the path of repression or aggression in childhood to projection in folk-tales. Folk-tales are considered by some anthropologists as projective systems (e.g. Kardiner, 1945) or tests and, as is well-known, they have been thus used in the study of achievement motivation by McClelland and Friedman (1952).

Method

1. Field observations of child-rearing procedures were rated by students for severity of independence-training and indulgence of aggression (the relevant variables).

N.B. There was considerable unreliability of rating.

2. Stories and folk-tales of the culture were also rated for the occurrence of various behaviour systems, e.g. succorance, nurturance and aggression (see Whiting, 1963).

Results. In these stories aggression was by far the commonest theme – as judged by all raters. Furthermore, despite the unreliability of the judges, it does appear that aggression is suppressed as far as possible in the child-rearing procedures of this tribe.

Comments and conclusions

Price-Williams (1965), in a complex interpretation of these results demanding considerable knowledge and insight into the background of this tribe, argues that these findings support the claim of Spiro (1961) that such witchcraft practices, as attributing illness to outside agencies, are a cultural defence mechanism of projection or displacement. Although this particular paper is too speculative to be regarded as firm objective evidence for projection, it does nevertheless illustrate, as did Whiting and Child (1953), the possibilities inherent in their method for the cross-cultural study of psychoanalytic phenomena. Nevertheless, as was stated earlier in the cross-cultural study of personality (see p. 60), this investigation could be regarded as more evidence for the claim that such studies are a dangerous chimera.

CONCLUSIONS CONCERNING PROJECTION

None of these empirical objective studies supports the mechanism of projection. It may be that methodological difficulties account for this but nevertheless, despite the intuitive attraction of the notion, there is as yet no firm evidence in its favour – but see the objective studies of paranoia (p. 265).

IDENTIFICATION WITH THE AGGRESSOR

In our discussion of identification as a developmental process in the formation of the super-ego (see p. 138), it was pointed out that in Freudian theory identification is thought to occur through fear of the castrating father. Bandura (1969) pours scorn on this concept on the grounds that in everyday life imitation certainly takes place without this fear. The laboratory studies of imitative behaviour carried out by Bandura and colleagues have not, however, specifically tested this hypothesis of aggressive identification as a defence. Anna Freud (1946) regards it as an important defence mechanism, quoting clinical examples of children identifying with dentists and other threatening figures. It is to be noted that the examples of identification used by Bandura and Anna Freud differ in one important respect: in Bandura's examples there is no defensive purpose in the imitative behaviour.

Clinical evidence for the concept of identification is not hard to find. Bettelheim (1943) regards the behaviour of the inmates of concentration camps as examples of this mechanism while Sarnoff (1962) considers that Jewish anti-Semitism is an illustration of it. Objective evidence is scanty. Sarnoff (1951) has, however, conducted one such study of Jewish anti-Semitism.

The work of Sarnoff

Subjects. 45 highly anti-Semitic Jewish students and 55 neutral Jewish students were selected by means of an anti-Semitism questionnaire. This was the measure of identification with the aggressor.

Hypotheses

1. Anti-Semites should have negative feelings to parents. This is, according to Sarnoff (1951), because such feelings are an antecedent to the development of this defence mechanism.

This hypothesis is faulty in that *by definition* Jewish anti-Semites (unless converts to the religion) would be hostile to their parents.

2. Anti-Semites should be insecure and anxious. This is because anxiety feelings are the cause of the identification with a source of strength.

3. Anti-Semites should be more passive in the face of hostility. This follows from the notion of identification. A person who resists hostility is unlikely to identify with hostile or aggressive people.

Method. Personality questionnaires were used to assess anxiety, insecurity, feelings to parents and attitudes towards aggression.

Results. All these hypotheses, derived from psychoanalytic theory, were supported.

Comments and conclusions

The fact that these hypotheses were supported must be regarded as confirmation of psychoanalytic theory. Nevertheless it must be admitted that the hypotheses are rather distant from the actual identificatory process itself as studied by Bandura in the laboratory. Thus, just as hypothesis one could be predicted without the notion of identification with the aggressor so it can be argued that hypothesis two, for example, could be interpreted differently. Thus if insecurity and anxiety are regarded as symptoms of neuroticism it could be inferred that anti-Semitism is itself a sign being, presumably, irrational. The concept of identification is one explanation of these observed correlations, but equally it could be argued that anti-Semitism is the result of a neurotic projection of feelings (as in paranoia) – hence its relation with anxiety.

REACTION-FORMATION

Sarnoff (1960)

Sarnoff has also carried out a study of reaction-formation – a notoriously difficult concept to verify objectively.

Rationale of study. Cynicism, it was argued by Sarnoff, is a reaction-formation against feelings of affection. If other people are unpleasant then negative be-haviour towards them is permissible. On this assumption, people with strong reaction-formations against affection, i.e. cynics, should become anxious when they are confronted by stimuli evoking affectionate responses. To reduce anxiety by increased reaction-formation cynics should become more cynical.

Hypothesis. Subjects with a strong reaction-formation (HRF) should become more cynical than subjects with a weak reaction-formation (LRF) after affection has been aroused.

Subjects. 81 male undergraduates.

Method. A cynicism scale (CS) and a measure of reaction-formation (RF) were administered to the subjects. These were then assigned at random to two treatments. One group saw a play which was chosen to arouse affection (HA). The low arousal group heard a tape-recording of the same piece. Then subjects again filled in the cynicism scale.

Results. Both HRF and LRF groups tended to become less cynical after both conditions – a finding contrary to hypothesis. However the high group did shift less than the low group in the aroused condition. There was a small correlation between the reaction-formation score and the cynicism score.

Comments

Sarnoff (1962) in discussing this experiment claims that the shift in scores and the correlation between reaction-formation and cynicism supports Freudian theory. However it cannot be denied that the main hypothesis was not supported. This seems hardly surprising in that the original assumption of this study, that cynicism is a reaction-formation against affection, may well be false. This experiment shows considerable experimental ingenuity and dialectical skill in deriving hypotheses. However it seems too far removed from psychoanalytic theory to be an adequate test of it.

SUBLIMATION

Wallach (1960) and Wallach and Greenberg (1960) have published two studies pertaining to the defence mechanism of sublimation as it affects liking for music. Since both these investigations used the same sample they cannot be considered to be independent.

FREUDIAN THEORY OF SUBLIMATION IN MUSIC

Very simply, in psychoanalytic theory listening to music can provide an outlet for repressed sexuality. Hence liking for music is a sublimation of sexuality.

The study of Wallach and Greenberg (1960)

Rationale. If the Freudian theory be correct, anxious introverts should express more sexuality by listening to music than anxious extroverts. This is because the anxiety of the introvert indicates that his introversion is not a good defence and introverts cannot express their sexuality alone. On the other hand, non-anxious introverts should express very little sexuality in listening to music since their non-anxiety indicates their defences are sound.

Hypotheses

1. Highly anxious introverts should show greater symbolic sexual arousal to music than highly anxious extroverts.

2. The opposite should be the case for low anxious introverts and extroverts.

Subjects. 73 female students.

Method. These subjects wrote stories in response to three pieces of jazz which had been previously rated for their ability to arouse the listener sexually. They then stated their preference for the music and completed the Maudsley Personality Inventory and the Minnesota TSE Test (Evans and McConnell, 1951).

Scoring. These stories were scored for sexual symbolic arousal, using the method of Clark and Sensibar (1958) and Beardslee and Fogelson (1958). This involves counting the incidence in the stories of motion, peak, penetration, rhythm and symbolic content. The validity of these indices of sexual arousal is derived from Clark and Sensibar who found them related to gazing on pictures of nude women in a sample of men. Wallach and Greenberg themselves support the validity of these scores by showing that they are all intercorrelated. In addition the incidence of sexual events was noted.

Results. Both hypotheses were supported. Introverts who were anxious were more strongly sexually aroused by jazz than extroverts.

The research of Wallach (1960)

Subjects. As in the previous study.

Music. Three classical pieces, two by Ravel, one by Debussy.

Method. As above these subjects had to write stories in response to each piece of music. One month later subjects had to choose which of these three pieces they liked best and to rate them on a seven-point rating scale for preference. In addition the MPI was administered to the students.

Scoring. The stories in response to this serious music were again scored for symbolic sexual arousal and manifest sexual content.

Results. An analysis of variance on the symbolic sexuality scores showed degree of preference and degree of anxiety to be significant factors. Thus sexual arousal was related to both these variables. Correlations were also computed between sexual arousal and these variables: sexual arousal and anxiety correlated ·3, sexual arousal and preference correlated ·32.

Comments on both studies

Taken together these investigations support the Freudian claim that liking for music is a sublimation of sexuality. The fact that the relationship is not higher between sexual arousal and preference is not an argument against Freudian theory. As Waelder (1965) points out, the fact that there are ego components in appreciation of the arts (understanding of harmony, contrapuntal devices, for example) is the bribe for the super-ego to allow listening to proceed. It is these complex intellectual skills that make a liking for music respectable. An illustration of the point is the generally accepted difference between pornography and high art.

CONCLUSIONS

These investigations by Walach could not be held, on their own, to prove that sublimation of sexuality accounts for pleasure in music. Nevertheless they have shown that symbolic sexual arousal and preference are linked as would be expected from the psychoanalytic theory. These investigations may be regarded, therefore, as support for the concept of sublimation and also for the Freudian theory of art (see p. 200).

THE WORK OF GLESER AND IHILEVICH (1969)

Gleser and Ihilevich have developed what they claim to be an objective measure of defence mechanisms. If this were shown to be valid it would be a most important advance in the elucidation of psychoanalytic theory.

Rationale of the test

Having scrutinised the descriptions of defence mechanisms the authors decided that five categories would embrace them all and it is these five basic defences that the test purports to measure:

1. *Turning against object* (TAO), e.g. identification with the aggressor, displacement.
2. *Projection* (PRO).
3. *Principalisation* (PRN), e.g. intellectualisation, isolation, rationalisation.
4. *Turning against self* (TAS), e.g. masochism.
5. *Reversal* (REV), e.g. denial, repression, reaction-formation.

Description of the test

Ten stories are included, two per conflict area. The conflict areas are:

(*a*) authority
(*b*) independence
(*c*) competition
(*d*) situational, and
(*e*) masculinity (for males) or femininity (for females).

For each story there are four questions tapping actual behaviour, fantasy behaviour, thoughts and feelings. For each of these questions there are five possible responses tapping the five defences to which subjects have to indicate the most and least liked.

Scoring rationale. Three psychologists and seven social workers only agreed 60% of the time as to what defence a response indicated on TAS, REV and PRN. There was even less agreement on the other scales.

COMMENTS AND CONCLUSIONS

The fact that there was so little agreement as to what defence a response indicated means that in its present form the test cannot be considered useful. Nevertheless it may provide an objective measure of defence mechanisms on further development. *A priori* it seems an ingenious scheme. Ideally, instead of classifying defences subjectively, an objective classification based on a factor analysis of correlations between items tapping individual defences would have been preferable. This could overcome the lack of agreement as to what defences a response was tapping since reference to its factor loadings would make this clear.

Clearly, evidence of its validity must be presented and disagreements between scorers as to the implications of responses removed, before the test can be used seriously. Nevertheless it does appear to be a potentially useful measure of defence mechanisms.

CONCLUSIONS CONCERNING ALL STUDIES OF DEFENCE MECHANISMS
OTHER THEN REPRESSION

It is clear from our discussion of the empirical studies reported in this chapter that methodological difficulties, not unexpectedly, have proved too much for most investigators. Few indeed have even dared to surmount them. In the case of projection none of the studies is sufficiently well designed to test the theory. The work of Price-Williams (1965) is not so much defective in design as too speculative to provide firm evidence. The studies of reaction-formation and identification with the aggressor are all too defective to be used as evidence. Only the studies of sublimation by Wallach (1960) and Wallach and Greenberg (1960) are satisfactory. Nevertheless on their own they are sufficient only to *support* not prove the Freudian theory.

The basic difficulty is, of course, that defence mechanisms are internal processes which may be inferred from behaviour rather than observed. These inferences are difficult to draw with any precision without a wealth of clinical data which cannot constitute objective evidence. Nevertheless the fact remains that from these studies it must be admitted that there is *no objective verification for projection, reaction-formation, or identification with the aggressor*. These have not been refuted either owing to methodological problems. *There is, however, some support for the concept of sublimation.*

SOME OTHER RELATED PSYCHOANALYTIC HYPOTHESES

In this chapter, studies of the Freudian theory of slips of the tongue, wit and humour and artistic creativity will also be reviewed. Their position here is not arbitrary for each, as will be seen, represents a breach of defence mechanisms and hence a glimpse into the unconscious. They therefore constitute a link between the major portion of this chapter and the next which is concerned with dreams which constitute in Freudian theory as complete a breakdown of ego defences as may be observed outside psychosis.

SLIPS OF THE TONGUE

Freudian theory

In *The Psychopathology of Everyday Life*, Freud (1901) devotes considerable attention to slips of the tongue. He does not consider these errors to be random or due to the similarities between adjoining words. Freud believes such slips to be due to unconscious mental activity. Careful analysis of the errors by free association would reveal their unconscious determination in each case. An unconscious thought striving to emerge distorts the conscious intent. Freud gives an example: Brill told a patient she was incompetent (his true opinion) to run her own affairs when he intended to say competent. In psychoanalytic theory, therefore, slips of the tongue are evidence of the failure of defence mechanisms, brief glimpses of the unconscious. They are examined here, under defence mechanisms of which they constitute a breach not an example, as has been discussed above. Strictly, perhaps, they are better included under dreams but this huge subject deserves separate treatment.

The work of Veness (1962)

Veness carried out an experimental investigation into this theory although on a small and restricted sample.

Subjects. 32 females. These were acquaintances of the author, secretaries and lecturers in the university. Female subjects were used to ease the embarrassment of a female experimenter.

Words. Eight lists of words, matched for frequency in the Thorndike-Lorge word list (Thorndike and Lorge, 1944) and for ease of pronunciation, were used. Half the words were neutral, half emotive, as rated independently by three judges.

Method. The eight typed lists were presented to each subject who had to speak one word, then utter an association to it, speak the next word, and so on to the end, in time with a metronome set to beat 60 times a minute. Two judges scored the experiment as it went on.

Scores. Missed beats, slips of the tongue and delayed reactions (faults) were recorded for each subject.

Results

(a) *Slips*. Only 41 slips were made in all – almost equally divided between emotional and neutral words. Furthermore over half of these were made by five subjects. This was too small a number to provide an adequate sample for statistical analysis. There were more slips to emotional words than neutral and to the associations to neutral than emotional words.

(b) *Missed beats*. Although there were more missed beats (sig. ·01 level) for the emotional words there was also a high correlation for missed beats between the lists.

(c) *Faults*. Here the variance was attributed by analysis of variance both to differences between subjects and between lists.

From this Veness concludes that the Freudian theory underlying slips of the tongue was not confirmed.

Comments and conclusions

Veness recognises the problem that emotional words may not be emotional to some subjects and that neutral words may be emotional to others. Nevertheless, this aside, the experiment may not provide an adequate test of the theory. According to the theory the unconscious breaks out and overcomes our defences, hence the more errors when we are tired or thinking of something else. In this study, by virtue of the experimental conditions subjects are concentrating on the words. Thus errors will be likely to be reduced, an argument which accounts for the low number recorded. However if the theory were correct more errors would still be expected to occur with the emotional words.

This experiment entirely fails to support Freudian theory. However, as was discussed in our study of repression (see p. 166), it would have been better to have selected words which were relevant to the problems of each subject to test the theory adequately.

WIT AND HUMOUR

Outline of the psychoanalytic theory

In 'Jokes and their relation to the unconscious' (1905b), and also in the paper 'Humour' (1927b), Freud proposed the psychoanalytic theory of wit and humour. It is somewhat akin to the theory of parapraxis (Freud, 1901) in that the joke allows material to pass the super-ego (or censor, as at this state of psychoanalysis it was known), which in an ordinary situation it would not do. The explosive quality of the laughter is related to the strength of the unconscious impulses being satisfied through the content of the joke. In addition Freud attempts to distinguish between wit and humour. Humour is defined as the situation where the principal character reacts to intolerable problems with a verbal jest rather than resignation or hostility. Humour is the characteristic response of well-adjusted individuals. Wit, on the other hand, especially hostile wit, is favoured by maladjusted individuals. Typically hostile wit deals with people in a highly derogatory fashion, the wit concealing the true hostility. Thus wit and humour allow the expression of repressed wishes and other material of the id.

Importance of the theory

This theory of humour is not an important part of psychoanalysis from the viewpoint of theory. It could be proven entirely false in every detail and the basic structure of Freudian theory could remain unshaken. For this reason the description given above has been abbreviated. It has been included in this book because, from the point of view of understanding an interesting portion of human behaviour and for the light it throws on literature and verbal skills, it is of considerable importance.

Empirical hypotheses of the theory

There appear to be a large number of testable hypotheses which can be drawn from this theory. The hypotheses set out below are not considered to be the total number of possible deductions but are rather examples to which the reader can add his own.

1. Individuals finding aggressive jokes the funniest will be those whose aggression is normally repressed.
2. Similarly those who find sexual jokes the most amusing will be those whose sexuality is normally repressed.
3. Highly repressed individuals (with a very strong super-ego) will be humour-less (they will not dare to laugh at jokes).
4. Psychopaths, similarly, will not find jokes amusing (they have no need to express their repressions in this way).
5. Witty people will have strong unconscious aggression.
6. Wits will be more neurotic than the normal population.

The work of Cattell – the IPAT Humour Test

The IPAT Humour test of personality has been developed by Cattell and his associates from a series of empirical studies of humour. (Cattell and Luborsky, 1947; Luborsky and Cattell, 1947; Cattell and Luborsky, 1952). Originally (Cattell and Luborsky, 1952) there were two forms to this test: in form A subjects have to choose from pairs of jokes which they think is the funnier, while in form B the subjects rate jokes for humour on a two-point scale. Since both forms do not correlate highly the authors suggest that in any application of the test both forms be used. 91 pairs of jokes are used in form A, 112 jokes in form B.

Measures derived from the test

From a study of the intercorrelations between jokes on around 100 subjects 13 clusters were isolated. A cluster was defined such that the jokes within it had to correlate more than ·17 with each other and less than this with jokes outside it. These clusters of jokes were then related to scores on the Guilford-Martin test (see p. 38) (Luborsky and Cattell, 1947). Ten of these clusters were identified and used as the test variables – debonair sexual uninhibitedness, good-natured play, tough self-compusure, gruesomeness, hostile derogation, resignation, cold realism, ponderous humour, whimsical retort and mistreatment humour.

Cattell and Luborsky (1947) found that jokes could not be rated reliably for their underlying impulses (e.g. aggression or masochism) but that once these dimensions had been empirically defined jokes could be assigned to them with some accuracy.

Both these early forms of the test were vitiated by a lack of clear evidence of validity. The manual to the test (Cattell and Luborsky, 1952) refers constantly to the articles by Cattell and Luborsky (1947) and Luborsky and Cattell (1947) which however refer only to 69 of the items in the two forms of the test (Lubin and Loos, 1953). Furthermore their references to correlations with the 16 PF test are too vague to be useful. Wittenborn (1953) also points to a possible logical flaw in the test, namely that if custom stales the humour of a joke subjects are likely to find unfunny the very jokes they characteristically use!

Cattell (1957) reports briefly some later findings with this test, findings which still have not been fully reported in the literature. The research discussed above was unusual for Cattell in that it was based on cluster analysis rather than his beloved factor analysis, and was beset with the problem of instability from population to population. Form A and Form B have therefore been subjected to a full factor analysis and a new C Form was constructed. This work has resulted in 10 factors which seem reasonably stable – the ten described above (see p. 195). However as Cattell (1957) points out even these are not stable with extreme samples as Pichot (1954) found with paranoids.

Comments and conclusions

Neither the handbook to the test, the articles cited in it, nor the description of the factorial studies with the IPAT Humour test give sufficient detail for an accurate assessment of the validity of these factors to be made, so that the test must be regarded as purely experimental. The rationale of this test has been examined because in the handbook to it Cattell and Luborsky (1952) claim that the results support the Freudian hypotheses concerning humour. However we are forced to agree with Lubin and Loos (1953) that there is no factual evidence to support this assertion. Indeed the only relation this test would seem to have with the Freudian theory of humour is the basic assumption that humour is in some way related to personality.

It must, therefore, be concluded that despite the claims of the authors this test is not really relevant to the psychoanalytic theory of humour.

The work of O'Connell

O'Connell (1960, 1962, 1964) has investigated the psychology of humour with a scale developed to test certain psychoanalytic hypotheses. This is known as the Wit and Humour Appreciation Test (WHAT).

O'Connell (1960) had 332 subjects complete the Worchel (1957) Self-Concept Inventory (for predicting maladjustment) in which self and ideal adjustment is rated. A number of these subjects was then put in a stressful situation where they were made to feel failure and insulted. All the sample then completed the WHAT in which jokes have to be rated on a four-point like-dislike scale.

Hypotheses and results. Men preferred hostile wit more than did women. Women, however, showed a greater preference for nonsense wit than did men.

O'Connell (1960) admits that the derivation of this finding from psychoanalytic theory is not clear. However such a hypothesis is in fact made by Grotjan (1957). To test further Freudian hypotheses an analysis of variance of the WHAT scores was computed with the following main factors: high and low self-ideal discrepancy on the Worchel (1957) test, sex, and stress, no stress. The main findings from this analysis were:

(a) In the non-stressful situation the maladjusted men appreciated hostile wit more than did the well-adjusted men. However in the stressful situation this was reversed and the maladjusted did not favour hostile wit.

This supports Freudian theory. It has already been noted that a liking for hostile wit is symptomatic of maladjustment in psychoanalytic theory and it could be expected that in a stressful situation the maladjusted would repress everything.

(b) This finding did not hold for women. Adjusted women preferred hostile wit on both occasions.

(c) The well-adjusted subjects preferred humour.

This finding supports Freudian theory.

(d) There was no confirmation that well-adjusted subjects preferred nonsense to hostile wit.

O'Connell (1960) argues that these results support the Freudian distinction between wit and humour and that, in accord with psychoanalytic theory, in some circumstances wit does reduce tension.

To what extent this study by O'Connell supports Freudian theory depends heavily on the validity of the WHAT. Are the categories of wit and humour, for example, really distinct? O'Connell (1962) describes the rationale and construction of the test so that it is possible to evaluate these results.

Construction of the WHAT

65 jokes were independently classified on the criteria of psychoanalysis by 11 clinical psychologists into humour, hostile wit and nonsense wit. 32 of these jokes were reliably classified so that, when two were rejected at random, ten jokes were left in each of these categories.

The split-half reliability was ·84 and the test-retest reliability was ·8.

These are very impressive reliability coefficients for a personality test and compare well with those of the well-established measures. It is certainly a more reliable test than the IPAT Humour test discussed above. It is extremely interesting that the psychologists in the O'Connell (1962) study were able to classify the jokes with such accuracy because Cattell and Luborsky (1947) found that their raters were unable to do so although these latter used content rather than categories of humour and wit.

Using a chi-square analysis (sex and adjusted or maladjusted), O'Connell (1962) examined the individual items of his test. This analysis supported the claim in the psychoanalytic theory that adjusted subjects preferred humour and that men preferred hostile wit. However his sample in this study was the same as in the earlier research.

The fact that the WHAT is so reliable is impressive. However O'Connell has presented no evidence, other than that 11 psychologists agree, that these three categories of jokes are in fact separate and valid measures. Without this, the support for Freudian theory that the results appear to give cannot be upheld. In any case the only clear findings confirming the theory were that maladjusted subjects did not enjoy humour as much as adjusted ones.

The study by O'Connell (1964)

In this investigation O'Connell had 6 clinical psychologists choose, from a pool of 49 items purporting to be either wit of humour, those items which they regarded as humour (in the Freudian sense). 10 of these humorous items were used in a multi-dimensional study of the Freudian concept of humour with 100 undergraduates. These subjects compared each joke with every other (80 comparisons in all) and the ratings were subjected to factor analysis, following the procedures suggested by Messick and Abelson (1956).

Results. Four factors underlying liking for humorous jokes were revealed – loss of face, gallows humour, being pursued, and non-fatal loss.

O'Connell concluded that Freudian theories of humour were supported in that gallows humour emerged as a factor. However he regarded this study as evidence that the theory needed elaboration since there were three other factors.

These conclusions do not appear to be warranted by this evidence. After all the original six judges used psychoanalytic criteria (gallows humour) to select the items. The emergence, therefore, of a factor of gallows humour supports the accuracy of their subjective judgements. In effect the factor confirms the claim that there is a class of jokes with gallows humour content. Psychoanalytic theory is not needed to discover this. What would be needed to demonstrate the Freudian theory by this method would be a factor analysis of a large sample of jokes. If a clear factor emerged loading on jokes with gallows humour, orthogonal to jokes pertaining to wit, and if it could be further shown that different people liked these two types of jokes and neurotics favoured wit, then support would be adduced for Freudian theory.

Conclusions to the work of O'Connell

These investigations by O'Connell are worthy of note in that they demonstrate that the psychoanalytic theory of wit and humour can be investigated objectively. Nevertheless, as yet they have not given sound confirmation for the theory apart from the finding that maladjusted men do prefer wit to humour. Thus this research must be praised because it is pregnant with possibilities rather than for the fruits of its labours.

The work of Gollob and Levine (1967)

These authors investigated the effects of distraction in the enjoyment of aggressive humour.

Rationale of the study. As we have seen in our description of the Freudian theory of wit and humour, there are ego and id components in the enjoyment of jokes. Thus the technique of the joke is enjoyed by the ego whereas the id appreciates the expression of forbidden aggressive or sexual impulses. However if the impulses expressed in the joke are too obvious enjoyment ceases. Thus a good joke must distract the ego and super-ego from the fact that impulses are being expressed. Remember that it is a cardinal point of Freudian theory (Freud, 1925a) that anxiety is a signal that id material is approaching consciousness and anxiety is antithetical to the enjoyment of jokes. Gollob and Levine tested the Freudian claim that distraction is important in enjoyment of humour by having subjects rate cartoons for humour before and after concentrating on their content. Aggressive cartoons should be more affected by this procedure than non-aggressive ones.

Subjects. 14 female college students.

Cartoons. 8 very aggressive, 8 least aggressive and 8 nonsense cartoons.

Method. These cartoons were rated on an 8-point scale for humour and four from each group were selected on the basis of their mean humour rating score. Ten days later subjects had to say what was funny about each cartoon (thus destroying any distracting qualities) and they re-rated them for humour.

Results. In accord with the Freudian hypothesis, after studying the contents, the ratings for the aggressive cartoons dropped more than for the others. This result was repeated in a second study where the 12 cartoons were used in both presentations.

Comments and conclusions

The hypothesis drawn from Freudian theory that distraction is an important factor in the enjoyment of aggressive humour is certainly supported by these results. It is possible to argue, without recourse to psychoanalytic theory, that aggressive humour seems less funny than other types of joke on analysis. However the question as to why this should be is still left unanswered. This study by Gollob and Levine supports one aspect of the Freudian theory of humour – the importance of distraction from the 'real' content of the joke in the enjoyment of a joke.

The work of Lamb (1968)

Lamb investigated the personality correlates of humour enjoyment following the arousal of sexual feelings.

Sample. 40 males saw photographs of nude women; 40 controls saw neutral photographs.

Measures. After arousal subjects rated cartoons for humour.

Results. The experimental, aroused group enjoyed the cartoons more than the control group. Among the aroused subjects those who were high on a questionnaire measure of feelings of guilt about sex rated the cartoons more highly than did the control group. From this it was argued that sex guilt is an important factor in the enjoyment of humour.

Comments and conclusions

The relevance of this study to the Freudian theory of wit and humour is equivocal. Thus as Gollob and Levine (1967) have shown, distraction is important in the enjoyment of jokes. Now it could be argued that by arousing sexual feelings, Lamb was increasing vigilance against sexual themes and that the aroused group would, therefore, enjoy the jokes less. On the other hand the fact that this group enjoyed the jokes more supports the broad Freudian notion that the enjoyment of humour is related to the repression of forbidden wishes. However, excessive reliance should not be placed on the results concerning sex guilt since the validity of the test of sexual anxiety is unknown. Since this subject is highly contaminated by social desirability, it is not easy to accept a measure on face validity alone. In conclusion this study by Lamb supports slightly the Freudian theory that humour is an expression of repressed wishes.

THE PSYCHOANALYTIC THEORY OF THE ARTS

Outline of the theory

'Before the problem of the creative artist analysis must, alas, lay down its arms.' Thus wrote Freud discussing the personality of Dostoevsky (Freud, 1928). Despite this modest disclaimer, psychoanalytic theory does in fact purport to embrace the creation of artistic works – visual, literary and musical. It has no especial theory of art but merely applies its usual analytic technique to the work of art much as is done in the study of dreams or wit and humour.

Thus in an early paper on poetry and daydreaming Freud (1908) makes the basic psychoanalytic position quite clear. Daydreams express the private fantasy wishes of the dreamers which most people normally strive to keep hidden because they are ashamed of them and because, even if communicated, they would tend to repel the audience. The man of literary talent however, by his *ars poetica*, expresses his fantasies in such a way that the audience takes great pleasure in them. Thus the poetic art is this ability to overcome our repulsion. Freud argues that the aesthetic pleasure of the formal structure of the work acts as a 'bribe' for us to enjoy the deeper pleasure of seeing basic, impulsive wishes acted out in the content. We can enjoy our own wishes without shame. In brief then, just as slips of the tongue and dreams express basic wishes, so too do the arts. Here the super-ego is quieted not only by disguise, as in dreams, but by the formal nature of the work. In this way we can vicariously and guiltlessly express our repressions.

Naturally the nature of these wishes underlying great art is no different from the nature of the wishes underlying all human behaviour. Freud (1928) points out that it is unlikely to be accidental that three of the great literary masterpieces of the world are concerned with the Oedipus complex – *Oedipus Rex*, *Hamlet* and *The Brothers Karamazov*.

The visual arts, too, are easily encompassed in this theory. Freud (1908) has attempted to link the actual desire to use paint with sublimated anal erotism. Fairbairn (1938) and Rickman (1940) have attempted to relate the symbolism of art, which they call art-work, to dream-work, i.e. both represent disguises for repressed material. Fairbairn, indeed, attempted to correlate the quality of a work of art with the amount of art-work in it. Pickford (1969) however has convincingly demonstrated, by using examples of psychiatric art where the art-work was remarkably clear, that no such correlation with aesthetic excellence can be true.

This relatively simple theory has been much developed, especially in this country, by Stokes and Ehrenzweig who are virtually psychoanalytic aestheticians and by Waelder in America. Thus in their view the weakness of orthodox psychoanalytic theory lies in its inability to deal with the formal aspects of art. As Waelder (1965) and Ehrenzweig (1967) point out, the original Freudian theory can account for the content of the art but not the form and, an even more serious defect, it cannot distinguish between a mediocre work and an excellent one (if the content be the same). This is what Freud (1928) means when he says that the problem of the creative artist remains unsolved. Even his point that the aesthetic pleasure is a bribe for the super-ego does not explain the nature of this aesthetic pleasure. In brief then orthodox Freudian theory can account for the content of great art but not its essence.

Ehrenzweig (1967) attempts in psychoanalytic terms to account for the very essence of art. For him great art is characterised by the syncretic vision of its author. Syncretic vision is undifferentiated, unconscious perception for the existence of which Ehrenzweig cites as evidence the work on perceptual defence and the Poetzl phenomenon (see p. 248). This unconscious vision, independent of logic and reason and to be observed in children's art, is what distinguishes the great works from the lesser, gives them their universal appeal. Sometimes this unconscious syncretic perception imposes on the work of art an apparent superficial chaos – the Ninth Symphony by Beethoven is regarded by Ehrenzweig as an outstanding example of the problems of order (disorder) caused by powerful unconscious creative processes. *The Hidden Order of Art* (Ehrenzweig, 1967) fully discusses the import of this view. Great art, then, in this view, is the untrammelled expression of the most profoundly unconscious drives and impulses, combined with, not stifled by ego-controlled techniques. Only to very few individuals is such a combination possible. Stokes (1965) also attempts to account for form within a psychoanalytic framework. His work, however, deserves only brief mention in this book since his theories have departed far from Freudian theory. His avowed mistress is Melanie Klein (see p. 330). His view of art is that it reflects the inner world of the artist – an inner world, dominated as in Kleinian theory, by introjections and introjected projections of the parent and the good and the bad breast.

Testability of the theory

So far no evidence for any part of this Freudian theory of art has been adduced. No studies have been carried out. The only investigation of even marginal relevance was that of Kline (1967c) which has been fully discussed earlier in this book (pp. 25-7). He found that a sample of painters had a lower score on a test of anal characteristics than other comparable groups – a result which supports the claim that painting is a sublimation of the desire to handle the faeces.

However the orthodox Freudian theory concerning the content of art is, at least in part, amenable to test. For example psychosexual testing of painters should reveal anal, oral and, say, Oedipal painters. Their paintings could then be surveyed for evidence of these fixations. The same technique could be applied to novelists. *Couples* (Updike, 1968) seems overtly concerned with oral erotism. We should hypothesise, therefore, that Updike would score high on oral measures. Readers can no doubt think up similar hypotheses for writers of their choice. Of course, it remains a fact that the judgement of what fixations a picture or story reveals is subjective. Nevertheless a number of independent judges to some extent overcomes this subjective element.

It is certainly clear in the paintings of Hieronymus Bosch or the etchings of Goya that processes are at work in these fantasies akin to dream-work and related to psychosexual fixations. Oral sadistic and anal sadistic images are common – consider, for example, the monstrous hooked beaks of many of these denizens of Hell. However, studies of this type, of the content of art-works, unrelated to accurate measures of the personality and/or background of the artist cannot be considered as evidence for the Freudian theory. These constitute but the data of the theory.

The second part of the theory, as proposed by Ehrenzweig (1967), does not seem amenable to test. Apart from the difficulty of deciding what is or is not great art – a quite different problem from that of the subjective nature of the assessment of orality in a picture – there is no way of proving that a picture is typical of unconscious as distinct from conscious perception. This is not because the statement that X is a product of the unconscious is non-empirical and thus not a subject of scientific study, in the way that the statement X is a great work of art is non-empirical and thus a subject for philosophy rather than science. It is because as yet we have no measure of whether a percept is conscious or un-conscious. Nor in the near future are we likely to develop one. Yet the statement is not meaningless. If we accept the assumption made by Ehrenzweig, certain consequences follow – for example teaching methods in the arts will be radically different from the Victorian approach based on careful life-drawings and develop-ment of techniques. Furthermore, if we accept it, our appreciation of modern abstract art, and also more formal styles, becomes changed. Nevertheless we must accept that Ehrenzweig's theories, and thus psychoanalytic theory in a developed form, is quite unscientific because it cannot be tested.

Summary

The orthodox Freudian theory of art applies only to the content of artistic productions rather than their form: it fails to establish the essential difference between a great work of art and a mundane production. Although it is a testable theory it has never been put to the test. Freudian theory, as developed by Ehrenzweig, can account for the essence of art. It cannot however be tested. For the entire psychoanalytic theory of art there exists no objective evidence whatever. However in that it gives insight into art, for some writers at least, it should not be abandoned. Here, indeed, is a field where research should be developed, for unlike many contemporary psychological theories psychoanalysis can embrace the arts.

9

Freudian dream theory

INTRODUCTION

Freudian dream theory has been most extensively developed especially in 'The interpretation of dreams' (Freud, 1900) and in the 'Introductory lectures on psychoanalysis' (Freud, 1916-17). This means that any outline of the theory must do it scant justice. Because of this complexity the outline itself will be analytic – categorised under various headings.

OUTLINE OF THE THEORY

'Every dream is an attempt to put aside disturbance of sleep by means of a wish fulfilment. The dream is thus the Guardian of Sleep' (Freud, 1940).

FORMATION OF DREAMS

Dreams may be provoked in two different ways:

1. An instinctual impulse which is as a rule suppressed (*i.e. an unconscious wish*) finds expression during sleep.
2. A desire left over from waking life obtains reinforcement during sleep from an unconscious element.

Dreams therefore may arise from the id or the ego (Freud, 1940).

NATURE OF THE DREAM CONTENT

Manifest dream material

This is the overt dream content as remembered by the dreamer. However in Freudian dream theory this manifest content is relatively trivial. What is important are the processes concealed behind it. This is known as *latent dream thought*. The process by which the manifest dream material is derived from the latent dream thoughts is the *dream-work*.

'The study of dream-work affords us an excellent example of the way in which unconscious material from the id forces itself upon the ego, becomes preconscious and owing to the efforts of the ego, undergoes the modifications which we call *dream distortion*' (Freud, 1940).

Dream-work, then, is an example of the unconscious working-over of preconscious mental processes, i.e. an example of primary processes at work.

204

Several mechanisms of dream-work have been described:

1. *Condensation* – the formation of unities from things which we keep separate in our waking thoughts.
2. *Displacement*. The most important thing in the manifest content may be trivial in the dream thoughts and vice versa.
3. Thoughts are transformed into visual images (Freud, 1916).
4. *Opposites*. The manifest dream may express a latent dream thought by its opposite (!). Freud tries to support this claim by recourse to linguistic examples, e.g. *altus* means high or deep, *sacer* means sacred or accursed.
5. *Secondary elaboration*. The attempt to give a coherent overall picture of the dream on recounting it.

All these mechanisms, indeed the latent dream thought itself, were discovered by getting the subject to free associate to the manifest dream content. However, it frequently happens that there are certain 'silent' elements in the manifest dream content to which no associations are possible (Freud, 1916). These 'silent' elements are the *symbols*.

 Dream symbols

'The number of things which are represented symbolically in dreams is not great. The human body as a whole, parents, children, brothers and sisters, birth, death, nakedness and one thing more' (Freud, 1916). Some examples of symbols are:

Object (*in latent dream*)	Manifest symbol
Human body	House
Male body	Smooth-fronted house
Female body	House with ledges and balconies
Parents	Emperor, empress, king and queen
Children	Little animals or vermin
Birth	Some reference to water
Dying	Setting out on a journey, travelling by train
Nakedness	Clothes and uniforms

However, the overwhelming majority of symbols in dreams are sexual symbols (Freud, 1916).

Whole male genitalia	Number three
Penis	Sticks, umbrellas, poles, trees, knives, daggers, lances, sabres, guns, pistols, revolvers, taps, watering cans, springs, pulley lamps, pencils, penholders, nail files, hammers, reptiles, fishes, serpents, hats and cloaks, machinery

Erection	Balloons, aeroplanes, the sensation of flying
Female genitalia	Pits, hollows, caves, jars, bottles, bones, chests, coffers, pockets, landslides, landscapes, jewel case
The womb	Cupboards, stores, rooms
Genital opening – female	Doors, gates, mouth
Woman	Wood, paper, tables, books, snails and mussels, churches and chapels
Breasts	Apples, peaches, fruit in general
Pubic hair	Woods and thickets
Sexual pleasures	Sweetmeats
Auto erotism	Play
Masturbation	Sliding, gliding, pulling off a branch
Castration fear	Falling out or extraction of teeth

WHY IS THERE DREAM-WORK AT ALL ?

'With the help of the unconscious every dream in the process of formation makes a demand upon the ego for the satisfaction of an instinct (if it originates from the id) or for the removal of a conflict . . . (if it originates from a residue of preconscious activity in the working life).' The sleeping ego desires to sleep, it regards the demand as a disturbance, and to remove the disturbance by replacing the demand by a fulfilment of a wish. 'This *replacement of a demand by the fulfilment of a wish remains the essential function of dream-work*' (Freud, 1940).

Freud admits that in the case of dreams arising from residues of the previous day it is often hard to detect the unconscious motive force and the wish fulfilment 'but we may assume it is always there'. For wish fulfilment is the motivation of dreams (Freud, 1916).

ANXIETY DREAMS AS WISH FULFILMENTS

Freud (1916) accounts for anxiety dreams in a number of ways.

1. The dream-work may not be entirely successful in creating a wish fulfilment so that a part of the painful latent thought enters the manifest content of the dream.

2. The very fulfilment of the wish may provoke anxiety.

3. Anxiety dreams often have a content in which there is no distortion: it has escaped the censorship. Thus the anxiety dream is the open fulfilment of a repressed wish. The anxiety indicates that the repressed wish was too strong for the censor. If the wish is only too likely to break through we wake up – in considerable anxiety – and the dream has failed to protect our sleep.

Every dream is an attempt to put aside a disturbance of sleep by means of a wish fulfilment. The dream is thus the guardian of sleep.

THE HYPOTHESES OF FREUDIAN DREAM THEORY

A. SYMBOLISM. Certain objects, especially sexual organs, are represented by other objects in dreams and in primary, unconscious thought processes. Since dream contents are primary processes symbolism can be observed outside dreams and, as we shall see, symbolism is best investigated outside dreams. This is because there is no reliable way of inducing dreams, except by hypnosis, so that dream content could be predicted. Unfortunately, as Tart (1965) makes clear, the process of hypnosis is not sufficiently well understood for hypnotically induced dreams to be equated with normal, nocturnal dreaming.

If, however, other parts of Freudian theory are assumed to be true, such as the Oedipus complex or castration complex, the content of dreams may be predicted – sex differences in content would be expected. Symbolism in dreams can be checked this way. For example a sex difference would be expected from psychoanalytic theory in the dreams of kings and queens.

B. DREAMS FULFIL WISHES. This part of Freudian theory can be tested, in theory at least, by comparing the dreams of subjects whose repressed wishes. have been independently assessed. Similarly dream deprivation would be expected to produce disorders of waking behaviour.

From this it is clear that it is exceedingly difficult to put Freudian dream theory to an adequate test. One of the major problems lies in the fact that psychoanalytic theory is derived from the *interpretation* of dreams. There seems to be, except in the case of symbolism, no other method of reaching similar conclusions. Hence an independent check not based on interpretation is hard to carry out. The most hopeful procedure probably lies in the study of criterion groups whose dreams may, from the nature of their problems and background, be predicted (in terms of psychoanalytic theory).

IMPORTANCE OF THE THEORY

Freud (1909) claims that the 'interpretation of dreams is in fact the royal road to a knowledge of the unconscious: it is the securest foundation of psychoanalysis and the field in which every worker must acquire his convictions and seek his training.' Although this is an early statement, Freud clearly holds broadly to this position. Much of the data of psychoanalysis on which Freudian theory was based was dream material. Dreams give us a chance to see primary processes at work. Since Freud (1940) has argued that unconscious mechanisms discovered from dreams help us to understand the neuroses and psychoses it is clear that dream theory is a fundamental part of psychoanalytic theory as a whole. If it be shown to be false, considerable doubt must be cast on much of psychoanalytic theory.

SECTION I – SYMBOLISM

As is clear from the psychoanalytic theory of dreams, an important element in interpretation is the claim that certain objects represent, or are symbols for, others. In the outline of the theory various examples of these were given. This part of the theory contains an obvious testable question: are certain objects represented by others as Freudian theory states? Although symbolism was originally derived from the analysis of dreams, to test the theory it is not necessary to consider only dream material. This is, of course, because dream material reflects the workings of the unconscious mind, the primary processes, which may be evinced in all behaviour even if less clearly.

THE EMPIRICAL EVIDENCE CONCERNING SYMBOLS

In this review of the objective evidence for the psychoanalytic theory of symbols, those studies not concerned with dreams will be first considered. The arrangement will be broadly chronological unless a research sparked off a series of other investigations; these will be examined together.

The work of Krout (1950): the Symbol Elaboration Test (SET)

In this investigation Krout administered 12 symbolic drawings to a sample of 169 subjects aged 6-69 years of whom 12 were American Indians. To give examples of the symbols used, a semi-circle represented femaleness, two counter-opposed semicircles stood for female society, a single straight line represented maleness and a diffuse mass was a symbol for anxiety. The subjects had to make drawings from these symbols and they were then questioned about them. There were thus three sources of data – the manner of drawing, the content of drawings and verbal associations. Based on purely subjective judgements of this data Krout concluded that these symbols were universal. As regards the sample, apart from the 12 Indian children there were 30 normal American white children, two small groups of normal adults (N 24 and 30), 13 children with behaviour problems and 60 adults undergoing psychotherapy.

Comments and conclusions

Clearly with such a small sample it is not possible, whatever the results, to claim that these symbols were universal: to do that, representative samples from all cultures would be necessary. Furthermore, the extremely subjective and interpretative nature of the scoring of the responses robs this study of real objectivity. Indeed, this investigation has only been discussed because it is an early forerunner of the kind of approach possible with the investigation of symbolism. Again, many of the symbols, combinations of lines and semi-circles stem more from the author's clinical experience and skill than from psychoanalytic theory.

This study cannot be regarded as support for the Freudian theory of symbols – it is far too subjective for that. It is, nonetheless, an interesting approach to the problem.

The work of Hammer (1953)

Hammer studied the Freudian theory of genital symbolism in a group of male patients who had been sterilised and a group of controls who had undergone other operations.

Test used. Hammer employed the HTP projective test (Buck, 1948). In this the subject is required to make a drawing of a house, a tree and a person. It yields a measure of genital symbolism, and hence castration anxiety, directly. From Freudian theory, for example, it would be predicted that those suffering from castration anxiety would in their pictures of the house omit the chimney (penis) or draw it billowing smoke. The tree might well be cut down or the head of the person cut off.

Experimental design. Since the sterilised subjects were prisoners HTP protocols were obtained from them on admission to prison, on admission to hospital, on the day of operation, and the day after operation. A similar sequence was obtained from the control group. Matching of the groups (20 in each) was not perfect – the experimental group was of lower intelligence.

Analysis of results. The Fisher Exact Probability Test was applied. The operation scores of the experimental group were compared with their original scores (obtained in the prison) and the operation scores of the surgical control group.

Results. The results strongly support the Freudian theory of genital symbolism. Examples of items differentiating the experimental group from the controls and their original scores at the ·05 level, or better, were: chimney missing, tree cut through, penis-like feet and the admisson on interview that the house needed a chimney.

Comments and conclusions

The assumption upon which this study rests is that patients undergoing sterilisation will feel fears of castration. This is the rationale for comparing them with surgical controls. The results support this claim. In doing so, as has been indicated, the Freudian theory of sexual symbolism has been strongly supported. The theory predicts certain differences in drawings between the groups and these were found. It is to be noted that the experimental design, comparing operation protocols with previous scores and a control group, is very neat. It seems unlikely that imperfect matching of the groups on intelligence and psychopathy (more in the experimental group) could have contributed to these predicted differences.

This study must be regarded as good evidence for the psychoanalytic theory of genital symbolism.

The work of McElroy (1954) and Jahoda (1956)

On the Freudian hypothesis that rounded shapes represent the female genital organs and pointed shapes the male, McElroy presented a 12 item test (each item consisting of one rounded and one pointed shape) to 380 boys and 399 girls. Subjects had to indicate for each item which of the two drawings they preferred.

As predicted from the Freudian theory, males preferred female shapes and females preferred male shapes, a preference which increased with age.

Although this study appears to confirm the Freudian theory it is not entirely satisfactory for a number of reasons as, indeed, McElroy himself admits. In the first place other hypotheses are possible to account for the results. It is possible that in some items the shapes had different associations for boys and girls which would account for the differential preference. Item 2, for example, portrayed a shield and a fleur de lys. It is also possible, if unconvincing, to account for the findings in terms of stimulus generalisation. So Jahoda, in an attempt to overcome these problems and to make a more critical test of the Freudian hypothesis (and also because he claimed there was an error in the computations), replicated this study in an alien culture – Ghana.

Owing to the nature of the society in Ghana a far more critical test of the psychoanalytic hypotheses was possible, since the alternative hypotheses were not tenable. Among the Ga, the tribe who constituted his sample of 858 middle school children (age range approximately 12-15 years) and 278 similar subjects in a further subsidiary experiment, there is far less repression of childhood sexual activity (e.g. Field, 1940) than is usual among Scottish children (McElroy's sample). Therefore sex differences in preference for shapes would be expected to be less pronounced.

In fact there were sex differences on only 5 of the 12 items. The Accra boys (town dwellers) did not change with age whereas the girls converged towards the boys' preference patterns. In the subsidiary experiment, where the children were afterwards questioned, it emerged that the preferred drawings were those that could be named. This, however, fails to account for the sex difference noted. Furthermore, the girls' preferences were not attributable to the quality of drawings as McElroy had suggested they might be. From this evidence Jahoda argued that only the psychoanalytic theory of symbolism had not been eliminated as being responsible for the sex differences in preferences. McElroy's other hypotheses had been shown to be false. As regards the older girls' decline in preference for male shapes, Jahoda argues that this is due to the fact that by this age the Ghanaian girl has had far more sexual experience than the boy.

Conclusions

These two experiments taken together must be regarded as support for the Freudian theory of symbolism, specifically that rounded shapes represent the female and pointed shapes the male sexual organs. The cross-cultural study in Ghana seems to rule out other alternative explanations accounting for the sex preferences observed. In general, therefore, Freudian theory is upheld.

Of the four studies so far examined, it will have been noted that three support the psychoanalytic theory while one (Krout, 1950) is neutral in this respect. Now an investigation must be discussed which claims to show that the theory is false. Apart from the interest of the results this study also sparked off other similar investigations.

The work of Levy (1954)

Levy put the theory of genital symbolism to the test in a sample of around 60 ten-year-old children. Two methods were used. In the first, children had to allocate names to figures symbolic of female or male sexual organs. The hypothesis was that were the theory correct female names should be given to rounded objects and male names to pointed ones. In the second method the sample was divided into two groups. One was given a paired associate learning task – the male names with the male symbols and the feminine names with the female symbols. The other was given the same task but with the genders reversed – female names and male objects. It was hypothesised that the first group would remember their material significantly better since, according to the theory, there ought to be already unconscious connections.

Results and conclusions

   (a) *Method* 1. Contrary to the Freudian hypothesis, male and female names were not matched to their respective symbols. Levy concluded from this that the Freudian theory was disproved.
   (b) *Method* 2. There was no significant difference in memory for the paired associates between the two groups.

From the results of this investigation Levy concluded that the Freudian theory of genital symbols was disproved.

Comments

At this point in the discussion it will suffice to say that on the face of it this study looks like convincing proof that in this sample of children, at least, there is no evidence whatever of symbolism. Certain objections have been made to the study and these will be taken up as they appear in the investigations stimulated by this work. Nevertheless the fact remains that this is evidence contrary to Freudian theory.

The work of Jacobs (1954)

Jacobs gave a list of symbols for the male and female sexual organs to a sample of 99 mental hospital patients, 27 student nurses and 12 hospital attendants, and asked them to assign a gender to each of the words.

Results and conclusions

The correct (in psychoanalytic theory) gender was assigned to the symbols far beyond the chance level. Normals were superior in this to his patient population. Jacobs regarded these results as supporting Freudian theory.

Comments

As Moos and Mussen (1959) point out, it is wrong to assume from these results that symbolism is impaired in psychotics. This is because psychotics often suffer from a general intellectual deficit which would of itself account for the results. In addition small samples of student nurses and hospital attendants are hardly sufficient as normal control groups. Nevertheless the overall result that there was a better than chance matching of gender to symbol does provide support for the Freudian theory.

The work of Starer (1955)

Starer replicated the work of Levy (1954) asking subjects to match names to rounded or pointed figures. He used a substantial sample of psychotics, mainly schizophrenics, and a control group of the inevitable student nurses.

Results

Contrary to the findings of Levy these patients matched figures to names significantly better than chance (by chi-square) thus providing more evidence in favour of psychoanalytic theory. Starer also claimed that he had the *impression* that inability to match names was increased by psychotic confusion.

Comments

These results directly support Freudian theory and are entirely opposed to those of Levy. In addition the clinical impression that the degree of psychotism impaired matching bears out the work of Jacobs (1954) already discussed. This investigation constitutes yet more evidence for the Freudian theory of symbolism.

The work of Mosak (1955)

Mosak adopted an entirely different and novel approach to the question of symbolism. He examined the gender of the words for the Freudian symbols in French, Spanish and German.

Results and conclusions

In French, 15 of 32 male symbols are feminine and 12 of the 26 female symbols are masculine. In Spanish the respective figures are 19 and 12 while in German these figures fall to 11 and 9.

Mosak concluded that these results threw considerable doubt on the veracity of the Freudian theory.

Comments

It is difficult to know what interpretation to place on this finding that the gender of sexual symbols in a number of European languages is not in accord with the psychoanalytic theory of symbols. Since the psychological origins of language are not well understood it may be presumptuous to expect such an accordance. Indeed it is not clear whether, from psychoanalytic theory, matching would be predicted. It is true that had the gender of words fitted the sexual symbols psychoanalytic investigators would have claimed it as support for the theory – on the grounds that it indicated the unconscious origins of language.

However, if the unconscious origins of language are the basis for the claim that male sexual symbols should be masculine then the gender of words derived from the same language, as French and Spanish are derived from Latin, should be the same. The fact that they are not is evidence that there are other factors in the acquisition of gender in the development of languages. Such an argument of course suggests a further more fundamental investigation: if unconscious factors are important in the origins of language, then symbols in the original languages, e.g. Sanskrit and Basque, ought to be the same. However, since it is evident that there are other factors than unconscious ones in the development of languages, Mosak's failure to find agreement between the theory of sexual symbolism and the gender of words cannot seriously be considered as disproof of the Freudian theory.

The work of Minturn (1965)

Minturn, in a rather more extensive investigation, also studied the gender of various symbolic words in a variety of languages.

Rationale. Minturn accepts that the gender of words is not likely to be entirely determined by their symbolic referents and therefore he subjected the Freudian theory to the test by examining the direction of gender classification of symbol words in *several* languages rather than the *magnitude* of this relationship in one language.

Symbols. Symbol words were selected from the studies by Hall (1966 for example, see pp. 229-35) rather than from orthodox psychoanalytic writings, because Hall's symbols were derived from normals not neurotics and reflected modern dreams rather than those early in the century. Hall's list, of course, very largely overlaps that of the psychoanalysts. 54 male and 60 female symbols were used – those rated by judges as unambiguously masculine or feminine.

Languages. From each branch of the Indo-European languages only one language was used in this study since in related languages, for example French and Italian, gender classification is not independent in that in both are derived from Latin. Since four non Indo-European languages were also used, the language sample was as shown below:

French (Romance), German (Germanic)
Russian (Slavic), Greek (Hellenic) } Indo-European
Irish (Celtic), Maharata (Indic)
Arabic (Semitic), Tunica (American Indian) } non Indo-European
Nama (Khoisan), Hausa (Uad-Hamitic)

Method. Fluent speakers of these 10 languages translated the symbols. In addition stratified random samples of nouns in each of the languages were classified for gender.

Results

Test 1. The expected frequencies for gender classification based on the random sample were compared with the observed frequencies for the classification of the symbolic words, and the probabilities of these differences were computed by the sign test. Four tests had high probabilities in the expected direction, the Tunican sample being significant at the 1% level (males). Only three female differences and one male difference were in the wrong direction.

Test 2. A chi-square analysis was computed to test the association between symbolic classification and actual gender. In 8 out of 10 cases the results were in the predicted direction (probability of such a result is 5%).

The Tunican sample is again significant at the 1% level.

Since it has been admitted that other variables affect gender than the symbolic significance of the words, constancy of results across languages is the crucial test. For female symbols the difference between observed and expected frequencies is correct only 5 out of 8 times (not significant) but for male symbols it is correct 7 out of 8 times (sig. 3% level.)

Thus it can be concluded that masculine symbols do tend to be classified as male in a wide variety of languages (not just the Germanic of Freud's original data) but also in non Indo-European languages, while female symbols are classified with less consistency as feminine.

Test 3. A chi-square analysis was performed comparing the gender of symbolic words with the expected frequency of neuter words in the language. Here the results were more equivocal since in some languages there was a greater frequency, in others less, of symbolic neutral words. The interpretation of this is complicated by the fact that neuter words, as symbolic words, are often the commonest in the languages.

Conclusions

The data presented in this study support the hypothesis derived from Freudian theory that symbolic words in a wide variety of languages do tend to be put into the gender appropriate to their sexual referent. This evidence therefore supports the notion of dream symbolism and the claim that such symbolism represents primary mental processes common to all men regardless of their linguistic background. That the evidence is not statistically more definitive must be attributed to the fact that gender in languages is influenced by other factors linguistic and non-linguistic.

The work of Mullen (1968)

Mullen attempted to investigate the universality (and by implication the validity) of Freudian and Jungian sexual symbols. This study suffers from the logical difficulty already mentioned in connection with the method of examining the gender of symbolic words in various languages – namely that since the gender of words in languages derived from a common source is often different some external influences must be affecting gender. Thus Mullen's finding that the gender of words symbolic in both Jungian and Freudian theory cannot be correctly predicted from either theory in French, German or Spanish cannot be regarded as refuting either theory. To use languages as a test of the theory, investigators must examine basic root languages. Here communality of gender would be not definitive proof but highly suggestive evidence. This study by Mullen cannot therefore be regarded as a true test of symbolism.

The work of Jones (1956)

Jones extended the work of Levy (1954) in a very sophisticated analysis of variance study aimed to eradicate certain faults in the previous work. First Jones claimed that failure of the Levy study could have been due to the fact that the names used were not equated for all their stimulus attributes. In addition it was pointed out that the children in Levy's investigation were not sexually mature, a fact which could be of some importance.

Design of the experiment. 10 male and 10 female students were used together with 10 male and 10 female psychotics. The main factors examined in the analysis of variance were sex, psychiatric classification and type of sexual symbol. Between-symbol differences were also examined.

Results. There were four main findings:

(a) Symbolism did occur – there were better than chance matching of names to symbols.
(b) The psychiatric groups matched less well than the students.
(c) Males were better than females. This finding was linked by Jones to the fact that males are more easily aroused by a variety of sexual stimuli than are females (Kinsey *et al.*, 1948).
(d) Although there was significant variation between symbols (not in accord with Freudian theory), this was due to the influence of one symbol alone – a box – a fact which cannot be held to invalidate the theory.

Comments

Again this study gives results contrary to those of Levy (1954). Freudian genital symbolism is indubitably supported. Clearly the age variable in symbolism needs

H

further investigation. The findings concerning psychotics confirm those of Jacobs (1954) and Starer (1955) although, as with those studies, the warning of Moos and Mussen (1959) must be borne in mind – that the observed differences reflect the general intellectual impairment of psychotics rather than a specific disability to use symbols. In conclusion the work of Jones must be regarded as confirming Freudian theory.

The work of Winter and Prescott (1957)

Starer (1955), as has been discussed above, had a clinical impression that psychotics matched names to symbolic objects less well than normals. Winter and Prescott, using the same technique as Starer, attempted to validate these findings.

Method. 55 female and 52 male hospitalised mental patients were administered the Starer (1955) test of symbolism and the MMPI.

Results. These psychotics matched names to objects significantly better than chance and Freudian theory was thus supported. However, correct matching was quite unrelated to any of the scores on the MMPI clinical scales. In addition the female psychotics in this study matched symbols to names as well as the normal females in the Starer study. Winter and Prescott concluded therefore that there was no relationship between the ability to match symbols and psychotic confusion.

Comments and conclusions

Although the fact that the matching of symbols to names was better than chance supports Freudian theory, the main finding that psychotism is unrelated to the ability to form symbols is not really supported by this evidence for two reasons:

(a) The fact that all the samples were psychotic means that it was very homogeneous thus depressing any correlations with the MMPI scales.

(b) The inadequacy of Starer's (1955) normal sample has already been mentioned (p. 212) so that any comparison with it, as in this study, is not meaningful.

Despite this, however, the study does support the Freudian theory of genital symbolism.

The work of Stennett and Thurlow (1958)

Stennett and Thurlow were interested in the discrepancy between the work of Starer (1955) and that of Levy (1954). They therefore investigated the question of whether the difference in results was due to the figures used by Levy differing in some unknown way from those of Starer.

Method. Both sets of figures were given to a group of 37 nurses.

Results. With both sets of stimuli matching was better than chance, Freudian theory was supported, and the failure of Levy to confirm the theory could not be laid at the door of the pictures he used. The authors concluded from this study that the age variable in matching names to symbols must be examined.

Comments and conclusions

This study does suggest that the reason for the discrepancy of the results of Levy (1954) might lie in the age of the sample. It must be remembered that all the other studies so far reviewed in this section confirm the theory. Furthermore, as Stennett and Thurlow point out, the cause of the discrepancy cannot be the normality of the sample (e.g. Jones, 1956). The nature of the stimulus material cannot be the cause and the only other difference (group rather than individual testing) is unlikely to be important.

This study supports Freudian theory and demonstrates that the age of the subjects may be a crucial factor in the development of the ability to symbolise.

The work of Accord (1962)

The influence of age on the ability to symbolise was studied by Accord. He administered the usual matching test to a total of 305 subjects divided into five groups by age. The groups were grades 3, 6, 9 and 12, plus an adult sample.

Results. Only the last two groups (i.e. those of 17 years and above) were able to put the name that first came to their mind to ten designs better than chance. The younger children, as was the case with Levy, were not able to match name and symbol.

Comments

This finding, that maturity is related to the ability to make the Freudian symbolic connections, neatly accounts for the discrepancy noted between the results of Levy (1954) and other investigators. This result still supports Freudian theory although, were it confirmed in further experiments, it would be necessary to make Freudian theory quite explicit on this point of age.

The work of Lessler (1962)

Lessler, using three groups of 20 males and 20 females with respective mean ages of 9·4, 14·4 and 20·2 years, also investigated age as an influence on symbolism.

Method. 20 Freudian symbols were presented to the subjects to be sorted into two piles as masculine or feminine. In addition 20 other symbols were presented, varying in texture (rough or smooth), but the results from this part of the investigation are not relevant to this book.

Results. Contrary to the work of Levy (1954) and Accord (1962) although more fully in accord with psychoanalytic theory, all three groups did significantly better than chance at assigning gender to these objects.

Comments

Clearly it is necessary to attempt to account for the discrepancy from the other result with children.

Cameron (1967) explains these results in terms of the fact that in this experiment the subjects did not have to match names from a list or name symbols themselves, procedures which alert subjects' defences. The procedure of merely sorting into two piles, being less disturbing, is more effective. If this hypothesis were correct it still does not convincingly account for the fact that the 'disturbing' technique works with adults. However, whatever the explanation for the fact that with the children in this sample genital symbolism appears to have been present, the experiment as a whole is further confirmation of psychoanalytic theory.

The work of Meissner (1958)

All but one of the investigations so far discussed have restricted themselves to but one aspect of the psychoanalytic theory of symbolism – genital symbolism. As an important extension of the work in this area, Meissner studied psychoanalytic death symbols.

Method. 20 words regarded in psychoanalytic theory as symbols of death, for example a bird, a journey across a bridge and an old man, together with 30 random control words from the Kent-Rosanoff list were presented to 40 Roman Catholic seminarians. Their GSR response to each word was collected and in addition they were asked to group all 50 words under common headings.

Results. There were more references to the symbol words under the heading of death than to the control words. Unfortunately no statistical test of this difference was made. More importantly there was a significantly greater amplitude of GSR to the death words than to the controls. Meissner regarded these results as confirming the Freudian theory.

Comments and conclusions

These GSR responses must be considered as good evidence for the Freudian death symbols, for they are difficult to fake or bring under rational control. It could be argued that some of the psychoanalytic death symbols take on their disturbing quality because they are, in everyday life, symbols of or connected with death – for example, black or the silent one. On the other hand it can be argued that this is in itself support for the Freudian theory. As regards the finding that the symbols were more frequently classified under death than their controls, little can be inferred without a statistical test.

This study is further support for the Freudian theory.

The work of Moos and Mussen (1959)

As has been previously pointed out, Moos and Mussen have objected to previous studies of symbolism among psychotics (e.g. Jacobs, 1954) because they consider that any deficit in ability to symbolise was due to a more general intellectual dysfunctioning. To put this to the test Moos and Mussen had three groups – psychotics, neurotics and surgical controls respectively (10 males in each) – indicate masculine or feminine to a number of psychoanalytic sexual symbols.

Results. All three groups matched symbol and gender better than chance. Moos and Mussen considered that this supported their claim because all groups were matched on age, education and, the crucial point, intellectual functioning as measured by the 40 word vocabulary test of the Shipley Institute for living Test.

Comments

This study, despite the size of the samples which would have only revealed large differences, does seem to support their claims regarding the inferior performance of psychotics. It also fully supports Freudian theory.

The work of Glotter and Reece (1962)

Glotter and Reece made a study of tactility and sexual symbolism in which four stimulus objects were presented to 30 students. There was one straight and one spherical object made of wood and a similar pair made of rubber. After feeling each object students responded on 20 scales of the semantic differential. The hard/soft dimension was highly significant for the concept of masculinity and femininity but the effects of form were confounded by weight and flexibility.

Comments and conclusions

In that the hard/soft dimension was relevant to the concept of masculinity it could be argued that this study supports Freudian theory. Nevertheless these two terms are related to masculinity in everyday life and psychoanalytic theory is not the parsimonious explanation of these results. Furthermore the fact that the effect of form was confounded by weight and flexibility means that the most important dimension of Freudian symbolism was confounded.

Although on the surface at least this study appears to confirm psychoanalytic theory it does not stand close scrutiny. Little relevant to Freudian theory may be concluded from it.

The work of Cameron (1967)

Cameron, in a study which has already been mentioned, carried out a most extensive study of symbolism in more than 2,000 children of age from 3 to 17 years.

Method. Children had to choose male or female symbols presented in pairs. The shapes were those used by McElroy (1954) and Jahoda (1956). 42 interviewers, randomly selected within areas, were used.

Hypotheses. Psychoanalytic theory predicts, as Fenichel (1945) emphasises, that individuals tend to prefer shapes representative of the sexual organs of the opposite sex. This, therefore, was the basic hypothesis investigated in this study. However in the light of Freudian psychosexual theory it was modified according to age, as set out below:

(a) Children below 4 years of age, being oral or anal, will show no preference for male or female symbols.

(*b*) Children 4 to 6 years of age, being at the phallic stage, will prefer shapes symbolic of the opposite sex.
(*c*) Children from 7 to 12 years of age, being at the latency period, will prefer shapes representative of the same sex.
(*d*) Children of 12 years and upwards, at the genital stage, will prefer symbols representative of the opposite sex.

One further hypothesis was made, namely that girls of thirteen and more would tend to have a greater preference for masculine shapes after latency because of the masculine orientation of the culture which younger phallic children would not perceive.

Results. The preference for symbols when tested by chi-square all fitted the Freudian hypotheses. Nevertheless it must be noted that the chi-squares although significant were small.

Comments

This investigation fully supports the Freudian theory of genital symbolism and, indirectly, psychosexual theory. Cameron attributes the failure of Levy (1954) and Accord (1962) to demonstrate symbolism in their samples of children to the fact that in their experiments the children were required to match symbols with names – a rational procedure. In this, ego defences could easily override the more primitive secondary processes of symbolisation. Preference on the other hand as used in this experiment is non-rational. Cameron points out that the other successful investigation with children, that of Lessler (1964), also required a non-rational procedure – sorting into piles.

Conclusions

From this experiment, carried out on very large samples of children, it can be argued that genital symbolism occurs in children of all ages. The failure of earlier investigations with children seems to be attributable to method. As a whole therefore, Freudian theory is again supported. But it must be pointed out that the results with the youngest children who showed no preference while fitting psychoanalytic theory are also consonant with the hypothesis that no symbolism occurs in young pre-school children.

OTHER DETERMINANTS OF GENDER

As we have seen from the attempts to examine the Freudian theory of symbolism by a study of the gender of symbolic words in various languages, there are clearly extra-symbolic determinants of gender. We finally turn to a number of studies which have investigated some of these factors.

The work of Lessler

Lessler (1964) and Lessler and Ericksen (1968) studied this problem among a sample of college students (1964) and school children (1968).

Lessler (1964)

Sample. 169 college students.

Symbols. They were chosen such that they could be classified as masculine or feminine in Freudian theory and as masculine or feminine through cultural influences. Thus Schonbar and Davitz (1960) in a study of the connotative meaning of sexual symbols found that choice of gender was determined by cultural factors: for example baseball bats were considered to be masculine because men exclusively played with them. To test this cultural hypothesis, Lessler developed a list of 40 symbols with obvious cultural content:

(*a*) Masculine in Freudian theory and by cultural content, e.g. baseball bat.
(*b*) Feminine in Freudian theory and by cultural content, e.g. powder puff.
(*c*) Masculine in Freudian theory but feminine by cultural content, e.g. rolling pin.
(*d*) Feminine in Freudian theory but masculine by cultural content, e.g. baseball.

He also devised 40 symbols where the cultural gender was more ambiguous (as rated by judges).

Finally he chose 20 symbols where there was no cultural bias.

Method. Subjects had to assign gender to these symbols.

Results
(*a*) Where the symbols had a cultural referent, that was used to assign gender to the word.
(*b*) Where there was no cultural bias, the symbols were sorted in accord with Freudian theory.

Comments and conclusions. Lessler argues that these findings may account for the disparity of results that we have already noted in the study of symbolism. Thus where in previous studies symbols were chosen which had cultural biases contrary to Freudian theory, that theory would not be supported. He argues that cultural factors were used to assign gender because it was more socially acceptable to do so, less threatening and more rational. The fact that in normals, at least, ego processes (cultural influence) override primary processes (selection of gender by symbols) is in no way contrary to psychoanalytic theory. Indeed, these results of Lessler are strong support for the Freudian theory of symbolism, which states that in the unconscious certain objects represent the sexual organs. These primary unconscious processes are usually only noticeable in psychosis, dreaming and in free association. Thus if Lessler had found that cultural factors did not influence the choice of gender then psychoanalytic theory would not be so well supported. In conclusion, this study strongly confirms Freudian theory.

Lessler and Ericksen (1968)

Lessler and Ericksen repeated this study on a sample of school children.

Sample. 142 boys, 164 girls in grades 1-6.

Symbols. As in previous study, but only half the numbers in each group were used.

Results were essentially similar to those reported for students. Thus where there was a clear cultural sex-role, that was used to assign gender. Otherwise Freudian symbolism was used. However female symbols were not correctly classified.

Comments and conclusions. This study fails to support the Freudian theory of sexual symbolism as regards the female sexual organs. It is difficult to produce a convincing reason for this particular finding in the light of the previous study.

The work of Jones and Lepson (1967)

Jones and Lepson carried out a similar test of the Freudian theory of symbolism using colour as the alternative classificatory cue.

Sample. 20 male and 20 female students and 20 male and 20 female psychiatric patients.

Symbols. Five pointed and five rounded figures (masculine and feminine). There was a black (strong colour and therefore masculine) and a grey series of each. Thus each system (shape or colour) could mediate a sexual response and in one half of each series there would be opposition of the two systems.

Method. Subjects had to assign gender to the shapes.

Results. Each system showed itself capable of mediating a choice of gender. Neither system appeared stronger than the other. These authors conclude that Freud was wrong to stress the primary generalisation features in his theory of symbolism.

Comments and conclusions

As was pointed out in our discussion of the work of Lessler, the fact that ego processes can account for the assignment of gender is not contrary to psycho-analytic theory. Thus this study, which shows that symbolic sorting can occur, does support Freudian theory. The claim of Jones and Lepson that Freud over-stressed symbolisation is not confirmed by this study since symbolisation is a primary process. The influence of colour is probably, by association of strong and masculine, best regarded as pre-conscious. This investigation is further support for the Freudian theory of symbolism and demonstrates yet another determinant of the assignment of gender – colour association.

The work of Worthy and Craddick (1969)

Worthy and Craddick investigated the gender of Freudian sexual symbols using the semantic differential.

Sample. 36 male and 36 female undergraduates.

Symbols. Typical Freudian symbolic words, e.g. umbrella and oven.

Measure. Subjects had to rate these for masculinity and femininity using the semantic differential.

Results. Some symbols were rated in accord with psychoanalytic theory but others were not.

Comments and conclusions

This study is difficult to interpret in that the precise significance of rating on the semantic differential is not known. Since this involves rating objects on a seven-point scale for masculinity or femininity, in effect it is little different from assigning gender to words. However two points are worthy of note. First, rating on a seven-point scale involves considerable thought compared with the forced choice decision about gender. As Cameron (1967) points out (see p. 219), this conscious ratiocination is liable to bring defensive processes into play. Hence the equivocal results. Again, as will be discussed below, there was no control in this study for the cultural components of the attribution of gender to words – a failing which could account for these findings (see Lessler, 1964). The conclusion must be, therefore, that the failure of this study to give complete support to the Freudian theory may be due to methodological problems.

COMMENTS ON ALL THESE STUDIES

Since the methodology and rationale of all the studies of symbolism reviewed has been similar there are a number of points of discussion common to all of them. These will now be considered.

1. To what extent were the symbols in these investigations an accurate reflection of psychoanalytic theory ?

Freudian dream theory, as may be seen from the outline of the theory at the beginning of this chapter, is absolutely explicit as regards symbolism: lists of symbols and what they represent are given as well as general principles such as pointed things representing the male genitalia. Not surprisingly, therefore, examination of the symbols in these investigations shows that most of them cannot be impugned on that account. The Krout (1950) Symbol Elaboration Test seems to deviate fairly strongly from classical Freudian theory (although not unwittingly) as do the textual symbols of Glotter and Reece (1962). It can safely be assumed that in the majority of experiments the symbols are psychoanalytic.

2. Is it a fair prediction from the psychoanalytic theory of genital symbolism that subjects should be able (in some form or other) to assign gender to the symbols ?

As Hall (1953) has made explicit in psychoanalytic theory, there are really two distinct accounts of why symbolism occurs. In one of them symbols are regarded as disguises for the objects they represent. In this way ideas and principally wishes can find conscious expression (as in dreams according to the Freudian theory) because symbolically disguised they can avoid the censor – the super-ego.

In the other account symbols are regarded as visual means to express abstract ideas, e.g. chastity represented as a lily. On both these accounts there is therefore a link in the unconscious between the symbol and the object. If the objects claimed to be sexual symbols really are so then it does seem a fair prediction that subjects should be able to assign gender to them better than by chance. It therefore does not seem reasonable to attempt to argue that the type of experiment reviewed in this section of the book is not a fair test of the psychoanalytic theory. It is of interest to note that the procedure of Levy (1954), where the prediction was made that masculine names and masculine symbols would be better remembered than feminine names and the same symbols, appears to be a good test of this unconscious link, despite its failure to confirm the Freudian theory.

The more specific point of just how this assigning of gender should be carried out has already been discussed in respect of each of the studies individually. Suffice it to say here that it appears that the less rational the procedure is the more likely it is that the Freudian theory will be confirmed. In short it is argued that these experiments are a fair test of the psychoanalytic theory of symbolism.

CONCLUSIONS

Since it can be accepted that these experiments are a fair test of the theory what conclusions may be drawn from them? The main finding is satisfactorily clear.

1.   Among adults sexual symbolism occurs

All the studies with adult subjects have demonstrated genital symbolism. There have been no findings contrary to theory.

1a. Sexual symbolism does not seem to be different from normal among
     psychotics

This is an important area of research since in Freudian theory (Freud, 1924b) psychotics are characterised by the emergence of repressed material and primary processes into the conscious. Whereas earlier workers (Jacobs, 1954; Starer, 1955) had found differences, Moos and Mussen (1959) showed that it was due to a general mental dysfunction rather than a specific disability that psychotics were inferior. In any case if primary processes are nearer consciousness in psychotics it could be argued that psychotics should be superior at symbolism, itself a primary process.

1b. Sexual symbolism probably does occur in prepubescent children

The work of Cameron (1967) with large samples of children appears to show that even among young children sexual symbolism occurs. Nevertheless it must be stated that his findings are bound up with psychoanalytic psychosexual theory and if the predictions made from this are not acceptable the Cameron study shows only that sexual symbolism occurs with adults (conclusion 1 – which is not in doubt). Levy (1954) had failed to confirm Freudian theory with children and Accord (1962), in a study of the age variable, also found that prepubescent children failed to symbolise. Lessler (1962) found the opposite result, however, as did Jones (1961). This discrepancy was imputed to method: matching names – a rational procedure – was thought to invoke defences, while sorting into piles (Lessler) and preference (Cameron) was considered not to do so – hence the successful results. Thus owing to these disparate results, the problems of methodology and the fact that the work of Cameron (1967) is bound up in other parts of Freudian theory, conclusion 1b may be stated only tentatively.

2. Symbolism of death occurs

This conclusion is based on one study only – that of Meissner (1956) which concerned only a small sample of students. The fact that GSRs to death symbols were larger than to neutral words is at least evidence that they provoked anxiety. Clearly conclusion 2 must remain tentative until further work is carried out.

FURTHER POINTS

It is to be noted that these studies of symbolism deal mainly with one aspect of it (albeit a very important one) – sexual symbolism. One further study deals with death symbols. Thus other aspects of Freudian symbolism remain unproven. It can be argued however, that since the whole of the theory was derived from the same original data – the dreams of patients undergoing analysis – the fact that one part of it has been substantially validated makes it unlikely that the other parts would not be correct. Nevertheless it is clear much work remains to be done.

Thus the first part of the study of symbolism, based on material not collected from dreams, has supported Freudian theory. It is now necessary to consider work based on the study of dreams. In this section symbolism will not be studied on its own but rather as one part of the phenomenology of dreams.

SUMMARY OF SECTION I

In Section 1 some objective studies of the psychoanalytic theory of symbolism have been reviewed. In this section only investigations not directly concerned with dreams were examined. The basic methodology of most of the researches was to get subjects to assign gender to Freudian symbols for male and female genitalia. Although there were certain problems inherent in this method, notably that the more rational the procedure the more ego defences seemed to be involved, it was considered that such experiments constituted a good test of the Freudian theory. The basic conclusion to emerge from these studies was that among adults Freudian sexual symbolism does in fact occur and that it probably does so among children as well. It was noted that only one study attempted to examine symbolism other than sexual – death symbolism. There can be no doubt that these studies strongly support the Freudian theory of sexual symbolism.

Summary of conclusions from Section 1

Hypothesis	Support	Investigation
Sexual symbolism in adults	Strong	Hammer (1953)
		McElroy (1954)
		Jahoda (1956)
		Jacobs (1954)
		Starer (1955)
		Jones (1956)
		Winter and Prescott (1957)
		Stennett and Thurlow (1958)
		Accord (1962)
		Lessler (1962)
		Moos and Mussen (1959)
		Cameron (1967)
Sexual symbolism not different in psychotics	Strong	Moos and Mussen (1959)
Sexual symbolism in children	Strong	Lessler (1962, 1964)
		Cameron (1967)
Death symbolism in adults	Fair	Meissner (1958)

SECTION 2 – REMs AND EEG

To help the reader unacquainted with the concept of rapid eye movement (REM) sleep, a brief description of the main findings from the electro encephalograph (EEG) study of sleep now follows. Two approaches have been used in the empirical study of dream content (apart from psychoanalytic free association):

1. Subjects on awakening in the morning are required to fill in report forms about their dreams.
2. Subjects are awoken during REM sleep and dream reports are then obtained.

EEG STUDIES OF SLEEP AND DREAMING

A full and detailed discussion would be out of place both because much of it would not be relevant to psychoanalytic theory and because, since Aserinsky and Kleitman (1955) first linked rapid eye movements with dreaming, there has been such an outpouring of research in this area.

Stages of sleep

1. As a subject falls asleep the EEG record shows increasing desynchrony with occasional waves of less than 8 cycles per sec. There are low-amplitude high-frequency waves and fast frequencies.

1-REM. This shows the same characteristic EEG pattern as above but is accompanied by *rapid eye movements* and *loss of muscle tone*. Aserinsky and Kleitman (1955) also found associated with these REM periods increased heart rate and changes in the pattern of breathing. Snyder (1963) claims that the truly distinctive feature of REM periods are the 'saw-tooth' shaped waves overlapping the rapid eye movements. Although there can be no doubt that dreaming occurs during REM periods as was pointed out by Aserinsky and Kleitman, as a result of later research, there is also no doubt that mentation, though of a less bizarre and dream-like character, does occur at other stages of sleep; see, for example, the study by Foulkes (1964).

2. Stage 2 is characterised by 'sleep spindles' – pointed waves of 14-16 cycles per sec. which occur against a background of low-voltage activity, in frequent bursts.

3. In this are found high-amplitude waves of 1-2 cycles per sec. together with the sleep spindles of stage 2.

4. This stage is typified by large-amplitude waves of 1-3 cycles per sec.

Stages 1 to 4 excluding REM sleep may be regarded as on a depth continuum. Characteristically, changes from stage to stage are in sequential order when moving towards stage 4 (although REM periods usually emerge from stage 2 sleep) but are abrupt when returning from stage 4. Stages are usually less than 15 minutes in length except for REM sleep. Usually most of stage 4 sleep occurs in the early part of the night whereas much of the REM sleep occurs late (Webb, 1968).

Thus EEG studies have shown the cyclic nature of the sleep process and the fact that dreaming is largely associated with one particular stage of sleep, the REM stage, although mentation occurs at other stages.

It is hoped that this brief and inevitably simplified summary will give the reader sufficient background to appreciate the implications of the EEG studies of dreaming that are to be reviewed later in the chapter.

DISADVANTAGES OF METHOD I (RECORDING DREAMS IN THE MORNING)

A disadvantage of the first method is simply one of memory: it is sometimes impossible to remember the content of any dream in the morning even though one can remember dreaming. Furthermore, since in normal sleep there are several REM periods, the common occurrence of believing one has had no dreams is unlikely to be true. It is more likely that they have been completely forgotten. Again the fact that there are several REM periods each night implies the strong possibility of several dreams each night so that any dream report recorded in the morning is likely to be either a composite of these dreams or the recall of only one REM period. In addition to all these problems, one of the actual Freudian mechanisms it would be hoped to investigate with such studies could well effect reports – secondary elaboration (see p. 205). A final disadvantage of this method lies in human weakness. The possibility must be faced that subjects will not bother to complete their dream reports or will fill them in much later than they should, possibly even inventing data.

ADVANTAGES OF METHOD 1

It is possible to build up very large samples of dreams both from special groups and the general population. There are two strategies: large numbers of dreams may be obtained from the same individuals or one dream may be recorded from each of a very large sample.

DISADVANTAGES OF METHOD 2 (EEG STUDIES)

For this method an EEG laboratory with sleeping facilities for subjects is necessary. The whole procedure of recording EEGs for eight-hour periods is extremely costly and laborious. The amount of paper on which the EEG is recorded over an eight-hour period is huge. There are therefore storage and marking problems. These difficulties and the fact that each EEG machine can only deal with a small number of subjects, if there is to be simultaneous recording, means that only very small samples may be used. Few studies use more than 20 subjects. There are other obvious administrative difficulties in this second method. There must be comfortable sleeping facilities for the subjects. Many subjects are, of course, unwilling to spend their nights in the sleeping laboratory and it is arguable that volunteers for this procedure do not constitute a normal sample. Equally it is not easy for psychologists, especially those employed as university teachers, to spend their nights in sleep research and their days in normal work. Nor do night hours appeal to those engaged purely on research. Webb (1968) contains an eloquent account of the personal difficulties of those engaged on sleep research.

ADVANTAGES OF METHOD 2

Dream reports elicited during an REM period are usually fuller and more dream-like (in Freudian terms less affected by secondary elaboration) than those obtained after a full night's sleep. In addition it is possible to obtain dream reports from all the REM periods. It is also possible to study experimentally the effects of external stimuli on dream content as in, for example, the work of Berger (1963). In addition, it is possible to induce dream deprivation by wakening subjects immediately an REM period begins – a method in some ways superior to the use of drugs where results are inevitably confused by possible side-effects of the drug itself.

In the next section the results of dream studies relevant to Freudian theory will be examined. First those investigations in which the first method was used will be discussed. Since Hall at the Institute of Dream Research has launched a truly massive attack on the phenomenology of dreams, in which more than

10,000 dreams have been subjected to detailed content analysis, it is fitting to deal with his work first.

THE WORK OF HALL (FROM 1953)

The most extensive investigations into the phenomenology of dreams have undoubtedly been carried out by Hall and his associates, now at the Institute of Dream Research. Their basic technique is to have subjects recall their dreams on specially prepared dream report forms as soon as possible on waking. This has enabled them to analyse for manifest content more than 10,000 dreams from a very large number of subjects. Hall (1953 and 1966), in the *Meaning of Dreams*, has presented his main conclusions in an entertaining and easily readable form. Unfortunately, however, he does not refer in detail to any of the original data so that for the purposes of this chapter it is necessary to examine some of the individual research papers of which the book was a summary.

Before any of these studies is reviewed in detail a number of points needs to be made clear. First, Hall studies only the manifest content of the dream, i.e. the reported dream material. He does not seek to uncover the latent content. Nevertheless he does attempt to 'understand' the dream, for to Hall the dream is a key to understanding the dreamer's conflicts. For example, in 1966 he writes 'This, above all, is what dreams are, an authentic record of a mind made anxious by conflict.' For Hall the interpretation of dreams is largely carried out by examining not one of a subject's dreams but a whole series. He writes 'From a single dream we may learn a few things about the dreamer but not until we have studied a number of his dreams are we able to paint a valid picture of his essential character.' Essentially the understanding of a dream is based on a hunch and if the intuitions resulting from interpretation of each of a series of dreams are internally consistent and sensible, then the dreams are considered to be correctly understood.

For the purpose of this book, what is interesting about the work of Hall is not so much the interpretation (for which there is little objective validity) but the fact that he has collected so many dreams from a large normal sample and that he has, in some cases, specifically tested hypotheses directly derived from Freudian theory. The normality of his sample means that the results may be more widely generalised without injury to scientific rigour than may, for example, the observations of analysts about their patients. The immense number of dreams collected means that statistical tests may be employed to elucidate any differences in dream-content observed between groups, and thus to test hypotheses.

Results from studies of Freudian hypotheses

A. *The dream of being attacked – Hall (1955)*

Hall (1955) investigated the significance of the dream of being attacked. In two previous studies Harris (1948, 1951) had attempted to test the Freudian hypothesis that dreams of being attacked represented a fear of castration by the father and that the dream of falling was a fear of losing maternal love. This was done with a small number of subjects by hypothesising that those who had the first dream would find difficulty in expressing aggression to their fathers whereas those who had the second would have difficulty in expressing aggression towards their mothers. Harris, in fact, despite the size of his sample, found support for these hypotheses and thus, indirectly, the Freudian hypothesis. Hall (1955) put these hypotheses to a more stringent test.

517 subjects were asked whether they had ever had either of the two dreams (being attacked and falling), which was the more unpleasant, and with which parent they found it easier to argue. The first results were contrary to Freudian theory in that females who had only one kind of dream were more likely to dream of being attacked, while males with only one dream were more likely to dream of falling. Yet castration fear is characteristically male, a fear of loss of love, female (Freud, 1933).

Again contrary to the Freudian hypothesis was the fact that females found the dream of being attacked significantly more unpleasant than the dream of falling while for males there was no significant difference. Furthermore, and again contrary to the psychoanalytic hypothesis, for both sexes the mother was more easy to argue with than the father. The hypothesis that those who can argue more easily with the father will be dreamers of falling (predominantly) was supported at the ·05 level for males but not for females. Though significant the difference was not large. To sum up, these results do not support the claim that the dream of being attacked symbolises fear of castration.

Hall then made a content analysis of 106 dreams of being attacked. Typically, the dreamer responds in a passive way to an unprovoked attack by a male or a group of men. From this Hall concludes that the dream of being attacked is equivalent to *being castrated*, not fear of castration – hence the feeling, in the content analysis, of being weak and impotent. This hypothesis fits the data far better since for women castration has already taken place (Freud, 1926) – hence women would dream this more. Indeed Hall develops the theme that the dream of being attacked symbolises *being castrated* (the attack itself) and femininity, the passivity of the dreamer. Femininity is characterised in Freudian theory by

(a) passive aims (Freud, 1931)
(b) a sense of inferiority (Freud, 1926)
(c) masochism (Freud, 1931).

All these points are typified in the inability of the dreamer to fight back his attackers. Thus a content analysis of dreams of being attacked supports the claim that for both sexes it embodies the psychoanalytic concept of femininity and that the attack itself represents being castrated rather than fear of castration.

Conclusions. This study by Hall (1955) is a good example of how predictions of dream content may be made from Freudian theory using both dream theory and other parts of psychoanalysis, in this case the theory of femininity. The findings support the theory. However it must be pointed out that, in this case at least, the links between femininity and the dream content are not obvious but a tribute rather to the skill of Hall in seeing relationships and educing correlates. Hall has shown the results can be seen as congruent with theory. They do not disprove it but they are not sufficient to support it with any degree of confidence.

B. 1. *Evidence relevant to the Oedipus complex*

Hall and Domhoff (1963) pooled the results of 11 investigations and reported a ubiquitous sex difference in the dreams of 1,399 men and 1,418 women. 64% of the characters in the dream narratives of the men (3,874 in number) were male, whereas in the dream narratives of the women (3,065 in number) only 52% were male. Similar findings have been made for the Hopi of the southwest United States and for the Yiv Yoront of Australia.

As a supplement to this study, a small sample of students was asked to write the initials of persons they liked and disliked (one minute). For males the percentage of male names was far greater than for females. In addition it was noted that in short stories by men 75% of the characters were male – a figure which fell to only 54% in stories by women.

Similarly, Hall and Domhoff (1962a, b) found that aggression in the dreams of men was more directed against males than females, whereas in the dreams of women aggression was directed equally against both sexes. The reverse (Hall and Domhoff, 1962b) was true of friendly acts. Here in the dreams of men they were directed significantly more towards females than males. In the case of the dreams of women, there was again an even split.

As with the previous study it is difficult to draw precise conclusions from these findings. The fact that male aggression is directed towards males and friendliness towards females could be regarded as evidence for the Oedipus complex, characterised by jealousy and hatred of the father by the son. Hall and Domhoff interpret the ubiquitous sex difference of more males in male dreams as support for the Oedipus complex because they follow Hall's theory (1966) that dreams reveal conflict. But there is some circularity here – men dream more of males – males have conflict with their fathers through the Oedipus complex – dreams show conflicts. Thus it would not be fair to invoke this sex difference as support for the Oedipus complex.

Conclusions. The finding that male dreams are characterised by aggression against males does appear to confirm Oedipal theory, although this is only manifest content. The ubiquitous sex difference confirms Oedipal theory only if dreams are regarded as evidence of conflict (Hall, 1966), a theory which needs further verification. These studies therefore provide only modest support for Freudian theory.

B. 2. *Further evidence relevant to the Oedipus complex – Hall (1963)*

Hall (1963) made a further study relevant to the Oedipus complex in an investigation of the incidence of male strangers in dreams. The psychoanalytic hypotheses underlying the paper are clearly stated and are embodied in the central part of psychoanalytic theory:

(a) that in girls the fantasy of a 'good' mother and a 'bad' father is not altogether obliterated by the castration complex (for the Freudian theory, see p. 96)

(b) for the boy, father is 'bad' – the Oedipus complex.

Thus the early concept of father, in psychoanalytic terms, is of a feared stranger. Therefore, if dreams reflect early conflicts (Hall, 1966) he will be represented in the dream by a male stranger unknown to the dreamer.

From these psychoanalytic hypotheses five empirical hypotheses were drawn. There will be:

1. More male strangers in dreams than female.
2. More male strangers in male dreams than in female dreams.
3. More aggressive encounters with male strangers than female strangers.
4. Higher proportion of such encounters in male than female dreams.
5. To male strangers in dreams more free associations of fathers and authority figures.

It is to be noticed that this investigation is a model of how from general psychoanalytic theory (Oedipus and castration complex) testable hypotheses concerning dream content may be drawn. The only other assumption made is that dreams are concerned with early conflict – a theory which is not contrary, though not specific, to psychoanalytic theory.

Samples. Various samples were used. There were two samples of children. One 2-12 years of age, the other 13-18 years. Three samples of young adults and one of mature people, 30-80 years old, were also included. From most samples one dream per subject was examined, and sample sizes were all greater than 200, many more than 400, evenly split by sex. One sample consisting of 27 men from whom 492 dreams were analysed and 28 women who supplied 525 dreams was also included.

Results. In most of these groups the first four hypotheses were confirmed at beyond the ·05 level. Hypothesis 3 was significant in only 15 of the 36 comparisons but, since the numbers of aggressions were small and the direction of difference was always correct, Hall is satisfied that the hypothesis was confirmed.

Hypothesis 4 was confirmed clearly only in group six with the largest number of dream reports where the difference was highly significant – beyond the ·001 level. As regards the last hypothesis concerning free association, Hall cites Rees (1959) who collected free associations to 10 dreams of 12 male and 12 female students. While the numbers were too small to reach significance, more father and authority-free associations than any other were in fact given to male strangers.

From these findings Hall concludes that four hypotheses were confirmed – the first four – while hypothesis 5 received marginal confirmation. He argues that it is irrelevant to ask whether any other theory could have predicted these results – the fact is that psychoanalytic theory *did* predict them. The eduction of *ad hoc* theories is usually unsatisfactory. If all studies of psychoanalytic hypotheses were considered together, the collection of *ad hoc* hypotheses would not be parsimonious either. Thus, while for any one experiment the psychoanalytic hypothesis may defy the law of Occam's razor, for a number of experiments this would not necessarily be the case since their explication might well involve an equal number of *ad hoc* hypotheses.

Comments and conclusions. This study, as has been mentioned, is a good example of how clear, testable hypotheses may be derived from psychoanalytic theory. The fact that they were largely confirmed is not only support for Oedipal theory but for Freudian dream theory. If these results are accepted it would be impossible to argue, for example, that the mental content while dreaming is the result of random firing or stimulation of the brain during the REM period while protein is being synthesised (Oswald, 1969). On the contrary, the dream content appears to conform to a meaningful pattern. As suggested in the outline of Freudian dream theory, the dream allows normally repressed impulses expression (in this case Oedipal aggression towards the father). In this instance the Hall theory that old childhood conflicts are re-enacted in dreams is not far different from the orthodox psychoanalytic claim that the dream allows expression of a repressed wish. These findings, therefore, must be regarded as good evidence for psychoanalytic dream theory and as evidence for the Oedipus complex.

C. *Further evidence relevant to the castration complex*

Hall and Van de Castle (1963) made a further investigation (see Hall, 1955, p. 229) of the evidence from dreams for the castration complex. The hypothesis derived from the psychoanalytic theory of the Oedipus complex and castration complex (see p. 113 et seq.) was that male dreamers would report more dreams expressive of castration anxiety than of castration wishes or penis envy: for females the pattern would be reversed. This hypothesis is easily deduced from the Freudian theory and would appear from that point of view to be quite unexceptional.

Sample. 120 college students in three groups of 40 (20 male and 20 female). A total of 953 dreams was analysed.

Measures. Clearly the validity of the measures used for castration anxiety, castration wish and penis envy is crucial to evaluating this study. The dream reports were searched for evidence of any of these three states. Examination of the criteria used shows them to be well in accord with psychoanalytic dream theory (dream work). Examples of the criteria are given below.

(a) Castration anxiety
1. Actual or threatened loss, removal or injury to a specific part of the dreamer's body. Similarly threatened, or actual, stabbing or cutting.
2. Any defect of a part of dreamer's body.
3. Loss or injury or defect of any animal or object belonging to dreamer.

4. Inability of dreamer to use penis or symbol of penis.
5. Male dreamer is female in any way, e.g. clothes.

(b) *Castration wish.* As above but to another person *not* dreamer.

(c) *Criteria for penis envy*

1. Acquisition by dreamer of penis or phallic symbol.
2. Dreamer envies or admires a man's physical characteristic or performance.
3. Female dreamer becomes male in some way.

It will be noticed that most of these criteria embody phallic symbolism.

Inter-marker reliability of scoring. 87-96%. This is a satisfactory figure.

Results. X^2 was used to test the hypothesis which was supported beyond the ·001 level ($X^2 = 24$). 50% of females had no castration anxiety score, for example, compared with only 8% of males in this position.

Two further small studies were carried out which should be mentioned.

Freud (1917) argued that the penis wish implicit in penis envy becomes a wish for a baby, then a wish for a man. Hall, therefore, put the hypothesis derived from this – that girls have more dreams of babies and getting married than do men – to the test. Although it was strongly confirmed, in this case, as Hall points out, other alternative hypotheses are possible. Finally a further study showed that the incidence of castration anxiety, castration wishes and penis envy in the dreams of older men was very similar to that among college students.

Comments and conclusions. The major finding of this study strongly supports Freudian theory and the existence of male castration anxiety. As in the previous investigation (1963), Hall is careful to point out that it is possible to produce *ad hoc* theories to account for these results. Nevertheless what more can be expected of a theory than that it predict correctly? For example, he points out that injury can be expected to be a more frequent part of male dreams in that in their everyday life and even hobbies men undertake more dangerous things than women. In short, it must be accepted that these findings support Freudian theory – both dream theory and developmental hypotheses. It is also to be noted that these results are sound evidence for symbolism.

D. *Evidence relevant to the development of the super-ego*

The psychoanalytic theory of the development of the super-ego in men and women (see p. 96), strongly implies that women develop a less severe and less well internalised super-ego (e.g. Freud, 1931). From this Hall (1964) derived the hypothesis that more women would be the victims of aggression in dreams than men (their super-ego being external) whereas men would more often suffer a misfortune. This he tested by examining, as usual, the dream reports of men and women.

Sample. Around 1,500 male dreams and 1,500 female dreams were subjected to content analysis.

Results. The hypothesis was supported at the ·01 level.

Conclusions. As Hall indicates in the title to this paper, these results may be regarded as *modest* confirmation of the differential development of the super-ego in men and women. Confirmation is justified in that the prediction was supported but it is not powerful enough to support the whole theory. This finding is but one tile in the mosaic of construct validation.

Conclusions from Hall's empirical studies

Taken together these studies illustrate the problems of testing Freudian theory. Thus Hall's 1955 investigation of the dream of being attacked involves Freudian attributes of femininity and attempts to show that these are present in the manifest content of the dreams. This is only a subjective judgement, however, and although ingenious cannot be regarded as strong or objective evidence in favour of the theory. The 1963 study of the Oedipus complex, on the other hand, derives precise testable hypotheses from Oedipal theory concerning the objective content of dreams – e.g. either strangers are in the dream or they are not. Thus confirmation of this hypothesis must be considered as good evidence both for developmental and dream theory in psychoanalysis.

On the criteria, therefore, of clearly defined hypotheses capable of clear and objective measurement two of these studies may be regarded as supporting Freudian theory:

1. Hall (1963). Strangers in dreams: an empirical confirmation of the Oedipus complex.
2. Hall and Van de Castle (1963). An empirical demonstration of the castration complex in dreams.

The other dream studies reported in the previous section cannot be held to be strong support for the theory. Either the hypotheses are too tenuous or the subjective element in measurement too great to stand close scrutiny. Nevertheless, the fact that the results, as they stand, do support the theory cannot be ignored. These studies may be regarded as slender support – useful in the total consideration of all the evidence but unsatisfactory on their own.

Relevance to dream theory of Hall's studies

The fact that Freudian phenomena such as the Oedipus complex can be observed in the content of dreams indicates that there is psychological meaning in them, that they are not the results of random firing in certain areas of the brain. Since in psychoanalytic dream theory, wishes normally repressed find expression in dreams together with other repressed material, the occurrence of Oedipal aggression and penis envy would be expected. Thus these studies by Hall support the Freudian claim that the dream is the 'royal road to the unconscious'. In addition, they support the concepts of the Oedipus and castration complexes. Further study of these investigations may be found in the chapter on these complexes (pp. 112-14).

THE WORK OF LEE (1958)

Lee studied the dreams of 600 Zulu subjects (120 of these in great detail) and provided some powerful evidence in favour of Freudian dream theory. An interesting point about this cross-cultural study is the fact that it is not possible to argue that these subjects were influenced in reporting or remembering their dreams by Freudian or Jungian dream theory! – a common jibe at psychoanalytic clinical case studies. If influenced at all in this way it would be by the Zulu dream diviners who interpret dreams which in their culture are regarded as of great importance (Gallaway, 1868, quoted by Lee, 1958).

Subjects. 600 rural Zulus. Of these 120 female subjects were subjected to further interview.

Method. The 600 subjects were asked how much they dreamed and the content of their dreaming. In the more intensive interviews of the sub-sample, the women were asked to describe in detail two dreams. Other information was also obtained from these subjects. Thus manifest content, in Freudian terms, was the subject of the study.

Results

Many dreams had an apparent lack of latent content – i.e. the manifest content of the dream appeared to express the wish.

Lee shows that Freudian dream theory can accommodate such a finding. Thus Freud (1935) in 'An autobiographical study' argues that young children often have such undistorted dreams because repressions are not yet fully developed. Adults too can have such infantile dreams if the need is imperative. Thus a crucial test of Lee's interpretation of these Zulu dreams is to establish to what extent the dream wishes did in fact reflect imperative needs.

To test the relationship between dream material and imperative needs, the dream content was related to the obstetric history of the subjects (more than 400 women).

(*a*) Dreamers of 'a baby' had much the worst record of married infertility. Those who had borne children had lost more than half of them and these were the youngest group (if the eldest, the deaths of their children would not have been so surprising).

Lee shows that in Zulu society there is a powerful psychological need for a baby. Failure to produce one brings contempt. Eysenck (1954) has tried to argue that the Freudian claim that dreams represent wishes is disproved by the fact that hungry people do not produce hunger dreams. However, as Lee neatly argues, this evidence tests the hypothesis that dreams reflect all wishes, which is *not* the Freudian theory. This study by Lee shows that in the case of these young Zulu girls, dreams of a baby do indeed reflect an imperative need. This finding must be regarded, therefore, as support for the Freudian claim that dreams represent wishes.

b) Sufferers from pseudocyesis (false pregnancy), which was common in the area, also tended to have the direct baby dream which again supports the Freudian notion.

(c) Nine of the 21 subjects who had 'baby' dreams said a baby was their main wish, and four said children were their main desire. Of the 97 others only 18 gave either baby or children as their wish. This difference is significant at the 1% level. Thus further support for Freudian theory comes from this finding.

(d) Lee presents further data linking dreams of still water and flooding to conflicting desires for more children (a cultural norm) among those who already have sufficient of their own. Since this interpretation is largely speculative it will not be examined in further detail. Nor indeed will his other findings relating dreams of snakes and toholoske (a kind of Priapic river god) since they suffer to some extent from the same fault as orthodox psychoanalytic dream interpretations, being speculative and essentially untestable.

Comments and conclusions

This study by Lee is powerful evidence that in a sample of Zulu women certain common dreams do reflect wishes, in accordance with psychoanalytic theory. It also supports the Freudian claim that certain imperative needs may be directly expressed in the manifest content of the dream. In this sample there can be little fear that the results were biased by the subjects' knowledge of Freudian theory.

THE PHYSIOLOGY OF DREAMING

Snyder (1963, 1965) has claimed that dreaming, in man, is the subjective concomitant of a pervasive and distinctive physiological state. This state, most obviously typified by rapid eye movements is, according to Snyder, as qualitatively different from sleep as is waking from sleep. There are, therefore, three biological states in man, and indeed mammals. Dement (1963) makes this point with complete clarity.

(a) *Awakeness*. This enables the organism to act on the environment.
(b) *Sleep* (slow wave sleep stages 2, 3, 4). This very probably enables the organism to recuperate.
(c) *REM*. Function not truly known.

CHARACTERISTICS OF THIS THIRD STATE – REMS

Since our interest in REMs stems from the fact that dreaming in its most typical, bizarre form occurs in them, a brief description of the major physiological characteristics of REMs must suffice. Snyder (1965) has an excellent summary. *The eyes* are in intermittent frantic activity, first related to dreaming by Aserinsky and Kleitman (1955). *Breathing* is shallow, rapid and irregular. In the face and hands there are twitch-like, muscular movements. This twitching occurs in animals also (e.g. in the opossum) as a constant twitching of ears, snout muscles and digits. Pet lovers have all observed similar things in their dogs and cats. The pulse tends to increase in man (Aserinsky and Kleitman, 1955) as does systolic blood pressure (Snyder *et al.*, 1963). In man there is an EEG pattern of 2-3 per sec 'saw-toothed' shaped waves preceding or overlapping the clusters of eye-movements. This EEG pattern is never seen outside REMs. Furthermore, there is almost complete loss of muscle-tone – i.e. the organism is paralysed. In men 85% of these REMs are accompanied by penile erection (Fisher, 1965, Karacan *et al.*, 1966).

OCCURRENCE OF REMS IN ANIMALS AND MAN

In organisms lower in the phylogenetic scale than mammals it is unlikely that REMs occur. Klein (1963) found no REMs in the tortoise (reptile) although a very brief period has been seen in a bird. Among mammals, however, REMs have been found: cats, dogs, rabbits, rats, sheep, monkeys and chimpanzees (Klein, 1963). Even the marsupial opossum (Snyder, 1964), low in the mammalian scale, has REMs. Based on an examination of many investigations, Fisher (1965) shows that in man there is a decided age trend in the amount of REM sleep per night. Thus a premature (30-week) infant spent 80% of its sleep time in REM sleep. Between 33-5 weeks this fell to 67%. The neonate typically spends 50% of its sleep in REM sleep, a figure which drops to 35% at one year, 30% at 3 years to 20% at 5 years. This 20% appears reasonably constant until late in life. At 50-70 years the figure falls again to 13-18% and one 100-year-old man spent only 13% of his sleep time in REM sleep.

These figures and the fact that mammals undergo REM sleep are of great importance in appreciating the significance of REM sleep for the psychoanalytic theory of dreaming. This will be discussed later (see pp. 254-9).

PHYSIOLOGICAL MECHANISMS INVOLVED IN REMS

Jouvet has carried out much research on the physiology of sleep and REMs. He claims (1967) that the overall results of his experiments

> reveal that the structures *sufficient* for the periodical appearance of the major behavioural and EEG signs of PS (paradoxical sleep – the term favoured by Jouvet but to be equated with REMs) are located at the level of the pons. Another series of experiments shows that some pontine structures are equally necessary. . . .

Dement *et al.* (1967) and Jouvet (1967) both argue from the complex mass of evidence that in some way during REMs a neurochemical substance, a monoamine, is being metabolised. This chemical, which piles up during REM deprivation, is thought to underlie the effects of such deprivation. Some evidence for this comes from the fact that cerebro-spinal fluid from a cat deprived of REM sleep, when injected into a normal cat, produces an increase in REM sleep (Dement *et al.*, 1967).

RELATION OF REMS TO DREAMING

From the viewpoint of psychoanalytic dream theory, the importance of the discovery by Aserinsky and Kleitman (1955) that REMs were associated with dreaming cannot be too strongly emphasised: for the first time it enabled some kind of objectivity to be brought into the study of dreaming since it indicated when a subject was, or was not, dreaming.

Dement and Kleitman (1957)

Dement and Kleitman made a rigorous examination of this relationship. Seven male subjects and two females participated in the study. Three approaches were used:

1. Dream recall from REM and NREM periods was elicited without direct contact between the experimenter and subject.
2. A subjective estimate of the length of the dream was correlated with the length of the REM period before awakening, and
3. The pattern of eye movements was related to dream content.

Results

As Dement and Kleitman had previously found, REMs and the characteristic EEG were associated in all subjects (see section on physiology of dreaming, p. 227). REMs had a mean duration of 20 minutes (range 3-50) and REMs late at night tended to be longer. For every individual there was a regular cycle of REMs, on average every 92 minutes.

The main findings in relation to the three problems examined in this paper were:

1a. Very high recall in REM awakenings, very little in NREM.

1b. This recall dropped precipitately on cessation of REMs.

2. Positive relationship between estimated length of dream and whether waking was after 5 or 15 minutes. Also a positive relationship between length of dream narrative and length of REM (·71 to ·40 with 5 subjects).

3. There was a relationship between eye movements and content of dream reports. Examples will best make this clear. Subjects were woken after one minute of continuous eye-movement in either the vertical or the horizontal plane. Alternatively they were woken after one minute's fixation. In fact there was only one period of horizontal movement observed. In the dream report immediately elicited people had been throwing tomatoes at each other. In two cases there was a period of inactivity followed by large movements and in each of these the subject was driving a car. On the basis of these results Dement and Kleitman (1957) concluded that REMs were so closely related to dreaming that it was possible to use them as objective measures of dreaming.

There can be little doubt that this experiment is solid evidence for the relationship between REMs and dreaming and there is little point, therefore, in examining earlier or merely confirmatory experiments. Nevertheless further studies have shown these findings to be somewhat over-simplified and the more recent elaborations will now be considered, although it must be stressed at this point that these further studies are elaborations and that the broad findings have been confirmed.

Dement and Wolpert (1958)

Dement and Wolpert investigated the relationship of eye-movements, bodily motility and external stimuli to the content of dreams using as raw data 204 dream reports from 14 men and 2 women.

Results

Chi-square analyses showed that there was little bodily movement associated with continuous dreaming whereas for fragmented dreams there was much movement. The amount of eye movement was related to the activity or passivity of the dream and, as was reported by Dement and Kleitman (1957), the direction of eye movement, whether it was horizontal or vertical, was related to the dream content. Finally it was found that some stimuli were incorporated into dreams: a water spray 42% of the time, a tone only 9% of the time and the arousing stimulus, a bell, not at all.

Conclusions

This study is further support for the fact that eye movements and muscular activity of the REMs are not random activations of the central nervous system but are, on the contrary, related to the processes of dreaming.

DREAM REPORTS FROM REM AND NREM PERIODS OF SLEEP

Work of Foulkes (1960, 1962)

Foulkes (1960) in his doctoral dissertation investigated the question of when dreams occur in three subjects over 25 nights. In this study he found that dreaming occurred outside REM periods but was of a qualitatively different kind: REM dreaming was mainly perceptual, NREM dreaming conceptual. Foulkes (1962) extended this study using 8 male subjects who were awoken at various stages of sleep over a period of 57 nights. They were asked to classify their dreams into 'thoughts' or 'dreams', the criterion for dreams being the presence of sensory imagery.

Results

There was recall in 74% of awakenings from NREMs and in 87% of awakenings from REMs. From NREMs there was 'thinking' rather than dreaming. Foulkes attempts to align his findings with those of Dement and Kleitman (1957), discussed above, by claiming that these writers had a more stringent criterion for dreaming than his. When he asked his subjects for dreams rather than reports of what was 'going through their minds' much less material was elicited.

Conclusions

Thus it appears that dreaming as normally defined – bizarre and hallucinatory mental events – does occur during REM periods but that, in addition, a more mundane kind of mentation also takes place during NREM periods.

A number of studies have investigated the relatedness of the mental activity occurring during sleep. Thus, for example, Dement and Wolpert (1958) examined the dreams from 8 subjects over 38 nights. On any night dreams were not duplicated and there was not a truly continuous series of dreams. Nevertheless, the manifest content of dreams on the same night was related and in 7 out of 38 sequences all dreams were united by a common theme. In fact, these authors likened the dreams to the different chapters of a book. This tendency for there to be some kind of relationship between dreams of the same night is generally confirmed by the other researches in this field (e.g. Trosman *et al.*, 1960; Offenkrantz and Rechtschaffen, 1963; Rechtschaffen, Verdone and Wheaton, 1963).

Rechtschaffen, Vogel and Shaikun (1963)

In the light of these findings concerning the relatedness of dream material during the same night and the work of Foulkes (1960 and 1962) concerning REM and NREM mentation, which has already been discussed, Rechtschaffen, Vogel and Shaikun (1963) made a further and most interesting investigation of this problem. They examined three questions:

(a) The relationship of NREM mentation of the same night (for the other studies had concentrated on REM dream reports), and
(b) the relation of REM and NREM material of the same night. Finally,
(c) they were interested in investigating the nature of any such relationships.

As is the case with almost all these EEG studies of dreaming, for reasons of objectivity the manifest content of dreams, not the latent content, was investigated.

Sample. There were two samples:

(a) 2 subjects for three nights were subjected to awakenings every 30 or 90 minutes. The time interval was chosen at random.
(b) 17 subjects from whom, in all, the dreams of 30 nights were investigated. Since the results from both these samples were similar the results will be discussed together.

Results

A. Identical or almost identical manifest elements are repeated in reports of NREM awakenings.
B. NREM and REM elements are also similar.

C. In each report the elements have different contents. There is no continuous narrative.

D. The manifest element appears in the first NREM report. Therefore the report cannot be a hangover from the first REM period – i.e. a memory of a previous dream.

Conclusions

There is an obvious problem in this study that the actual dream-reporting early on in the night could influence later dream reports. Nevertheless, as will be discussed more fully in the section on the implications of these studies for psychoanalytic dream theory, NREM mentation is not unlike the Freudian day-residues of dreaming which are secondary or pre-conscious processes, and REM mentation is precisely what would be considered a primary process. This relationship of common elements in REM and NREM mentation is again similar to the relation between day-residues and dreaming proper suggested by Freud in the 'Metaphysical supplement to the theory of dreams' (Freud, 1917).

It should be noted that in addition to the studies by Foulkes (1960, 1962) and Rechtschaffen, Vogel and Shaikun (1963) where NREM mentation was observed, other researches have confirmed this finding, notably Rechtschaffen, Verdone and Wheaton (1963), Foulkes and Rechtschaffen (1964) and Kamija (1961). Although the subjects in the second Rechtschaffen (1963) study were the same, in part, as those of the first (1963), there can be no doubt that mentation is not, as was first thought, restricted to REM periods.

Foulkes (1964) in an attempt to summarise the findings and implications of all these studies emphasises the resemblance already referred to between NREM mentation and day residues and REM dreams and secondary processes. REM dreams, he argues, are distortions of NREM dreams.

EYE MOVEMENT AND DREAM CONTENT

Of major importance in a study of the relation between REM periods and dreaming is clearly the relationship between eye movements and dream content. In the original investigations by Dement and Kleitman (1957) it was shown that vertical eye movements corresponded to reports of vertical activity in dreams, as did horizontal eye movements. This was confirmed by Dement and Wolpert (1958). Even more impressive evidence for the fact that REMs are associated with the hallucinatory imagery of dreaming was offered by Roffwarg et al. (1962). These authors elicited dream reports from REM periods of sleep. Where the dreamer felt that his recall was good an independent reader of the dream report was able to predict what the pattern of REMs would be. In one case eye movements compensated for an hallucinatory head movement – where a subject was climbing stairs holding a cat. If eye movements in dreams do in fact scan visual imagery, the question of REMs in the blind, especially the congenitally blind, is clearly relevant evidence.

REMS IN THE BLIND

Berger *et al.* (1962) carried out an investigation of just this point. They found no evidence of REMs in their sample of congenitally blind subjects. Amadeo and Gomez (1964) on the other hand, found exactly the opposite in a study of subjects with life-long blindness. Fisher (1965) accounts for this apparent contradiction in terms of method. He cites a study he carried out with Gross and Feldman (Fisher, Gross and Feldman, 1965) with subjects suffering from retrolental fibrophasia. These subjects showed no REMs when tested by the usual method. This is because in this disease the retina is destroyed and there is no corneo-retinal potential. By using a different method REM activity was observed.

Conclusions

The conclusion must be drawn, therefore, that REMs occur in the congenitally blind. This does not contradict the previous findings that REMs are scanning hallucinatory images, especially when the findings of infant REMs and mammalian REMs are taken into account. REMs are presumably, as Fisher (1965) argues, a phylogenetically ancient mechanism which has been taken over by the phylogenetically more recent visual dreaming.

DREAM DEPRIVATION AND THE NEED TO DREAM

If, as psychoanalytic dream theory claims, every dream expresses a wish which replaces some instinctual demand, unable in waking life to find expression but in dreaming able to evade the censoring super-ego, then dream deprivation should produce on waking what could be regarded as substitute symptoms. Demands unexpressed at night should therefore force themselves through in other ways.

When Dement and Kleitman (1957) apparently showed that dreaming was synchronous with REM sleep and did not occur at other stages of sleep, an obvious method of testing Freudian hypotheses by dream deprivation was suggested. Subjects could be selectively deprived of REM sleep alone: the effects of fatigue or simple sleep deprivation could be controlled by, at a later stage, selectively depriving subjects of NREM sleep and comparing the effects. Dement (1960, 1963), Dement *et al.* (1967), Berger and Oswald (1962) have carried out such procedures with human subjects while Jouvet (1960, 1965) has made extensive studies of REM sleep (rather than dream) deprivation in cats. Since the papers of Dement (1963) and Dement *et al.* (1967) are, in part, reviews of past work in the field, it is simplest to examine these rather than review in detail earlier work which later findings have contradicted.

Dement (1960), in a study where 20 subjects were deprived first of REM sleep and then of NREM sleep, noted that deprivation of REM sleep produced a tendency for REM sleep to appear more frequently. On the recovery night the amount of REM sleep was greater than the subject's normal amount. In addition, compared with controls moderate psychological disturbances were observed in those deprived of REM sleep – anxiety, irritability and difficulty in concentration.

Dement interpreted these results as a need to dream. Fisher and Dement (1963) attempted to fit these results into the psychoanalytic theory of dreaming. They argued REM sleep was concomitant with instinctual id drive discharge processes which would lead to hallucinatory dreams. Sufficient dream deprivation should therefore produce psychotic symptoms, delusions and hallucinations. However 13 nights' REM deprivation (in the case of one subject) did not produce any such symptoms. In fact he was becoming fatigued and could not be awakened for REM deprivation.

Dement (1963), in the review paper already referred to, argues that the simple interpretation of this early work as showing a *need to dream* cannot stand scrutiny

(a) because REM sleep has been shown to occur in sub-humans,
(b) because of the emergence of the concept of a third biologic state (Snyder, 1963 and 1965, see pp. 237-8) of which REMs are but one indication and
(c) because mentation has been shown to occur in NREM periods (see p. 241).

Thus any results can only be interpreted as due to *REM* not *dream* deprivation.

In addition Dement (1963) points to a methodological weakness in these studies, namely that small amounts of REM sleep could have occurred because subjects were woken when the characteristic EEG pattern and eye movements had begun. However in cats, at least, Jouvet and Mounier (1960) have shown that even a little paradoxical or REM sleep reduces their hyper-excitability (the main effects of REM deprivation in cats). However, Berger (1961) had noted that EMG* suppression took place a few seconds before REM activation and Dement (1963), using this EMG suppression (measured from neck muscles) as a signal for waking subjects to induce REM deprivation, quotes three case studies to illustrate its effects:

1. In one case 95% REM deprivation for 8 nights produced almost no effect except slight drowsiness.

2. In his second subject dexedrine was also used to reduce REMs chemically. This was necessary because of habituation to the arousing stimulus and the greater press for REM sleep on deprivation which means that long periods of deprivation become difficult to produce. After night 14 there was a sudden dramatic change in the personality of the subject. A taciturn, moral man became garrulous, expressed annoyance and anger and impulsively wanted to do things, such as go to a night club and cheat the waitress, that he otherwise would not contemplate.

3. Dexedrine was again used with this subject whose NREM sleep time was equal to or above normal – a fact which makes fatigue unlikely as a cause of these results. He endured 16 nights' REM deprivation. Again after the 14th night there was an abrupt change. He became paranoid and thought his friends were disparaging him.

On the recovery night in all cases REM sleep showed a great increase in frequency. Dement (1963) argues that it is unlikely that these changes in the last two subjects were due to the dexedrine, they must be imputed to REM depriva-

---

* EMG (electromyograph) is the measurement of electrical current in the musculature.

tion. Clearly, the slight changes noted in earlier experiments were due to the small amounts of REM deprivation – 14 days of 95% deprivation seems critical.

The conclusions to be drawn from this paper will be discussed after the work of Dement *et al.* (1967) has been examined. This paper reviews all the animal and human REM deprivation studies up to this date and provides an excellent summary of the work done. According to these authors the main results of REM deprivation in both animals and men are:

1. *REM increases in frequency:* as deprivation goes on more arousals become necessary and when left there is a long period of REM. This was found in the work of Dement (1960, 1963) which has already been discussed by Kales *et al.* (1964) and by Sampson (1965). This increase in REM time on recovery has also been found with animals. For example, Jouvet *et al.* (1964), in their study of cats, found that after 30 days or more deprivation the recovery curves remain the same. In addition the intensity of the REM state appears to increase (great increase in brain temperature and blood flow).

The next three findings are not important from the viewpoint of relevance to psychoanalytic theory, so they will simply be listed.

2. More rapid recovery of potential evoked by the second of a pair of clicks in the cat.

3. Drop in the seizure threshold, for rats.

4. Rise in heart rate for cats (with lesions in nucleus pontis caudalis).

5. In cats, up to as long as 70 days' deprivation produced no impairment of motor performance and no fatigue.

6. In cats, the eating drive was increased.

7. In cats, compulsive mounting of anaesthetised cats. In rats 80% of REM deprived animals (only 14% in control group) attempted to mount a female.

8. On 6 subjects, there were some changes on TAT scores, but deprivation was only six days and Dement's (1963) data implies that a longer period is needed to be effective.

9. In cats, seizures seemed to compensate for REM periods. For 9 human subjects similar results were observed although the data were less consistent. Furthermore an epileptic patient, who was also REM deprived for four nights, showed an increase in the number of seizure discharges in his EEG.

Dement *et al.* (1967) conclude from these results that REM deprivation leads to increased excitability in the organism. As was mentioned in the section on the physiology of REMs these authors link the findings to a neurochemical theory involving the build up of monoamines in the organism when REM deprived. It is noteworthy that the concept of hyper-excitability hypothesised to account for the findings is insufficient to explicate the two case studies quoted by Dement (1963).

Conclusions from REM deprivation studies

The fact that REM is but an indicant of a biological state means that REM deprivation studies deprive organisms of being in that state. This means that

REM deprivation studies are *more* than just dream deprivation studies. The fact that organisms low (relatively) in the phylogenetic scale, such as the opossum, have REM states almost certainly implies that their function is more than that of dreaming but is originally at any rate biological. This, coupled with the finding that there is a relationship between REM deprivation in man and epileptic seizure, also means that even for man there is a basic physiological necessity for undergoing REM periods. Since, too, it has been shown that mentation does occur outside REM periods in other stages of sleep REM deprivation must not be equated with dream deprivation. Thus it must be argued that REM deprivation studies are not adequate tests of psychoanalytic theories of dreaming. This is disappointing in view of the interesting and suggestive data obtained by Dement (1963) with his prolonged deprivation studies of human subjects.

However, this irrelevance to Freudian theory certainly only applies to the REM *deprivation* studies. There is no doubt that study of dream reports elicited during REM periods, when clearly the most striking dreaming takes place, is relevant and this will be discussed in a subsequent section. What is stressed now is that neither the positive nor the negative (e.g. Kales *et al.*, 1964) results of REM deprivation studies are in fact relevant to Freudian dream theory.

PENILE ERECTION DURING REM PERIODS

If Freudian dream theory were correct in assuming that instinctual demands were expressed in dreaming, then the observation that penile erections accompanied REM periods deserves careful scrutiny especially since it would be hypothesised, from the study of psychoanalytic theory, that sexual demands would be very common at least in Western society.

Ohlmeyer *et al.* (1944 and 1947) reported cyclic erection during sleep several years before Aserinsky and Kleitman (1955) had noted the crucial link between REMs and sleep, so that there was no attempt in either of these papers to relate such cyclic erections to dreaming or REM. Fisher *et al.* (1965), however, found that full or partial erections accompanied 95% of REM periods observed. Furthermore, erections very rarely occurred outside REM periods in other NREM phases of sleep. Various methods of penile measurement were used – this was necessary because of the problems involved in placing anything on the penis without affecting its size – including observations of some of the sleepers in the nude. In fact, erection took place two minutes before the REM period began and detumescence set in about one minute before the end of the REM period.

Karacan *et al.* (*1966*)

Karacan *et al.* carried out a highly interesting study of these nightly penile erections – an investigation which has an important bearing on the question as to whether such erections are evidence for sexual impulses during REM periods or rather for a more generalised physiological excitement. Since, in waking life, anxiety can cause temporary impotence, in sleep anxiety in the dream experience could well inhibit or prevent erection. The following hypothesis was, therefore, put to the test: *Less anxious dreams would be reported by subjects awoken from REM periods with full erection than by subjects awoken with irregular or no erection.*

Sample. 16 paid volunteer students. Each spent six nights in the laboratory.

Measures

1. *The Nowlis Check List (Nowlis, 1963)*

This is an adjective check list which has been factored into 7 dimensions, of which anxiety is one. To use the Nowlis measure the dreamer rates his dream 1 to 3 for each word of the list.

2. *The Gottschalk rating scale (Gottschalk and Gleser, 1969)*

This is a scale used for rating the anxiety of the dream content.

These were the two measures of anxiety used in this investigation in an attempt to lessen the subjectivity of the dream judgements.

3. *Measurements of the penis.* Three categories were employed:

A. *Regular erection*   this was when the penis reached its maximum extent and continued thus until awakening. 42% of REM periods (N = 100) were thus classified.

B. *Irregular erection*   this was when the amplitude of the penis fluctuated or detumescence had begun before awakening. 37% (N = 91) of REMs were thus classified.

C. *No erection*   20% (N = 46) of REMs were thus classified.

There were thus 237 REM periods examined of which 80% were accompanied by penile erection. It was noteworthy that there were only 19 NREM erections.

Results

1. The anxiety score for A. dreams (regular erection) as measured by the Gottschalk test was significantly higher than the anxiety score for other dreams.
2. There was no significant difference on the Nowlis test.

The erection cycle did not appear to be affected by coitus – in that subjects who came to the laboratory having just performed coitus showed the usual erection cycle. Nor did nocturnal emissions produce detumescence.

Conclusions

In view of the problems of attempting to score dreams for anxiety, the fact that one such objective measure is related to penile erection may be taken as evidence for the relationship of dream content to penile erection.

Implications for Freudian theory

This study appears to indicate that the penile erections are related to the dream content, a finding which supports the idea that instinctual impulses are expressed in dreaming, as Freudian theory suggests. This view is endorsed by Fisher (1965)

I

who stated that rapid erection has been found to accompany erotic dream content while detumescence was associated with dreams having castration anxiety content. Although this study by Karacan *et al* must be held to support Freudian theory, the evidence will be considered again in the section on the implications of all these REM studies for psychoanalytic dream theory (p. 258) where other material concerning erection must be considered.

EXTERNAL INFLUENCE ON DREAM CONTENT AND REMS (OTHER THAN DRUGS)

The effects of drugs on REMs and dream content is not considered relevant to the psychoanalytic theory of dreaming. This is because it is fully accepted that all behaviour must have its neurological and biochemical correlates. However to know what these are tells us nothing about the behaviour. Consequently the fact that drug A can or cannot affect the process of dreaming is quite irrelevant to *any psychological theory* of dreaming. No doubt while dreaming certain neurochemical processes are going on, and no doubt these may be interrupted by chemical interference.

The relevance to Freudian theory of experiments showing the influence of external stimuli on dream content is also not entirely straightforward. This is, of course, because the wish which is substituted for the gratification of the instinctual impulse is expressed through the *latent* rather than the *manifest* content of the dreams. Most dream investigators have not been committed to Freudian theory and, in the interests of precision and objectivity, have deliberately restricted themselves to the manifest content. For this reason studies of this type will be given only brief consideration.

Ramsey (1953) has made an excellent survey of the work carried out on dreams up to 1953. Most of the findings, however, are vitiated by the fact that they all depend on dream reports on awakening in the morning – inevitably, since the relationship between REM and dreaming was not then known. This means that it is unclear as to whether the reports refer to REM or NREM mentation and also, inevitably, that a large number of dreams never get reported. However Maury (1861) reported that stimuli, such as perfumes and water drops on his forehead, did influence the manifest content of his dreams. Poetzl (1917) found that subjects to whom pictures were presented tachistoscopically dreamed of details which they had been unable to report immediately after seeing the picture. This curious finding is known as *the Poetzl phenomenon*.

Studies of the Poetzl phenomenon

Shevrin and Luborsky (1958) investigated the Poetzl phenomenon with 27 subjects. After seeing the picture (1/5 sec) subjects had to report the dreams of the night. From those who offered no dreams an 'image' of the picture was obtained. The number of new elements (compared with their original description) in either the dream or the image was regarded as a measure of preconscious perception. Poetzl's claim that dream imagery excludes conscious perception in favour of preconscious was supported.

Shevrin and Luborsky regard this Poetzl phenomenon as support for Freudian dream theory in that the 'neutral' nature of this preconscious perception allows it to be used as a cover for unconscious ideas that would otherwise be suppressed. Thus a correlation was observed of ·57 between preconscious recall and peak unpleasantness as rated by a judge. Fisher (1954, 1960) has also found evidence for the Poetzl phenomenon.

Waxenberg *et al.* (1962), however, have considerable doubts about the occurrence of the Poetzl phenomenon. First they note that although Fisher (1954) claimed that he had confirmed the phenomenon in 30 experiments he gave no details of the experimental procedures used. Furthermore, they point out that Shevrin and Luborsky (1958), despite their claim to have supported Poetzl, in fact did not do so. Thus in his original paper Poetzl (1917) showed that it was the unreported parts of stimuli which had been presented tachistoscopically which tended to occur in dreams, whereas Shevrin and Luborsky found that the more subjects saw initially, the more was seen in the dream. Waxenberg *et al.* (1962) therefore put the Poetzl phenomenon to further test on a sample of 24 medical students who at weekly intervals were shown a different picture tachistoscopically and asked to draw it. It was suggested that they might later dream about it and 34 dream experiences were collected.

Five judges working independently failed to support the Poetzl hypothesis in that they were unable to match dreams to drawings better than by chance using either the complementary hypothesis or trying to match by similarity. Waxenberg *et al.* (1962) thus conclude that the existence of the Poetzl phenomenon is doubtful.

Actually, an earlier study by Johnson and Eriksen (1961) had also put the existence of the Poetzl phenomenon into some doubt. These authors had found that the daydreams of subjects were conceptually similar to their descriptions of tachistoscopic stimuli – a finding which was considered confirmatory of the Poetzl phenomenon (N.B. the objection of Waxenberg *et al.*, 1962 to this formulation). However, the daydreams of subjects who had not seen the stimuli were not different from the experimental group as regards the presence of related items. This finding means, in simple terms, that the judgement of conceptual similarity was too general or too ingenious.

Tart (1965), however, thinks that these results may be due to 'the demand characteristic' of the situation. The concept of demand characteristic (Orne, 1962) according to Tart vitiates many studies of dreaming in that the very nature of the experimental procedures and the questions asked by the experimenter, suggests answers to the subjects. It is thus a specific form of experimental bias.

Conclusions from studies of the Poetzl phenomenon

Despite the claims of Fisher (1954) and Shevrin and Luborsky (1958) much more firm evidence needs to be provided before the Poetzl phenomenon may be accepted. Thus interesting support for preconscious perception in dreaming must be abandoned.

The work of Dement and Wolpert (1958)

In a study already discussed (p. 240) Dement and Wolpert presented stimuli during REM sleep. A pure tone was incorporated into 9% of the trials, a light into 23% of the trials, and drops of water into 42% of the trials. There was no effect if stimuli were presented during NREM sleep.

Conclusions

This study illustrates clearly the faults and problems of work on the influence upon dreams done without EEG monitoring of sleep – i.e. all work before 1955. Clearly, even stimuli which have a profound effect when presented in REM sleep would produce no effect when presented during other phases. In addition, since recall of dreams after the REM period is finished is slight, dream reports on awakening in the morning are not sound evidence. This means that since stimuli presented in NREM periods produce no effect, dreams must be regarded only as the guardians of REM sleep, not, as Freud stated, of sleep. In addition, since dreams occur every night and since, in normal life, stimuli during REM periods are few in number, the generality of experiments such as this must be regarded as slight.

Berger (1963b), however, conducted an experiment into the effects of external stimuli on dreaming which has far more implications for Freudian theory and it will be examined, therefore, in greater detail.

The work of Berger (1963)

Berger (1963a), in his doctoral dissertation on the psychophysiology of sleep and dreaming noticed, *en passant*, that words and phrases spoken below the threshold of waking were incorporated into dreams elicited soon after. He decided to investigate more systematically what was little more than a clinical impression. The results and description of the study are set out below.

Sample. 4 male and 4 female students. Their past girl- or boy-friends were known as was the type of relationship each subject had with them.

Stimuli. The names of two friends + two neutral names (neutrality previously determined by the criterion of GSR response). These names were uttered below the threshold of waking during an REM period. 20 seconds afterwards a dream was elicited.

Treatment of data. Subjects were asked to match dreams to stimuli as was one independent judge.

Hypotheses

A. Potentially arousing stimuli (names associated with dreamer) will be experienced as belonging to the dream or distorted to fit in with it.

B. Names should be matched to dreams better than by chance (both by dreamer and judge).

C. Names with emotional significance will be matched more frequently.

Results. Subjects and judge both matched names to dreams better than chance. The sex of the subject and the emotional quality of the stimulus did not affect the matching.

Of the 48 dreams influenced by a stimulus, 31 worked through *assonance*, 6 by *association*, 8 *directly* and 3 by *representation*. The examples given by Berger (1963b), some of which are set out below, may perhaps be regarded as experimental illustrations of Freudian dreamwork.

Assonance. Jenny became 'Jemmy', Edward became 'Out a Gourd'. Naomi became 'An aim to ski', Gillian became 'A woman from Chile' – i.e. a Chilian.

Association. Richard became 'Had been to a shop for a sale'. Association: Richards was the name of a shop to which the subject had recently been for a sale.

Direct. A background voice utters the name in the dream.

Representation. The person appears directly or disguised in the dream.

Discussion. Berger argues that these results support the Freudian view that dreams are the guardian of sleep. However, as was the case with the Dement and Wolpert (1958) study, these results can only be interpreted as showing that dreams are the guardians of REM sleep. For stimuli presented during NREM periods do not influence dreams. However, it is clear that the external stimulus is woven into the dream. It does not provoke it. According to Berger the stimuli are incorporated into the dream to rob them of reality: for example, the dream that names are being whispered to them or that they even wake up. This last is very reminiscent of Freud's example of the nursemaid's dream to illustrate its function as guardian of sleep.

Sexual symbolism. A few of the dreams where the symbol was incorporated contained Freudian sexual symbols (see p. 205). This only occurred to an emotional stimulus – usually the current boy- or girl-friend.

Examples. Eileen and *a big lamp*: *A snake of fairy lights, snaking in and out*: digging out *a gourd like a round cucumber*. Smoking a *cigar*: the *cigarette*, frayed and burnt, *I inhaled*. These are clear examples of sexual symbolism and it is very interesting to note that none occurred to non-emotional stimuli.

Discussion and conclusions

The distortions noted seem characteristic of dream-work and the fact that the stimuli were incorporated into the dreams supports the Freudian claim that dreams are the guardian of (REM) sleep. The symbolism is also good support for Freudian theory especially because it was found only with emotional names, where sexual impulses were more probable. Nevertheless, the fact that such stimuli are effective only if presented during REM periods seems to limit, as was the case with Dement and Wolpert (1958), the generality of the findings. Surely pre-sleep or diurnal influences must be more relevant. Nevertheless with that proviso, this study must be regarded as good evidence for certain aspects of the psychoanalytic theory of dreaming.

The work of Foulkes and Rechtschaffen (1964)

These authors studied the pre-sleep determinants of dream content on a sample of 24 subjects. One night, subjects saw a violent episode of a TV film: on another night they saw a non-violent episode: dream periods were identified by REMs and reports of a dream were immediately elicited. In addition to this these subjects completed the TAT, the MMPI and rating scales concerning their dreams.

Results

After the violent film, dream reports were significantly longer, clearer, more imaginative and more emotional than after the peaceful episode. They were not more unpleasant or more violent. Imagination as measured by the TAT had a correlation of ·4 with dream recall. There was also a significant correlation between some of the clinical scales of the MMPI and the dream-like quality of the dreams. There was little direct incorporation of the content of either film into any of the dream reports. Finally there was little similarity between TAT and dream fantasy material concerning instinctual impulses.

Discussion

Foulkes and Rechtschaffen argue that the violent film was more arousing (since the dream reports were more brilliant) although, somehow, the film content was disassociated from the arousal it produced. However if NREM reports are combined with the REM dreams there is no difference between the dreams produced by the two films. They also argue that the MMPI correlations are consistent with Freudian theory in that dream experience helps the expression of affect, which becomes more important with increasing pathology. Since these correlations could be interpreted as evidence that dream *reports* are correlated with psychopathology, the eye-movement activity itself was correlated with the MMPI scales. No correlation was found, however. It should be pointed out that REMs have been related to content and activity and passivity (see pp. 239-40) but not to dream-like quality so that no correlation should, perhaps, have been expected.

Comments and conclusions

This investigation is worthy of study because it deals with a problem which may be generalised to normal life. Clearly we are all subject to environmental stimulation before sleep yet its effects on dreams are not known. It thus differs from other studies so far examined which have concentrated on the effects of stimuli presented during REM periods. First of all these results are implicitly in flat contradiction to the Poetzl phenomenon. Foulkes and Rechtschaffen (1964) are aware of this but by no means regard the Poetzl phenomenon as a proven fact.

They follow Johnson and Eriksen (1961) who review a number of studies of the Poetzl phenomenon and discredit it on the grounds of methodology.

It should be pointed out that the correlations between the MMPI, the TAT and the dream rating scales should be interpreted with the utmost caution on a sample as small as this in view of the low reliability of these personality tests.

The correlation between the bizarre quality of the dreams and the MMPI clinical scales is some support for Freudian theory. The failure to confirm the Poetzl phenomenon is, however, really contrary to psychoanalytic theory since dreams 'use' preconscious material to evade the super-ego. To be really relevant to the theory these dreams need examination from the viewpoint of *latent* content, where no differences would be expected between groups since latent content reflects personality rather than environment. This study has been carefully examined because it illustrates the problems of testing Freudian dream theory without first having precise predictions derived from it in terms of manifest content (as does Hall) or without examining the latent content.

Hypnotic suggestion and dream content

Fisher (1953) and Tart (1965) have both shown that post-hypnotic suggestion can influence the content of dreams. Tart (1965) claims, indeed, that for some subjects (a minority) it is the most powerful and precise method of affecting dreams. For others, however, it has no effect. These studies will not be further discussed since their relevance to psychoanalytic theory is enigmatic in view of the fact that hypnotic suggestion is not itself well understood psychologically.

Other variables influencing dream content and REM

A number of other variables has been shown to influence dream content or REM itself. However, a brief list of these will suffice since the relevance of these findings to Freudian dream theory is small.

(*a*) *Social isolation.* Wood (1962), quoted by Tart (1965), showed in his doctoral thesis that the social isolation of subjects before sleep produced dreams in which more than usual social intercourses took place.

(*b*) *The dream laboratory.* It is now an established fact of REM and EEG research into dreams that the first laboratory night is affected by the experimental situation: both the content of the dreams, which tend to be about the laboratory (e.g. Dement, Kahn and Roffwarg, 1965), and the process of REM sleep itself, the first cycle of which is usually missed out (e.g. Dement and Kleitman, 1955, Snyder, 1963). As a result of this, data from the first experimental night should not be used in investigations. Except for the fact that these findings indicate that anxiety (presumably) can affect the overt content of dreams and inhibit dreaming itself, as was stated earlier, it is difficult to demonstrate their relevance to Freudian theory. Altshuler (1966), however, regards the fact that anxious subjects (Dement, 1963) tend to miss more REM sleep on the first night than do non-anxious subjects as evidence *against* the psychoanalytic theory of dreams. Increased anxiety should lead to increased dreaming.

Internal stimuli and dreaming – thirst and hunger

Dement and Wolpert (1958) in a study already discussed (see p. 240), subjected some of their subjects to water and food deprivation because of its relevance to the relationship between REMs and dreaming. This had no effect on either REM time or content. A similar finding was reported by Rechtschaffen (1964).

Comments and conclusions

These studies are not convincing since the amount of deprivation for ethical and practical reasons (subjects are likely to be needed for further experiments) was not considerable. If Freudian theory were correct, hunger and thirst motifs should have been noted in the dreams, provided deprivation was effective. Anecdotal evidence quoted by Hall (1966) concerning the Himalayan expedition of Hunt and the reports of other explorers (e.g. Cherry-Garrard, 1970) suggest that dreams are affected by the absence of pleasant rather than nutritious food. O'Neil (1964), on the other hand, did find that dream reports of four groups differing in food and drink customs and nutritional state revealed differences in accordance with psychoanalytic theory. These were not, however, REM dream reports. Clearly more research needs to be done in this area.

SUMMARY OF FINDINGS IN THE EEG AND REM STUDY OF SLEEP AND DREAMING

To facilitate comprehension of the discussion of the implications of all these findings for psychoanalytic theory a tabular summary of the main results will be found opposite.

IMPLICATIONS FOR FREUDIAN THEORY

Findings 3 and 4

The fact that REM states occur in mammals and in infants more frequently and as a greater proportion of the total sleep time than in adults, implies inevitably that REMs are not psychogenically caused. In Freudian theory there is no psychic structure at birth. REMs are therefore one symptom of a basic physiological process. However we must be careful not to confuse REMs with dreaming. REMs may be a physiological correlate of dreaming but dreaming itself is a psychological event. It is a self-evident fact that psychological events have such physiological processes. Thus, for example, vision implies physiological activity in the retina, the optic chiasma and the visual cortex. But the study of such neural activity tells us nothing about the experience, what was seen and the implications of it for the observer. Thus it is with REMs: the fact alone that they occur in lower organisms is not in itself contrary to Freudian theory.

Results	Investigator	Comments
1. REM a distinct biologic state distinct from sleep and wakefulness.	Snyder (1963, 1965)	Based on review of literature.
2. REM associated with dream reports.	Aserinsky and Kleitman (1955)	The first of many such observations.
3. REM occurs in many other animals.	Klein (1963)	
4. The younger the organism the greater the proportion of REM sleep.	Fisher (1965)	Based on review of literature.
5. Positive mechanism involved in REM.	Jouvet (e.g. 1967)	Based on animal studies.
6. Relation between eye movements and dream content.	Roffwarg *et al.* (1962)	
7. Thought-like mentation from NREM sleep. Dream-like mentation from REM sleep.	Foulkes (1962)	
8. Dream material of same night related.	Rechtschaffen *et al.* (1963)	
9. REM deprivation produces psychotic-like effects.	Dement (1963)	Not necessarily dream deprivation.
10. REM deprivation produces increased attempts at REM.	Dement (1963)	
11. Penile erection associated with REM sleep.	Fisher (1965)	
12. Penile erection can be affected by dream content.	Karacan *et al.* (1966)	
13. The Poetzl phenomenon.	Poetzl (1917)	Methodological problems may vitiate results.
14. Stimuli presented during REM sleep may be incorporated into dreams.	Berger (1963)	Examples of Freudian dream work.
15. Effects of the first laboratory night.	Dement *et al.* (1965)	

Finding 2

The fact that REMs are associated with reports of 'dreaming' rather than thinking' is of great methodological importance for the scientific study of dreams.

It means that very full dream reports may be obtained. This is especially important since waking after the REMs have finished usually results in very poor memory of dreams. This means that the dreams which Freud was able to analyse are but fragments of the total dreaming experience of his patients – often of the last REM period. The use of REM awakenings should allow the relationship between dream content and the personality and life of the dreamer to be examined more accurately.

Finding 6

Eye movements are related to dream content. If then it is accepted that REMs are a symptom of a basic physiological process, and are not caused by the act of dreaming, then findings 2 and 6, which hint at an intimate relationship between dreaming and REM periods, remain to be explained. Fisher (1965) proposes that REMs are a prepared mechanism ready at birth which is later taken over for the visual scanning of hallucinations.

Finding 5

The implication of the caudal pontile nucleus in REM sleep, a structure which is part of the pontile reticular formation (the reason why Jouvet, 1967 also used the term mid-brain sleep) is of some interest for Freudian theory. In the earlier chapter on the evidence for the hypothesised psychic structure of ego, id and super-ego (pp. 129-30), some very tentative physiological bases of such a division were examined. It is to be noted, therefore, that this pontile nucleus is connected to the hypothalamus which has been suggested as the possible neural correlate of the id (see p. 130). In Freudian theory of course the drive for dreaming originates there. Consequently while it is in no way claimed that the physiological work on REM states by Jouvet and his collaborators confirms Freudian dream theory, it is contended that such work in no way runs counter to the theories, and fits in with what little is so far known.

Findings 7, 8, 9 and 1

From these findings there are several points which are of great relevance to the elucidation of Freudian theory. Since it has been shown that mentation or dreaming (even if not of a bizarre or hallucinatory nature) occurs in NREM periods, it cannot really be argued that deprivation of REM sleep is dream deprivation. At most it is deprivation of 'dream-like' dreams. Thus finding 7 considerably weakens the results of Dement (1963) whose subjects after 15 days deprivation of REM sleep began to develop psychotic-like symptoms.

Needless to say, attempts to deprive subjects of all dream time in both REM and NREM periods could not be used to assess the effects of dream deprivation since any such effects would be inextricably confounded with fatigue due to sleep loss.

Finding 1, that REMs are really a third distinct biologic state, also means that REM deprivation studies are not good dream deprivation studies. If REMs are a symptom of a basic physiological process of which dreaming is a concomitant, then the effects of REM dreaming cannot by any logical process be accounted for by dream deprivation. To do this (ignoring for a moment the fact of NREM mentation) would require, for example, a drug which abolished dreaming without abolishing REMs and the other physiological processes.

From these two arguments, therefore, based on the occurrence of NREM mentation and the fact of the biologic state of REM, current dream deprivation studies may not be regarded as adequate tests of psychoanalytic dream theory.

Findings 7 and 8, however, which suggest that REM and NREM mentation of the same night is related, are important as regards Freudian theory. In addition all these studies show that REM dreaming is typically dream-like whereas NREM dreaming is quite mundane and often referred to by subjects as thinking rather than dreaming. In fact, therefore, empirical observation has yielded two distinct types of dream. Psychoanalytic dream theory is certainly not upset by this result since in 'The interpretation of dreams' Freud (1900) distinguishes between day residues and dreams. Furthermore the distinction is very similar to that between the 'thinking' and 'dreaming' of the two stages of sleep.

Rechtschaffen *et al.* (1963) have clearly shown that NREM and REM dream material is related. This fits the Freudian claim that internal processes (NREM mentation) can instigate dreams. For in dream theory preconscious day-residues can form the point of contact for unconscious dream thoughts. NREM mentation may therefore be the conscious representation of such day-residues. This would certainly fit the thought-like character of NREM mentation. Foulkes (1964) and Rechtschaffen *et al.* (1963) both incline to this view. Of course it follows, as Foulkes points out, that the collection of NREM dream material, the raw data, as it were, for the dream-work, would facilitate the Freudian interpretation of dreams.

In summary, therefore, it may be said that findings 7 and 8 accord well with the Freudian concepts of day-residues and dreaming.

Finding 10

It has already been shown in this section that the need for REM sleep cannot be equated with a need for dreaming. Snyder (1963, 1965) interprets the need for REM sleep in physiological terms – there is a need for a physiological process which occurs during REM periods. This is also the view of Dement *et al.* (1967). It is assumed that under REM deprivation there is a build up of some neurochemical substance which would otherwise be metabolised. However it was pointed out in the opening paragraph of this section that REM studies and Freudian dream theory are really separate realms of discourse and in this case we must guard against confusion. This finding, once REM and dreaming deprivation have been separated, is not in fact relevant to Freudian theory.

Findings 11 and 12

These two results dealing with penile erection and REM periods are, superficially at least, powerfully in accord with psychoanalytic theory. Berger and

Oswald (1962) remark that had psychoanalysts read the journals in which the early results were announced, they would most certainly have used them as ammunition for the cause. Fisher (1965), who has carried out research in this area, has examined the implications of the results for Freudian theory in considerable detail. Broadly he regards the erection which starts just before the REM period *not simply as a symptom of sexual excitement but as an index of activation in the limbic area.* (The limbic area has been discussed in the section on ego, super-ego and id – see p. 130; it is part of the mid-brain and includes the hypothalamus.) To support the possibility of non-sexual erection, Fisher cites the work of Ramsey (1943) who showed that non-sexual stimuli could produce erection in boys, and also the Kinsey report (Kinsey *et al.*, 1948) in which similar observations may be found. In addition Fisher (1965) argues that the morning erection, which is often thought to be caused by a full bladder, is, in fact, the final REM erection. This is important since such morning erections are often experienced as non-erotic, and impotent men can have such erections (Kinsey *et al.*, 1948). Thus Fisher supports the claim that erection during REM periods is not necessarily proof positive of the sexual aetiology of all dreaming.

Against this, rapid erection has been observed where the erotic nature of the dream was very strong and detumescence where there was castration anxiety, and Karacan *et al.* (1966) reported that anxiety in dreams affected erection (although very recent sexual intercourse did not appear to do so).

Perhaps the best conclusion concerning penile erection and REM periods is to admit, along with Fisher (1965), that originally it may be but an index of limbic activity (a description which could also be applied to it during sexual excitement), but that as with the rapid eye movements, it can be affected by dream content. It is probably the case that erection *per se* does not imply the sexual aetiology of dreaming. The fact that it can be affected by some dreams certainly imputes psychological significance to dream content and to this extent the phenomenon is in accord with psychoanalytic theory.

Findings 13 and 14

The finding that stimuli presented during REM sleep may be incorporated into the dream whereas at other stages of sleep they either have no effect or wake the sleeper is in fact relevant to Freudian theory. As has already been pointed out this means that dreams are the guardians of REM sleep, not sleep in general. However Altshuler (1966) says that even in this they are inefficient since up to 50% (Dement, 1963) of REM periods include occasions in which the subject is awake. Berger's (1963) study does appear to illustrate experimentally the very process of dream-work and must be regarded, therefore, as good evidence for Freudian theory. The examples of symbolism were also impressive.

The importance of the Poetzl phenomenon is more enigmatic. If the methodological problems of the studies could be ignored and the results accepted, it does mean that there is some objective evidence for the claim that preconscious perception is the basis of dream imagery. It does not, however, bear on the aetiology in the Freudian theory – that preconscious imagery helps the avoidance of repression. However, in view of the problems associated with it, it is probably wise not to put too much reliance on the results.

Finding 15

As was discussed in the section on the first laboratory night, the fact that anxiety appears to inhibit REM sleep is contrary to Freudian theory in that anxiety should lead to less rather than more sleep.

CONCLUSIONS FROM STUDIES OF REM SLEEP

In considering the implications of REM sleep studies for the psychoanalytic theory of dreams, great care must be taken not to confuse two universes of discourse – the psychological and the physiological. Studies of REM and NREM mentation indicate that dream material during REM periods does appear to be worked over in a manner similar to Freud's description of primary processes. Dream deprivation studies (based on REM deprivation) must be treated with great caution since REM deprivation clearly involves far more than just dream deprivation.

Perhaps the greatest value of REM studies for psychoanalytic theory lies in the fact that they offer a technique for obtaining access to a far greater proportion of dream material and with greater accuracy than was ever possible with recall on the succeeding day. They also offer up hope of experimental study of factors affecting dream content. Clearly the most exciting work in this area still remains to be done.

10

Psychoanalytic theory of neurosis, psychosis and other emotional and psychogenic disturbances

INTRODUCTION

It must be frankly admitted at the outset that empirical study of Freudian theory in this area is extremely difficult. For example, Freud (1923) in 'The ego and the id', claims that the neurotic conflict takes place between the id and the ego. Again, in 'Neurosis and psychosis' (1924) he argues that the neurotic obeys the external world and represses the instinct whereas the psychotic denies the external world and obeys the instinct. Since, as was made clear in the discussion of the dynamic view of the mind (p. 138), there are at present no adequate measures of either ego or id, and since there are not as yet any satisfactory classifications of behaviours into either of these categories, it is obvious that the broad molar psychoanalytic approach to emotional disturbances is not readily put to the empirical test. In one sense, therefore, the theory must be regarded as unscientific – testable hypotheses are not derivable from it.

The whole basis of psychoanalytic theory was discovered from the study of patients with hysteria, a major psychiatric nosological category, so that it is perhaps surprising that examination of this field should yield so little in the way of testable hypotheses. The paucity of clear-cut material is, however, more apparent than real. The fact is that the basis of psychoanalytic theory *was* derived from studies of neurosis and psychosis and this basis has already been empirically examined in the earlier sections of this book. Furthermore very careful study of the work of Freud, aided by the indefatigable Fenichel (1945), does in fact reveal a number of clear testable propositions concerning various types of emotional disturbance, neurosis and psychosis. As is to be expected in so sexually-oriented a theory, there is a large number of such hypotheses concerning sexual anomalies.

In the next section a list of testable Freudian hypotheses will be given. They will be grouped according to widely used psychiatric classifications and the source of each will be stated. Where necessary, some brief comments will be given to indicate how the hypothesis fits into the broader Freudian theory. In this chapter, therefore, we have departed from the regular format of 'outline of theory' followed by 'hypotheses'. This is because an outline of theory section would be very cumbrous (Fenichel runs to 500 pages!) and because the hypotheses would not be self-evident from the theory.

260

THE HYPOTHESES

A. Neuroses and psychoses

A.1. *Coitus interruptus is a major precipitating factor in anxiety neurosis.*
   Source: 'Sexuality in the aetiology of the neuroses' (Freud, 1898). 'On the grounds for detaching a particular syndrome from neurasthenia under the description anxiety neurosis' (Freud, 1895c).

A.2. *Neurasthenia due to excessive masturbation.*
   Source: 'My views on the part played by sexuality in the aetiology of the neuroses' (Freud, 1906).

A.3. *Oedipus complex very important in conversion hysteria.*
   Source: 'Further observations on the neuropsychoses of defence' (Freud, 1896).

A.4. *Regression to anal-sadistic level typical in obsessional neurosis.*
   Source: 'Notes upon a case of obsessional neurosis' (Freud, 1909b). 'The predisposition to obsessional neurosis' (Freud, 1913b).

A.5. *Oedipus complex central to obsessional neurosis.*
   Source: See A.4.

A.6. *Oral fixation always evidenced in depression.*
   Source: 'Mourning and melancholia' (Freud, 1917b).

A.7. *Narcissism also found in depression.*
   Source: See A.6.

A.8. *Paranoid delusions caused by projection of homosexual feelings.*
   Source: 'Psychoanalytic notes on an autobiographical account of a case of paranoia (dementia paranoides)' (Freud, 1911).

Comments

There is no need of explanatory notes for the hypotheses concerning neuroses and psychoses since all the psychoanalytic concepts invoked have already been discussed earlier in the book and the evidence for them has also been examined. Some of these hypotheses are among the earliest speculations of psychoanalysis. Brief descriptions of the psychiatric categories used in this section are given below.

Since the problems of psychiatric classification are so great and since there is considerable disparity between, for example, the Freudian classifications used in the hypotheses given above and the Schneiderian phenomenological school (Schneider, 1958), the brief clinical descriptions must, of necessity, be taken from psychoanalytic workers. In fact these descriptions are based on the work of Glover (1949).

A.1. *Anxiety neurosis.* 'The characteristic feature is a great increase in anxiety readiness' (Glover, 1949). Anxiety reaching even to panic develops for no apparent reason. Often, in addition, there is irritability, moodiness, restless sleep and anxious dreaming. There are frequently cardiovascular, respiratory and gastro-intestinal disturbances.

A.2. *Neurasthenia.* The two main features are chronic fatigue and fatigue readiness. There is lack of interest, inability to concentrate and no initiative – a combination of apathy, weakness and indifference. Sleep is disturbed and there is marked hypochondria.

A.3. *Hysteria (conversion).* The typical symptoms of conversion hysterias are somatic. They can affect any organ and can vary in intensity from mild cramps to complete paralysis. The symptoms may be translated – i.e. they have a psychic meaning and represent a body language (Freud, 'The aetiology of hysteria', 1896b). This distinguishes them from psychosomatic symptoms. It is to be noted that this particular psychoanalytic hypothesis was not considered empirical and testable. Conversion hysterias must be carefully distinguished from *anxiety hysterias* which are often expressed as phobias of particular objects or situations.

A.4. *Obsessional neuroses.* Typical symptoms are thoughts or actions which the patient feels compelled to consider or carry out against his will. Housewives may spend hours cleaning and re-cleaning the stairs, others are forced to consider again and again the precise meaning of a word or phrase. Sometimes before a particular action, e.g. going to bed, obsessive rituals must be carried out which often are long and complex. Care must be taken to distinguish these ego-dystonic *symptoms* which the patient knows to be absurd with ego-syntonic obsessional traits of which the patient is often proud, e.g. the orderliness of an efficient clerk. This distinction has been fully examined by Sandler and Hazari, 1960; Kline, 1967b and Pichot and Perse, 1967.

A.6 *Depression.* Depression quite often alternates in manic-depressive patients with mania. The symptoms are an exaggerated form of the normal feeling. Listlessness, indolence, sadness, a feeling of complete unworthiness, that everything is useless, are typical symptoms of depression and attempted suicide is common.

A.8. *Paranoia.* This is a chronic state, characterised by fixed delusional symptoms usually of persecution with or without hallucination and often separated from the rest of the personality which may be unaffected and otherwise normal. The delusions often create a desire for litigation and literally at any cost.

B. Sexual anomalies

B.9. *Impotence is based on the unconscious sexual attachment to the mother* (the Oedipus complex).
Source: 'Three essays on sexuality' (Freud, 1905a).

B.10. *The castration complex is a major factor in male homosexuality.*
Source: 'Analysis of a phobia in a five-year-old boy' (Freud, 1909a).

B.11. *Homosexuals identify with their mothers.*
Source: 'The ego and the id' (Freud, 1923).

B.12. *Homosexuals are hypothesised to have weak fathers.*
   Source: See B.11.

Identification in psychoanalytic theory is likely to occur with the major frustrating figure in the child's life – identification through fear of loss of love. Hence if B.11 is true, B.12 follows, since strong domineering mothers are likely to create the identification noticed, and this domination implies weak fathers. A similar argument applies to hypothesis B.15 set out below – as regards its first part. The empirical studies of identification have been discussed in Chapter 7, pp. 138-50.

B.13. *Homosexuals who choose young boys are fixated at the phallic level.*
   Source: 'Three essays on sexuality' (Freud, 1905a).
B.14. *Homosexuals (who express their anal erotism directly) should have few anal traits.*
   Source: 'Character and anal erotism' (Freud, 1908a).
B.15. *Identification with the father and the castration complex are major factors in female homosexuality.*
   Source: 'Female sexuality' (Freud, 1931).
B.16. *Two factors are basic to fetishism: the castration complex and denial.*
   Source: 'Fetishism' (Freud, 1927a).
B.17. *Pyromaniacs (and firemen) fixated at the phallic level.*
   Source: 'The acquisition of control over fire' (Freud, 1932).

In psychoanalytic theory there is an association between fire and urethral and phallic erotism, hence the pyromaniacs of the B.17 hypothesis. The present author has, somewhat gratuitously perhaps, added firemen to it. But surely a glance at the brazen helmets and the clanging bells, the dazzling red of the vehicles, the remarkable contrivance in place of stairs in the fire station, the hoses and ladders is sufficient to make the insertion worthy of test?

C. Psychogenic and other disturbances

C.18. *Peptic ulcer reflects oral conflicts.*
C.19. *Ulcerative colitis reflects anal conflicts.*

These two hypotheses, C.18 and C.19, although easily derivable from Freudian theory, were not explicitly thus stated by Freud. They are the results of long study of the problems by the Chicago school of psychoanalysis, notably Alexander (1934). They are directly in the classical Freudian tradition however in that, if shown to be true, they would directly support Freudian theory.

C.20. *Stutterers have an anal fixation.*
   Source: 'The psychoanalytic theory of neurosis (Fenichel, 1945).
C.21. *Tics are related to anal and narcissistic fixations.*
   Source: Fenichel, *ibid.*

As with C.18 and C.19, hypotheses C.20 and C.21 are not explicitly stated by

Freud but are easily derived from Freudian theory. In the case of the stutterers, it is the 'retentive' tendency of the anally fixated that stops words coming out.

C.22. *Psychogenic disturbances of vision are symptoms of repressed impulses to look at or be looked at (exhibitionism and voyeurism).*
Source: 'The psychoanalytic view of psychogenic disturbance of vision' (Freud 1910b).
C.23. *Passion for gambling related to masturbation conflicts.*
Source: Fenichel, *op. cit.*

Hypothesis C.23 is a somewhat wild assertion based on a small number of case studies, put in for interest only and as an example of the problems of attempting to validate the more extreme positions of the followers of Freud.

STUDIES OF THE FREUDIAN THEORY OF PARANOID SCHIZOPHRENIA

DEFINITION OF PARANOID SCHIZOPHRENIA

Of all the schizophrenias, which are characterised by disturbances of thinking, the blunting and incongruity of emotions, disturbances of volition – e.g. negativism, catatonic symptoms, delusions and hallucinations – paranoid schizophrenia is the most homogeneous (Mayer-Gross *et al.*, 1961). The leading symptoms are *primary delusions, secondary delusional interpretations* and, in some cases, *hallucinations*. These, indeed, may be the only symptoms. These delusions and their interpretations are *persecutory in nature*.

FREUDIAN THEORY

The psychoanalytic theory of paranoid schizophrenia is derived from Freud's study of the autobiography of Dr Schreber (Freud, 1911). According to his interpretation of this case material, the persecutory delusions are due to *repressed homosexuality* and the defence mechanism of *projection*. The thought-process of the paranoid schizophrenic may, therefore, be stated thus: 'I love him' becomes, by a reaction-formation as a defence against homosexuality, 'I hate him' which by projection becomes 'he hates me'.

EMPIRICAL PROPOSITIONS AND CONSEQUENCES OF THE PSYCHO-ANALYTIC THEORY

From the psychoanalytic theory of paranoid schizophrenia a number of testable hypotheses may be derived.

1. Paranoid schizophrenics should show evidence of repressed homosexuality.
2. Male paranoid schizophrenics should have male persecutors.
3. Female paranoid schizophrenics should have female persecutors.

EMPIRICAL STUDIES OF PARANOID SCHIZOPHRENIA

The work of Norman (1948)

Norman carried out a clinical study of schizophrenic and paranoid schizophrenic patients in an attempt to establish the incidence of homosexuality in the two groups.

Sample. 75 paranoid schizophrenics and 25 non-paranoid schizophrenics.

Method. The patients were given a clinical examination under sodium amytal, followed by a further interview the next day 'to eliminate fantasy'. Sodium amytal, it is to be noted, is one of the so-called 'truth' drugs.

Results. Of the paranoid patients, 24% were consciously homosexual and 31% gave evidence of symbolic homosexuality during the clinical examination. The corresponding figures were 12% and 16% respectively for the control group. Norman considers that these results support the Freudian theory although they do not prove the aetiology.

Comments

Clinical studies of this kind may only just be regarded as objective evidence. They are not replicable since no tests or fixed interview schedules were used. The validity of results obtained with sodium amytal, especially when fantasies had afterwards to be rejected, is also open to doubt. The only claim to respectability of this study is that it deals with a large number of specified cases. It has been quoted, therefore, to illustrate the difficulties of obtaining clinical evidence of a reputable kind. If the data are trustworthy the fact that not all paranoid patients were homosexual and that some non-paranoid patients were homosexual casts doubt on the Freudian claim that homosexuality is causative in paranoid schizophrenia. It does, however, support the claim that homosexuality is an important factor in it. A further point arises as to whether the incidence of *actual expressed* homosexuality is relevant to the psychoanalytic theory which is concerned with *repressed* homosexuality. It could be argued that it is possible to repress and express homosexuality, i.e. not express it completely, but strictly the theory demands the investigation of repressed homosexuality only.

Conclusions

The unobjective data of this study make firm conclusions difficult to draw. To attempt to support or refute theory from such data would be hazardous. Nevertheless compared with controls paranoid schizophrenics do show more signs of homosexuality. To this extent psychoanalytic theory is supported. Such homosexuality however cannot, from this study, cause the paranoia.

In brief, as far as clinical studies can, this work by Norman (1948) supports the implication of homosexuality in paranoid schizophrenia, but it is weak evidence.

The work of Klein and Horwitz (1949)

Since this is another clinical study where the data are of an unobjective kind it may be very briefly discussed. Case material from 40 female and 40 male schizophrenics was examined for evidence of homosexuality. In 20% of cases this was discovered. However in the absence of a control group of any kind the significance of this figure is unknown.

Conclusions

Without a control group and with data of unknown validity and replicability the fact that this study implicates homosexuality in paranoid schizophrenia is only the very slightest support for Freudian theory. More objective evidence than that supplied by these two relatively large clinical studies is necessary.

The work of Aronson (1953)

Aronson used the Blacky Pictures (Blum, 1949) in a study of the Freudian theory of paranoia.

Sample. 30 paranoid schizophrenics, 30 non-paranoid schizophrenics and 30 normals.

Test. The Blacky Pictures.

Results. The paranoid-schizophrenics were more disturbed than the *normals*, on the following dimensions of the Blacky Pictures: oral erotism, oral sadism, anal retentiveness, masturbation guilt, castration anxiety, identification processes, internalisation of guilt, narcissistic love object and anaclitic love object. They were more disturbed than the non-paranoid schizophrenics on anal erotism and the internalisation of guilt.

Comments

The validity and reliability of the Blacky Pictures have already been discussed in Chapter 5 (see p. 80), and will therefore not be examined again now. There is some evidence for their validity, of which this study is an important part, in that it shows that the Blacky Pictures can discriminate, as measures of psychosexual fixation should do, normals from neurotics.

The Blacky Pictures themselves contain no direct measure of homosexuality. However it is possible to argue from the Freudian theory of homosexuality (Freud, 1909a) that homosexuals would be more disturbed in the dimensions of *castration anxiety* – especially as this is the most important factor in becoming homosexual, the refusal to face the fact that there are beings without a penis – *Oedipal intensity* and *identification*. Aronson (1953), in a series of extremely involved arguments, puts the case for even more differences on other dimensions. However, Freudian theory is so diffuse that such tenuous logical convolutions are not convincing: indeed it might well be possible to demonstrate the opposite. Thus it is very significant from the point of view of Freudian theory that the paranoid schizophrenics were not higher on the dimensions which are clearly related to the psychoanalytic theory of homosexuality than the non-paranoid schizophrenics. On the evidence of their being higher on anal retentiveness and internalisation of guilt it could not be argued that the paranoids were more homosexual than the non-paranoids. Thus Freudian theory is not supported.

It is also interesting to note that Oedipal intensity did not differentiate the neurotics (or psychotics) from the normals although, according to psycho-analytic theory, the Oedipus complex is the kernel of neurosis (Freud, 1916).

Conclusions

Although this investigation supports in general the discriminative power of the Blacky Pictures with normals and neurotics and hence the importance of psycho-sexual development in psychological disorders, it cannot be said to support the Freudian theory of paranoia. If paranoid schizophrenics were to be distinguished from non-paranoid schizophrenics by being homosexual, differences on castration anxiety would be expected from the Blacky Pictures. These differences were not found.

Therefore this study by Aronson fails to support the Freudian theory of paranoid schizophrenia. Indeed, if the Blacky Pictures are valid this investigation refutes the theory.

The work of Zeichner (1955)

Zeichner tested two hypotheses derivable from the Freudian theory of paranoid schizophrenia:

1. that paranoids would be more confused over sexual identification than normals or non-paranoid schizophrenics, and
2. that paranoids would identify more with females than either of the two control groups.

Sample. 15 paranoid, 15 non-paranoid schizophrenics, 15 normals.

Tests. Rorschach and TAT. All statistical comparisons were done by chi-square.

Results. The paranoids were more confused than the other two groups as regards sexual identification. However, although the experimental group were more feminine than the normal controls, they were only more feminine than the schizophrenics at the ·06 level – just below the usual significance level.

Comments and conclusions

These results support the Freudian theory. However the small size of the samples and the dubious, unproven validity of both the Rorschach and the TAT make it difficult to put much weight on the findings.

The work of Daston (1956)

Daston used an experimental technique – the perception of homosexual words presented tachistoscopically – to test the psychoanalytic theory. The hypothesis he derived was that paranoids should recognise homosexual words more quickly than controls because, according to theory, they should have a greater awareness and sensitivity to such stimuli.

Sample. 25 paranoid, 25 non-paranoid schizophrenics, 25 normal controls.

Method. Homosexual, heterosexual and non-sexual words with pleasant, unpleasant or neutral connotations, as rated by judges, were shown to the subjects through a tachistoscope. Recognition times were then subjected to analysis of variance and co-variance (with baseline recognition times held constant).

Words used. Homosexual words were: fruit, fairy, pansy, homos, blown, rectum, sissy, sucked, queer. Their heterosexual equivalents were: caress, bosom, breast, piece, pick-up, screw, fucked, whore, rapist. Some non-sexual, neutral words were also shown.

Results. The paranoid schizophrenics were significantly quicker than normals or non-paranoid schizophrenics on the recognition of homosexual words. There was no difference between schizophrenics and normals.

Comments

This experiment is similar in conception to many of the studies of perceptual defence which have already been discussed in the chapter on defence mechanisms (see p. 165). Many of the objections to those studies are not applicable here however because of the finding that there was no difference between schizophrenics and normals. Thus it cannot be argued that the slowness of recognition be due to the sexual or socially undesirable nature of the response, which normals were loth to put down. If this were the case the non-paranoid schizophrenics would have been quicker as well. Again the argument that the rarity of the non-neutral words accounts for the results cannot be adduced. This rarity would equally affect all groups: indeed *both* the neurotic groups, if this were a factor, would be expected to be slower, for it may be the case (e.g. Moos and Mussen, 1959) that schizophrenia dulls general cognitive efficiency.

Since, therefore, it is not possible to explain the results as artefacts of the experimental technique, this result must be considered to be powerful evidence for the implication of homosexuality in paranoid schizophrenia. Since too the non-paranoid schizophrenics were not different from the normals the homosexuality cannot be linked to schizophrenia in general.

Conclusions

In this investigation Daston (1956) has provided good evidence for the psychoanalytic claim that homosexuality is an important factor in paranoid schizophrenia – for the results could not be explained on any other hypothesis. It must be noted, however, that this experiment does not bear on the aetiological significance of homosexuality in paranoia. In brief this experiment is strong support for one aspect of Freudian theory.

The work of Zamansky (1958)

Zamansky carried out what is probably the best known objective investigation into homosexuality and paranoia. The experimental technique was clever and the derivation of the hypotheses from the psychoanalytic theory subtle yet precise.

Sample. 20 male psychotic paranoids and 20 non-paranoid schizoid psychotics. Both groups were hospitalised.

Experimental measure. Time spent looking at pictures presented in pairs of males and females (time on male minus time on female).

Hypotheses. Since it had been previously shown by Zamansky that homosexuals did spend longer looking at male than female pictures, it could be hypothesised *that paranoids would spend more time looking at male pictures than a control group.* Freudian ego-defence theory states that defence mechanisms prevent the emergence of unacceptable impulses into consciousness. Two further hypotheses were therefore drawn up:

1. *Paranoids would fixate less on threatening pairs of pictures,* and
2. *Paranoids, when asked to select liked pictures, a process in which ego-defence would be involved, would select fewer male pictures than when their liking was measured by time of fixation.*

In addition the experiment attempted to answer the question of whether the homosexuality was due to the rejection of women (the Freudian theory – castration anxiety) or the attraction of men. If it were attraction, the hypothesis was set up that *paranoids would spend longer looking at males if a male and neutral pair of pictures was presented.* If it were rejection, *paranoids would fixate longer on the neutral of a female and neutral pair.*

Pairs of pictures. 9 male-female pairs, 4 male-neutral pairs, 4 female-neutral pairs, 4 threatening male (e.g. two men kissing) and 4 threatening female pairs and 4 neutral-neutral pairs. There was high agreement among raters for the threat-value of the pictures.

Results

(a) Male *v.* female pairs. The paranoids fixated significantly longer ($t = 5\cdot34$ sig. $\cdot01$ level). The hypothesis was supported.
(b) Threatening male *v.* female. No significant difference. Hypothesis not supported.
(c) Attraction score of paranoids would be greater than their stated preference. Hypothesis supported $t = 4\cdot40$. No difference in controls.
(d) Male *v.* neutral pairs. Paranoids fixated significantly longer on males ($t = 2\cdot18$ sig. $\cdot05$ level). Hypothesis supported.
(e) Female *v.* neutral pairs. No significant difference.

Comments

The fact that paranoids fixated longer on the male pictures than did the controls is impressive evidence that homosexuality is implicated in paranoia, especially since homosexuals have been shown thus to fixate. Results of this kind cannot, as with tests such as the Rorschach or Blacky Pictures, be impugned on grounds of dubious validity. Furthermore no other theory could predict such a finding. This result is, therefore, powerful support for the psychoanalytic theory. Result (c), that the attraction score was greater for paranoids – but not for schizophrenics – than the stated preference for pictures, is also good evidence for the work of ego-defences and the claim of Freudian theory that in paranoia the homosexuality is repressed. This experimental evidence is a far more precise test of the theory than the clinical surveys of the incidence of homosexual activity among paranoid schizophrenics. Finding (*b*) on the other hand fails to confirm the notion of ego-defence in that no differences were found between the groups. It is possible, of course, that the pictures were not as threatening to homosexuals as they appeared to the clinical psychologists. Clearly more research is needed into this type of measure of ego-defence. The last two findings (*d*) and (*e*) support the claim that homosexuals are attracted to men rather than repelled by women. However it is arguable that this part of the experiment is less well designed to test psychoanalytic theory than the earlier part of it. In Freudian theory, rejection of women comes about in homosexuality through castration anxiety – the rejection of the idea of beings without a penis. This fear is only likely to be effective in the case of a sexual object. Since the neutral pictures were designed specifically not to a rouse sexual desire, the female pictures may well not have provoked castration anxiety in this context.

Conclusion

Zamansky (1958) has provided powerful support for the psychoanalytic theory of paranoia. He has produced good evidence for the importance of homosexuality in this form of psychosis and for the fact that this homosexuality is repressed (despite the failure of one of his measures of this). The evidence that homosexuals do not reject women is perhaps not quite so watertight. However Zamansky notes that this finding fits the work of Knight (1940) who argued that the homosexuality of paranoids was due to reaction-formation against hostile Oedipal wishes against the father. This, however, is a departure from orthodox Freudian theory.

In brief, therefore, Zamansky may be regarded as having offered good support for the psychoanalytic theory that repressed homosexuality lies behind paranoid schizophrenia.

The work of Klaf and Davis (1960)

Since this is a clinical study it may be briefly examined. It is worthy of note, however, in that it uses statistical techniques to evaluate the data and tests one hypothesis which is not generally investigated.

Sample. 150 paranoid schizophrenics and 150 non-paranoid controls.

Data. Case records of the sample groups.

Statistical analysis. Chi-square tests between the groups.

Results. Significantly more of the paranoids had revealed homosexual preoccupation during therapeutic sessions (41% compared with 9%). Homosexual experiences were also twice as frequent (X^2 sig.). In addition 82% of the paranoids had male persecutors. Only 26% had delusions with sexual content. The control group, being non-psychotic, had no delusions.

Comments and conclusions

The non-schizophrenic controls are unsatisfactory in that differences could be due either to being paranoid or schizophrenic. The case file data too are of unknown validity and reliability. Nevertheless the fact of homosexual preoccupations and male persecutors does support Freudian theory. Whether or not incidence of overt homosexuality is evidence of the *repressed* homosexuality demanded by Freudian theory has already been discussed. If homosexuality is repressed the sexual content of delusions might not be high. This study, despite its shortcomings, does offer some support for Freudian theory.

The work of Klaf (1961)

Klaf approached the problem of paranoid homosexuality by conducting a clinical study of overt homosexuals to determine the extent of their paranoid ideation.

Sample and data. The case files of 100 homosexuals were examined.
Results. Paranoid ideation was found in 24% of males and 18% of females.

Comments and conclusions

This study appears to bear on the question of paranoia and homosexuality. However, it is illogical to argue that if paranoids are homosexual, homosexuals should be paranoid. In addition the difference between repressed and overt sexuality has been ignored. Furthermore paranoid ideation among homosexuals is more parsimoniously explained in the light of the social problems of being homosexual in a heterosexual society. It is therefore concluded that this study is valueless as regards the psychoanalytic theory of paranoia.

The work of Moore and Selzer (1963)

Moore and Selzer, in another clinical study, attempted to remedy the deficiency of the control group of Klaf and Davis (1960) by using as controls non-paranoid schizophrenics.

Sample. 128 paranoid and 177 non-paranoid schizophrenics.
Data. Case files of the two groups.
Results. To a significantly greater degree than controls, the paranoid sample showed a greater incidence of homosexuality, a greater preoccupation with homosexuality during the therapeutic sessions and were more often judged by psychiatrists and psychologists to be latently homosexual.

Comments and conclusions

Within the limits of this kind of clinical survey, Freudian theory is supported by these findings. However it must be noted that *some* non-paranoid schizophrenics had similar homosexual backgrounds. Moore and Selzer conclude from this that homosexuality cannot therefore be aetiological in paranoia. This however is an inadmissible case. If *projection* is not the chosen defence mechanism, by theory paranoia will not develop. Thus the incidence of homosexuality in some non-paranoid schizophrenics does not weaken the Freudian theory. This study therefore gives very limited clinical support for the psychoanalytic theory of paranoia.

The work of Watson (1965)

Watson, aware of the weakness of the clinical studies – they were concerned with *overt* homosexuality – investigated the incidence of repressed homosexuality among a small sample of paranoid schizophrenics.

Hypotheses. Since, in Freudian theory, homosexuality in paranoids is repressed, the following hypotheses may be drawn up:

(a) Paranoids should be lower than controls on a true-false, face-valid awareness of homosexuality scale.
(b) Paranoids should have response latencies to TAT-like pictures, with and without homosexual content, different from those of controls.
(c) Paranoids should be higher than controls on the MMPI Mf scale (whose items are unthreatening).

Sample. 27 paranoid, 23 non-paranoid schizophrenics.

Tests. MMPI, L, F, K and Mf scales, some TAT-like pictures and a homosexual awareness scale.

Method. The L, F, and K scales of the MMPI were used to select out from the sample those subjects whose attitudes to test-taking, for example defensiveness and putting the socially desirable response, were likely to distort the results.

Results

(a) The paranoids were lower ($t = 2 \cdot 85$ sig. at the $\cdot 01$ level) on the homosexual awareness scale.
(b) Paranoids had a higher latency ratio for homosexual pictures ($t = 2 \cdot 28$ sig. at $\cdot 05$ level).
(c) Paranoids were lower on the Mf scale of the MMPI than the controls (diff. not sig.).

Thus the first two findings confirmed the hypothesis: the third finding was contrary to prediction.

Comments and conclusions

The confirmation of hypotheses (a) and (b) is again powerful support for the psychoanalytic theory of repressed homosexuality being linked with paranoid schizophrenia. The failure of the third hypothesis to stand investigation could be due to the invalidity of the Mf scale. Indeed, as Grygier (1957a) points out in a survey of the psychometric techniques available for the assessment of homosexuality, despite its construction by empirical methods (criterion keying) the Mf scale reads suspiciously like a mid-West stereotype of a real man and a good woman. A simpler explanation could be that the MMPI Mf scale is in fact threatening to repressed (as distinct from overt) homosexuals – hence the low score.

Despite the problem of the failure of the third hypothesis to receive support, this study by Watson (1965) must be regarded as good evidence for the Freudian theory.

The work of Wolowitz (1965)

In an interesting study Wolowitz investigated a conflict theory of homosexuality in male paranoids. However it assumed that approach involves a wish to be dependent on powerful men and to appropriate their power through magical sexual aggression whereas avoidance involves castration fear by powerful males. This theory seems too far removed from classical psychoanalysis to be relevant. Nonetheless, he tried to compare predictions from this theory and from the orthodox theory by having a sample of paranoids and controls move photographs of men and women, whose power had been previously rated, in a tube-like apparatus until they looked 'best'. On classical theory men should always be placed nearer than women regardless of power rating: on the conflict theory male photographs should be displaced further away as their power increases. The results supported the conflict theory and Wolowitz concluded that attraction to men was based on power.

Comments and conclusions

This study has been only briefly summarised because of the curious nature of the theory it sought to prove and because of the unknown validity of the measurement technique. How valid was the 'power rating'? How do we know that such a rating was not inversely related to the sexual attractiveness of the men? Is placing a picture near or far a measure of sexual attraction?

Without further research on the techniques, especially the 'power' rating, these results can be regarded only as ingenious and interesting, not as evidence against the Freudian theory.

DISCUSSION AND CONCLUSIONS FROM EMPIRICAL STUDIES OF PARANOID SCHIZOPHRENIA

A. Clinical studies

Even where large samples of patients are used and statistical analysis of the results carried out, it is clear that clinical studies are beset by problems:

1. The reliability and validity of the case material.
2. The reliability and validity of the interpretations of these data, e.g. evidence for 'latent homosexuality'.
3. The relevance of homosexual activity to the Freudian claim that *repressed* homosexuality is important in the development of paranoia.
4. The contaminating effects of the fact that, in some cases at least, the investigators had also carried out the psychotherapy.

These difficulties inevitably mean that all results must be treated with very great caution. The one good point of the studies resides in the large samples used. Nevertheless it is of interest that in general these clinical studies do support the psychoanalytic theory in as much as homosexuality appears to be an important factor in paranoid schizophrenia. The fact that, albeit to a much smaller degree, homosexuality was implicated in schizophrenia does not disprove the Freudian theory. What is clearly needed is a study of the defence mechanisms used against it. If it could be shown that paranoids characteristically employed projection as a means of defence whereas the non-paranoid schizophrenics did not, there would be support for the theory or, if this was not the case, refutation. The final conclusion, therefore, from these clinical studies must be *that to a very limited extent, they support the psychoanalytic theory of paranoid schizophrenia.*

B.1. Objective studies using tests

With this type of investigation all depends upon the samples and the validity of the tests used. In all the three researches examined the samples were small and the validity of the tests by no means well proven. Thus the Rorschach and TAT as used by Zeichner (1955) are not universally accepted, a statement which must also apply to the projective pictures used by Watson (1965). The Blacky Pictures (Aronson, 1953) do not even contain a direct measure of homosexuality repressed or overt. The psychometric measures such as the MMPI are also open to question especially in the light of the problems of response sets (e.g. Cronbach, 1946 and 1950). As with the clinical studies, therefore, the results must be regarded with caution.

In fact two studies do support the theory (Zeichner, 1955, Watson, 1965) while the work of Aronson (1953) fails to confirm it. Of all these the research by Watson is the most persuasive in that his hypothesis embraced the concept of repressed, not overt, homosexuality and his measure of homosexuality – reaction time to pictures – would appear to be valid since reaction time is generally considered a fair indicator of emotional involvement (e.g. Jung, 1918 and the Kent-Rosanoff word association list).

Thus from these studies with tests, it may generally be concluded *that psychoanalytic theory is confirmed but that great weight cannot be put upon the results.*

B.2. Objective experimental studies

If the sampling is acceptable, experimental studies must provide the most powerful evidence, provided only that the experimental procedures are good derivations from the psychoanalytic theory. If this is the case the results must either confirm or refute the theory. Thus the fact that Daston (1956) found that paranoids recognised homosexual words more quickly than controls must be regarded as powerful evidence that homosexuality is implicated in paranoia. The results cannot be interpreted in any other way. Similarly the work of Zamansky (1958) is impressive support. Thus his finding that paranoids fixate longer than controls on homosexual pictures agrees with Daston (1956). However, his finding that an attraction score was higher than a stated preference score for homosexual partners is evidence that the homosexuality is repressed. The work of Wolowitz (1965), on the other hand, illustrates the problems in the experimental method in that the hypotheses he tested do not seem very close or relevant to the underlying theory.

In summary then, *two of the experimental studies are impressive support for psychoanalytic theory.*

Summary

Clinical studies of paranoid schizophrenia and objective studies using tests give support for the Freudian theory but need to be treated with caution. The experimental studies, however, provide good evidence for the psychoanalytic theory. In brief the Freudian theory of paranoid schizophrenia is confirmed.

Tabular summary of studies of paranoid schizophrenia

Investigation	Comments	Result
Norman (1948)	Clinical: case records	Some support
Klein and Horwitz (1949)	Clinical: case records and no control group Methodologically weak	No support
Aronson (1953)	Blacky pictures used	No support
Zeichner (1955)	TAT and Rorschach	Some support
Daston (1956)	Experimental: reaction-times	Strong support
Zamansky (1958)	Experimental	Strong support
Klaf and Davis (1960)	Clinical: poor control-group	Some support
Klaf (1961)	Clinical: illogical hypothesis	No support
Moore and Selzer (1963)	Clinical	Some support
Watson (1965)	TAT, MMPI and reaction-times	Support
Wolowitz (1965)	Experimental: complex derivation of hypotheses	No support

ORAL CONFLICT AND SCHIZOPHRENIA

The work of Bergman *et al.*

Bergman *et al.* (1968) studied the strength of oral conflict among schizophrenics. These authors claim that oral conflict is an important factor in schizophrenia in psychoanalytic theory, although Fenichel (1945) clearly indicates that regression is seen as the main feature of this disease. However since regression to a narcissistic stage implies regression to an oral stage, oral conflict can be implicated in schizophrenia. Nevertheless it must be admitted that oral conflict is not a central issue in the development of schizophrenia in Freudian theory.

Sample

Study 1. 26 male and 29 female schizophrenics and normal controls.

Study 2. 33 male and 27 female schizophrenics, 16 neurotics, 23 depressives, 12 co-twins, 27 biological parents and 14 adoptive parents.

Measures. The authors reasoned that oral conflict would show itself in impairment in oral behaviour. Thus three measures of oral behaviour were used, which in a previous study (Bergman *et al.*, 1967) had shown themselves to be related negatively to the MMPI R scale which may be considered to be a measure of repression. These oral tests were:

Sucking. Strength of suck on a pipe.

Swallowing. 4 sizes of pill were presented – the biggest one that could be swallowed was noted.

Biting. Time taken to bite through a hose.

Vital capacity, i.e. lung capacity, was also measured, as was manual strength.

Results. In the first study male schizophrenics had a significant deficit in sucking strength compared with normals, a deficit which was not so marked in the second study. Female schizophrenics showed this deficit in both studies. The second investigation showed that neurotics, depressives and the familial blood relatives of schizophrenics did not differ from normals in sucking strength. The authors conclude that oral conflict is a factor in schizophrenia.

Comments and conclusions

A nice feature of this study is the measure of oral conflict. As must now be only too evident to the reader of this book, a major weakness of so many investigations into psychoanalytic hypotheses is the validity of the tests, especially when these consist of questionnaire items. In this case the validity cannot be impugned. The test is an example of the required behaviour and if oral conflict has any behavioural implications, i.e. is a useful concept, it must evince itself in decrements of oral behaviour. Of course it could be that other factors such as embarrassment (which the authors discount) influenced the sucking of schizophrenics. However it is still pertinent to ask, if this be the case, why schizophrenics and not others are thus affected. Thus these results may be taken as evidence of oral conflict in schizophrenia.

In psychoanalytic theory (see p. 261) oral fixation is strongly implicated in depression. The finding, therefore, that depressives were no different from normals and less conflicted than schizophrenics is not really in accord with psychoanalytic theory. It is also curious that other oral behaviours were not similarly affected. The sex difference, which was evident in their previous study (Bergman *et al.*, 1967), where sucking strength was related to personality variables in females but physical variables in males, is also an inexplicable feature for an oral test.

These difficulties and problems mentioned in the last paragraph mean that although the results may be regarded as evidence for oral conflict in schizophrenia, they must be treated as suggestive rather than definitive. In addition it must be remembered that oral conflict is not a major point in the Freudian theory of schizophrenia. It seems to us, in conclusion, that this study is memorable more for the ingenuity of its measures than the power of its results.

STUDIES OF THE FREUDIAN THEORY OF HOMOSEXUALITY

THE THEORY

The basis of the Freudian theory may be found in the castration complex. The homosexual male refuses to admit that there are beings without a penis and therefore devotes his attention to males. According to Fenichel (1945), the female homosexual has a similar castration fear. In addition cross-sex identification aids homosexual object choice.

Empirically then, homosexuals suffer from castration anxiety and identify with the opposite sexual parent.

INVESTIGATIONS OF THE FREUDIAN THEORY

The work of Grygier

In three publications (Carstairs and Grygier, 1957, Grygier, 1957a and Grygier, 1958) Grygier has discussed problems inherent in the empirical study of homosexuality and reported some preliminary results with his own personality test, the Dynamic Personality Inventory (1961). In a previous chapter on Freudian psychosexual theory the construction and validity of this test have been fully discussed (see p. 19). The conclusion reached, it will be remembered, was based on a study by Kline (1968b) that the validity of the Dynamic Personality Inventory was open to doubt. Nevertheless it is one of the few instruments capable of testing psychoanalytic theory and the results obtained with it deserve scrutiny.

Carstairs and Grygier (1957); Grygier (1957a)

In the study reported in these two papers a small group of homosexuals was compared with normals on the DPI scales.

Sample. 203 normals and 30 neurotic homosexuals.

Test. DPI.

Results. The homosexuals were significantly higher on narcissism and feminine identification. Half the homosexual sample showed a reversal of sexual identification.

Comments and conclusions. This study was unsatisfactory because the experimental group was both homosexual and neurotic. It is obvious, therefore, that any differences from the normal group could be attributed either to neurosis or homosexuality. Although the results – that homosexuals were more narcissistic and identified with women rather than men – support Freudian theory (indeed narcissistic fixation is an element in the psychoanalytic theory) the main theoretical claim relating to castration anxiety was not supported. This is important since it is this anxiety that leads to the feminine identification and hence the homosexuality. Thus even if the error of the non-neurotic control group is ignored, this study by Grygier cannot be said to confirm the Freudian theory. It does, however, indicate that the DPI may be a useful test for discriminating homosexuals.

Grygier (1958)

In an attempt to improve his control group, Grygier compared neurotic homosexuals with neurotic heterosexuals. Thus any differences were now attributable to homosexuality.

Sample. 20 homosexual neurotics and 22 heterosexual neurotics.

Results. The homosexuals were high (significantly higher than the control group) on *need for warmth* (Wp). They were significantly higher than controls and normals, indeed as high as women, on *narcissism* and *feminine identification*.

Comments and conclusions. These results with the DPI confirm the findings from the earlier study. Again they support the utility of this personality test as a measure of homosexuality. They do not, however, confirm the psychoanalytic theory that castration anxiety is fundamental to homosexuality.

Conclusions from the three studies by Grygier

Although the DPI seems capable of discriminating homosexuals from heterosexuals, psychoanalytic theory is not entirely supported. Whether this be due to the invalidity of the test or the failure of the theory cannot be determined from this work. Nevertheless psychoanalytic theory cannot be said to be supported by these investigations.

The work of Lindner (1953)

Lindner made a psychological study of 67 prisoners guilty of sexual offences.

Sample. 67 prisoners convicted for offences of: homosexuality (37), sodomy (10), rape (9), pedophilia (8), exhibitionism (1), carnal knowledge (1) and contributing to the delinquency of minors (1). The controls used were matched for age, race, IQ, marital status, number of crimes and length of sentence.

Test. The Blacky Pictures.

Results. The sex criminals were differentiated by the chi-square test from the controls on 9 of the 13 variables. The sexual offenders were higher on: oral erotism, Oedipus complex, masturbation guilt, castration complex, sibling rivalry and guilt feelings (·001 level), oral sadism and narcissistic love object (·01 level) and anaclitic love object (·05 level). However the Blacky Pictures were unable to differentiate any of the sub-groups within the sex offenders nor could they discriminate between the homosexual (homosexuals and sodomites) offenders and the others.

Comments and conclusions

Although in the most general terms this study by Lindner supports psychoanalytic theory in that sexual offenders were more disturbed in psychosexual development than non-sexual offenders, in specific terms it fails to do so. The fact that homosexuals were not differentiated from heterosexuals, certainly on the castration anxiety card, is contrary to theory. Whether this failure be due to the test or the theory is difficult to determine. However some positive results have been obtained with the Blacky Pictures and there is, as has been discussed in an earlier chapter (see p. 82), some evidence for their construct validity.

It must be concluded, therefore, that this study by Lindner (1953) fails to support the psychoanalytic theory of homosexuality. It is of interest to note here that Thomas (1951), in an unpublished doctoral dissertation cited by Taulbee and Stenmark (1968), also failed to support the psychoanalytic theory of homosexuality in a study with the Blacky Pictures.

In a research already fully discussed in our study of the evidence for the castration complex (see p. 102), Schwartz (1956) compared a sample of 20 homosexuals with a normal control group on indices of the castration complex derived from the TAT test. The validity and reliability of these measures is not considerable so that the fact that three of the scores differentiated the groups cannot be considered as anything but very limited support for the Freudian claim that castration anxiety is an important factor in homosexuality.

The work of Bieber *et al.* (1962)

Bieber *et al.* carried out a large clinical study of 106 homosexuals and controls. All subjects were undergoing analysis which varied from strictly Freudian to 'cultural' – a term applied to those psychiatrists who regard the Oedipus complex as pathological rather than the inevitable result of the nuclear family constellation.

The main body of results will not, however, be discussed here since it was derived from data which cannot be held to be scientific despite the fact that they were subjected to very detailed statistical analysis.

Data. 77 psychoanalysts of whom 58 contributed data on the homosexual group took part in this investigation. They filled in three questionnaires about homosexual patients and controls.

Examples of questions. Did patient regard his father as an admirable person? Did mother humiliate patient?

Comments and conclusions

From this brief description of the methodology it appears that the data refer only to the analysts' clinical impressions of the patients. All these responses must be inferred from the therapeutic session. The statistical results therefore refer, in truth, to analysts' conceptions of homosexual patients contrasted with controls. Furthermore, since the data were contributed by so large a number of analysts, comparability between protocols is suspect. Thus in our view Bieber's study cannot be regarded as objective evidence of homosexual behaviour, despite the statistical analysis and the control group: rather it is a study of analytic views of homosexuals and controls.

However, the final part of the study was concerned with the therapeutic outcome of these 106 homosexual patients. This part does constitute an objective test of the psychoanalytic treatment of homosexuality and is discussed in the next chapter (see p. 314).

The work of Goldberg and Milstein (1965)

Goldberg and Milstein carried out a perceptual investigation into the psycho-analytic theory of latent homosexuality in women.

Sample. 15 low latent homosexual women and 10 high latent homosexual women. These groups were selected by the MMPI.

Method. Six pictures were shown to the groups by tachistoscope. Three pictures were rated as non-threatening to both groups – a clothed male, a clothed female and an ambiguous figure. Three pictures were rated on psychoanalytic theory as threatening to the high group – a nude male (fear of female genitalia), a nude female and two nude females.

Hypothesis. By *selective vigilance* (Blum, 1954, see p. 176) people should be sensitive to cues relevant to repressed impulses. However, when impulses begin to approach consciousness a second process occurs – *ego defence* – and at this point individuals try not to perceive the impulses. With these two concepts (related to psychoanalytic theory) the hypothesis was formed that the high homo-sexual group would show *longer latencies for the highly threatening pictures* (*perceptual defence*) but *shorter latencies for the low threat pictures* (*selective vigilance*).

Results. The hypothesis was confirmed.

Comments and conclusions

Psychoanalytic theory concerning the defensive processes in homosexuality in women was supported by this study. It also supports the claim that castration anxiety (the unclothed male) is important in female homosexuality. The design of the experiment precludes sexual anxiety from being the source of variance since this would have equally affected both groups. This study supports, there-fore, the psychoanalytic theory of the role of the ego defences in female homo-sexuality.

The work of Kline (1967c)

Kline studied the Freudian claim (Freud, 1908a) that as homosexuals express their anal erotism directly, they should therefore possess few anal traits.

Sample. 13 homosexual men referred to a clinic for treatment.

Test. Ai3, a measure of the anal character.

Results. The mean score of the homosexuals was not significantly different from that of comparable student groups. The non-significant differences were also in the wrong direction.

Comments and conclusions

The validity of Ai3 as a measure of the anal character has already been fully discussed (p. 26) and it appears to be a valid test. The sample of homosexuals was small but all were rated by the psychologist in charge of them as Kinsey 3 or more. The Kinsey scale of homosexuality (Kinsey *et al.*, 1948), which attempts to measure the amount of homosexual behaviour and feeling within individuals, has 3 as its middle ranking. It means that 50% of sexual outlets and feelings are homosexual. Thus the homosexuality of the sample can hardly be impugned. It must be concluded that this study entirely fails to support the Freudian hypothesis.

The work of De Luca (1967)

De Luca attempted to examine the psychosexual constitution of male homosexuals by means of the Blacky Pictures.

Sample. 20 male homosexuals and 40 male controls.

Test. The Blacky Pictures (Blum, 1949).

Scoring system. Blum's (1962) factor-analytic scoring system was used (see p. 83).

Results. The homosexuals were differentiated on only one of the 30 factors.

Comments and conclusions

Since according to psychoanalytic theory, as we have seen, a number of psychosexual differences would be predicted between homosexuals and normals – for example, differences in castration anxiety, Oedipal conflict and parental identification – the fact that only one of the thirty factors discriminated significantly certainly fails to support the theory. Since also, in our discussion of the Blacky Pictures (see p. 83), it appeared that there is some evidence for the validity of this projective technique, it is difficult in this case to impute the failure to confirm psychoanalytic theory to the test rather than the theory.

Thus this study by De Luca certainly fails to confirm Freudian developmental hypotheses concerning male homosexuality.

CONCLUSIONS FROM ALL THE STUDIES CONCERNING THE THEORY OF HOMOSEXUALITY

Only one of these studies, that of Goldberg and Milstein (1965), supports psychoanalytic theory regarding homosexuality and that was concerned more perhaps with its concomitant defensive mechanisms for which good evidence exists (see Chapters 6 and 8). For the main Freudian hypothesis that homosexuality is a result of the castration complex—castration anxiety—there is no support. Thus, although it may be due to methodological weaknesses, it must be concluded that *there is no objective evidence supporting the Freudian theory of homosexuality.*

PSYCHOSOMATIC DISORDERS

Alexander (1950) and Alexander and French (1948), at the Chicago Institute of Psychoanalysis, have concentrated on developing Freudian theory to give a specific understanding of certain diseases or disorders which are known to be affected by psychological events. The diseases subjected to special study have been asthma, peptic ulcer and ulcerative colitis. Although strictly a development of orthodox Freudian theory, it is such an easily taken step which introduces little new into the theory, that objective study of their claims must lead to a better appreciation of the orthodox Freudian concepts involved. This application of psychoanalytic theory to psychosomatic disorders has not gone uncriticised by non-analytic psychiatrists. Thus, for example, Mayer-Gross, Slater and Roth (1961) write that 'The psychoanalytic interpretation of psychosomatic disorders is, of all applications of Freudian theory, the least satisfactory . . .'

OBJECTIVE STUDIES OF THE PSYCHOANALYTIC THEORY OF ASTHMA

The work of Stein and Ottenberg (1958)

Stein and Ottenberg investigated the role of odours in asthma.

Samples. Two methods were used. For method 1 the sample was 25 asthmatics; for method 2, 20 asthmatics and 20 controls were studied.

Methods

1. Asthmatics were interviewed about the role of odours in their attacks. Judges then classified substances which were mentioned as oral or anal.

2. 19 odorous substances were presented to asthmatics and controls. Free associations were then elicited to the smells.

Results

Method 1. In this sample 5% of attacks were provoked by smells of food; 75% of attacks were provoked by smells on a continuum clean-unclean; 13% of attacks by substances such as the scent of flowers. From this Stein and Ottenberg concluded that the majority of attacks were provoked by smells which could be classified as anal derivative.

Method 2. The free associations to smells of the asthmatic group were significantly more blocked than were the free associations of the controls. From this it was argued by the authors that such smells were a source of conflict for the asthmatic group.

From both these results Stein and Ottenberg (1958) concluded that asthma was a psychological defence against activation of childhood conflicts (anal) by odours. Hence the anal phase of development was implicated in asthma.

Comments and conclusions

If the anal significance of clean-unclean smells is accepted, then this investigation does implicate anality in asthma. It cannot be the case that such smells naturally create chronic bronchial disturbances since a control group was used in the experiment. This study therefore supports the psychoanalytic anal aetiology of asthmatics.

The work of Margolis (1961)

Margolis investigated the mother-child relationship in bronchial asthma.

Samples. 25 mothers of asthmatic children, 25 mothers of children suffering from rheumatic fever, and 25 mothers of normal children.

Tests. The mothers were given the Blacky Pictures and a test of parent-child relationships.

Results. The 'asthmatic' mothers were higher than the other groups on Oedipal conflict and oral erotism.

Comments and conclusions

This study sought explicitly to test the hypothesis of French and Alexander (1941) that behind the asthmatic attack lies excessive dependence on anal longing for the mother. It would appear a better strategy to examine such a claim by testing the children rather than the mothers. The fact that the asthmatic mothers were more Oedipal gives only very slight confirmation of the hypothesis. This study cannot be held to support psychoanalytic theory.

The work of Pollie (1964)

Pollie carried out a projective study of conflict and defence in both bronchial asthmatics and patients suffering from peptic ulcers.

Sample. 61 patients with duodenal ulcer, 46 asthma patients, 52 patients with gastro-intestinal symptoms and 20 normal controls (medical students).

Tests. The Blacky Pictures and the related Defence Preference Inquiry.

Results. The asthmatics were less defensive than ulcer patients: avoidance rather than reaction-formation was their preferred mode of defence. Over-attachment to the mother was also noted.

Comments and conclusions

The validity of the Defence Preference Inventory is not well established so that the conclusions concerning defensive processes cannot be accepted un-critically. The authors claim that these results support French and Alexander (1941), especially the finding concerning the mother-child relationship. However they cannot be regarded as good evidence for classical psychoanalytic theory since this mother relationship is usually associated with oral fixation (Fenichel, 1945). Thus differences on Blacky anal and oral cards would be expected. In brief, this study supports the psychoanalytic claim that the mother-child relationship is disturbed in asthma but does not confirm the pregenital fixation which is a part of such disturbance.

The work of Seiden (1965)

Seiden administered the Blacky Pictures to a sample of asthmatic children to determine whether the age of onset of the attacks was related to the level of fixation. Unfortunately, this is a very brief report in the *American Psychologist* so that it is difficult to evaluate the study.

Sample. 45 asthmatic children. Three groups, defined by age of onset as oral, anal and phallic.

Test. Blacky Pictures (old scoring system).

Results. Freudian theory, that asthma is related to pregenital fixation, was supported in that each group showed the strongest conflict in the area related to the age of onset of attacks.

Comments and conclusions

This study by Seiden indicates that onset of asthma is related to 'current psycho-sexual difficulties'. Pregenital fixations are therefore implicated. However, without a control group of normals and, for preference, other psychosomatic groups, further conclusions cannot be drawn.

Conclusions from all the studies of the psychoanalytic theory of asthma

The general tenor of these studies implicates psychosexual developmental factors in asthma. This certainly fits psychoanalytic theory. However as Fenichel (1945) admits, what differentiates the development of a pregenital conversion neurosis (e.g. asthma) or a compulsion neurosis is not fully understood. Furthermore pregenital fixation is a factor in a large number of abnormalities in psycho-analytic theory. Thus the objective findings reported here can only be regarded as very tenuous support for Freudian theory which is by no means explicit. French and Alexander (1941) argue that the asthmatic attack is a reaction to the danger of separation from the mother, an equivalent of a cry of rage, and that mastery of fear of being left alone governs the asthmatic's life. This however is a long way from orthodox Freudian theory. In summary, therefore, these objective studies of asthma give only vague support for psychoanalytic theory which on this point is itself vague.

PEPTIC ULCER AND ULCERATIVE COLITIS

Psychoanalytic theory, in the case of peptic ulcer at least, is certainly better defined than is the case with asthma. Fenichel (1945), summarising Freudian beliefs, argues that the peptic ulcer patient is hungry for love. This hunger causes the mucous membrane of the stomach to secrete – hence the ulcer – and is related to repressed oral erotism.

Similarly ulcerative colitis represents the result of anal (rather than oral) conflicts. Fenichel (1945) points out that colitis may be the result of the organism being constantly under eliminative and retentive pressure, just as the peptic ulcer results from receptive pressure. This relationship between peptic ulcers and ulcerative colitis, reception and retention or elimination, was powerfully developed to embrace all the neuroses by Alexander (1935) in the concept of vector analysis. However vector analysis is a long way from orthodox psychoanalytic theory and its investigation is beyond the scope of this chapter.

What is clear, therefore, from this brief discussion of the psychoanalytic theory of peptic ulcer and ulcerative colitis is that oral and anal influences are to be expected in these disorders.

OBJECTIVE STUDIES OF PEPTIC ULCER AND ULCERATIVE COLITIS

Studies using the Blacky Pictures

A series of studies of peptic ulcer patients was carried out beginning with Blum and Kaufmann (1952) and ending with an investigation by Berger (1959). Since each of these studies is related the discussion and conclusions will be common to all of them.

The work of Blum and Kaufmann (1952)

Sample. 14 male peptic ulcer patients + controls.

Results. All 14 patients were disturbed for oral eroticism – on the criterion of the spontaneous story. However on the multiple-choice questions two trends were found:

1. Half the sample put, as expected, the disturbed response.
2. Half the sample put the conflict-free response.

Blum and Kaufmann argued from these findings that there were two patterns of dynamics in ulcer patients: *primary*, where the oral conflict is close to conscious and *reactive*, where there is an attempt at denial of dependency.

The work of Marquis, Sinnett and Winter (1952)

Sample. 16 male ulcer patients.

Results. These authors report similar results to those of Blum and Kaufmann (1952). The peptic ulcer patients were characterised by oral disturbances. Again a reactive type, where the dependency was denied and a primary type was recognised. No control group was used, however, so that the importance of the oral conflict is difficult to gauge.

The work of Streitfield (1954)

Sample. 20 ulcer patients and 20 non-gastro-intestinal psychosomatic controls.

Results. Oral erotism scores on the Blacky Test did not distinguish the ulcer group from the control group, as would be expected from psychoanalytic theory.

There were however, from the Rorschach test, stronger oral aggressive wishes in the ulcer patients.

The work of Winter (1955)

Winter developed further the findings already reported.

Sample. 68 peptic ulcer patients.

Results. Two separate scales for measuring the primary and reactive ulcer patients were constructed from responses to the Blacky Pictures. The primary pattern was one of overt, immature dependence. The reactive pattern was self-sufficient, high achieving and determinedly independent. These two Blacky scales were validated against the Rorschach test. Winter concluded that the Blacky Pictures could discriminate two patterns of ulcer dynamics, the primary and the reactive, this last being the typical ulcer personality. This study therefore confirms the findings of Blum and Kaufmann (1952) and Marquis *et al.* (1952).

The work of Bernstein and Chase (1955)

Bernstein and Chase objected to the study of Blum and Kaufmann on the grounds that the half of the sample who made neutral choices on the enquiry items had not in fact been diagnosed as reactive by any independent judge or criterion: they were reactive because they chose the neutral items. It is therefore circular to use neutral items to discriminate reactive ulcer patients. So they further investigated the problem.

Sample. 20 peptic ulcer patients, 20 psychosomatic non-ulcer patients, 20 surgical patients.

Results. Contrary to the majority of findings but in agreement with Streitfield (1945), the ulcer patients could not be discriminated from the others on the Blacky Pictures. Furthermore, Bernstein and Chase could find no evidence for differentiating a primary or a reactive pattern.

The work of Berger (1959)

Berger points out that the primary and reactive patterns described by Blum and Kaufmann (1952) and Marquis *et al.* (1952) were worked out from the same small group of subjects. Furthermore, although Winter (1955) cross-validated the Blacky indices of primary and reactive patterns on 68 ulcer patients, no control group was used. Berger therefore administered these scales to a control group and compared the results with those of Winter.

Sample. 30 surgical, non-ulcer patients.

Results. On the original primary scale of Winter this surgical control group differed to some extent from Winter's ulcer patients: on the reactive scale there was even better discrimination. However on the revised scales, as developed by Winter, the surgical controls were not significantly different from Winter's ulcer patients. Berger therefore concluded that Winter's claim of two personality patterns in patients suffering from peptic ulcer was correct, but that these patterns were also to be found in non-ulcer cases.

Conclusions from these studies using the Blacky Pictures

The position is that three investigators, Streitfield (1954), Bernstein and Chase (1955) and Berger (1959), fail to support the psychoanalytic theory of peptic ulcers and fail to find either a prominent position for oral fixation or two distinctive personality patterns. Blum and Kaufmann (1952) and Marquis *et al.* (1952), using the same sample, and Winter (1955) do however support the theory. The fact that Berger found patterns in surgical controls similar to those of Winter, who had no control group, rather discounts the work of Winter. Such patterns are of little value if they are not peculiar to ulcer patients. This only leaves the studies by Blum and Kaufmann and Marquis *et al.* on 16 patients, to support the theory. Thus the weight of the evidence from these studies of ulcer patients with the Blacky Pictures does not support psychoanalytic theory. Only two early studies (with the same sample) favour Freud. Later studies fail to replicate the findings.

Other studies

The work of Mednick, Garner and Stone (1959)

Mednick *et al.* carried out an ingenious investigation of Alexander's specificity theory. The study is relevant to this chapter in that this theory was derived from psychoanalytic theory, but it deserves only brief mention because it is not truly testing Freudian theory. Ulcerative colitis patients, it was hypothesised, on a complex task, would *initially show a devil-may-care attitude,* produce *a fantastic performance or give up entirely,* and afterwards would show *projection* in explaining their performance. Ulcer patients, on the other hand, would be *initially optimistic,* would *persist in the task until it was completed,* and would afterwards *deny any dependence* on the help of the experimenters.

Experimental task. Amidst a complex mass of electronic machinery a pursuit-rotor task had to be performed.

Measures. Questionnaire measures of initial attitude and post-task defences were taken.

Results. None of these hypotheses was confirmed.

Discussion and comments. To the extent that Alexander's themes are dependent on psychoanalytic theories this failure to confirm the theories fails to confirm psychoanalytic theory. Even if the initial and post-task measures were not valid, the actual behaviour during the task did not support the theory. This study certainly runs counter to psychoanalytic psychosomatic theory.

The work of Pollie (1964)

This investigation with the Blacky Pictures has already been reviewed in our discussion of the studies of bronchial asthma. The experimental details may be found on p. 283.

Sample. 61 patients with duodenal ulcers.

Results. Compared with control groups of asthma patients, gastro-intestinal patients and a small group of normal controls, the ulcer patients showed great defensiveness in almost all conflict areas. They were not, however, differentiated from the other groups on oral erotism.

Comments and conclusions. The fact that the ulcer patients were not higher than the controls on oral erotism is certainly contrary to Freudian theory. However, the fact that they were so defensive could account for this low score. Thus it will be remembered that in those studies where the primary and reactive patterns of ulcer dynamics were noted (e.g. Marquis *et al.*, 1952), the reactive type was characterised by just this fact: he picked neutral choices on the questions attached to the oral card. Thus his overall oral erotism score, using the orthodox scoring manual, would not be high. This defensiveness could account for the low scores obtained for ulcer patients in this study by Pollie. On the other hand, as we have seen, the validity of such reactive scores is strongly open to doubt. It must be concluded, therefore, that this study fails to support the Freudian theory of gastric ulceration.

The work of Wolowitz

Wolowitz (1967) and Wolowitz and Wagonfeld (1968) have produced two studies of the psychoanalytic theory of peptic ulcer, as explicitly formulated by Alexander (1950). Unlike the majority of empirical investigations in this area, they used not the Blacky Pictures but the Food Preference Inventory (Wolowitz, 1964). This test which, it is claimed, taps oral passive or oral sadistic involvement consists of a number of forced choice items concerning food preferences where the subject has to choose a hot sweet liquid food (passive) or a sharp, sour dry one (sadistic) – rice pudding or pickles. It is thus not, in content at least, unlike the corresponding scales of the Dynamic Personality Inventory (Grygier, 1961) which is not well validated (e.g. Kline, 1968b, Stringer, 1970). The validity of the FPI rests on the fact that it discriminated alcoholics from controls (Story, 1963; see p. 296).

Rationale of the studies. Since peptic ulcer is a symptom of oral fixation, the hypothesis can be made that peptic ulcer patients will score more highly on the oral passive scale of the FPI than comparable controls.

Sample in study 1 (Wolowitz, 1967). 20 male peptic ulcer patients and 23 psychiatric controls.

Results. 17 of the ulcer patients were above the median on the FPI and 18 controls below the median – a difference significant at the ·005 level.

The psychiatric controls were an obvious objection to this study. To improve the experimental design the second investigation was carried out by Wolowitz and Wagonfeld (1968).

Sample. 38 peptic ulcer patients and 62 patients with gastro-intestinal complaints other than peptic ulcer.

Results. Again the peptic ulcer patients were higher on the oral passive scale than the controls (t = 4·01, sig. at the ·01 level).

Comments (both studies). The results of the first study are probably better ignored, not merely because the control group were psychiatric rather than normal, but because they were not also suffering from gastro-intestinal complaints. It is well known that ulcer sufferers are frequently recommended to milky diets in an effort to prevent the ulcer worsening, and indeed preference for such foods on the part of ulcer patients could merely indicate the fact that they tend to cause less discomfort than other foods. Such an explanation could easily account for the findings of the first study, especially since the onset of peptic ulcer is frequently insidious rather than acute.

This interpretation of the observed differences on the FPI is less applicable to the second study where the controls were also suffering from gastro-intestinal complaints, especially where these were also insidious. However the results only indicate that peptic ulcer patients prefer soft pappy foods rather than sour spicy food. Whether this indicates oral passivity is another question. We cannot assume that it does since this link is a part of the psychoanalytic theory we are attempting to verify.

Conclusions

Nevertheless the fact remains that from psychoanalytic theory we should hypothesise peptic ulcer patients as oral passive and by a further theoretical jump as liking soft foods. This prediction has been clearly confirmed – a prediction unlikely to be made from any other theory. Thus these studies by Wolowitz, especially the second by Wolowitz and Wagonfeld (1968), must be held to confirm the psychoanalytic theory of peptic ulcer.

Conclusions from all studies of peptic ulcer and ulcerative colitis

The majority of the investigations discussed in this section fail to support psychoanalytic theory. Those that do depend on ignoring the normal scoring system for the Blacky Pictures and counting neutral responses as reactive. Blum (1962), in his factor-analytic study of the Blacky Pictures, provides a rationale for this procedure in that a 'defensive' factor loaded on such neutral items can be observed. On the other hand Berger's (1959) study does not lend empirical support to scales derived from this approach to scoring.

It must be concluded therefore, that in the case of peptic ulcers and ulcerative colitis the evidence does not confirm psychoanalytic theory, except for the studies of Wolowitz using a food preference inventory.

INVESTIGATIONS OF THE PSYCHOANALYTIC THEORY OF STUTTERING
Theory

Fenichel (1945) claims that the psychoanalysis of stutterers reveals the anal sadistic universe of wishes as the basis for the symptom. Speaking has an anal sadistic significance. In addition phallic, oral and exhibitionistic impulses play a part, though minor to that of the anal components.

The work of Merchant (1952)

Blum and Hunt (1952), in their study of the validity of the Blacky Pictures, cite this unpublished study of stuttering by Merchant.

Sample. 20 stutterers and 20 controls.

Results. Stutterers were significantly higher on the following scores of the Blacky Pictures: oral erotism, oral sadism, castration anxiety and penis envy, identification, guilt feelings and anaclitic love object. They were lower on anal expulsiveness.

Comments and conclusions

This study supports the implication of the minor components (oral and phallic erotism) in stuttering. It is reasonable to take scores on the castration complex and penis envy card as indicative of phallic fixation. It does not, however, confirm the most important psychoanalytic claim – that relating to anal sadism. This investigation cannot therefore be regarded as support, except in a very minor way, for Freudian theory.

The work of Carp (1962)

Carp also used the Blacky Pictures to investigate the psychosexual development of stutterers.

Sample. 20 stutterers and 20 student controls at a Midwestern college.

Results. The experimental group were higher on oral sadism, the spontaneous story of the oral erotic card, and phallic erotism. On anal retentiveness there was no difference, while they were lower on anal expulsiveness.

Comments and conclusions

This study is very similar to that of Merchant. It again fails to support the main psychoanalytic hypothesis, although oral and phallic components do appear to play a part in stuttering.

Conclusions from both studies

These studies fail to support the major psychoanalytic propositions concerning stuttering. Obviously further study is required with the oral pictures to see whether stutterers can be separated from, for example, ulcer patients. The final conclusion concerning stuttering must be 'no support'.

APPENDICITIS

The work of Eylon (1967)

As Eylon points out, most writers on psychosomatic medicine, for example Alexander (1950), Alexander and French (1948), Lief *et al.* (1963), contain no reference to appendicitis. However, Dunbar (1954) does discuss pseudo-appendicitis and, in connection with this, Eylon draws attention to the fact that pathologists regard chronic inflammation of the appendix as rare (e.g. Robbins, 1962).

Hypothesis tested. The basic hypothesis tested by Eylon was that 'some event in real life gives rise to birth fantasies which initiate acute pain in the right iliac fossa, leading to the diagnosis of acute appendicitis and appendectomy'. Such real life events are: childbirth, forthcoming childbirth or weddings among people who are psychologically close to the patient.

These hypotheses were derived partially from the few case studies of appendicitis and birth fantasy by Inman (1958, 1962), who did not, however, have any pathologists' findings on the appendices to support his speculative theories.

Freud (1905), in the case history of Dora, related appendicitis to birth fantasy. Eylon supplies the precise quotation 'Her supposed attack of appendicitis had thus enabled the patient . . . to realise a fantasy of childbirth.'

Sample. 35 appendectomy patients where both pre- and post-operative diagnosis was appendicitis. A matched group of 35 controls was used.

Birth data. Obtained by interview based on an open-ended questionnaire.

Results

1a. There was a significant association ($P < \cdot 005$) between birth events and appendectomy.
1b. No such relationship existed between birth events and other operations.
2. Proportion of normal appendices in patients with and without birth events was the same. However this was an artefact of the sampling in that post- and pre-operative diagnosis had to be appendicitis.
3. Young females did not have more appendectomies than other operations.

Comments and conclusions

The main finding, that birth events were related to appendectomy as distinct from other surgical operations, suggests strongly that psychogenic factors influence appendicitis. This is striking support for the Freudian claim. It is difficult to think of any other theory that could predict such results. This study must be regarded, therefore, as good evidence for this aspect of Freudian theory. As was pointed out under result 2, to a large extent the sampling precluded patients with normal appendices. It would have been interesting to see to what extent birth events were related to such appendectomies. Thus Eylon supports the Freudian theory relating birth fantasy to the onset of appendicitis.

ANOREXIA NERVOSA

A case study by Beech (1959)

Beech carried out an experimental case study on a woman of 27 suffering from anorexia nervosa. This investigation is examined because it is entirely replicable and because the data are objective. Obviously, however, further cases will have to be tested before any firm conclusions can be drawn.

Experimental technique. 25 neutral and 5 sexual words were presented below the threshold of hearing. An audible signal was sounded just before each word to which the subject had to free-associate.

Sex words. The 5 sex words were unequivocal: vagina, penis, breast, intercourse, sexual.

Hypothesis. There would be a greater possibility of food associations to sexual than neutral stimuli.

Results. This hypothesis was supported by the chi-square test. Three normals to whom the technique was also administered produced no food responses at all. Of course such a result, it could be argued, might be due to the link between sex and anxiety so that the chain of events was sex, anxiety, food. Again the link between sex and food could have been learned by the patient during previous psychotherapy.

Conclusions

In psychoanalytic theory oral problems naturally play a large part in the understanding of eating difficulties. Nevertheless the sexualisation of oral activity, as suggested in this study, would fit in well with Freudian theory. Oral fixation can lead to the oral expression of any kind of instinctual conflict (Fenichel, 1945). This study by Beech clearly cannot confirm psychoanalytic theory. However, further studies of this kind could perhaps produce some interesting support for the psychoanalytic theory of anorexia nervosa. This investigation must be regarded as highly suggestive.

ALCOHOLISM

Psychoanalytic theory

The psychoanalytic theory of alcoholism is clear. Fenichel (1945) writes 'The unconscious impulses in alcoholics typically are not only oral but homosexual in nature'. The orality, since drinking is involved, is logical enough. The homosexuality is not so obvious. Fenichel claims that the all-male heartiness and back slapping of the typical drinking man is everyday evidence for the latent homosexuality.

The work of Botwinick and Machover (1951)

These writers carried out a psychometric examination of latent homosexuality on a small sample of alcoholics.

Sample. 39 male alcoholics: age range 30-49 years.

Tests. MMPI Mf Scale and Form A of the Terman and Miles Attitudes and Interests analysis test.

Results. The alcoholics were not higher than non-alcoholics on these scales.

Comments and conclusions

Grygier (1957a), in a survey of all the then current measures of homosexuality, came to the conclusion that none of them was satisfactory. In an earlier section of this chapter – that concerned with the claimed link between paranoid schizophrenia and repressed homosexuality – it will be recalled that we found one of the major problems to be the assessment of *repressed* homosexuality. Indeed if the items of the Mf scale of the MMPI are too overtly homosexual, latent homosexuals would be expected to score lower and not higher than normals. Thus the failure of this study to confirm Freudian theory could have been due to the invalidity of the measures of homosexuality. Nevertheless this study by Botwinick and Machover clearly offers no support for Freudian theory.

The work of Scott (1958)

Scott investigated the role of homosexuality in alcoholism by examining the case records of 267 male and 33 female alcoholics. A very brief review of this study will be sufficient in view of the subjective nature of the data. As evidence for homosexuality, divorce and marriage rates were studied. Scott concluded that immaturity rather than homosexuality characterised their sexual relationships.

Conclusions

Despite the impressive number in its sample this study cannot be regarded as a serious refutation of Freudian theory. Again the problem turns round an adequate measure of homosexuality, particularly *latent* homosexuality.

The work of Machover, Puzzo and colleagues (1959)

Machover *et al.* conducted a number of studies of alcoholism of which two are relevant to the Freudian theory.

A. *Study of the alcoholic personality by Machover and Puzzo (1959)*

Sample. 23 remitted alcoholics and 23 non-remitted subjects. Mean age was 41·9 years and the mean WISC IQ was 119. All were male.

Measures. A large battery of projective and psychometric techniques was employed amongst which were the Blacky Pictures, the Rorschach and the TAT.

Statistical analysis. If a trait as measured by any of these tests occurred in 60% or more of the sample it was deemed typical of the alcoholic personality.

Results. Oral dependence and castration anxiety (variables relevant to psychoanalytic theory) were typical of these alcoholics.

Comments and conclusions. These results are regarded by Blum (1966) as supporting Freudian theory. However, the fact that there was no matched control group vitiates the results to a large extent.

B. *Study of latent homosexuality by Machover et al. (1959)*

Sample. As above, a homosexual control group and a normal control group.

Tests. Rorschach, Machover Figure drawing test and the MMPI Mf scale.

Results. With these tests the alcoholics (both groups) did not show greater homosexuality than the normal controls though remitted alcoholics were higher than the drinking alcoholics.

Comments and conclusions. These results cannot be held to refute Freudian theory in that none of these tests is regarded as a highly valid measure of repressed homosexuality.

Conclusions from both studies

The implication of orality and homosexuality in alcoholism has not been confirmed by this study. Also, the reliance on projective techniques and the MMPI Mf scale makes the results of this investigation of dubious validity.

The work of McCord et al. (1959)

These authors examined various theories of alcoholism in the light of evidence from a longitudinal study of young people.

Sample. 29 alcoholics and 158 men (not neurotics or criminals), the attenuated sample from the Cambridge-Somerville Youth Study (Witmer and Powers, 1951), all of whom had been investigated in great detail.

Measures
   A. *Orality:* thumbsucking after infancy, excessive early smoking, eating orgies, playing with the mouth.
   B. *Latent homosexuality:* feminine tendencies, doll playing, dressing up as girls. Overt homosexuality was also noted.

Results
   A. *Orality.* 59 boys were classified as oral on these measures. Of these 12% became alcoholic. 18% of the 128 non-oral boys became alcoholics. Freudian theory is not supported.
   B. *Homosexuality.* Of boys thus classified only 4% became alcoholics whereas 16% of the normals fell into this category. Two of the six overt homosexuals became alcoholics. Again Freudian theory was not supported.

Comments and conclusions

There can be no doubt that McCord *et al.* have cast the strongest doubt on the psychoanalytic theory of drinking. Certainly these indices of latent homosexuality and orality seem good: it is probably fair to say that had the results supported the theory Freudians would not have disputed them. However it could be argued that, although thumbsucking is an index of orality, fixation at the oral level is more likely to result where thumbsucking was *prevented* when it was desired. A mere counting of thumbs is not on its own sufficient. Furthermore the omission of neurotics and delinquents who might have also been alcoholics could have affected these results. The conclusion must be that Freudian theory is not supported and would be refuted if the indices used were a little more sensitive.

The work of Gibbins and Walters (1960)

Gibbins and Walters used a perceptual defence technique (see p. 165 et seq.) to investigate homosexuality as a factor in alcoholism, as Daston (1956) did in the case of paranoia (see p. 267). Three experiments were reported in this paper.

First experiment

Sample. 15 alcoholics, 15 controls and 10 homosexuals.

Method. Homosexual words and control words were exposed tachistoscopically to the subjects.

Score. The difference in recognition threshold between control and experimental words.

Results. There were no significant differences between the groups although, as predicted by psychoanalytic theory, the alcoholics were midway between the homosexual and normal groups.

Second experiment

Sample. The same numbers in groups were used but composed of new subjects.

Method. As in the first experiment, but this time the sexual words were unequivocal – breast, bowel, etc.

Results. There were significant differences between the groups but these were unrelated to the homosexuality of the words.

Third experiment

Sample. 13 drinkers, 20 controls and 16 homosexuals.

Stimuli. Symbolic pictures were shown (male and female sex symbols).

Results. Homosexuals and drinkers selected more male pictures than did the controls.

Conclusions from all these studies by Gibbins and Walters

Only the last experiment supports homosexuality as being a factor in alcoholism. However, in both the other experiments the drinkers were more homosexual than the normals. If we take into account the problems with this type of perceptual defence experiment, which we fully discussed in the chapter on repression (control words may be emotive, for example, the greater frequency of sexual words in reality than is apparent from a word-list), then it is hardly surprising that only the symbolic picture test produced significant results. Daston (1956), however, did show a difference with words in the case of paranoid schizophrenics.

We must conclude that these results support to a slight degree the implication of homosexuality with alcoholism. It would not appear to be as important here as in paranoia.

The work of Engeset *et al.* (1963)

These authors studied the incidence of peptic ulcer among abusers and non-abusers of alcohol in Norway.

Sample. 251 alcoholics and a random sample of 329 males.

Rationale. Since in psychoanalytic theory peptic ulcers and alcoholism are both related to oral fixation, more gastric ulcers would be expected among alcoholics than among normals.

Results. Significantly more (19·1%) abusers than non-abusers (13·1%) suffered or had suffered from ulcers. The difference was restricted to gastric ulcers and did not apply to duodenal ulcers.

Comments and conclusions

This study points to a relationship between the two phenomena – as predicted from Freudian theory. It does not, of course, demonstrate that the common factor is oral fixation. This study could be one piece of evidence in the construct validation of the Freudian theory.

The work of Bacon *et al.* (1965) – cross-cultural studies of drinking

Bacon *et al.* produced a series of related papers on drinking habits in a large sample of societies, using the cross-cultural methods of Whiting and Child (1953) which we have described in an earlier chapter (see p. 52). Their second paper contains the findings relevant to this chapter.

Sample. 139 societies.

Measures. Anthropological descriptions of these societies were rated for indulgence or severity of child-training practices. The measures of drinking were the presence and extent of ceremonial drinking, the general consumption of the society and the frequency of drunkenness.

Results. The correlations between these variables (ratings) showed that indulgence of dependency needs during infancy, childhood and adulthood and the diffusion of nurturance were each related to a low degree of drinking and insobriety.

Comments and conclusions

Since dependency is an aspect of the orally fixated personality, it should follow from Freudian theory that orally fixated persons whose dependency was not indulged would seek other oral gratifications – hence the correlation noted. This study is again one small piece of evidence supporting psychoanalytic theory.

Orality and alcoholism

The work of Story (1968)

Story examined the scores of alcoholics on a number of indices of orality.

Sample. 30 alcoholics and 30 normals.

Measures:

1. *Chain-association test.* Five oral and five non-oral words are presented to the subject who has to make 15 associations to each word. The time for this is noted as is the number of oral responses.
2. Seven oral and seven non-oral proverbs are presented to the subject who has to explain the meaning (from which an abstraction score is taken) and indicate agreement or otherwise.

Results. There were highly significant differences between the groups on the oral stimuli and the alcoholics were considerably worse at the oral tasks than at the non-oral tasks.

Comments. This study no doubt implicates problems over oral responses (e.g. eating, drinking, biting) among alcoholics. In a normal group we could postulate that responses did indicate orality in the Freudian sense of an over-concern with oral behaviour. However, we know such problems exist in an alcoholic group (drinking *is* the problem) and such responses tell us little new about the patients. To demonstrate orality in alcoholics we need a measure (e.g. of oral character) not overtly concerned with oral behaviour. This study therefore demonstrates that alcoholics have oral problems which Freudian theory predicts. It can only be regarded as slight support for Freudian theory, however, in that it fails to implicate other aspects of orality.

Nevertheless in fairness to the author, he did relate these scores to oral personality traits as part of his doctoral dissertation (1963). As reported by Wolowitz (1964), Story found that this same sample of alcoholics scored significantly higher on the Goldman-Eisler scales of orality (Goldman-Eisler, 1951) which have already been fully described and discussed (see p. 13).

If we take these two findings together we can argue that Story (1963, 1968) has truly implicated orality in alcoholism.

The work of Wolowitz and Barker (1968)

Wolowitz and Barker replicated the work of Storey (1963) – who reported that alcoholics scored higher than controls on the FPI – by using a non-patient alcoholic sample.

Sample. One extended family of 23 members: 14 alcoholics and 9 controls.

Rationale of Sample. This curious sample was chosen because the authors claim that the role of being a patient tends to make subjects dependent and affects their responses on the FPI as used by Story (1963).

Test. The FPI (Wolowitz, 1964) which is described on p. 288.

Results. The whole family was significantly higher than other samples tested by Wolowitz and reported in this book (see his work on ulcer patients, p. 289).

By the median test, the alcoholics of the family were significantly higher than the others.

Comments and conclusions. These findings support the previous study by Story (1963). Wolowitz and Barker have shown the results cannot be attributed to the dependent patient role. However, as with the study by Story (1968), the result only implicates food preferences in alcoholics even though such interests have been related to oral personality traits by Story (1963). Thus this investigation implicates orality in alcoholism if it is taken together with previous findings.

The work of Bertrand and Masling (1969)

These writers studied the incidence of orality in the Rorschach responses of heavy drinkers.

Sample. 20 heavy drinkers matched for age, education, intelligence and diagnosis with 20 other patients.

Measures. The Rorschach orality indices described by Schafer (1954). There are references to:

(a) *oral dependence:* e.g. foods, food sources, food objects, supplicants.

(b) *oral sadism:* e.g. oral assaults, destruction, aggression.

Results. The drinkers were significantly more oral dependent than the controls.

Comments. We have not usually considered the Rorschach as coming under the category of scientific evidence but this study differs somewhat in that the indices are, for oral dependency at least, unequivocally oral responses (in the main). Indeed Masling *et al.* (1968) found that such imagery in the Rorschach was related to the tendency to conform in the Asch experiment, where subjects are asked to make perceptual judgements clearly against the evidence but in conformity with other stooge subjects in the experiment. Hence the fact that drinkers make more food responses than controls is of relevance to the Freudian claim that drinkers are fixated at the oral level.

Conclusions from all studies of alcoholism

Of the ten studies reviewed in this section three run contrary to the theory (Botwinick and Machover, 1951; Scott, 1958 and McCord *et al.*, 1959). The others give some degree of support although in most cases only slight. Of the three refuting studies the first two are not good methodologically but the longitudinal study by McCord *et al.* is hard to fault despite the insensitivity of the measures. Of the supporting studies the best appears to be that of Gibbins and Walters (1960) whose perceptual defence technique had proved useful with paranoid schizophrenics. Yet even this gave only limited confirmation. As is so often the case with cross-cultural studies of Freudian concepts, the work of Bacon *et al.* (1965) promised more than it achieved.

Thus with slight confirmation from some studies, though with different kinds

of data (experimental, psychometric and cross-cultural), and definite disconfirmation from the longitudinal study, the final conclusion must be that there is
only very slight support for the Freudian theory of alcoholism.

ORALITY AND SMOKING

The work of McArthur *et al.* (1958)

These authors studied the psychology of smoking using as a sample 252 Harvard
alumni who had been selected in their sophomore year as suitable for forming a
panel of normals for research purposes.

Results. Most of the variables investigated were not relevant to the psychoanalytic theory of smoking. However, in their investigation of the ability to stop
smoking, one finding stands out and we can do no better than quote their words:
'A signal fact is this: ability to stop smoking is directly proportional to the
number of months our subjects were fed from their mother's breast!' (p. 272).
Thus light smokers who could stop were weaned at 8 months, heavy smokers
who could stop, at 6-8 months. Smokers (mainly heavy) who do not try to stop
were weaned at 5 months, and a similar group, who were unable to stop, at 4-8
months.

Comments and conclusions

These findings are powerful support for the implication of orality in smoking
and they are certainly in full accord with psychoanalytic predictions from the
concept of orality. Incidentally they run counter to the learning theory account
of thumbsucking (Sears and Wise, 1950, see p. 75) from which an opposite
result would be expected – the more sucking subjects had during infancy the
more sucking they would need later.

One argument against this study is that the weaning data was retrospective
and as we have shown, this recollected data is not accurate. However, inaccuracy
would be expected to blur the results so that these findings are even more striking.

This study must be regarded as confirming the Freudian theory that orality
is linked with smoking.

The work of Jacobs *et al.* (1965, 1966)

Jacobs *et al.* carried out two studies into the personality of smokers which are
relevant in part to this chapter in that one of the variables studied was orality.
Both these investigations will be examined together since the second was to some
extent a replication of the first.

Method. Questionnaires were constructed to measure maternal over-control,
maternal harshness and maternal coldness, danger-seeking, impetuousness,
defiance, emotional lability and orality. This last was measured by oral habits
such as nail biting.

Results and samples. In the first investigation, reported in the first paper, the sample consisted of 97 adult male electronic engineers. Heavy smokers (20+ per day) were higher on all variables except danger-seeking and significantly higher on orality.

In the second investigation of this first paper, where the sample was 136 factory workers, the results were not so clear-cut. Indeed the categories of 'heavy smoker' and 'moderate smoker' had to be combined to produce any differences compared with non-smokers. In their second paper Jacobs *et al.* (1966) studied a sample of 134 males and produced essentially similar results to the previous findings except that maternal malevolence was not implicated as a factor.

Comments and conclusions

These two papers have merited only brief discussion since the validity and reliability of the questionnaire measures is highly dubious. It will be recalled by readers how, in our earlier chapter on the influence of child-training procedure on adult personality (see pp. 45-6), the difficulty of obtaining accurate measures of such procedures was discussed. Jacobs *et al.* are content, however, to rely on adult recollection of maternal attitudes. Similarly their measure of orality lacks good evidence of validity (indeed any evidence). Certainly there was no check on social desirability as a response set.

Thus the fact that psychoanalytic theory is supported and heavy smokers were more oral than non-smokers cannot be regarded as evidence in favour of the theory, until evidence is forthcoming pertaining to the validity of these scales. Actually even this Freudian hypothesis is doubtful: if smokers express their orality by smoking we might predict them to be *less* not more oral than their non-smoking controls.

The work of Kimeldorf and Gewitz (1966)

Kimeldorf and Gewitz carried out a small-scale study of smoking among students.

Sample. 15 non-smokers and 7 smokers (more than 20 cigarettes a day).

Test. The Blacky Pictures – oral cards.

Scoring system. Blum's (1962) scoring system based on a factor analysis of the responses (see p. 83) was used.

Results. Smokers were higher than their controls on Blum's first two factors, oral craving and playfulness, a factor which was interpreted by Blum (1962) as defensive avoidance of hostility to the mother.

Comments and conclusions

The validity of the Blacky Pictures has already been fully discussed in this book (see pp. 80-83). There is probably more evidence for their validity as measures of psychosexual fixation than for any other test. Nevertheless results with the Blacky Pictures have to be accepted cautiously. The small size of the sample and the restricted population from which it was drawn both necessitate that these findings be regarded as only limited support for the Freudian theory.

The work of Veldman and Bown (1969)

Veldman and Bown studied the characteristics of smokers and non-smokers in a large sample of college freshmen.

Sample. 401 cigarette smokers were compared with 401 non-smokers. These two groups were matched for education, social background and ability.

Measures. 70 variables in all were used, although the only one relevant to our needs is the orality score.

Orality score. This was derived from 36 sentence completions which were administered to the subjects. The orality score comprised any reference to food, eating, drinking, and smoking. Veldman and Bown point out that the inclusion of this last item 'smoking' did not bias the results because in fact there were very few such sentence completions.

Results. Smokers were significantly higher on the orality score than were the control group. Males too scored significantly higher than females on this variable.

Comments and conclusions

As with the two studies by Jacobs *et al.* (1965, 1966), great caution must be shown in interpreting these results which appear to confirm psychoanalytic theory in that they link orality and smoking. Again it is the dubious nature of the oral scale which calls the findings into question. The authors admit that scoring food responses to the sentence completions as indices of orality was purely *a priori*: there is no evidence for validity and the reliability is unknown. Furthermore the discovery of a sex difference on this scale is not hopeful from the viewpoint of construct-validity. Thus these findings may be regarded as only slight support for psychoanalytic theory. In fairness to the theory, however, it is noteworthy that three investigations have found a positive correlation between orality and smoking, which if the scales were not valid is a surprising coincidence. Clearly what is needed above all is a well validated and reliable oral scale.

Alone, this study by Veldman and Bown is modest confirmation of Freudian theory. Together with the investigations of Jacobs, however, it amounts to a somewhat more solid support.

ENURESIS

The work of De Luca (1968)

De Luca investigated the psychosexual constitution of a sample of adolescent enuretics drawn from army trainees.

Sample. 20 enuretics and 40 controls.

Test. Blacky Pictures (Blum, 1949).

Scoring system. The factor-analytic system of Blum (1962).

Results. There were no significant differences on any of the 30 factors.

Comments and conclusions

In psychoanalytic theory enuresis is linked (see Fenichel, 1945) to unresolved Oedipal conflicts, castration fears and fixation at the phallic stage. Thus this failure of the Blacky Pictures – of which there is some evidence for validity (see pp. 82-3) – to discriminate enuretics from controls is certainly contrary to psychoanalytic theory. Whether the Blacky Pictures are sufficiently robust for this finding to constitute a refutation of psychoanalytic theory is, however, less certain. Nevertheless, this study by De Luca clearly fails to substantiate Freudian claims concerning the aetiology of enuresis.

THE PHOBIAS

The work of Dixon *et al.* (1957)

This investigation was a psychometric study of phobia in a sample of patients at the Tavistock Clinic.

Sample. 125 men and 125 women patients at the Tavistock Clinic.

Test. The Tavistock Self-Assessment Inventory (Sandler, 1954). Items referring to phobias were used.

Statistical analysis. Phi-coefficients of correlations were computed between the test items. The resulting correlation matrix was then subjected to a centroid factor analysis.

Results. Seven factors emerged accounting for just under 37% of the variance. The first two factors, a general factor and a bipolar factor, accounted for 22% of the variance. Dixon *et al.* argued that these findings showed that within a general framework of phobias there were two distinct groups of fears:

1. A fear of being left alone, of being helpless and lonely.
2. A fear of pain, operations, the dentist and accidental injury.

These two groups were differentiated by the second bipolar factor. Their relationship was demonstrated by the first general factor on which all items had positive loadings.

The separation phobia was characterised by items pertaining to fears about being left alone, crossing a bridge or street, open spaces, water, trains and the dark. The second part of the bipolar factor was concerned with accidental pain and injury, fears about the dentist, surgical operations and the like.

Comments and conclusions

Dixon *et al.* argue that this pattern of phobias, revealed by the factor analysis closely fits the Freudian theory of anxiety. Thus Freud (1925a), in 'Inhibitions, symptoms and anxiety', contrasts the anxiety over loss of love (the first group of phobias) with castration anxiety (the second group in this study). Thus according to Dixon *et al.* the separation phobias in the first group are symbolic forms of anxiety about separation from the mother, just as the other phobias are symbolic forms of castration anxiety. If their conclusions and interpretations of this factor analysis were acceptable, this study would constitute powerful and compelling evidence for psychoanalytic theory. However such an interpretation ignores some important methodological difficulties.

(*a*) *The validity of the test*. The items were selected from the Tavistock Self-Assessment inventory originally because they were face valid, that is they appeared to be relevant to phobias. However, as has been earlier discussed in the section on the psychometric study of personality (p. 14), face validity is not a good guide to true validity. Furthermore all items were keyed 'Yes' which could easily confound the true variance with the response set of acquiescence. In addition there was no check on the other main response set – the tendency to put, in questionnaires, the socially desirable response. Thus these two response sets could have considerably lowered the validity of the test (see Cronbach, 1946 and 1950) which rests alone on face validity.

(*b*) *Phi-coefficients*. Phi-coefficients of correlation, which are highly affected by the ratio of the two responses, were computed between all the items. Thus limits are set to the phi as soon as the dichotomy becomes uneven, e.g. 75% put 'Yes', 25% 'No'. Phi is at its most accurate when the response is evenly split – 50% put 'Yes', 50% 'No' to an item. Guilford (1956) contains a full discussion of this problem. It is particularly important when the resulting matrix of correlations is factored, as in the present study. Some writers indeed argue that the factorisation of a matrix of phi-coefficients yields merely 'difficulty' factors (Cattell, 1957). This means that the factors are comprised of items of similar difficulty or with a similar ratio of responses.

(*c*) *The centroid factor analysis*. As Harman (1964) demonstrates, with a matrix of positive correlations a centroid factor-analysis always yields a general factor followed by bipolar factors. Thus to claim that such a pattern, a statistical artefact, supports a theory is not acceptable. Clearly 'blind' rotation to simple structure would overcome this difficulty in that it can then be argued that the rotated solution is not a product of the method but the most simple fit to the data. If this then fits the theory, support for that theory is justified.

These three problems, which are common to the factor-analytic approach to personality measurement, make the interpretation by Dixon *et al.* (1957) appear rather too disingenuous. Nevertheless they do not entirely discount it. After all, the items loading on the bipolar factor do fit the theory – i.e. fall into two recognisable and predicted groups (even though less than one quarter of the variance of the items is accounted for).

It is thus concluded in the light of this discussion that this study by Dixon *et al.* gives qualified support to the psychoanalytic theory of phobias.

DEPRESSION

The work of Leckie and Withers (1967)

These authors carried out a psychometric study of depression of particular interest because they attempted to distinguish between liability to depressive illness and actual depressive symptoms. Psychoanalytic theory was the basis of the items in the questionnaires.

Tests used. 150 items were tried out from which 58 were selected mainly by item analysis. The items fall into three scales:

A. *11 Direct depressive items.* In themselves these items could indicate prevailing moods of patients.

  Examples 5. I seldom worry about my health.
       23. I work under a great deal of tension.

  The remaining scales were designed to test the psychoanalytic theory of depression.

B. *9 Threshold items.* These items were negatively correlated with the direct depressive scale.

  Examples 18. Deep down I regard myself as rather a poor specimen.
       46. I hardly ever feel envious.

C. *32 Indirect depressive items or unconcious items.*

  Examples 34. I very often get a gnawing feeling.
       52. I do not feel that any part of me is bad.

In addition 6 unscored items were included to lighten the depressing effects of reading the items.

Validity test of the three scales. The scales were given to 31 depressives and 31 matched controls. All three scales and the total score discriminated the two groups.

Test-retest reliability of the scales. For each scale this was around ·90 which is very satisfactory.

Cross-validation study. 67 psychiatric cases filled in these scales. The inventory was then scored to give a blind diagnosis. The scoring rationale constituted a test of psychoanalytic theory.

Rationale of scoring

(a) *High score on the unconscious items* indicates an underlying tendency to depressive illness.

(b) *The threshold items* indicate whether this tendency might materialise as depressive illness.
  A high score on the threshold items will lead to symptomatic depression.
  A low score on the threshold items plus a high score on the direct depressive items may reflect a *mood* of depression. However if such a patient had a low unconscious depression score, the overt depression would be considered a mood.

(c) *The direct depressive items.* A high score on these items reflects a prevailing depression.

Thus the crucial scale is the *threshold scale*. A high score on this indicates endogenous or reactive depression. The unconscious items then discriminate the endogenous (High) from the reactive (Low).

Results. There was a 73% agreement between the blind diagnoses and psychiatric ratings based on five months clinical experience with the patients. Endogenous depressives had the highest total scale score of any of the nosological categories.

Discussion

Leckie and Withers (1967) argue that these results support the Freudian theory. For example, in reference to the unconscious scale they claim that item 6, 'I sometimes get the feeling that I was terribly let down as a child' and item 12, 'I wonder whether something terrible must have been done to me when I was too young to remember it', tap primary narcissistic injury as defined in 'Mourning and melancholia' (Freud, 1917b). Similarly items 11, 'I find it difficult to remember the things I have read' and 34, 'I very often get a gnawing feeling', are intended to tap object loss through oral incorporation (Freud, 1917b). Other items attempt to tap the part played by anal sadism in the destruction of the internalised loved objects. Thus the scales go a long way in measuring apparently unmeasurable unconscious factors.

In the opinion of Leckie and Withers the threshold items determine whether a person will suffer from depression or not, despite his liability to depression as measured by the unconscious scale, because a low score on them indicates an ability to deal with the self-denigration which is so destructive a factor in depression.

The extent to which the three scales (tapping liability to depression, actual depressive symptoms and ability to handle some of the aggression – denigration) support Freudian theory by discriminating depressives from normals and other psychiatric cases, must now be considered. The fact that the items of the unconscious depression scale were drawn from Freudian theory and that the scale can discriminate depressives must be regarded as good evidence for the theory, especially since the scale is distinct from a description of depressive *symptoms* (which could otherwise account for the discrimination of the scale). However, whether an item such as 'I very often get a gnawing feeling' taps loss of orally incorporated objects is unproven. Clearly therefore much more work needs to be done with these scales to establish their construct validity.

Conclusions

These scales can discriminate depressives from normals and other neurotics. Their construction was based on the psychoanalytic theory of depression. This study therefore must be considered as supporting Freudian theory, although until further work is done with the scales the theory cannot be regarded as proven.

CONCLUSIONS FROM ALL STUDIES OF FREUDIAN THEORIES OF
NEUROSIS AND OTHER EMOTIONAL ABNORMALITIES

Summary of findings reported in this chapter

Paranoid schizophrenia	*Support* for link with repressed homosexuality
Homosexuality	*No support* for importance of castration anxiety
Asthma	*Almost no support:* vague implication of developmental difficulties
Peptic ulcer and colitis	*No support* for importance of oral and anal fixation
Stuttering	*No support* for importance of anal fixation
Appendicitis	*Support* for relationship with birth fantasies
Anorexia nervosa	*Slight support* based on an experimental case study
Alcoholism	*Slight support* for importance of repressed homosexuality and orality
Smoking	*Slight support* for importance of orality
Phobias	*Some support* for separation and castration anxiety
Depression	*Some support*

This summary makes it clear that attempts to impugn psychoanalytic theory in general are useless. Parts are supported, others are not. As should be clear from the discussions contained in the relevant sections, failure to find objective support may only mean that inadequate methods have been applied. Thus in paranoid schizophrenia experimental techniques have implicated repressed homosexuality. This has not been demonstrated in alcoholism where only questionnaire measures have been used.

The final conclusion is that more research must be devoted, in these areas, to explicit psychoanalytic hypotheses. At present, however, about half of those tested have been supported.

11

The effects of psychoanalytic therapy

A. OUTCOME STUDIES

Problems involved in the assessment of psychotherapeutic success

Since the study of the effects of any kind of psychotherapy involves considerable methodological problems and a large number of variables, it will be convenient to list these briefly before turning to a consideration of the empirical studies.

1. *Patient variables*. There is a tendency to consider patients as essentially homogeneous. Kiesler (1966) considers that the fallacy of patient uniformity undermines the validity of many studies of the outcome of psychotherapeutic procedures.

2. *Therapist variables*. Meehl (1955) has pointed out the problems involved in assuming homogeneity among therapists just because they belong to the same school. These problems are essentially the same as those confronting educational research into the efficacy of different teaching methods. Clearly, in evaluating the outcome of any method of psychotherapy, a large number of practitioners must be used or else an analysis of variance design accounting for differences between therapists should be drawn up. Possible solutions to the problems here discussed will be found below (p. 312).

3. *Criterion for success*. In psychological disorders there is no generally agreed fixed criterion for success – i.e. recovery of the patient. In medicine, for example, there would be a high reliability for assessing recovery from measles; in the case of obsessionality, on the other hand, there is no such agreement. This is particularly important in evaluating the success of psychoanalysis, especially as compared with therapies purportedly based on learning theory. In these, from learning theories themselves, removal of the symptom is the aim. For psychoanalysts this could not in any way be regarded as a cure. Hence measurement of recovery is a vital problem in this area.

4. *The use of control groups*. Most researchers in this area regard a contro group as a methodological *sine qua non* (e.g. Eysenck, 1960 and Cross, 1964). This is obviously true when attempting to attribute the outcome of any procedure to that procedure. Normally a control group receives no treatment. Nevertheless the problems of matching control groups are well known and are especially acute in the matching of patients when psychiatric diagnosis is itself unreliable.

5. *Spontaneous remission*. Eysenck (1952, 1960 and 1965), in view of the problems involving control groups, has used the concept of spontaneous remission

from neurosis to form a base-line from which to judge the success of therapies. He points out (1952) that the studies of Landis (1937), who followed up patients discharged from a custodial hospital where they received no psychotherapy, and of Denker (1947), who investigated patients treated by their own doctors, indicate that 70% of neurotic patients get better of their own accord. Therefore therapists must show a significantly higher success rate than 70% to claim success. Kiesler (1966), however, has denied the validity of this concept of spontaneous remission, as have numerous other writers. This will be fully discussed below (see p. 311).

In evaluating the outcome of psychotherapy the most basic of these problems is the *criterion for success*. As Malan (1959) points out, subjective methods of assessment such as improved/not improved are poor because they fail to do justice to quantitative differences. On the other hand many quantitative assessments fail to do justice to qualitative differences. In addition it should be stressed that the use of tests for assessing improvements due to treatment where scores before and after therapy are employed demands tests of very high test-retest reliability. This quality is notably lacking from the most popular clinical tests – the TAT and the Rorschach among projective tests (see Zubin *et al.*, 1965), and the MMPI among psychometric tests.

Possible solutions

Kiesler (1966) makes explicit the implications of these problems – the solution by analysis of variance design. *Main* factors would therefore be *types of patient* (hysterical, obsessional, etc.) and *school of therapy* (psychoanalysis, Rogerian, control group, etc.). However, account would be taken of individual differences between therapists within schools and between individuals. Such a design would yield interactions between types of patient and school of therapy.

However, such a design means that adequate measures of success more sensitive than a rating scale would have to be devised, since the scores subjected to the analysis of variance would be 'improvement' scores on a number of criterion measures. In addition this solution needs, *in toto*, a number of adequately matched patients of each nosological category for each therapist in the study. The *practical* problems of this theoretically elegant solution are therefore considerable. However, consideration of outcome or criterion scores alone, without control of these factors, is clearly inadequate. On account of these problems of sampling and measurement another approach has been adopted – examination of the therapeutic process itself.

B. STUDIES OF THE THERAPEUTIC PROCESS

Truax and his associates (e.g. Truax, 1963; Truax and Carkhuff, 1964), working with the concept of constructive personality change (Rogers, 1957), which is the intended outcome of Rogerian psychotherapy, have been energetic workers in this field where the effects of the therapeutic process itself are examined. Their work will be reviewed only briefly since it is mainly concerned with the work of Rogers. However it is relevant to psychoanalytic therapy in that as a *method* it can be applied to any psychotherapeutic procedure.

Constructive personality change – the intended outcome

This is measured by conventional psychological tests such as the F scale of the Authoritarian Personality (Adorno *et al.*, 1950), the MMPI, the Rorschach and the TAT. This part of their approach is identical with the outcome studies and is subject to the same weaknesses both of unreliability and validity.

Therapist variables

Truax has measured the *therapist's self-congruence, his unconditional positive regard for the patient*, and his *accurate empathy*. These measures were blind ratings from four main samples of taped therapeutic sessions. Again this involves the measurement problem of rating scales (e.g. Vernon, 1953).

Patient variables

From the same tape the patient's *depth of self-examination* is rated. All scores are then related to the criterion outcome scores.

From this it can be seen that although these particular variables are relevant to Rogerian rather than Freudian theory there is no intrinsic reason why a similar method could not be applied to psychoanalytic sessions. In addition this method also comes closer to the analysis of variance method of examining the outcome of therapy, which was suggested by Kiesler (1966) as an ideal solution in that the effects of therapist and patient differences are not assumed to be randomly distributed.

With this brief outline of the problems and advantages of both methods it will now be possible to evaluate the empirical studies which bear on the effectiveness of psychoanalytic therapy.

A. STUDIES OF THE OUTCOME OF PSYCHOANALYTIC THERAPY

THE WORK OF EYSENCK

Eysenck (1952, 1960 and 1965) has launched three savage attacks on the effectiveness of all types of psychotherapy in general, except that based on learning theory. He is particularly severe on pyschoanalytic therapy which he regards as worse than useless – in fact definitely deleterious to a patient's well being. Since this view has become accepted in some quarters, the evidence quoted by Eysenck (1952) must be carefully examined.

Spontaneous remission

Eysenck, as has been previously noted, claimed that 70% of the patients discharged from custodial care without treatment recovered. This figure was based on the study of Landis (1937). Denker (1947), following up patients on insurance company lists and treated by their own physicians (who were not, of course, psychiatrists), found a similar recovery rate. From these two studies Eysenck (1952) argued that 70% of neurotic disorders got better without treatment – spontaneous remission. Effective psychotherapy, therefore, must needs better this figure. This base-line of 70% recovery was used because at this time there were no studies of psychotherapeutic success using control groups.

Eysenck's (1952) figures for the success of psychoanalytic therapy were based on five studies – Fenichel (1930), who reported on 484 cases; Kessel and Hyman (1933), who used 34 subjects; Jones (1936), 59 subjects; Alexander (1937), 141 subjects and Knight (1941), who used 42 cases. Eysenck thus had psychoanalytic success rates on a total sample of 760 cases – a not unimpressive figure. Of these 760 patients, 335 were rated by these authors as either cured, greatly improved or slightly improved – a 44% success rate. In comparison with this 64% of patients treated eclectically were regarded as successes. The precise base-line rate was 72%. Thus the more treatment given (for psychoanalytic treatment is the longest), the worse the results. The very low figure for psychoanalytic treatment is partly due to the fact that patients who broke off the lengthy treatment before completion were regarded as failures. If these are ignored, the success rate for psychoanalysis rises to 66% or about the same as eclectic treatment.

Conclusions

Even if the improved rate for psychoanalysis (66%) is accepted it is still worse than no treatment and the argument that the more prolonged the treatment the worse the result still holds. In addition, since there is a good chance that a patient will not complete his psychoanalytic therapy, on these figures it would not be possible to recommend psychoanalytic therapy. It could, indeed, be regarded as positively harmful.

Comments

This paper produced a flood of enraged protest from psychotherapists of all persuasions. If, as Eysenck (1965) later claimed, the case was overstated to provoke research it must be considered a very successful paper. It would not be relevant to examine all the attempts to refute Eysenck and show that psychotherapy was effective. Two papers, however, those of Luborsky (1954) and Rosenzweig (1954), challenge the data for spontaneous remission and the consequent base-line for success. Since Rosenzweig's paper also contains many of the other objections raised in the refutatory papers, it must be carefully considered.

The comments on Eysenck's (1952) paper by Rosenzweig (1954)

(a) Definition of neurosis and interpretation of results

In his 1952 paper Eysenck, for purposes of comparison, was forced to classify results under headings on a scale running from cured to discontinued and failed.

Furthermore he only concerned himself with pyschoneuroses. He therefore had to interpret the results given in the reports. Rosenzweig argues that this interpretation was idiosyncratic. For example, while Eysenck claims that there were 484 cases, the total number of cases in Fenichel's (1930) paper was in fact 604, which is not a small discrepancy. Again, while Eysenck's interpretation of this report led to a success figure of only 39%, Landis (1937) interpreted the same results as a 58% rate of success. In brief, Rosenzweig considers that Eysenck has completely ignored the problem of the definition of a psychoneurosis.

(b) Spontaneous remission

Rosenzweig argues that there is no evidence to gauge precisely how ill were the patients on the insurance company lists examined by Denker (1947). But he also suggests, with some justice, that in view of the fact that they only saw their own doctors and did not require hospitalisation, they were probably less ill than the psychoanalytic patients. The patients studied by Landis, on the other hand, were probably more ill. However their discharge from hospital was on totally different criteria from those employed by a psychoanalyst. Thus Landis (1937) writes that hospitalisation yields 'sufficient improvement for favourable discharge' (quoted by Rosenzweig, 1954) whereas for Fenichel (1945) recovery was defined as a change entirely explicable by the psychoanalyst in terms of Freudian theory. Rosenzweig therefore claims that comparisons between the 'success' rates of two such groups is meaningless as success is so differently defined.

In addition, it is doubtful whether Denker's or Landis' patients were in fact untreated. Denker (1947) even admits that the patients were not so well treated as they would have been by expert eclectic psychiatrists.

Conclusions

The conclusions that follow from this paper are that the base rate of spontaneous remission so ingeniously derived by Eysenck is by no means so clear-cut as he would have us believe. This is due to the problems of working out a comparable figure for successful treatment by psychoanalysts and to the fact that the so-called 'untreated' patients were in fact treated. In addition, the criterion for recovery is so different from school to school of psychotherapy that comparison is not meaningful.

Comments

Even if, therefore, we agree with Kiesler (1966) that spontaneous remission is a myth propagated mainly by Eysenck, this in no way demonstrates the efficacy of psychoanalytic therapy. In summary, therefore, Eysenck (1952) has not entirely destroyed any rational belief in the efficacy of psychoanalytic therapy, although the process obviously still requires much research.

The work of Eysenck (1960)

Eysenck (1960) made a further review of studies of the success of psychotherapy. In this paper he concentrated on investigations which complied to some extent

L

with the minimum requirements laid down by Meehl (1955) for the evaluation of psychotherapy. These are

(a) the use of a control group – a requirement which rules out the studies of psychoanalysis already mentioned
(b) an objective and uncontaminated pre- and post-therapy evaluation
(c) follow-up evaluation.

Since, however, only one paper was thus rigorously designed he examined all those reports where control groups had been used. Because only one of the reports, that of Barron and Leary (1955), dealt with analytic therapy (psycho-analytically orientated) this paper is not as relevant to this chapter as the earlier work. Again Eysenck claimed that psychotherapy was not useful, with the exception of behaviour therapy as practised by Wolpe.

Similarly the latest review by Eysenck (1965) is not concerned with psycho-analytic therapy. In conclusion, these three papers by Eysenck demonstrate clearly that psychotherapy is by no means as efficient as its adherent would desire. They do not however, as has been stated, indicate that psychoanalytic therapy is useless.

OTHER REVIEWS OF PSYCHOANALYTIC THERAPY AND ITS OUTCOME

Because of the difficulties of matching different criteria of success, Malan (1959) has suggested that special criteria for psychoanalytic therapy should be set up, it being irrelevant that other schools of psychotherapy do not have similar objectives. He suggests nine basic principles for the evaluation of results:

1. True assessment depends on a knowledge of all the disturbances in a patient and the changes in each.
2. Disturbances may be subtle and unknown to the patient.
3. Such disturbances may be discovered only after psychodynamic hypotheses concerning the case have been drawn up.
4. The most important evidence must come from the patient's life (tests are only a supplement).
5. The point of breakdown is not usually the beginning of the illness. Therefore the base-line from which to assess recovery must be the health of the patient some time before breakdown.
6. The criteria which must be fulfilled for true resolution of the neurotic conflict must be stated.
7. These criteria should be laid down before treatment.
8. Results should be judged quantitatively in terms of these criteria.
9. Occurrences in therapy should not be allowed to over-ride these criteria.

As Malan most fairly admits, this scheme of evaluation is similar to that advocated by Wallerstein *et al.* (1956). There are several points worthy of note about this method.

A scheme such as this obviates the crudity of attempting to rate recovery as successful or not, as Eysenck (1952) was compelled to do in his attempt to find overall rates of success for various schools of psychotherapy. It takes into account the patient variable. Since, too, predictions dependent on theory are made, the therapist variable becomes an error variable since therapist variance will destroy prediction. Thus some of the sources of error in outcome studies are taken into account.

On the debit side, however, it is not possible to compare any group with an untreated control group or with the therapeutic procedures of other schools. This scheme is an attempt to combine the best features of subjective assessment, since the outcome is strictly geared to each patient, and objective assessment, since quantification of results is suggested. The emphasis on life data is salutary. The example quoted by Malan refers to homosexuality in a boy, which appeared to be cured. However this could have been due merely to improved external conditions – he went to help his father in his work and thus gave up the Oedipal conflict. Only later behaviour could determine whether this was, therefore, true improvement.

Unfortunately, as with many of the studies to be examined in this chapter, the chief interest of this paper lies in its methodological possibilities rather than any practical results so far achieved with it. Yet even this is important. Up till now there have been no adequate studies of the effects of psychoanalytic therapy, perhaps indeed of any psychotherapy. Clearly, therefore, any potentially useful method of assessment deserves note especially since psychoanalytic therapy may have been unfairly condemned as a result of inadequate methods.

Other reviews of the outcome of psychotherapy add little relevant to a study of psychoanalytic therapy mainly because of the shortage of quantified reports using control groups (e.g. Cross, 1964). Indeed, Fox (1961) makes the point that there is a strong negative correlation between the rigour of the research design in reports of the effects of psychotherapy and positive, favourable results.

SUMMARY OF STUDIES OF THE OUTCOME OF PSYCHOANALYTIC THERAPY

Since in this book we have attempted to examine the objective scientific evidence pertaining to psychoanalysis, in this chapter we have been inevitably highly restricted in the reports that could be considered. Studies of the outcome of psychoanalytic therapy where even the minimum standards of methodology, using control groups and quantification of results (as suggested by Meehl, 1955), are satisfied, simply do not exist. This is the reason why Eysenck's (1952) paper is so important: with great ingenuity he manages to impose a crude quantification on psychoanalytic results and to produce instead of a control group a base-line of minimum performance. Unfortunately, as Rosenzweig (1954) has made clear, neither the quantification nor the concept of spontaneous remission really stands critical examination. Malan's (1959) study is important in that it suggests a possible method for evaluating the outcome, which takes into account some of the variables which are known to affect it. Thus the net result of the studies of the outcome of psychoanalytic therapy is very small and little is yet known about its efficiency.

INVESTIGATION OF THE THERAPEUTIC EFFECTS OF PSYCHOANALYSIS ON HOMOSEXUALITY

The work of Bieber *et al.* (1962)

This study has already been discussed (see p. 280) in connection with the psychoanalytic theory of homosexuality. The follow-up results are of great interest, since they indicate that therapy may be successful.

Results

Of the 106 patients,

(a) 29 (27%) became exclusively heterosexual.
   19% of the exclusively homosexual patients achieved this change and 50% of the bisexual patients.
(b) The longer the treatment, the more likely was this change to exclusive heterosexuality to come about.
(c) Objective factors for a favourable prognosis were: bisexuality of patient, length of analysis and early age at beginning of analysis (before 35 years). Important also was the desire to become heterosexual. Other favourable indicators, which can be regarded as non-objective because they reflect only the analyst's opinion (e.g. patient idolises women), will not be discussed since the adequacy of the data based on analysts' reports is doubtful. This data problem has been discussed in the previous chapter.
(d) Factors which appeared unimportant for prognosis were the sex of the analyst, his theoretical orientation and the psychiatric diagnosis of the patient.

Comments

If we put value judgements aside and regard as a criterion of success the attainment by a homosexual of heterosexual activity, then the figure of 27% is certainly larger than other comparable success rates. Thus Woodward (1958) reports that only 7 out of 113 cases at the Portman Clinic showed an absence of homosexual inclination and increased heterosexual activity while Curran and Parr (1957) present a similarly low success rate. Indeed the Wolfenden Report (1957) appeared to accept the impossibility of such changes.

It must be noted, however, that these figures were gathered by the analysts at the *end of treatment*, so this study does not tell us how long these new sexual inclinations continued. Furthermore there was no control group for this part of the study. The control group was used only to compare the attributes of homosexuals. For the investigation of therapeutic success a different control group (consisting of untreated homosexuals of whom some wish to change) is necessary. Nevertheless this lack of control group is not as important as it might at first appear since the subjects can, to a certain extent, serve as their own controls. An examination of their previous sexual history shows that no similar exclusively heterosexual behaviour had occurred. In addition, other studies of homosexuals (e.g. Woodward, 1958) indicate that such changes in sexual orientation are not normal events.

Conclusions

This study by Bieber demonstrates that long periods of analytic therapy can change the homosexual behaviour of some patients who want to become heterosexual. The success rate at termination of therapy was higher than in comparable studies. But before any firm conclusions could be drawn, long-term evaluation and study of a comparable untreated group would be necessary.

The work of Meyer (1966)

Meyer attempted to show that the success rate achieved by Bieber *et al.* with their homosexual sample was superior to that with behaviour therapy, as reported by Freund (1960) in Eysenck (1960). Meyer frankly admits, however, that there were differences in the two samples and that the method used by Freund was not perhaps the most efficient for the treatment of homosexuality. A chi-square analysis of success and type of treatment demonstrates that psychoanalysis was significantly better than behaviour therapy. An important difference in the two samples was their motivation to become heterosexual. Freund's sample was certainly less motivated, a fact which could well account for the resulting inferiority of his therapy.

B. STUDIES OF THE THERAPEUTIC PROCESS ITSELF

The problems involved in making judgements simply about the outcome of psychotherapy have already been indicated. The main one is probably the criterion of success to be adopted. This is peculiarly difficult for psychoanalysis since the criterion of change explicable in terms of Freudian theory is hardly comparable with that of other schools. It also means that control groups cannot be used for comparison. This is, of course, because untreated groups could not possibly be assessed in terms of such dynamic changes. The use of control groups is also difficult. Most psychiatrists would regard the assignment of a patient to an untreated control group as unethical although Eysenck (1960) argues that this view presupposes (contrary to evidence) that there is some value in psychotherapy. However the use of patients on a waiting list as controls (e.g. Rogers and Dymond, 1954), is more acceptable, unless the treatment, as in psychoanalysis, is prolonged. All the normal control group problems of matching still exist even if a group can be obtained.

For all these reasons, therefore, interest has turned among a number of investigators towards a study of the psychotherapeutic process. Very influential in research in this area is the work of Truax.

STUDIES BY TRUAX

As was stated above (p. 309), only a brief mention of this work will be made since it is specific to the psychotherapeutic concepts of Rogers (1957) in his school of non-directive therapy. That it is discussed at all is due to the fact that, in theory at least, the methodology could be applied to the study of psychoanalytic therapy.

Brief summary of findings

Truax (1963), studying recorded samples of psychotherapeutic sessions with 14 schizophrenic patients, found that therapists who were rated high for positive regard for patients, empathy and congruence produced improvements in their patients whereas therapists rated low on these variables produced deterioration. This means that the quality of therapist is a vital matter in the psychotherapeutic process.

Comments and conclusions

The importance of this result, especially with reference to the general findings concerning the outcome of psychotherapy as propounded by Eysenck (1952, 1960 and 1965) – that psychotherapy is not useful – cannot be missed. The failure of psychotherapy to produce results may be due to the fact that some patients improve and others deteriorate, thus cancelling out the effects; this is what occurred in Truax's study. His control group was the same as his experimental group on the criterion scores, but the variance of the experimental was significantly larger. This is a further argument against the first method of examining the overall results of psychotherapy. Bergin (1963) quotes the study of Cartwright *et al.* (1960) who used an own control design where patients had matched periods of therapy and no therapy. Again there was no significant difference in mean score on the criterion variables but the variance in the experimental sessions was greater.

It must be concluded therefore that in this type of therapy at least, and with schizophrenic patients, the quality of the therapist is a major factor in the results. A bad therapist may do harm. Certainly studies of effects of psychotherapy with the therapist variable uncontrolled are of doubtful value.

A weakness of these studies, from the viewpoint of their application to psychoanalytic therapy, resides in the nature of the criterion variables which are scores on the MMPI and the TAT test (among other similar scales) none of which is suitable for the assessment of psychoanalytic therapy.

Nevertheless, this method of studying the process of the therapeutic session as well as the outcome, is clearly applicable, in principle, to psychoanalytic sessions and studies of these will now be examined.

The work of Bellak (Bellak, 1958; Bellak and Smith, 1965)

These two papers will be discussed together since the 1958 article is in effect a summary of the earlier paper.

Method. Psychoanalytic sessions were recorded. Two psychoanalysts then made independent judgements on what had occurred while two other psychoanalysts made independent predictions of the next psychoanalytic hour. Statistical comparisons of agreement and disagreement were then made. In this way, according to Bellak (1958), psychoanalysis becomes a public event (in the sense that the term is used in the philosophy of science).

Patients and judges. Two patients were recorded for 50 sessions: two analysts made predictions and two analysts made judgements of the tapes. Predictors and judges were continuously swopped around. Every four weeks correlations were computed between judgements and predictions.

Results. On many variables there were good correlations (tetrachoric). This means, according to Bellak (1958), that there is good agreement as to how five analysts describe in psychoanalytic language the psychodynamics of a patient.

Examples of variables considered. Positive transference, oral striving, homosexuality, repression and projection. For each of these variables the judges had to indicate presence or absence in both conscious and unconscious form. The judges of the recorded session indicated the present status of these variables. Those predicting the analytic sessions indicated their status, for the next hour, the next week and the next month. In addition, multiple-choice questionnaires were used to elucidate the themes of the sessions.

Advantages of the method. According to Bellak there are numerous advantages in studying the psychoanalytic process by this method.

1. *There is no need of control groups.* This is clearly true since all that is being attempted is the prediction of behaviour from psychoanalytic theory. If behaviour as specific as that shown in the analytic hour can be predicted, then it must be regarded as support for the theory.

2. *No criterion needed for success.* This is again the case because the investigation involves the prediction of behaviour. At the end of the treatment it could well be possible to say whether the outcome (predicted or not) was an improvement or deterioration, but that would not affect the study of the process itself. Thus, unlike the work of Truax (1963), which studies the process of psychotherapy in relation to the success, Bellak studies the process only, attempting to predict its course.

3. *The long duration of the investigation.* Bellak attempts to argue that this makes spontaneous remission irrelevant. However, since we have shown that spontaneous remission refers only to recovery due to treatment by non-psychiatrists this point does not seem particularly important. It could be claimed,

however, that spontaneous remission, if it occurred, would be noted in the Bellak method by failure to predict behaviour in the analytic hour.

4. *One case can be the population under investigation.* This is important from the practical point of view since it is often difficult to gather sufficiently large and homogeneous samples of patients for convincing statistical analysis. Repeated observations on one case are respectable psychometrically and form the basis of P factor analysis – the technique advocated by Cattell (1957) for the investigation of clinical and psychiatric problems.

5. *The judges are psychoanalysts.* This is important in the study of psycho-analysis, since the objective validation of psychoanalytic concepts by psychologists is frequently subjected to criticism by psychoanalysts on the grounds that the psychologists have misapplied or misunderstood the theory. Since judgements and predictions, in the Bellak method, are by psychoanalysts this argument (which is irrefutable, if unfair) no longer obtains.

6. *Whole behaviours are examined.* Tests and rating scales are usually only samples of the behaviour we wish to measure as in, say, an individual intelligence test, such as the WAIS. Sometimes indeed they are correlates of such behaviour: an example of these would be the objective tests of Cattell (Cattell and Warbur-ton, 1967). Other tests such as the MMPI are merely self-reports of behaviour. Clearly, therefore, examination of the actual behaviour during the session, if quantified and specified, is superior to any of the above methods. Bellak's scheme of short-term prediction allows for this last type of observation.

7. *Such a scheme of short-term prediction can be used to evaluate any interaction.* It would be possible to compare other schools of psychotherapy in this way. Those where predictions were never verified could be dismissed as worthless.

Comments

Bellak believes that this method of short-term prediction is the best way of validating psychoanalytic therapy and theory. Indeed this claim is reiterated in a later paper (Bellak, 1961). If the method is looked at with the problems outlined at the beginning of this chapter in mind, it will be seen that it obviates many of the difficulties. The patient and therapist variables are both taken into account. The necessity of finding adequate control groups is removed as is the problem of spontaneous remission. The criterion of success does not have to be defined in this evaluation of psychoanalysis. However this is probably its weakest point. After all, logically it is possible to predict an interminable number of sessions in which deterioration or no improvement occurred. In this case the method would appear to validate psychoanalytic theory in that predictions would be supported and agreement noted among judges. However this objection is more theoretical than real since psychoanalytic theory normally predicts success; for the psycho-analytic session, as a therapeutic method, is based on psychoanalytic theory.

Is short-term prediction a method of verifying psychoanalytic theory ? Bellak claims that it is possible to validate psychoanalytic theory in the true scientific fashion by using this method. His grounds are that prediction of events is the standard scientific test for theory; hence the ability to predict the content of psychoanalytic sessions must support psychoanalytic theory. This is especially true when the fact that each prediction, entered on the prediction sheet for each session, must be supported by theory to obviate accurate guessing through insight into the particular method of the analyst conducting the case.

Certainly the results obtained by Bellak and Smith (1956) indicate that a good part of the psychoanalytic sessions could be predicted from the theory. However, to say that such predictions, even when based on theory, support the theory is to ignore other explanations of such results. For instance, if the analyst concerned were in fact reinforcing certain verbalisations of the patient (the Greenspoon effect, Greenspoon, 1955) the judges could well predict that other similar points would be reinforced. The flexibility of Freudian theory is such that experts in it would find little difficulty in using it to support their predictions. Again experts in psychoanalytic theory could use it to support insights that came from clinical intuition of the interaction recorded between patient and therapist.

Conclusions

It seems to this author, therefore, that the study by Bellak (1958) is impressive support for Freudian theory although other *ad hoc* hypotheses can be adduced to account for the results. The actual results in this study with two patients are clearly not extensive enough to accept or reject psychoanalytic therapy. As so often, therefore, it must be concluded that more research needs to be done. Nevertheless, as a method of investigating psychoanalytic therapy this seems to be most promising.

The work of Knapp (1963)

Knapp also reports the results of 600 short-term predictions of behaviour during therapy for four patients undergoing psychoanalysis, and for several patients in psychotherapy.

Method. The predictions were made by Knapp, who also carried out the psychotherapy, and by an independent collaborator. Sessions were recorded on tape. Predictions were classified as *verified, wrong* or *no evidence.*

Results. As Knapp points out, the mathematical distribution of outcomes was unclear, a fact which made statistical analysis difficult. Nevertheless he concludes that with all patients there was a better than chance prediction of events.

Examples of predictions

Prediction: Patient will be depressed before next session.
Outcome: Patient reports that she felt her life had been wasted. Prediction was verified.
Prediction: Patient would arrive between 10-20 minutes late for session.
Outcome: Patient arrives 12 minutes late. Prediction was again verified.

Some predictions were even made during the analytic hour and were not written down but recorded in the mind. These were, however, a minority.

Comments

This study by Knapp, although interesting, is far less rigorous than that reported by Bellak (1958) and is consequently less impressive evidence for psychoanalytic theory than the previous work. The main weakness lies in the fact that Knapp himself was taking the psychoanalytic sessions and making the predictions. This kind of experimenter contamination can clearly lead to all kinds of experimental bias (Rosenthal, 1964) of which the Greenspoon effect, already mentioned in connection with the work of Bellak, is but one example. Furthermore, in this study it is difficult to separate predictions based on clinical insight from those derived from Freudian theory.

Conclusions

The methodology of this investigation is not rigorous enough to use it as evidence for or against Freudian theory. It is, however, worthy of note, in that it exemplifies how a study of the psychotherapeutic process itself could lead to a verification of psychoanalytic claims.

CONCLUSIONS FROM ALL STUDIES

The conclusions to be drawn from these studies of psychoanalytic therapeutic success may be summarised under a number of headings.

1. Studies of the outcome alone of psychoanalytic therapy are too crude because the criteria of success from school to school and of any control groups are inevitably too disparate.
2. The use of the concept of spontaneous remission to form a base-line, above which successful psychotherapy must rise, is of dubious validity.
3. Short-term prediction of behaviour during the psychoanalytic sessions, as used by Bellak (1958), seems to offer *the best method* of evaluating psychoanalytic therapy. This should clearly elucidate what kinds of patient can be treated successfully by such procedures.

FINAL COMMENTS

If, therefore, we are correct in arguing that the best method for evaluating the effects of psychoanalytic therapy is to examine the psychoanalytic session itself, it is disturbing to note that Crown (1968), in a paper designed to propound the merits of psychoanalysis, still argued that the psychoanalytic hour should remain inviolate – no tapes or cameras.

Thus while it is true to say that the studies reported in this chapter have done little to elucidate the value of psychoanalytic therapy, at least it may be argued that a viable research method has emerged. In addition some misconceptions about the value of psychoanalytic therapy, based on inadequate methodology and conceptualisation of the problems, have been revealed.

Nevertheless it is clear that the present state of knowledge concerning the effectiveness of psychoanalytic therapy is little advanced from the days of Fenichel (1945) who wrote, commenting on his own report (1930) from the Berlin Psychoanalytic Institute and on studies of analytic success rates by Coriat (1917), Oberndorf (1942) and Sadger (1929) – that there is little doubt that psychoanalytic therapy leaves much to be desired.

12

The neo-Freudians and other analytic psychologies

INTRODUCTION

As is well known, in the course of the development of psychoanalysis by Freud, a number of his followers, of whom the most famous were Jung and Adler, broke with Freud on points of psychoanalytic theory. These analysts proceeded to found their own schools or branches of psychoanalysis. Thus, centred in Zürich, Jung developed Analytical psychology while Adler expounded his Individual psychology. Other analysts again, while they formed no distinctive school, concentrated on certain aspects of psychoanalytic theory to the exclusion of others so that their brand of psychoanalysis cannot be considered part of the orthodox theory – for instance Rank, who regarded the birth trauma as of crucial importance in the psychological development. All these writers are often referred to (e.g. Brown, 1961) as early schismatics.

During the thirties and forties, as psychoanalysis continued to develop, two divergent systems came into being: the Continental school, representing the orthodox position and typified by the work of Anna Freud (driven by the Nazis into Britain), and the British school influenced most by the work of Melanie Klein. Furthermore in America there have grown up a number of systems of dynamic psychology which have concentrated to a greater extent than has orthodox psychoanalysis on the psychology of the ego. The main progenitors of these systems are Horney, Fromm and Sullivan. These psychiatrists are known as neo-Freudians although it has been said that, in their concentration on social factors, they are perhaps better called neo-Adlerians.

AIM OF THE CHAPTER

The complexity and volume of the works of Jung alone, quite apart from the other writers mentioned in the introduction, make any kind of detailed review of their work impossible in one chapter. However the procedure adopted has been to outline the main divergences of these writers from orthodox Freudian theory, as discussed in this book, and to scrutinise these divergences in the light of the experimental evidence relevant to the portion of Freudian theory concerned. For example, good evidence has been adduced for repression (see pp. 165-81); thus any theorist whose divergence includes the exclusion of that concept could not be regarded as well supported. On the other hand, no study has been able to demonstrate the existence of a phallic character (see pp. 13-44). The theorist, therefore, who rejects this concept would be supported by the empirical evidence. Inevitably, some of the theories reviewed here demand their own body of experimental studies for support or disconfirmation, but this will not be attempted here since it is irrelevant to the purposes of this book – to examine Freudian theory. Furthermore since the influence of these other theories has been less, little empirical work in fact exists.

JUNG*

THE JUNGIAN MENTAL STRUCTURE

As we have seen (p. 126), in psychoanalytic theory there is a tripartite mental structure of ego, super-ego and id. Conscious and unconscious mental activity is held to occur.

Jung postulates three mental systems:

(a) *The conscious.* This is concerned with the individual's relation to the real world around us. This is the outward appearance of the personality and is called the *persona.*

(b) *The personal unconscious.* This is, in part, the opposite of the persona. Thus the brave man is unconsciously cowardly. It consists of repressed, neglected and unrealised qualities. Thus, as Brown (1961) says, the personal unconscious is compensatory in function. Just as the conscious, seen by the world, is called the persona, so the personal unconscious, the opposite, is called *the shadow.* If too strongly repressed by social conventions, for example, the shadow is likely to burst forth and overwhelm the conscious.

(c) *The collective unconscious.* This is the deepest layer of the mind. It contains the collective beliefs and myths of the race to which an individual belongs. Even deeper down it contains the universal unconscious common to all men (Brown, 1961). These universals are called *archetypes.* One archetype that a man has is the *anima* – the archetype of woman, by which he 'apprehends the nature of woman' (Jung, 1953). A woman has a corresponding archetype of man, the *animus.* One of the aims of Jungian psychotherapy is to help a person know his anima or animus, to plumb the depths of the racial unconscious and thus to become more fully himself. Other archetypes are the wise old man and the great mother. Possession by these archetypes is called by Jung *inflation* and produces psychotic delusions of grandeur.

BALANCE IN JUNGIAN THEORY

In Freudian theory the ideal balance of the dynamic forces in the mental structure, the aim of psychotherapy, is control by the ego: 'Where id was, there shall

* The description of Jung's system is based on the writings of Jung and summaries and discussions by Brown (1961), Lindzey and Hall (1965), Glover (1950), Fordham (1959) and Blum (1953).

ego be' (Freud, 1933). In the psychopath, for example, the id has gained control, in the obsessional neurotic, the super-ego is too powerful.

In Jungian theory the ideal is a balance between conscious and unconscious. Thus the influence of reason (consciousness) is important, but so too is the influence of the unconscious. If a blend of reason and vitality can be struck, a new centre of personality emerges – *the self*. The self, as Fordham (1959) points out, is not used by Jung in its everyday sense but is used in the sense of the Eastern mystics. In *The Secret of the Golden Flower* (Jung and Wilhelm, 1931) Jung develops the theme of what the self truly is. It seems to mean complete acceptance of both oneself and the world around. Fordham quotes the Jungian mystical description: 'The self is not only the centre but also the circumference that encloses consciousness and the unconscious; it is the centre of this totality as the ego is the centre of consciousness' (Jung, 1940).

Clearly this brief description of the mental apparatus as conceived by Jung must do violence to the mystical complexity of his full concept. Nevertheless the main points have been presented.

Comments

Jung's concept of the collective unconscious – the inherited racial foundation of the whole structure of personality (Hall and Lindzey, 1957) – perhaps differentiates his theories most profoundly from those of Freud. Unfortunately modern genetics cannot support the possibility of the inheritance of acquired characteristics, a necessary implication of the collective unconscious. It is to be noted that Freud (1913) also postulated inherited memory traces to account for symbolisation in dreams. However, unlike Jung, Freud made no use of the concept in his general theory and the fact of symbolisation may be accounted for without recourse to inherited memories. Jung, as we have seen, placed great emphasis on the collective unconscious since it contains all the 'wisdom and experience of uncounted centuries' (Jung, 1953) and is the creator of the self.

In Chapter 7, surveying the empirical evidence for the Freudian theory of ego, super-ego and id, it was noted that factor analysis by Cattell and his associates had yielded three factors which could be identified with the Freudian constructs. Furthermore, at least the basic theory was in accord with modern concepts of the neurophysiology of the brain. In addition, a test (the IES test) had been developed to measure the behaviours relevant to each part of the mental apparatus. Thus, difficult as it obviously is to provide empirical evidence for this type of theory, there is some support for the psychoanalytic concepts. Jung's concepts on the other hand cannot be put to the empirical test. Indeed the anima and animus resemble more the Platonic $\epsilon' \iota \delta' \eta$ which, of their nature, can only be conceived.

In short, for the Freudian theory, which is hard enough to test but has some degree of support, Jung has substituted an untestable system which flies in the face of current genetics.

CONTENTS OF THE UNCONSCIOUS

The concept of unconscious mental activity was not invented by Freud. His contribution was to specify what such contents were, e.g. the Oedipus complex, the castration complex, repressed sexual desires and aggressions. Jung, too, has specified the contents of the unconscious. The personal unconscious contains repressed and neglected ideas and abilities, the racial or collective unconscious, the wisdom of ages in the form of *archetypes*. The archetypes identified include birth, rebirth, death, power, magic, unity, the hero, the child, God, the demon, the earth matter, the wise old man, the animal (Jung, quoted by Hall and Lindzey, 1957). As indicated, archetypes can take possession of the individual: Bertrand Russell might be thought to have been possessed by the archetype of the wise old man. Certain archetypes, such as the anima, animus, shadow and persona, operate almost as separate systems. Thus the ego frequently identifies with the persona, and the shadow (man's animal side) is frequently repressed into the personal unconscious.

Comments

Freud's theories of Oedipal and castration complexes can be subjected to empirical test; the antecedent conditions of such complexes are specified and so are the consequences. These theories of archetypes are not thus testable. All individuals must have them, being racially inherited, but the evidence for them comes from their appearance in myths and dreams and psychotic episodes. As Brown (1961) points out, the concept of archetypes depends on reasoning from the particular symbol to a generalised idea in the platonic sense. Indeed, as is the case with dream symbols, there is no need to postulate a collective unconscious for these common themes are explicable in terms of the common experiences of men in different societies. The only evidence for archetypes is their actual occurrence in conscious behaviour.

For example, the occurrence of the Odysseus theme in various cultures is evidence for an archetype of the lost prince. No other kind of evidence can support the construct. It is, therefore, untestable. On the other hand the basic contents of the unconscious in Freudian theory, such as the Oedipus complex and castration complex, have a certain amount of empirical support, both in cross-cultural and experimental studies and from the study of dreams by Hall and his associates.

Jung (1955), in *Psychology and Alchemy*, demonstrates in a long series of dreams from one patient similarities between his dream symbolism and the symbols of mediaeval alchemy – evidence, he claims, for the racial unconscious and the existence of archetypes.

Freud's dream theories, on the other hand, claim that the dreams represent the disguised wishes of the dreamer, and that most of the dream symbols represent not archetypes but the sexual organs. In Chapter 9, where the evidence for dream theory was reviewed, we discussed a considerable amount of work supporting the Freudian theory of symbolism (e.g. Lessler, 1962), the enormous empirical dream studies of Hall (1966) which support dream symbolism and the Oedipus and castration complexes, and finally the EEG studies of dream activity. These again, especially Berger (1963), provide support for the Freudian theory of dreams.

Jung, however, with an untestable theory of archetypes which is inevitably contrary to modern genetics since the whole concept of the racial unconscious implies the inheritance of acquired characteristics, diverges from Freud at a point where Freudian theory is strongly supported.

From this study of two basic differences between Jung and Freud, the concept of the racial or collective unconscious and the notion of archetypes, it is clear that in place of the Freudian theory which to some extent at least, has empirical support, and which *can* be tested, Jung has substituted two untestable hypotheses. This is a good illustration of the reasons why this book, apart from this brief chapter, has been restricted to orthodox psychoanalytic theory. As must be clear, Freudian theory itself has little empirical support originating from psycho-analysis. Deviations from it, therefore, if based on clinical evidence would not be likely to be useful. What is needed is rather to attempt to utilise those parts of psychoanalytic theory which have been confirmed.

JUNGIAN CONCEPTS OF EXTRAVERSION AND INTROVERSION

Jung (1949) first coined the terms extraverted, to describe the person mainly interested in the external world, and introverted, which applied to the person more concerned with his internal subjective world. For Jung, most people would be classified into types in that their persona was either extraverted or introverted and the opposite tendency existed in the personal unconscious. In addition, since Jung (1949) also recognised four basic psychological functions – thinking, feeling, sensing and intuiting – the stage is set for eight basic personality types – the extraverted thinker, feeler, the introverted thinker, feeler and so on. For Jung considered that one of these functions was especially developed in each person.

Comments

This classification, in Freudian terms, is an ego psychology – a branch of psychology that was not highly developed in orthodox psychoanalytic theory. This, undoubtedly, is a part of Jungian psychology which is well supported by the empirical studies of personality reviewed in this book (see Chapter 4).

Here it will be remembered that Cattell, Eysenck and Guilford each isolated an extraversion-introversion factor, and a social introversion scale occurs in the MMPI. While these studies support the basic concept of extraversion-introver-sion there is not much support for the quadruple functional division although it is to be noted that one test of these Jungian types has been developed (thus at least demonstrating their testability) – the Myers-Briggs Type Indicator (Briggs and Myers, 1962).

It is clear, therefore, that the concept of extraversion-introversion as a dimension of personality has very powerful support. However the factorially devised dimension is not identical with that of Jung. A most essential difference is that the empirical derivation is a dimension on which the majority of people score around the middle. The Jungian scheme, a typology, would strictly require a bimodal, not a normal, distribution. Nevertheless this divergence by Jung into the psychology of the ego proved basically sound. It is a pity, therefore, that it played relatively little part in his overall system.

CONCLUSIONS CONCERNING JUNG

As was indicated in the introduction to this chapter, to do justice to the immensity and complexity of Jungian theory in part of a chapter is not possible. Thus a few major points of Jung which differ markedly from orthodox psychoanalytic theory have been discussed. His basic theory, including the inherited racial unconscious, is harder to test empirically than that of Freud and is not in accord with modern opinions concerning genetics. On the other hand, the Freudian theory of ego, id and super-ego does have a modicum of support. As regards extraversion-introversion, for which there is no psychoanalytic equivalent, Jung is supported by the evidence although his typological notions have not been confirmed.

Before we leave the analytic psychology of Jung, one further point needs to be mentioned. It is generally accepted that Jung first split off from Freud on account of Freud's pansexualism. Jung, indeed, claimed this to be a most important reason in a personal communciation to Hall and Lindzey (Hall and Lindzey, 1957). Readers may therefore object that this point should surely have been explicitly dealt with. Implicitly it has been covered. Freud's concept of the id, repository of the Oedipus complex and repressed instinctual impulses (pansexual) has been contrasted with the Jungian concept – the collective unconscious. What evidence there is favours the Freudian version. However in this book, as was made clear in the opening chapter, the technique used has been to break down the Freudian concepts into explicit or implicit empirical testable hypotheses. Thus such broad questions as to whether the libido is primarily sexual or not have not been considered. Nevertheless the Cattell studies of drive (ergs) do support the importance of sexual drive.

ADLER

THE INDIVIDUAL PSYCHOLOGY OF ADLER

Like Jung, Adler broke with Freud partly on account of Freud's emphasis on the importance of sexuality. In place of the Freudian struggle between ego, id and super-ego, Adler's view of man was more optimistic: basically socially oriented, man struggles to realise his creative self. An examination of some of the most important terms in Adler's psychology will demonstrate clearly his divergence from Freud.

The inferiority complex

Adler will be immortalised, if for no other reason, by this term alone. In his view the individual is always striving towards goals, realistic or unattainable. His view of man is thus teleological. Constant failure to reach his goals produces in an individual feelings of inferiority – the inferiority complex. Thus Adler (1930) says . . . 'I begin to see clearly in every psychical phenomenon *the striving for superiority* . . . .' To Adler the feeling of inferiority is inevitable for a child – he is inferior. Often this inferiority real or imagined is met by *compensation*. Organ inferiority, a concept by which Adler tried to account for particular organic symptoms, is often thus countered by compensation. Had Demosthenes not stuttered, there would have been no *Philippics*. An example of compensation is the *masculine protest*, seen in the aggressive masculinity of the stereotypic suffragette. Thus then the striving for superiority is a basic driving force of behaviour – 'the great upward drive' (Adler, 1930).

Goals

'Individual psychology insists absolutely on the indispensability of finalism for the undertaking of all psychological phenomena. . . . The final goal alone can explain man's behaviour . . .' (Adler, 1930). Indeed what distinguishes neurotics from normal people is the realism of their goals. Neurotics are neurotic because they aim at the unattainable. Another feature of neurotic goals is that they are selfish or lack *social interest*. Social interest refers to the socialisation of the striving for superiority. Thus the goal of becoming headmaster is, presumably, socialised, oriented to the good of society. Without social interest this goal might be transformed to that of gang-leader – oriented to selfish gain.

Style of life

This represents the *way* in which these strivings to overcome inferiority take place, and thus is the source of individual differences among people. It is formed early on in childhood and, once formed, influences our whole perception of the world. Partly it is the child's compensation for his inferiority and is closely related to the kinds of goal he has set himself (which depend upon where he feels inferior). This style of life, the personality resulting from the goals adopted and the methods of overcoming inferiority in respect of them, is what has to be changed in the neurotic personality. This is the function of psychotherapy and it may be done by either changing goals to one which the individual can attain, or changing his means of compensation for inferiority.

COMMENTS

Adler broke away from Freud in 1911 and his individual psychology bears little relation to psychoanalysis. In effect it is an ego psychology only. Thus although the style of life is adopted early in childhood and the goals of the individual may be unconscious, they are unconscious only in the sense that they are unverbalised.

What has been abandoned from Freudian theory, therefore, is the whole concept of the motivating power of repressed sexuality and aggression, the Oedipus and castration complexes and the importance of infantile sexuality. As we have seen from the studies discussed in this book, Adler is on safe ground in so doing to the extent that it is these unconscious elements that are so difficult to put to the empirical test. Nevertheless it must be pointed out that a limited amount of empirical evidence does exist for the castration and Oedipus complexes (see p. 116), for sexual symbolism (see p. 226), for id and super-ego (see p. 138) and for the application of these concepts to an understanding of neurosis (see p. 306) and even the arts (see p. 190).

In place of this Adler has erected a striving for superiority based on early family background and tinged, in the normal, adapted individual, with social interest which appears to be innate. Empirical and theoretical studies of personality such as those of Eysenck, Cattell and Guilford (pp. 31-9) do not in fact support the claim that striving for superiority is a major factor in personality. Cattell (1965), however, has isolated an erg of self assertion, though this is only one among many. At this point, in fairness to Adler, a body of research conducted by McClelland and his associates on the achievement motive, may also be related to Adler's ideas of striving for superiority (see for example McClelland, 1961). Cattell, however, relates this achievement motive empirically to self assertion, self-sentiment and super-ego. A weakness of Adlerian theory, as has been discussed by Brown (1961), is that the attractive simplicity of the theory involves the defect that, in respect of neurosis, it is quite unable to explain how different symptoms develop in different people. If the goal is wrong, the style of life misdirected, there is nothing to account for obsessional rather than hysterical symptoms.

CONCLUSIONS TO ADLER

Adler's individual psychology is hardly a branch of psychoanalytic theory since it is concentrated on the psychology of the ego. For Adler, man is therefore essentially a rational animal. There can be no doubt that one of the most attractive features of Freudian theory – its immense explanatory power – has therefore been abandoned. Furthermore, as the evidence in this book shows, such total rejection is probably not justified. On the other hand Adler's emphasis on the social determinants of personality – for the style of life is entirely socially determined – and the importance of the ego in behaviour, were needed improvements

in psychoanalysis. Indeed it is interesting to note that orthodox modern psycho-
analysts are now trying to develop their own psychology of the ego, for example
Anna Freud (1946) and Hartman, Kris and Lowenstein (1947). It still remains
to be seen whether Adler's emphasis on the struggle for superiority is justified.
In the light of the evidence, however, it must be concluded that, salutary as
Adler's emphasis on ego psychology was, his theories abandoned too much of
Freudian theory and robbed it, perhaps, of what was most interesting and
valuable.

MELANIE KLEIN

HER THEORIES

A brief mention must now be made of the theories of Melanie Klein. These
are interesting because the majority of modern developments of psychoanalytic
theory have, like Adler, turned their attention to the ego and its mode of development as an individual grows up within a culture, whereas Klein has very much
concentrated on the early infantile determinants of behaviour and its instinctual
basis. These developments are also important in that they have exerted a profound influence on a number of British analysts, notably Winnicott and Bowlby
(see Winnicott, 1957 or Bowlby, 1969 for example). Indeed, Brown (1961) calls
the analysts thus influenced the British School. Despite its influence and its
intrinsic interest, however, only a bare summary of the main differences between Melanie Klein's work and that of Freud will be given because, as will become clear, her theories are inherently untestable.

The raw data on which Melanie Klein based her theories

Freudian theories of infantile development, despite the case of Little Hans
(Freud, 1909), came largely from the free associations and dream material of
adults. Melanie Klein, however, analysed children using an interpretation of
their play and their verbalisations about their play. Using this play-association
technique Klein was able to analyse children from two years upwards. Many
orthodox analysts reject the theories derived from the play method because they
do not believe it can open up the unconscious in the same way as the standard
free-association technique (which was generally used with highly intelligent and
articulate patients). Fenichel (1945), however, does say the method may work.
If the original data obtained by Freud is regarded as of dubious reliability, then
an example of a child analysis will show how much more interpretative this is.
Segal (1964) quotes an example of one of her analyses of a child of five:

> . . . she started spreading glue on the floor of the playroom and her shoes . . .
> I interpreted that she wanted to glue herself to the floor so as not to be sent
> away at the end of the session. . . . She confirmed this interpretation verbally
> and then proceeded to smear the glue in a more messy and dirty fashion, saying
> with great satisfaction 'But it's also a "sick" right on your floor'. I inter-

preted that she wanted to glue herself not only to the inside of the room, but also to the inside of my body, where new babies grew, and to mess it and dirty it with the "sick".

There is little point in questioning the correctness or otherwise of this interpretation. It is quoted to show how very subjective and interpretative are the original 'data' for the theories of Melanie Klein. Such data are not sufficient to construct a theory of personality development. Yet much of Melanie Klein's theorising concerns infantile personality development in the first six months. Since classical, free-association techniques did not normally recapture such early memories, it is difficult to imagine how even scientifically respectable techniques could reveal such early memories or fantasies (if indeed they exist).

Her basic conclusions

The super-ego begins its development in earliest infancy. It is not, as in Freudian theory, the heir of the Oedipus complex. In early infancy the infant is orally aggressive. This aggression, the fantasy of biting the mother, is projected on to the mother, who is therefore seen as a violent hostile figure. This in turn creates anxiety. Aggression (which is innate) is of more importance than sex in the theories of Melanie Klein. Flugel (1945), describing this portion of the theory, writes that 'He wants ('cannibalistically') to incorporate the nipple and the breast and later to consume the contents of the mother's body (this last being perhaps one of the most startling of Klein's discoveries).'

Jones (1923) regarded this fantasied aggression of the infant as a far more important determinant of that infant's development than the actual aggression of the parent in the way he handles the child.

As Flugel makes clear, this projection of aggression on to the mother is crucial to the development of the super-ego, because in Kleinian theory in addition to projection (the mental analogue of defaecation) the child also indulges in introjection (the mental analogue of eating). Originally indeed the child introjects the 'good' breast and projects the 'bad'. By introjection these violent aggressions projected on to persons or objects are incorporated into the self. These introjections constitute the beginnings of the super-ego. Hence the super-ego is developed over a long period from earliest infancy. Hence too the barbaric severity of the super-ego, noted by Freud (1933) and attributed by him to the fact that it is the parents' super-ego which is introjected. To Melanie Klein, of course, this severity is but a reflection of the child's own savage impulses projected on to others and again introjected.

Comments

The data from these play sessions with children are not sufficient basis for any respectable theory. As the example from Segal (1964) showed, there is an enormous amount of interpretation by the analyst. However with children of this age it is difficult to see how more satisfactory data might be obtained. After all, intelligence testing, which is one of the most valid and reliable forms of assessment in psychology, is at its weakest with young children – however excellent the baby tests such as those of Griffiths (1951) and Psyche Cattell (1940) are.

Klein is, of course, a thorough-going psychoanalyst. She accepts most of the major tenets of psychoanalytic theory, including even the death instinct. Her divergence from classical theory lies in the developmental sphere, the fact that she attributes so much importance to the first six months of life, and claims that the super-ego has clearly begun its development. Since this occurs through the ego defence processes of projection and introjection a further divergence from orthodox theory is implied. In orthodox theory the ego develops slowly from the id during childhood. In Kleinian theory the ego is already sufficiently developed at birth to project and introject.

Melanie Klein's theory and the empirical evidence

By the evidence adduced in this book for the Freudian theory of the mental apparatus and the defence mechanisms of introjection and projection, it is to be noted that both theories are equally supported. This is because the evidence does not attempt to establish at what age these structures and defences appear. To choose between the theories, therefore, on rational empirical grounds would need a specific critical test. For example super-ego behaviour would be expected by Freudian theory *not* to occur in children of three years old; by Kleinian theory it could be expected. In principle, therefore, a critical test could be devised. At present however no such test can be devised in practice. This is because the precise testing of such behaviour in young children is not possible. Studies of specific moral behaviours, e.g. cheating, are not really relevant to the psychoanalytic theory since not cheating can be due to feelings of guilt (super-ego) or fear (ego). That is why factor-analytic studies of super-ego and ego activity are superior to purely observational studies. If a factor common to a large number of moralistic actions can be isolated it may be interpreted as a super-ego factor. However this technique requires a large number of quantified variables which cannot be obtained from young children.

CONCLUSIONS TO MELANIE KLEIN

Empirical evidence gives equal support to the theories of orthodox psychoanalysis and those of Melanie Klein. At present no critical tests can be devised for the two hypotheses because it would involve the testing of young infants. The data, however, on which Melanie Klein based her theory are highly dubious even by the standards of psychoanalysis. Her theories, therefore, cannot rationally be accepted. On the evidence it is possible to argue for the construct of a super-ego. There is little evidence concerning its origins. Nevertheless regarding the theories of Klein, we must agree with Flugel (1945) who wrote '. . . which (the findings of Melanie Klein) when described in forthright scientific language are apt sometimes to appear so far-fetched, weird and sinister as to be scarcely credible.'

FROMM

HIS THEORIES

Unlike Freud, whose main concern was with the psychology of the individual, Fromm was equally interested in individuals and society. At present, however, we shall concern ourselves with his views of man, concentrating on his points of divergence from Freud.

In *The Fear of Freedom*, Fromm (1942) outlines his debt to and his disagreements with Freud. Basic to Fromm's ideas are '. . . some of the fundamental discoveries of Freud, particularly those concerning the operation of unconscious forces in man's character and their dependence on external influence . . . .' However, contrary to the Freudian view that man's relationship with others is always a means to an end, the satisfaction of biologically given drives, Fromm holds that '. . . these drives which make for the *differences* in men's characters, like love and hatred, the lust for power and the yearning for submission, the enjoyment of sensuous pleasure and the fear of it are all *products of the social process*' (our italics). He continues, 'Man's nature, his passions, and anxieties are a cultural product . . .'. Thus then, for Freud biological man, for Fromm social man.

The clearest exposition of Fromm's view of man is to be found in *Man for Himself* (1949). Here his divergences from Freud become quite clear.

Character

Fromm's (1949) theory of character formation follows that of Freud (see pp. 6-12) quite closely, as he himself admits, but with the fundamental difference that

> . . . the basis of character is not seen in various types of libido organisation (e.g. repressed anal erotism produces the anal character) but in specific kinds of a person's relatedness to the world. In the process of living, man relates himself to the world.

> 1. by acquiring and assimilating things, and
> 2. by relating himself to people (and himself).

> The former I shall call the process of assimilation, the latter that of socialisation.

Fromm continues

> These orientations by which the individual relates himself to the world, constitute the core of his character: character can be defined as the (relatively permanent) form in which human energy is canalised in the process of assimilation and socialisation. (*Ibid.*)

Fromm (1949, p. 111) draws up a chart of the various character types.

		Descriptions	
Assimilation	*Socialisation*	*Positive aspect*	*Negative aspect*
1. Non-productive orientation			
a. Receiving (Accepting)	Masochistic (Loyalty)	Optimistic, responsive	Wishful thinking, passive
b. Exploiting (Taking)	Sadistic (Authority)	Impulsive, active	Aggressive, rash
c. Hoarding (Preserving)	Destructive (Assertiveness)	Cautious, orderly	Pedantic, obsessional
d. Marketing (Exchanging)	Indifferent (Fairness)	Adequate, purposeful	Indiscriminating, opportunistic
2. Productive orientation			
Working	Loving, Reasoning	No similar description attached	A development of true spontaneity

Fromm points out that most people are blends of these orientations and that the non-productive characters are clinically similar to the pre-genital character types of Freud (see p. 6). The difference lies in the hypotheses concerning their aetiology.

For example, the hoarding character of Fromm is very similar to the anal character of Freud. However, the anal character (Freud, 1908) is the result of reaction-formation and sublimation of repressed anal erotism. To Fromm the retentive nature of the hoarding orientation is merely a reflection of his general relation to the world. He is mean with money, not as a substitute for faeces, but because he is mean with everything, including faeces.

The productive orientation is the ideal development, equivalent to the genital character of Freud. In a later work Fromm (1965) uses two further concepts to describe character. *The necrophilous character* – 'the malignant form of the character structure of which Freud's anal character is the benign form . . . . is attracted to and fascinated by all that is not alive, all that is dead; corpses, decay, faeces, dirt.' It is related to the death instinct. This is contrasted with the *biophilous orientation* to be found in the productive character and typified by a love of life.

Fromm's theories in the light of the evidence

Fromm's character typology is professedly the equivalent of the Freudian psychosexual theory of personality development (see pp. 6-12). There, it will be remembered, it was argued that implicit in the psychosexual theory were two hypotheses capable of empirical validation:

(*a*) that certain personality syndromes exist, and
(*b*) that these are the result of repressed pre-genital erotism.

Fromm's theory of characters or orientations is therefore virtually the same as

Freud's regarding the first hypothesis but quite different regarding the second.

A considerable body of evidence supports the existence of the personality syndromes: Goldman-Eisler (1953) supports the oral character, Beloff (1957) and Kline (1969a) confirm the anal character. So far there has been no confirmation of the phallic personality or Fromm's marketing orientation. This evidence equally supports, therefore, the receptive and exploiting orientations (oral dependent and sadistic) the hoarding orientation (anal character) and necrophilous character.

The second hypothesis, concerning the aetiology of these syndromes, is the point of difference. Studies such as those of Beloff and Goldman-Eisler are not helpful here since, even if child-rearing processes are implicated in the aetiology of the syndromes (thus supporting repressed pregenital erotism), Fromm has argued that the general social background of parsimony and retention makes 'anal' mothers give severe pot training. However the studies with the Blacky Pictures (Blum, 1949), discussed earlier in this book (pp. 79-88), where responses to a lactating and defaecating dog are related to various aspects of personality development, are relevant to this difference between Fromm and Freud. Thus Kline's (1968a) finding that anal characteristics were related to the anal dimension of the Blacky Pictures and McNeil and Blum's (1952) research into handwriting and anal scores on the Blacky Pictures support the Freudian hypothesis. Thus, although the evidence for the link between repressed pregenital erotism and personality development is slight, what little there is must favour Freud rather than Fromm.

Conclusions

Fromm's theory of character is in reality little different, other than in nomenclature, from that of Freud. The evidence for the personality syndromes gives both views equal support. There is little firm evidence, as yet, in favour of either of the hypotheses concerning the development of these personalities. What little there is supports the Freudian theory, although Beloff (1957) did find that anal traits between mother and child were correlated (as would be predicted from Fromm's theories).

The Oedipus complex

As was the case with personality development, Fromm accepts the clinical finding of Freudian theory – the existence of the Oedipus complex – but desexualises its origins considering it to be the result of the social forces of the typical Western family structure. For Freud, the Oedipus complex was the sexual rivalry for the mother of father and son. Fear of castration by the father (as a punishment) created its repression which was finalised by the development of the super-ego (see p. 95 for the theory). Fromm admits that the discovery of fixation to the mother 'is, indeed, one of the most far-reaching discoveries in the science of Man. But in this area . . . Freud narrowed his discovery and its consequences by being compelled to couch it in terms of his libido theory' (1965, p. 95). Fromm continues 'Incestuous (Oedipal) wishes are not primarily a result of sexual desires but constitute one of the most fundamental tendencies of man: the wish to remain, to return to where he came from, the fear of being free . . .' (p. 107). In an earlier paper Fromm (1948) had argued that Oedipal rivalry with the father was due to the fact that Western society was patriarchal and authoritarian: the conflict was due to this harsh treatment, meted out by the father to the son. As support, anthropological evidence was quoted to show that the Oedipal complex did not occur in matriarchal societies – that it was not universal.

Comments

Because Fromm accepts the fact of the Oedipus complex but disagrees with Freud regarding its interpretation, the approach adopted in this book – to examine the objective evidence for the clinical findings of psychoanalysis – does not readily favour one or other of the two views. Nevertheless it must be stated that many psychologists do not even accept the fact of the Oedipus complex (e.g. Valentine, 1960). However certain points concerning Fromm's concepts of the Oedipus complex must be discussed. Orthodox psychoanalysis accepts the fact that the Oedipus complex is dependent upon the typical Western family constellation. Thus Fenichel (1945) says '. . . the sexual conflicts of children would be different if they did not live together with their parents and a few brothers and sisters, exposed to the typical family conflicts of sexual excitation and frustration. Different environments provoke different reactions' (p. 98). Consequently Fromm's (1948) argument as demonstrated by anthropological studies (e.g. Malinowski, 1927), that the Oedipus complex is not universal, does not destroy the psychoanalytic theory. It does, of course, destroy the psychoanalytic hypothesis that the Oedipus complex originates in a phylogenetic memory of the patricide of the primal horde (Freud, 1913). However, unlike Jung, Freud makes little use of this phylogenetic hypothesis in his general theory. It must also be pointed out that although Malinowski's findings are accepted, the evidence presented is really only clinical in nature and does not reach the standards of objectivity and reliability desirable in scientific research. However the attempt to rebut the evidence by Jones (1925) is, equally, entirely unconvincing. Thus what Fromm has done is to stress the importance of the social (familial) influence on the Oedipus complex.

However, Fromm's denial of the sexual nature of the Oedipus complex clearly needs further examination: is rivalry of the father the result of sexual jealousy or authoritarian treatment?

The evidence we have examined supporting the Oedipus complex (see pp. 97-116), slight as it is, tends towards an aetiology based on sexual jealousy. Thus the study by Friedman (1952) was interesting because of the sexual symbolism in the responses of the children – girls indicated that their fathers would mount some steps and enter a room. Certainly too, the work of Stephens (1961, 1962) stresses the sexual aetiology of the Oedipus complex.

Again the study by Whiting *et al.* (1958), where long post-partum sexual taboo was found to be related to totemism, which is in Freudian theory an acting-out of the Oedipus complex (Freud, 1913), very strongly points to the sexual nature of the Oedipus complex. Thus the evidence favours a sexual interpretation of the Oedipus complex.

Conclusions

As we have seen, Fromm accepts the fact that there is such a phenomenon as the Oedipus complex. His divergence from Freud lies in the hypothesised origin, which Fromm claims is simply the family environment which in patriarchal societies causes resentment of the father by the son. Fromm (1965) claims that fixation on the mother is a symptom of an inherited tendency to be dependent. What little evidence bears on the interpretation strongly supports the Freudian view of the sexual nature of the Oedipal tie with the mother. It should be pointed out that Fromm's view of an inherited tendency to be dependent is, like all instinct theories, very circular. Behaviour A occurs due to inherited tendency A1: A also provides the evidence for A1. Finally it must be stated that the universality of the Oedipus complex is not an essential plank in psychoanalytic theory.

Thus logically Fromm's theory is inferior to that of Freud and is less supported by the empirical evidence.

Super-ego

Fromm (1949) discusses the super-ego not from Freud's topological viewpoint but from the angle of its empirical manifestations, i.e. as conscience. He recognises two forms of conscience:

A. *Authoritarian conscience.* 'The authoritarian conscience is the voice of an internalised external authority, the parents, the state or whoever the authorities in a culture happen to be' (pp. 143-4). A little later Fromm writes 'The authoritarian conscience is what Freud has described as the super-ego; but . . . this is only one form of conscience . . .' (p. 144).

B. *Humanistic conscience.* 'Humanistic conscience represents not only the expression of our true selves; it contains also the essence of our moral experience in life' (p. 159). Again on the same page, 'Humanistic conscience is the expression of man's self-interest and integrity . . . .'

These two forms of conscience appear in every person. 'The problem is to distinguish their respective strength and their interrelation' (p. 165).

Comments

Once again Fromm adopts the clinical findings of Freud but this time adds something of his own. Little can be said about the humanistic conscience because, essentially, it is extremely hard to put to the empirical test. Presumably, if all classes of moral behaviour were subjected to factor analysis, the emergence of *two* factors rather than a general factor of conscience or super-ego would favour the theory of Fromm. The factor analyses of Cattell and Pawlik (1964) support a Freudian theory in that only one super-ego factor was found together with an ego and id factor.

Nevertheless, apart from the Cattell studies, the empirical investigations have not been such as to be relevant to Fromm's theory, so that no evidence can be adduced to support or refute it.

Mechanisms of escape

Fromm (1942) describes several mechanisms of escape, which Blum (1953) considers to be the equivalent of the Freudian defence mechanisms, and which Fromm himself likens to the concept of neurotic trends utilised by Horney (1939). These mechanisms of escape result from 'the insecurity of the isolated individual'. They are attempts to overcome the aloneness of the individual, characterised by '. . . the more or less complete surrender of individuality and the integrity of the self. Thus it is not a solution which leads to happiness and positive freedom: it is, in principle, a solution which is to be found in all neurotic phenomena' (p. 121). Three main mechanisms are discussed by Fromm:

1. *The masochistic-sadistic striving* – a striving for submission or domination which are caused by 'unbearable aloneness'. Fromm says this defence mechanism is different from that of Adler (striving for superiority) because Adler's is entirely conscious whereas the drive for submission and domination, is, for Fromm, unconscious – the terror of aloneness and insignificance.

2. *Destructiveness.* This mechanism too originates from feelings of 'individual powerlessness and isolation. . . . If I succeed in removing it (the world outside), I remain isolated . . . but I cannot be crushed by the overwhelming power of the objects outside myself' (p. 154). This mechanism is to be seen everywhere in action, disguised as 'Love, duty, conscience and patriotism'. However it has to be distinguished from destructiveness which is rational – a reaction to a genuine attack. For Fromm '*destructiveness is the outcome of unlived life*' (p. 156). Thus the more constricting a society is, the more destruction will be found within it.

3. *Automaton conformity.* This is the solution that the 'majority of normal individuals find in modern society' (p. 160). The individual ceases to be himself, he adopts the kind of personality offered to him by cultural patterns. Thus for Fromm national differences are real.

Comments

Freud did not regard sadism, masochism (sadism turned towards the self) or destructiveness as defence mechanisms. For him they became emanations of the death instinct. This has not been discussed in this book since the concept is simply not open to empirical validation. However neither destructiveness nor sadism play an important part in Freudian theory. Nor is the evidence adduced for Freudian defence mechanisms relevant to Fromm's concepts. In fact, the claim that terror of being alone is the cause of sado-masochism and destructiveness is hard to test empirically. Even the consequence that more of these defensive processes would be observed in a restrictive society (ignoring problems of defining this) would not definitely prove the thesis. Essentially these are un-testable and therefore unscientific speculations. As regards automaton conform-ity, this implies that in every different society would be found different person-ality types. Cross-cultural research with the Blacky Defence Preference Inventory (discussed on p. 183) points to the dangers of assuming that such national stereo-types in fact exist. Within-nation differences may be greater than between-nation differences.

Conclusions

To regard sadism and destructiveness, as Fromm does, as due to fear of isolation (when no operational definition of this is given) is to propound untestable hypotheses. Their importance in the development of behaviour is not supported by general studies of personality such as those conducted by Cattell, although dominance is an important factor (which could equally support Adlerian theory). The evidence in favour of Freudian defence mechanisms, especially repression, is such that to abandon them is to lose concepts with considerable empirical support. Naturally the evidence for Freudian mechanisms is not relevant to these very different mechanisms proposed by Fromm. In conclusion therefore, Fromm's concepts are not supported by evidence and are inherently untestable.

CONCLUSIONS CONCERNING FROMM'S THEORIES

As must be clear, with the exception of his mechanisms of escape Fromm has accepted the clinical observations of Freud concerning personality types, the Oedipus complex and the super-ego. Where he differs is in his interpretation. Freud interprets the findings in terms of libido theory; Fromm in terms of social factors. Fromm however is not explicit as to how these social factors produce their effects. Since the empirical consequences of the two theories are so similar the evidence cited in this book generally equally supports both. However where there is evidence concerning the aetiology of the phenomena, the Freudian theory has been generally favoured.

KAREN HORNEY

HER THEORIES

Like Fromm, Horney stresses the social rather than the biological determinants of personality and rejects the libido theory.

Penis envy

Freud (1933), in the 'New introductory lectures in psychoanalysis', regards penis envy as the crucial concept in the psychology of women (see p. 96 for the theory). Horney (1939) emphatically denies this. Thus she writes (p. 108) 'The wish to be a man, as Alfred Adler has pointed out, may be the expression of a wish for all those qualities or privileges which, in our culture, are regarded as masculine, such as strength, courage, independence, success, sexual freedom, right to choose a partner.' She continues (pp. 109-10) 'In short, interpretations in terms of penis envy, bar the way to an understanding of fundamental difficulties such as ambition, and of the whole personality structure linked up with them.' Here then, as Blum (1953) points out, are shades of Adler – the masculine protest and the emphasis on cultural factors.

Comments

In Freudian theory penis envy begins around the age of three at the phallic stage. It is biologically rooted in that it stems from the inferiority of the clitoris compared with the penis. However Fenichel (1945) agrees with Horney in that he accepts that the effects of this primary penis envy may be modified by social factors. Thus penis envy in our culture is reinforced by the fact that the male *does* have privileges. In other cultures where the female is the dominant sex, the psychological effects of penis envy may be cancelled out. Clearly, as Blum (1953) suggests, studies of penis envy in other cultures are needed. The major difference, therefore, between Freud and Horney is not that Freud failed to take into account social factors, rightly stressed by the neo-Freudians, but that for Horney penis envy is irrelevant to the understanding of women. If a woman wishes for a penis, it is merely symbolic of wishing for masculine privileges. Thus, like Adler's concept of the masculine protest, Horney has substituted for penis envy, an ego psychology of struggling for status – ambition.

Conclusions

The studies of the castration complex have been reviewed in Chapter 6 (pp. 97-116). Levin (1966) investigated penis envy in a group of career women but used the Rorschach test, the validity of which is a matter of doubt. Kreitler and Kreitler (1966) found no evidence of penis envy in their sample of children. However the interviews were conducted by untrained personnel so that the results are again open to doubt. Nevertheless there is, at present, no firm evidence for penis envy. No studies relevant to the Adlerian-Horney concept have been conducted. Cross-cultural research using quantitative techniques and longitudinal studies is clearly called for.

The Oedipus complex

Horney does not deny that the Oedipus complex may be seen in large numbers of people. However she rejects its biological foundation and regards it instead 'as a product of describable conditions' (1939, p. 82). 'One of them is, briefly, sexual stimulation by the parents. . . . The other series of conditions is entirely different in nature . . . it is connected . . . with its (the child's) anxiety' (*ibid.*). This anxiety, according to Horney, arises from the conflict in the child between its dependency on its parents and its hostile impulses. It is thus aimed at security. She claims that the 'vast majority of infantile attachments to parents, as they are retrospectively revealed in the analysis of adult neurotics, belongs to this group' (*ibid.*, p. 83).

Comments

As was the case with Fromm, Horney accepts the clinical facts of the Oedipus complex but denies its universality and to a large extent its sexual nature. The typical neurotic Oedipus complex is, for Horney, a bid for security. Only those Oedipus complexes based on parental stimulation are sexual in nature. As was made clear in the discussion of Fromm (see p. 336), psychoanalysts, e.g. Fenichel (1945), do not accept the biological phylogenetic foundation of the Oedipus complex, nor is such a Lamarckian belief necessary for Freudian theory. Thus the real point of difference between Horney and Freud lies in the interpretation of the Oedipus complex: sexuality or security.

The empirical evidence

The empirical evidence has been mainly concerned to demonstrate whether or not an Oedipus complex could be said to exist. Thus such evidence cannot bear on the relative value of the two theories. Since, however, Horney has a sexual Oedipus complex as well as a security-oriented version, the evidence for its sexual nature (Friedman, 1952 and Whiting *et al.*, 1958) again equally supports both theories. Thus at present no rational decision can be made between them since no empirical test of Horney's concept has been carried out.

Horney's theory of neurosis

The basis of neurosis for Horney was not the Oedipus complex but *basic anxiety*. Basic anxiety is defined in *The Neurotic Personality of Our Time* (Horney, 1937) as 'a feeling of being small, insignificant, helpless, endangered in a world that is out to abuse, cheat, attack, humiliate, betray, envy'. One notices the similarity to Adler's concept of inferiority feelings (see p. 328). This basic anxiety is unconscious, i.e. below the level of awareness of the subject. Horney (1942) describes ten neurotic trends developed in an effort to overcome this basic anxiety. The most important are:

1. The neurotic need for affection
2. The neurotic need for power
3. Neurotic withdrawal
4. Neurotic submissiveness.

Horney (1945) later classifies these needs into three categories:

(*a*) Moving towards people – the compliant type
(*b*) Moving away from people – the detached type
(*c*) Moving against people – the aggressive type.

All these three attitudes are present in individuals, but the normal person handles his conflicting demands in a rational and flexible manner, the neurotic rigidly.

Thus the neurotic may externalise certain attitudes by projection or he may create an idealised image of himself so that he sees only his good points. An example of idealised image, quoted by Mullahy (1948), is the large, middle-aged woman who sees herself as a slender young girl. Externalisation is more than projection for, as Mullahy points out, *all* one's feelings are experienced in others. Profound disturbance at political oppression (really one's own oppression) exemplifies this defence.

Comments

Basic anxiety as defined by Horney is a reinterpretation of Adler's feelings of inferiority in that both are seen to arise from marked positions of inferiority. To Adler this means that the individual strives to become superior, to Horney that he strives for security. The creation of externalised images again closely resembles Adler's fictive goal, an unrealistic style of life. Externalisation resembles projection (in the Freudian sense). Thus with these concepts Horney has but reinterpreted the clinical findings of Adler and Freud. It is to be noted too that in orthodox psychoanalytic terms basic anxiety is oral anxiety – fear that supplies will dry up – and would be likely to produce the oral pessimist.

The character types thought by Horney to be derived from three basic defences again have much in common with the typology derived from libido theory by Freud, with Fromm's analysis of character and also with Jung. Thus the compliant type is similar to Freud's oral erotic character (see p. 9) and Fromm's receiving orientation (see p. 334), the aggressive type resembles Freud's oral sadistic character and Fromm's exploiting orientation, while the detached type resembles Jung's extravert (see p. 326).

THE EVIDENCE

The evidence cited in this book has concerned itself broadly with attempting to establish the accuracy of Freud's clinical findings since it was argued that there is little point in researching into the interpretation of findings which turn out to be grossly inaccurate. Thus in the main where Freud and Horney overlap, the evidence cannot decide between them, and where they differ there is, in fact, little evidence. The evidence for the character types has been reviewed (see p. 44) and in that Horney overlaps with Freud and Jung she is supported. There is no evidence relating these types to moving away from or towards people and it seems an unverifiable hypothesis. On the other hand, as we have shown, studies with the Blacky Pictures (Blum, 1949) do provide evidence for the libido theory. There is the further point that rejection of libido theory makes the understanding of dream material, especially sexual symbolism (for which the evidence is considerable) (see p. 251), unconvincing.

Basic anxiety, often caused by maternal rejection (Horney, 1937), has perhaps been put to an empirical test in the studies of the effects of maternal separation. These studies have been reviewed (see pp. 116-25) and it was found that they were vitiated by their inadequate methodology. Nevertheless, as Bowlby *et al.* (1956) admit, the effects of maternal separation are not necessarily lasting. This finding militates against the importance of basic anxiety as the driving force behind neurotic behaviour.

CONCLUSIONS

The conclusions concerning Horney are similar to those drawn about Fromm. Since both accept many of the clinical findings of Freud, the evidence cited in this book tends to support them equally with Freud. The denial of sexuality (not so complete in Horney as in Fromm) runs against the tide of the evidence which is not however very considerable. Perhaps the chief value of Horney lies in her concentration on the social factors – for example, denying the universality of the Oedipus complex – work which has been generally accepted in orthodox psychoanalytic theory.

CONCLUSIONS CONCERNING THE WORK OF THESE DIVERGENT ANALYSTS

From the viewpoint of the empirical evidence is the work of these divergent analysts an improvement upon orthodox theory? Jung's major contributions – the collective unconscious and the theory of archetypes – appear to be unverifiable. They are therefore better considered as metaphysics and cannot be regarded as an improvement on orthodox theory. His theory of character types is however verifiable and, in name at least, has received support. Thus extraversion, though now rather differently defined, has turned out to be a major variable in the description of personality. This seems to be Jung's sole addition to knowledge of personality.

Adler, on the other hand, with his stress on the social influences on the development of personality – for he considers a man's style of life to be a major determinant of behaviour – and his emphasis on ego behaviour, has had a salutary influence on psychoanalysis. Thus the phylogenetic Lamarckian racial memory of the Oedipus complex has been abandoned in favour of an explanation of the Oedipus complex in terms of family life. On the other hand, Adler's major concepts that struggling for superiority is the driving force of behaviour, or that neuroses can be explained in terms of goals, have not been validated. Incidentally it should be noted that to call Adlerian psychology teleological is false since the goals are themselves determined by the style of life determined in its turn by the family situation.

The work of Melanie Klein, which is a true extension of psychoanalytic theory in that the full implications of libido theory are accepted, and which accepts the basic findings of Freud but throws them back to an earlier stage which is then subjected to detailed analysis, is by current techniques not verifiable.

M

Finally Horney and Fromm, who are really neo-Adlerians in that they reject libido theory and the importance of sexuality but emphasise the cultural determinants of development, accept many of the clinical findings of Freud but reject his interpretation, which does however appear to have some support.

Studies with the Blacky Pictures in general support the libido theory. Kline (1968), for example, found scores on the anal dimension of the Blacky Pictures related to anal characteristics. This is confirmation for Freudian theory. Similarly the oral character was related to weaning procedures by Goldman-Eisler (1953). As explanations, the neo-Freudian accounts of the hoarding character, for example, are weak – he is mean with money because he is generally mean. This is, of course, circuitous and fails to account for other traits in the syndrome. In addition considerable evidence supports Freudian dream symbolism (see especially Berger, 1963), the castration complex (Sarnoff and Corwin, 1959) all of which are inexplicable in terms of a non-sexual unconscious and a non-sexual libido.

In conclusion, therefore, it must be admitted that the work of the divergent analysts is no improvement on Freud. Certainly their data are no more carefully collected or quantified. The most important of them, Adler and Fromm, present what are virtually ego psychologies. However for this kind of psychology far better methods of data collection are available. Many of their hypotheses are unverifiable interpretations of inadequate material. Certainly there is little empirical support for their claims.

If we regard Freudian theory as valuable because of its explanatory power and its scope, then the rational procedure must be first to verify the clinical findings and then to attempt to incorporate them into a theory. To accept findings uncritically, as these neo-Freudian have done, and to reinterpret them in untestable form does not appear a useful procedure.

For Freudian theory, however, one useful gain has resulted. Psychoanalysts have examined the social determinants of development (and thus abandoned unsupportable phylogenetic hypotheses) and have attempted to develop an ego psychology. It must be stressed that this is useful for *Freudian theory*, rather than psychology, for quantification and precision of data are still missing from modern psychoanalysis.

13

The status of Freudian theory in the light of the evidence

In this final chapter we shall examine the status of psychoanalytic theory in the light of the evidence from the objective studies discussed in the previous sections. For example, if the concepts supported by these investigations are so few and so unrelated to each other that no coherent link between them can be found, it will be better, clearly, to incorporate them into the body of established psychology. If, on the other hand, sufficient Freudian theory has demonstrated validity such that academic psychology cannot easily accommodate the findings, it is equally obvious that the retention of the theory is justified.

Summary of verified concepts

Concept	*Exemplar* *Investigations and page no.*	Comments
1. Oral character	Goldman-Eisler (1950), p. 13	
2. Anal character	Kline (1969a), p. 25	
3. Oral erotism. No links between personality and child- training procedures	Levy (1928), p. 74)	Severe methodological difficulties. Theoretical problem of psycho- sexual constitution See p. 6
4. Oedipus complex	Friedman (1952), p. 99	
5. Castration complex	Stephens (1961), p. 108	
6. Id-ego – super-ego	Cattell and Pawlik (1964), p. 134	*N.B.* Validity of experi- mental personality variables uncertain
7. Repression	Dixon (1958b), p. 175	
8. Sexual symbolism outside dreams	Jahoda (1956), p. 210	
9. Psychological mean- ing of dreams	Hall (1966), p. 235	
10. Sexual symbolism in dreams	Berger (1963), p. 250	
11. Sexual nature of dreams	Karacan *et al.* (1966), p. 246	
12. Paranoia and homo- sexuality	Zamansky (1958), p. 268	

Summary of verified concepts—(contd.)

Concept	Exemplar Investigations and page no.	Comments
13. Appendicitis and birth fantasy	Eylon (1967), p. 290	
14. Phobias	Dixon *et al.* (1957), p. 302	
15. Depression	Leckie and Withers (1967), p. 303	

The first point to emerge from this tabular summary is that any blanket rejection of Freudian theory as a whole (e.g. Eysenck, 1952) simply flies in the face of the evidence. Nor can it be objected that, among the myriad observations and deductions made by Freud in the course of his studies, some were bound to be true, for the fact is that these concepts are, for the most part, cardinal points of Freudian theory. Only the hypotheses concerning neuroses cannot fall under that heading.

Nevertheless it would be wrong to assume that, because these concepts have been to some extent verified, the whole or even the majority of psychoanalytic theory must be accepted on the grounds that failure to confirm the rest is due to the methodological problems of verification. In some cases the objective evidence has severely delimited the concept so that Freudian theory needs to be modified accordingly. This indeed would be an ideal outcome of the scientific study of psychoanalysis – namely that Freudian theory became thus modified and adapted in the light of the evidence. Some of these modifications and limitations must now be discussed so that we can see more precisely just what parts of the theory are supported.

THE ORAL AND ANAL CHARACTER

Miles (1954) argued that it was a mistaken strategy to study psychosexual personality syndromes only because their childhood antecedents had been hypothesised in Freudian theory. Nevertheless the interest of these personality constellations lies in the fact that, were Freudian theory true, some powerful determinants of adult behaviour would be known. If the oral and anal character are unrelated to pregenital erotism or infant-rearing procedures their importance would be diminished, because empirical studies of personality such as those of Cattell and Eysenck have shown that such personality constellations account for only a minor part of the variance in personality measurement. Thus it is disappointing to note that the objective studies of psychosexual theory have demonstrated only that the adult personality constellations exist and have, except for two studies, universally failed to link them to infant-rearing procedures or pregenital erotism.

In the light of this evidence it would seem reasonable to abandon the terms oral and anal. The obsessional personality is a syndrome fully recognised in non-psychoanalytic psychiatry and is very similar to the anal character. Fenichel (1945), indeed, describes an obsessional character in terms indistinguishable from those he uses to describe the anal character. The oral character could be called the dependent personality. Nevertheless, if the psychoanalytic aetiology be abandoned, the question still remains as to why, in the anal character for example, the disparate and logically unconnected traits of obstinacy, orderliness, and parsimony should be found together. Here the neo-Freudians such as Horney, or Fromm (1942, 1965) with his hoarding and necrophilous characters who simply resemble their parents, are far from convincing. This failure to understand how such syndromes of personality traits come into being is a serious defect of a non-sexual concept of oral and anal characters. Eysenck (1967, for example) accounts for his two main factors of extraversion and neuroticism in terms of excitability of the central nervous system and lability of the autonomic system.

Oral erotism

Before abandoning the anal or oral aetiology of these personality constellations it must be remembered that there does seem to be evidence for oral erotism as evinced by thumbsucking if feeding is completed with but little sucking activity. The fact that there is, therefore, early in life a need to suck strongly supports the Freudian concept of oral erotism. As has been discussed in the relevant chapter (pp. 78-9), there have been no comparable studies of anal erotism because of the practical rather than logical difficulties of obtaining the requisite evidence. Furthermore studies attempting to link personality characteristics with infant-rearing problems are beset with severe methodological difficulties.

A final difficulty of investigating the psychosexual theory of personality development lies in the theory itself. Freud (1905) makes it clear that there is a constitutional factor in psychosexual development. Thus some individuals will be strongly oral erotic, others strongly anal erotic. This means, of course, that studies attempting to link pot-training procedures or methods of weaning to personality characteristics, without taking this constitutional factor into account, are not properly testing the theory. Blum (1953) refers to this aspect of the theory in a somewhat disparaging tone as the fudge factor. However if there *is* a constitutional factor, the fact that it makes scientific testing difficult is irrelevant. Nor can it be dismissed merely because of this.

Thus in the light of the evidence it would be wrong to abandon psychosexual theory. The mass of negative evidence is due largely to the problems of methodology.

Conclusion

Some of the personality syndromes postulated by Freud have been shown to exist. Their links to repressed pregenital erotism have not been demonstrated but the theory has not yet been refuted.

OEDIPUS AND CASTRATION COMPLEXES

Freud regarded his discovery of the Oedipus complex as his supreme achievement, a discovery fit to rank beside that of electricity and the wheel. It is therefore ironic, not to say tragic that, only four years after the death of Freud, Sears (1943) should write that the Oedipus complex was a grotesquerie of Freud's imagination. We have however cited some evidence (Friedman, 1952, Hall, 1963) for the Oedipus complex. Nevertheless it must be admitted that this evidence, though confirming the Freudian concept, does not establish the Oedipus complex as the central conflict of mental life or show it to be the kernel of neurosis. Far more modestly, it shows in one case that boys and girls do have sexual feelings towards the opposite sex parent of which they are largely unaware. In the other example the study of dream content indicates that the Oedipal situation is a source of psychological conflict in that it regularly appears in dreams. This, therefore, is an example of where the objective evidence so far confirms the Freudian theory but suggests that Freud may have attached too much importance to it.

Stephens' (1961) study of the castration complex is most impressive. Here the full scope of the Freudian concept as it affects the customs of whole societies has been put to the test. The fact that this cross-cultural study confirms the castration complex means that this particular concept has not been delimited.

ID, EGO AND SUPER-EGO

Presumably the perfect proof of this part of psychoanalytic theory would be the demonstration of three physiological systems in the brain which subsumed the activities characteristic of ego, super-ego and id. This has not been done. However the empirical studies, using objective personality devices of Cattell at the IPAT laboratories, have revealed three third-order factors which resemble to some extent the tripartite division of Freud (Cattell and Pawlik, 1964). Further support for this division comes from Cattell's studies of interests (Cattell, 1957) and the isolation of alpha, beta and gamma factors. These studies, as yet, are not definitive proof but rather are strikingly suggestive. If the validity of these objective test devices could be fully established and the results replicated on large samples, impressive support for this aspect of the theory could be mustered.

REPRESSION

Little needs to be said about this defence mechanism. It seems to us that the experimental studies of Dixon (1958a, b) and Blum (1955) are laboratory demonstrations of repression, as denial of entry into consciousness, in action. It is disappointing from the viewpoint of psychoanalytic theory that the other defences have not been confirmed to the same degree. Nevertheless repression is probably the most important of these defence mechanisms in Freudian theory since the whole dynamic view of mental life turns upon this concept. Thus the fact that it has been so powerfully supported means that one of the corner-stones of psychoanalytic theory as a whole still remains.

SEXUAL SYMBOLISM

This has been amply demonstrated to occur both within and outside dreams. Whether it must be regarded as a disguise to evade the censor, as Freud maintained, or whether, more simply, symbolism generally is the result of a visual transformation of abstractions, as Hall suggests, has not been decided by the empirical evidence. The fact that sexual symbolism has been verified means that the insights into art and literature offered by psychoanalytic theory need not be dismissed out of hand.

DREAM THEORY

The large-scale studies by Hall at the Institute of Dream Research make it clear that dream content has some kind of psychological meaning for the individual. Certainly Freudian theory was supported in that by using the concepts of Oedipal and castration complexes differential dream content for the two sexes was successfully predicted. Nevertheless the Freudian claim that dreams contain a wish has not been confidently verified, partly because the very subjective interpretation of dream content (to reach latent dream content) cannot, justifiably, be regarded as a scientific procedure. However the study by Lee (1958) among the Zulu does support this claim.

Although the 'need to dream', such as it is, is clearly physiological rather than psychological – that is, some essential metabolic process appears to go on during REM periods – and clearly dreams are the guardians of REM sleep rather than sleep itself, as postulated by Freud, the fact that dream content influences penile erections is evidence for the sexual nature of this type of dream. The finding, however, that REM periods are usually accompanied by penile erection cannot be regarded as evidence for the sexual nature of all dreams since penile erection is probably symptomatic of a more general subcortical stimulation, rather than specific sexual excitation.

Thus the objective study of dreams has confirmed the sexual symbolism of dreams and the psychological importance of dream content to the individual. REM study of dreaming has not yet yielded much evidence relevant to Freudian theory although as a method it offers great hopes.

NEUROSES

Many of the Freudian claims concerning the neuroses have simply never been put to the objective test. This is largely because no adequate measuring instruments exist. Thus the hypotheses which have been tested are usually those where convenient measures are at hand rather than those most crucial to the theory.

It is noticeable that where experimental techniques can be used, as in the investigation of the homosexual element in paranoia, clear-cut results have been obtained in favour of the Freudian theory. Some support has been adduced also for Freudian theory concerning depression, phobias and appendicitis. It is a curious fact that, although Freudian theory was developed from the study of neurotics and psychotics, there seems to be more objective evidence supporting the basic concepts of the theory than there is in favour of the particular theories underlying mental disturbances.

CONCLUSIONS

From a study of the objective evidence we are left with some confirmation of a tripartite division of mental activity into ego, super-ego and id. Developmental theory is supported in that oral erotism, Oedipus and castration complexes appear to occur. Furthermore adult personality patterns like the oral and anal character can be generally observed. There seems no doubt that the defence mechanism repression is commonly used and sexual symbolism is a verified phenomenon both within and outside dreams which do indeed seem concerned with basic human conflicts. In addition to this certain Freudian hypotheses concerning neuroses have been supported.

From these conclusions it seems clear that far too much that is distinctively Freudian has been verified for the rejection of the whole psychoanalytic theory to be possible. Furthermore it is to be noted that there are few good experiments which actually refute the theory. For example, as has been said, the fact that no link between infant-rearing procedures and adult personality has been shown, is at least in part due to severe methodological problems. Similarly many areas which have not been confirmed have not been put to the test.

The Blacky Pictures, to illustrate the point, contain a measure of the Oedipus complex. This is claimed by Freud (1916) to be the kernel of the neuroses, yet not one investigator has attempted the obvious check of seeing how neurotics and normals compare on this test other than the present author in a small pilot study (Kline, 1969b) which gave very limited support to the theory.

Two points must, however, be discussed before the status of Freudian theory can be evaluated. First we must consider those aspects of the theory which we have not touched on in this book. Finally we must try to establish whether or not the findings that have been verified could have been predicted from other psychological theories.

1. UNEXAMINED PARTS OF FREUDIAN THEORY

In the first chapter (see especially pp. 2-3), it was pointed out that the Freudian hypotheses examined in this book were the empirical and specific psychoanalytic propositions (Rapaport and Gill, 1959). However the fact is that much of psychoanalytic theory is, in this terminology, metapsychology of which the empirical propositions are the building blocks. It is this metapsychology, of course, which is characteristically difficult to test empirically and against which many of the objections on the grounds of scientific rigour have been aimed. Metapsychology has been ignored in this book both because in many cases it cannot be tested, and because, unless the original propositions are shown to be true, even attempting to test it seems useless.

Examples of metapsychological theory

The collective unconscious

Freud (1913) in 'Totem and taboo' put forward the tentative hypothesis that there is a kind of collective unconscious or mass psyche which accounts for the continuity of man's psychological life over the years. By means of this entity, whatever or wherever it is, man is able to inherit ideas, for example a memory of the primal horde and the original killing of the father.

Comments. As was made clear in our discussion of Jung (see p. 325) for whom the collective unconscious is an essential concept, this notion of a collective unconscious is quite untestable. The empirical consequences are not such as could ever prove the theory. For example, the similarity of the folk tales of all cultures does not necessitate such an explanatory concept. This mystical concept did not, fortunately, enter into the basic theory of psychoanalysis.

The inheritance of former experiences

Freud (1939) in his last work, *Moses and Monotheism*, suggested that Man brings with him into the world a heritage of ideational contents, memory traces of the experiences of former generations.

Comments. This hypothesis, related to that already discussed, is again not amenable to the scientific test. However it is not worth testing in that modern studies of genetics indicate that the inheritance of acquired characteristics (except by interference with DNA processes) is not possible. Lysenko seems finally to have been rejected. Furthermore to leave genetic arguments aside, even if individuals were reared up without contact with others, the fact of their ignorance of their archaic heritage could be put down to the linguistic and emotional disturbances that would inevitably, in psychoanalytic theory, result from this experimental rearing procedure. Thus the theory is not refutable.

Conclusions

Neither of these two hypotheses, which are clearly quite unscientific, are much used in general psychoanalytic theory. Thus they may be abandoned without loss to even the metapsychology of the general theory. It is interesting to note how closely these theories mirror early Platonic writing. Thus the notion of a collective mind occurs in the *Phaedo* and the doctrine of memnesis is 'proven' in the *Meno*, the subject of which, a poor unfortunate slave, is made to recall from his collective mind a geometric proof. A further noteworthy point is that the tripartite division of the soul is also to be found in the *Phaedrus* and *The Republic*. Although Freud's notions were based on observations, as he thought, it would be interesting to know how acquainted he was with these Platonic dialogues.

Eros and thanatos, the life and death instincts

Freud (1923) in 'The ego and the id' claims that in man there are two instinctual forces, eros and thanatos. The association and opposition of these two forces creates the very essence of life itself. The death instinct, to be found in all living matter, manifests itself as a tendency to return to the original inorganic state. Eros, on the other hand, represents the life force, the drive behind the sexual instincts.

Comments. Actually, as Fenichel (1945) states, psychoanalysts have tended to ignore this last formulation of Freud. Only Melanie Klein, indeed, seems to make any use of the concept of thanatos. These two concepts of eros and thanatos, as is the case with all instinct theories, cannot be put to any kind of empirical test. The only evidence that could be adduced in support of the death instinct is the fact that organisms die. Why do they die? Because of the death instinct for which the evidence is their death. The argument is thus circular. Even if two factors could be found to account for all human behaviour, this would not support the concept of life and death instincts. The fact is that these concepts have no empirical consequences other than life and death itself.

The only part of Freud's general theory that would appear to be affected by the rejection of eros and thanatos is the theory of sadism and masochism which are manifestations of thanatos turned, in the case of sadism, inwards to the self. Nevertheless if we wish psychoanalysis to become a scientific discipline it is necessary to abandon the concepts of life and death instincts.

The pleasure principle

Basic to Freudian theory is a concept which has not been put to the empirical test – the pleasure principle. In 'Beyond the pleasure principle' (Freud, 1920) it is made clear that the aim of mental functioning is pleasure, the reducing of tension within the nervous system.

Comments. Again this is not a testable aspect of the theory partly because Freud himself (1920) was not clear precisely how this occurred or how such tension could be measured. Nevertheless, although this principle underlies the workings of the psychical apparatus, failure to test it does not mean that Freudian theory has not really been tested, because the actual workings of this mental apparatus have been examined – Oedipus complex, repression, pregenital erotism and the like.

These examples, it is hoped, make it clear that in this book we have made no attempt to demonstrate the scientific validity of what are, perhaps, the most fundamental aspects of Freudian theory. These concepts, the metapsychology of psychoanalysis are, however, as we have shown, untestable and unscientific in that they have no empirical consequences. For this reason, therefore, it is argued that failure to test these concepts does not mean that we have not tested psychoanalytic theory. Indeed it emerges that these fundamental postulates can be removed without affecting the empirical propositions of the theory. Thus, for example, the finding that the castration complex is an important factor in the development of boys is not at all changed whether or not we regard the reason for this as being due to reduction of tension (the pleasure principle) or to some emanation of eros and thanatos. What is of interest is the fact of the castration complex, its antecedents and its consequences.

2. PREDICTION OF VERIFIED PSYCHOANALYTIC FINDINGS FROM OTHER THEORIES

Conant (1947) has made the point that theories tend to be displaced not by the discovery of dissonant facts but by the elaboration of an alternative theory. Despite the apparently large number of findings which do not neatly fit psychoanalysis, the fact remains that no alternative theory has been proposed. In the main this is because the idea of developing a theory to account for so huge a range of phenomena is not, as it was at the turn of the century, in accord with the scientific *Zeitgeist*. Indeed, Skinner (1954) is expressly and proudly atheoretical. Nevertheless operant conditioning as developed in the work of Skinner and his associates is clearly regarded by adherents of that school as containing the key to the understanding, prediction and control of human behaviour (Bolles, 1967). Certainly a school of behaviour therapy making use, as it claims, of operant conditioning techniques and Pavlovian conditioning has arisen, led in this country by Eysenck and Rachmann (Rachmann, 1965). Thus the question arises as to whether these verified findings of Freudian theory mean that the theory must be supported. If, for example, these findings could be predicted from operant conditioning there is no need to invoke Freudian theory. We can simply say that Freud made certain observations which, as it turned out, were correct.

Dollard and Miller (1950) have made what is probably the most determined attempt to interpret psychoanalytic theory in terms of the findings from studies of learning, although, as Breger and McGaugh (1965) point out, behaviour therapists have tended to ignore their work because the treatment derived from it is little different from psychoanalysis, and also because behaviour therapists do not even accept the accuracy of the findings interpreted by Dollard and Miller. It is therefore interesting to see to what extent the findings of Freudian theory which we have shown to be verified by objective evidence can be predicted from theories of learning.

Oral erotism

Dollard and Miller (1950) reject this concept on the basis of the study by Sears and Wise (1950, see p. 75). However, following Yarrow (1954) it was shown that this study did not invalidate the concept of oral erotism supported by Levy (1928, see p. 74). Hence the claim of Dollard and Miller that the 'specific desire for nursing at the breast or bottle is at least in part learned as a result of the primary reinforcement of getting food when hungry', is not supported in the light of later evidence. Learning theory, therefore, would not predict such a concept as oral erotism.

Oral and anal characters

Apart from the totally circular argument that these characters are the result of reinforcement schedules it would be difficult to account for them in terms of learning. The fact that anal characters seem to have parents with similar personalities perhaps might be explained in terms of imitation (Mowrer, 1950). Thus the talking budgerigar talks because it is then like its master, which is reinforcing. However, were this analysis the whole truth, children would be expected to resemble their parents to a far greater extent than in fact they do. Furthermore an analysis of personality in terms of learning by imitation would fail to explain why these particular syndromes rather than others occurred.

However, even if these syndromes cannot be satisfactorily understood in terms of learning theory, it must also be remembered that the psychoanalytic hypotheses linking them to repressed pregenital erotism and child-training procedures were not verified. Indeed had they been so the findings could have been interpreted in terms of learning theory also. Beloff (1957) argues that the anal character may be regarded as the result of overlearning and subsequent stimulus generalisation – what Eysenck (1947) hypothesises to be typical of introverts. The oral character could be interpreted in this way – dependency during feeding, for example, being strongly reinforced and continuing through life.

Oedipus and castration complexes

Dollard and Miller (1950) are able to incorporate both these concepts into the learning model. Very briefly they regard the Oedipal situation as one where overt sexual behaviour has been suppressed yet the child, through sex typing, has a vague expectation of reward from the opposite sex. Similarly fear of the father is aroused because the father is the source of discipline and has a unique relationship with his mother which the child is not allowed to share. The specific genital anxiety can arise from the fact that his motives are sexual (hence he fears a fitting punishment), from stories current in childhood lore and from observed sex differences. These fears bring about the resolution of the Oedipal conflict because 'When anxiety is greatly dominant over the approach tendencies, the conflicted individual strays away from his goal and but few of the acquired elements in the sexual appetite are aroused' (p. 147).

Thus, although the facts of the Oedipal and castration complex can be fitted into models derived from learning theories, a more important question is whether, in the absence of Freudian theory, any such predictions would have been made from these theories. This question underlines an essential point. The possible hypotheses to be derived from learning theories are almost as great in number as those that may be drawn from psychoanalytic theory. Furthermore, in the absence of knowledge of just what are particular reinforcers for individual human beings, it is not possible on the basis of learning theories alone to choose any particular hypothesis. Indeed it can be argued that what psychoanalysis is really concerned with, and these two concepts are good examples of it, is studying just what elements in the environment (the family situation) act as conditioned stimuli and reinforcers for the child's behaviour.

Repression

This is, of course, one of the key concepts in psychoanalysis. If repression could not be objectively verified, many other essential concepts would themselves automatically become suspect. Thus any other theory purporting to replace psychoanalysis must also be able to fit repression into its model. Dollard and Miller (1950) are easily able to accommodate this concept. They write: '. . . repression is the symptom of avoiding certain thoughts; it is reinforced by drive reduction . . .' (p. 201). The actual response that is reinforced by drive reduction (anxiety reduction) is to stop thinking. These formulations are the basis of their analysis of repression in terms of drive reduction theory and although they proceed to develop it in some detail this is unnecessary for our purpose. There can be little doubt that the mechanism of repression fits easily into learning theories of human behaviour, more easily indeed than the other Freudian concepts so far discussed.

Sexual symbolism

The fact of sexual symbolism also fits into a learning theory analysis of behaviour. Clearly it is a simple example of stimulus generalisation. On its own, stimulus generalisation fails to explain why it should be that the sexual organs are favourite objects of symbolisation. After all, on this theory a gun could represent a penis or a penis a gun – not the usual psychoanalytic interpretation! However if sexual symbolism is taken together with repression as it is in psychoanalytic theory, similar predictions about symbolism could be made from both learning theory and psychoanalysis. Thus there is no problem concerning sexual symbolism if learning theory models are preferred to Freudian theory.

Symbolism in dreams

The phenomenology of dreams is, however, a subject outside the bounds of learning theory. Here only the clinical dynamic psychologies such as those of

356 *Fact and Fantasy in Freudian Theory*

Freud or Jung attempt to account for the content of dreams and the reason for their occurrence for individual subjects. Jungian theory involving archetypes of the collective unconscious appears even less testable than Freudian hypotheses. Hall (1966) has postulated a theory of dreaming in which the content is related to the most basic conflicts and hence the most important events in men's lives. This, however, unlike the psychoanalytic theory of dreaming which is conceived as an expression of the unconscious – particularly clear because in sleep the super-ego is somewhat relaxed – is an *ad hoc* theory. It fails to explain why conflicts should be thus acted out in dreams. It is therefore probably still true to say that all for its inadequacies the psychoanalytic theory of dreaming is the most coherent. Learning theory is ill at ease in this field.

Paranoia and homosexuality

In Freudian theory the paranoid projects his repressed homosexuality (changed by reaction-formation into hatred) on to his fellow men; hence his persecutory delusions. Dollard and Miller (1950) explain this in terms of learning theory with the following example: the homosexual thoughts create anxiety and are repressed (see their rationale for repression). Because of this conflict the subject feels miserable in the presence of a particular colleague. This is rationalised as a dislike for the man which is regarded as mutual. This logical explanation reduces anxiety, caused by the fact that previously his feelings had been inexplicable. In addition the idea of dislike eliminates thoughts of love and is thus another source of reinforcement. From this it appears that the psychoanalytic formulation linking homosexuality and paranoia can be explained in terms of learning theory. However it is very much a *post-hoc* explanation. Given the facts of a paranoid's persecutory delusions, learning theory would not of itself *predict* repressed homosexuality and projection as a cause. Thus this example strengthens the case already put forward that psychoanalysis is concerned with the study of reinforcement. Learning theory, without a knowledge of what does and does not act as reinforcement for human beings, is quite inadequate for an understanding of human behaviour. Hence in this instance psychoanalysis may be regarded as completing the (*all important*) details of the learning process in this particular form of mental illness. Without this psychoanalytic knowledge learning theory would not be invoked. Thus it can be argued that in this instance Freudian theory is superior to learning theory.

Appendicitis and birth fantasies

This relationship, postulated by Freud and supported by Eylon (1967), must be regarded as one of the more surprising claims in psychoanalytic theory of the sort which has led to outright ridicule and disbelief. Suffice it to say that learning theory (as almost all other theories) would not be able to predict this finding.

Phobias

Freud (1925a) tries to discriminate between separation anxiety and castration anxiety. To some extent (see p. 302) Dixon *et al.* (1957) were able to support such a dichotomy with a factor analysis of certain questionnaire items from the Tavistock Self Assessment Inventory (Sandler, 1954). Phobias, of course, are the very meat and drink of the behaviour therapy school and it is with these complaints that their greatest successes are gained. Phobias, in terms of the learning theory model, are avoidance responses (reinforced by reduction in fear) often to quite inappropriate stimuli. The fact that such stimuli elicit these responses is, in part, a function of stimulus generalisation and higher-order conditioning.

The typical behaviour therapy treatment of phobias, in which by desensitisation the fear is gradually extinguished and then more appropriate responses are reinforced, again highlights the point previously made about psychoanalysis that it concentrates on the nature and origins of reinforcers and conditioned stimuli. Thus, pragmatically, behaviour therapy is interested only in the fact that maladaptive responses have been learned to, say, snakes and in the extinction of these responses. Freudian theory on the other hand, in the spirit of enquiry, is concerned implicitly with the question of how snakes can elicit such responses; it is concerned with the study of the nature of the stimulus generalisation (perhaps snakes to penis) and the reasons why there is fear reduction (perhaps the castration complex) and hence reinforcement. Thus while it is not denied that the learning theory model fits phobias well, it seems to us that psychoanalytic theory is concerned with the far more important and interesting task of examining the fundamental nature of the learning process in particular phobias.

Depression

Some support has been demonstrated for the psychoanalytic theory linking orality and narcissism with depression. In this area psychoanalytic theory is superior to learning theory models which seem unable to accommodate it. Dollard and Miller (1950) mention it on only one page, Eysenck and Rachmann (1965) have two references to it, in neither of which is the learning theory analysis mentioned. Franks (1969), in a book devoted to the appraisal and status of behaviour therapy, does not even contain one reference to it.

Id, ego, and super-ego

Dollard and Miller (1950) find no problem with the super-ego. They write 'Anxiety reactions, never labelled, are attached to stimuli, also unlabelled. When these stimuli recur later, the anxiety actions automatically occur. The resulting affect, Freud has called 'super-ego'.' They regard the ego as higher mental processes, e.g. thinking, planning and organising and make no explicit mention of the id. However they do talk about the unconscious which, they argue, means the unverbalised in Freudian theory. This unconscious includes the super-ego, of course, as well as the id. Nevertheless, for these writers the unconscious is characterised by its lack of verbal responses and cue-producing responses (e.g. counting) which are the essence of the higher-mental processes or the ego. Hence the importance in the unconscious of childhood experiences before such responses could be made. As Dollard and Miller point out, these definitions demand a somewhat extended concept of cue and response.

From this brief outline of one attempt to integrate the psychoanalytic theory of mental structure into a learning theory model, it will be clear that, even if vague, it is not entirely impossible. Of course it cannot be too strongly emphasised that this is a process which most learning theorists would not even attempt, since it is not in their view a profitable exercise. Mental structure is a field which theories of learning would not seek to embrace, with the exception of the super-ego. The super-ego is of relevance because in psychoanalytic theory it comes about through identification with the father by the child. Even if identification is not clearly defined it is clearly some sort of learning process. Mowrer (1950), in his interesting discussion of the concept of identification and its lack of clarity in orthodox Freudian formulations, makes the point that identification with the father may not come about as the result of the castration complex and the Oedipal conflict but that the identification may come first, through love of the father, and that this brings about the object choice of mother.

Thus although with the exception of the super-ego the Freudian concepts of mental structure are inherently foreign and irrelevant to theories of learning, as Dollard and Miller demonstrate, it is not impossible to fit them into such a theory.

FINALE

Three points have been emphasised in this chapter. Much of the metapsychology of psychoanalytic theory, it has been agreed, is unscientific in that it cannot be subjected to any kind of empirical test and so be refuted. Such concepts as the death instinct and the pleasure principle fall under this head. On the other hand we have shown much of psychoanalytic theory to consist of empirical propositions which can, logically at least, be tested. Most of this book has been concerned with sifting the objective evidence relevant to these propositions. Many of the Freudian concepts most important to psychoanalytic theory have been supported, for example repression and the Oedipus complex. Finally we have raised the fundamental question as to whether the verification of these Freudian concepts means that psychoanalytic theory should be retained. To this end, for those psychoanalytic propositions that were verified we examined the predictions made from theories of learning. Here it was found that in most cases the Freudian phenomena could be fitted into a model derived from theories of learning but that these theories on their own could not have predicted the clinical observations. This last point deserves further amplification since it is crucial to the status of Freudian theory.

Our discussion and analysis in terms of learning theory of the Freudian concepts which had been objectively confirmed revealed that in most cases, in effect, psychoanalytic theory had been concerned with the nature of the reinforcement which had led to the neurotic responses. Thus, in the example of phobias, in terms of learning theory the phobia represents a response which is essentially maladaptive and has been learned to an inappropriate stimulus. Behaviour therapy based on such an analysis clearly aims to extinguish this response by desensitisation and later to reinforce a more desirable alternative. Psychoanalytic theory on the other hand has been concerned in the case of phobias to examine the nature of the reinforcement which brings them about. Thus, and the work of Dixon *et al.* (1957) supports the claim, they are concerned with the castration complex (relief from this reinforces any response) and stimulus generalisation from sexual organs to snakes, in the case of snake phobias. Thus psychoanalytic theory gives insight into how such maladaptive learning occurs.

If this analysis be correct and psychoanalytic theory is in fact concerned with the details of the maladaptive learning processes underlying neurotic behaviour, then it is clearly essential that its findings be retained and examined. After all, the notion of reinforcers is somewhat empty if none can be found. It is therefore argued here that for the study of human behaviour psychoanalysis remains a vital instrument (though its findings must be properly verified). However it follows that if psychoanalytic theory is concerned with reinforcement, any resulting therapy may be better done in the style of behaviour therapy which seeks to 'unlearn' the badly learned. Psychoanalytic therapy in these terms is slow desensitisation by talking, whereas it may well be that deliberate reinforcement and extinction of responses is more efficient. However, to ignore psychoanalytic theory and to stress behaviour therapy pragmatically, because it works, without enquiring into the nature of the learning processes seems absurd.

So, far from regarding learning theory models and psychoanalytic theory as opposed, we consider them to be closely related – the Freudian theory supplying the details of the learning procedures. Without psychoanalytic theory, learning theory models of human behaviour would seem futile. It follows from this, therefore, that therapy must be based on psychoanalytic theory and behaviour therapy procedures. The status of psychoanalytic theory must now be clear. It must be retained not as a whole but only after rigorous objective research has revealed what parts are correct or false, or in need of modification. But, as has been shown in this book, much of it has been confirmed. Now, however, a huge task of research remains. If well done it could illuminate our understanding of human behaviour; if left undone, we shall be left to wander in a circular maze of undefined reinforcement.

References

ABERT, K., BALLY, C. and SCHADE, J.P. (1965) (eds.) *Sleep Mechanisms*. Amsterdam: Elsevier Pub. Co.

ABRAHAM, K. (1916) 'The first pregenital stage of the libido'. In *Selected Papers of Karl Abraham* (1965). London: Hogarth Press and Institute of Psychoanalysis.

ABRAHAM, K. (1921) 'Contributions to the theory of the anal character'. In *Selected Papers of Karl Abraham* (1965). London: Hogarth Press and Institute of Psychoanalysis.

ABRAHAM, K. (1924) 'Character-formation on the genital level of libido development'. In *Selected Papers of Karl Abraham* (1965). London: Hogarth Press and Institute of Psychoanalysis.

ABRAMSON, H. A. (1961) 'Intractable asthma: conflict of period of toilet training'. *J. Psychol.*, **52**, 223-9.

ABT, L. E. and REISS, M. (1964) (eds.) *Progress in Clinical Psychology*. New York: Grune & Stratton.

ACCORD, L. D. (1962) 'Sexual symbolism as a correlate of age'. *J. Consult. Psychol.*, **26**, 279-81.

ADCOCK, C. J. (1965) 'A comparison of the concepts of Eysenck and Cattell'. *Brit. J. Educ. Pyschol.*, **35**, 90-7.

ADELSON, J. and REDMOND, J. (1958) 'Personality differences in the capacity for verbal recall'. *J. Abnorm. Soc. Psychol.*, **57**, 244-8.

ADLER, A. (1930) *Individual Psychology*. In MURCHISON (1930).

ADORNO, T. W., FRENKEL-BRUNSWIK, E., LEVINSON, D. J. and SANDFORD, R. N. (1950) *The Authoritarian Personality*. New York: Harper & Row.

ALEXANDER, F. (1934) 'The influence of psychological factors upon gastrointestinal disturbances'. *Psychoanal. Quart.*, **3**, 501.

ALEXANDER, F. (1935) 'The logic of emotions and its dynamic background'. *Internat. J. Psychoanal.*, **16**, 399-413.

ALEXANDER, F. (1937) *Five Year Report of the Chicago Institute for Psychoanalysis*. 1932-7.

ALEXANDER, F. (1950) *Psychosomatic Medicine*. New York: Norton.

ALEXANDER, F. and FRENCH, T. M. (1948) *Studies in Psychosomatic Medicine*. New York: Ronald Press.

ALEXANDER, W. A. (1954) *A Study of Normal and Psychotic Subjects who Deviate in their Performance on the IES Tests*. Ph.D. thesis, Western Reserve Univ.

ALLEN, M. G. (1957) 'Childhood experience and adult personality: a cross-cultural study using the concept of ego strength'. *J. Soc. Psychol.*, **71**, 53-68.

ALPER, T. G., BLANE, H. T. and ABRAMS, B. K. (1955) 'Reactions of middle and lower class children to finger paints as a function of class differences in child-training practices'. *J. Abnorm. Soc. Psychol.*, **51**, 439-48.

ALTSHULER, K. Z. (1966) 'Comments on recent sleep research related to psycho-analytic theory'. *Arch. Gen. Psychiat.*, **15** (3), 235-9.

AMADEO, M. and GOMEZ, E. (1964) 'Eye movements and dreaming in subjects with life-long blindness'. *Paper at Annual meeting of Assn. Psychophysiol. Stud. Sleep.*

ANSHEN, R. N. (1948) *The Family: its Function and Destiny*, Vol. 5. New York: Harper Bros.

ANTHONY, J. E. (1957) 'An experimental approach to the psycho-pathology of childhood: encopresis'. *Brit. J. Med. Psych.*, **30**, 146-75.

ARGYLE, M. (1964) 'Introjection: a form of social learning'. *Brit. J. Psychol.*, **55**, 391-402.

ARGYLE, M. and ROBINSON, P. (1962) 'Two origins of achievement motivation'. *Brit. J. Soc. Clin. Psychol.*, **1**, 107-20.

ARNOLD, M. B. (1950) 'An excitatory theory of emotion'. In REYMERT, M. L. (1950).

ARONFREED, J. (1968) *Conduct and Conscience: the Socialization of Internalised Control over Behaviour*. New York: Academic Press.

ARONFREED, J. (1969) 'The concept of internalisation'. Chapter 4 in GOSLIN, D. A. (1969).

ARONSON, M. L. (1953) 'A study of the Freudian theory of paranoia by means of the Blacky Pictures.' *J. Proj. Tech.*, **17**, 3-19.

ASERINSKY, E. and KLEITMAN, N. (1955) 'Regularly occuring periods of eye motility, and concomitant phenomena, during sleep'. *J. Appl. Physiol.*, **8**, 1-10.

ATKINSON, J. W. (1958) (ed.) *Motives in Fantasy, Action and Society*. New York: Van Nostrand.

BACON, M. K., BARRY, H. and CHILD, K. (1965) 'A cross-cultural study of drinking. II: relations to other features of culture.' *Quart. J. Study. Alcohol. Supp.*, **3**, 29-48.

BANDURA, A. (1962) 'Social learning through imitation'. In JONES, M. R. (1962).

BANDURA, A. (1965) 'Influence of models' reinforcement contingencies on the acquisition of imitative responses'. *J. Pers. Soc. Psychol.*, **1**, 589-95.

BANDURA, A. (1969) 'Social learning theory of identificatory processes'. Chapter 3 in GOSLIN, D. A. (1969).

BANDURA, A., GRUSEC, J. E. and MENLOVE, F. L. (1966) 'Observational learning as a function of symbolisation and incentive set'. *Child Development*, **37**, 499-506.

BANDURA, A., GRUSEC, J. E. and MENLOVE, F. L. (1967) 'Some social determinants of self-monitoring reinforcement systems'. *J. Pers. Soc. Psychol.*, **5**, 449-55.

BANDURA, A. and HUSTON, A. C. (1961) 'Identification as a process of incidental learning'. *J. Abnorm. Soc. Psychol.*, **63**, 311-18.

BANDURA, A., ROSS, C. and ROSS, S. (1963) 'A comparative test of the status envy, social power, and secondary reinforcement theories of identificatory learning'. *J. Abnorm. Soc. Psychol.*, **67**, 601-7.

BANDURA, A. and WALTERS, R. H. (1963) *Social Learning and Personality Development*. New York: Holt, Rinehart & Winston.

BARNES, C. A. (1952) 'A statistical study of the Freudian theory of levels of psychosexual development'. *Genet. Psychol. Monogr.*, **45**, 109-74.

BARRON, F. and LEARY, T. F. (1955) 'Changes in psychoneurotic patients with and without psychotherapy'. *J. Consult. Psychol.*, **19**, 239-45.

BEARDSLEE, D. C. and FOGELSON, R. (1958) 'Sex differences in sexual imagery aroused by musical stimulation'. In ATKINSON, J. W. (1958).

BECK, A. T. (1962) 'Reliability of psychiatric diagnoses: a critique of systematic studies'. *Amer. J. Psychiat.*, **119**, 210-15.

BECK, A. T., WARD, G. H., MENDELSSON, M., MOCK, J. E. and ERBAUGH, J. K. (1962) 'Reliability of psychiatric diagnoses. II: a study of the consistency of clinical judgements and ratings'. *Amer. J. Psychiat.*, **119**, 351-7.

BECK, S. J. (1958) 'Review of the Blacky Pictures'. *J. Consult. Psychol.*, **20**, 487-8.

BEECH, H. R. (1959) 'An experimental investigation of sexual symbolism in anorexia nervosa employing a subliminal stimulation technique: preliminary report'. *Psychosom. Med.*, **21**, 277-80.

BELL, H. M. (1938) *The Bell Adjustment Inventory*. Stanford: Univ. of Stanford Press.

BELLAK, L. (1958) 'Studying the psychoanalytic process by the method of short-range prediction and judgement'. *Brit. J. Med. Psychol.*, **31**, 249-52.

BELLAK, L. (1961) 'Research in psychoanalysis'. *Psychoanal. Quart.*, **30**, 519-48.

BELLAK, L. and SMITH, M. B. (1956) 'An experimental exploration of the psychoanalytic process'. *Psychoanal. Quart.*, **25**, 385.

BELOFF, H. (1957) 'The structure and origin of the anal character'. *Genet. Psychol. Mongrs.*, **55**, 141-72.

BERES, D. and OBERS, S. (1950) 'The effects of extreme deprivation in infancy on psychic structure in adolescence'. *Psychoanal. Stud. Child.*, **5**, 121-40.

BERG, M. and COHEN, B. B. (1959) 'Early separation from the mother in schizophrenia'. *J. Nerv. Ment. Dis.*, **128**, 365-9.

BERGER, L. (1959) 'Cross-validation of "primary" and "reactive" personality patterns with non-ulcer surgical patients'. *J. Proj. Tech.*, **23**, 8-11.

BERGER, L. and EVERSTINE, L. (1962) 'Test-retest reliability of the Blacky Pictures Test'. *J. Proj. Tech.*, **26**, 225-6.

BERGER, R. J. (1961) 'Tonus of intrinsic laryngeal muscles during sleep and dreaming'. *Sci.*, **134**, 840.

BERGER, R. J. (1963) 'Experimental modification of dream content by meaningful verbal stimuli'. *Brit. J. Psychiat.*, **109**, 722-40.

BERGER, R. J. (1963a) Unpublished Ph.D. thesis, University of Edinburgh. Quoted by BERGER, R. J. (1963).

BERGER, R. J., OLLEY, P. and OSWALD, I. (1962) 'The EEG, eye-movements and dreams of the blind'. *Quart. J. Exp. Psychol.*, **14**, 183-6.

BERGER, R. J. and OSWALD, I. (1962) 'Effects of sleep deprivation on behaviour, subsequent sleep and dreaming'. *J. Ment. Sci.*, **108**, 457.

BERGIN, A. E. (1963) 'Negative results revisited'. *J. Consult. Psychol.*, **10**, 244-55.

BERGMAN, P., MALASKY, C. and ZAHN, T. P. (1967) 'Relation of sucking strength to personality variables'. *J. Consult. Psychol.*, **31**, (4), 426-8.

BERGMAN, P., MALASKY, C. and ZAHN, T. P. (1968) 'Oral functions in schizophrenia'. *J. Nerv. Ment. Dis.*, **146**, 351-9.

BERKLEY-HILL, O. (1921) 'The anal erotic factor in the religion, philosophy and character of the Hindus'. *Internat. J. Psychoanal.*, **2**, 306.

BERLYNE, D. (1961) *Conflict Arousal and Curiosity*. New York: McGraw-Hill.

BERNDT, R. and BERNDT, C. (1951) *Sexual Behaviour in West Arnhem-land*. New York: Viking Fund. Publications in Anthropology, XVI.

BERNSTEIN, A. (1955) 'Some relations between techniques of feeding and training during infancy and certain behaviour in childhood'. *Genet. Psychol. Monogr.*, **51**, 3-44.

BERNSTEIN, L. and CHASE, P. H. (1955) 'The discriminative ability of the Blacky Pictures with ulcer patients'. *J. Consult. Psychol.*, **19**, 377-80.

BERTRAND, S. and MASLING, J. (1969) 'Oral imagery and alcoholism'. *J. Abnorm. Psychol.*, **74**, 50-3.

BETTELHEIM, B. (1943) 'Individual and mass behaviour in extreme situations'. *J. Abnorm. Soc. Psychol.*, **38**, 417-52.

BIDDLE, W. E. (1957) 'Investigation of the Oedipus fantasy by hypnosis'. *Amer. J. Hypnosis*, **114**, 175.

BIEBER, I. *et al* (1962) *Homosexuality*. New York: Basic Books.

BIESHEUVEL, S. (1962) 'Personality tests for personnel selection and vocational guidance in Africa'. In TAYLOR, A. (1962).

BLOCK, W. E. and VENTUR, P. A. (1963) 'A study of the psychoanalytic concept of castration anxiety in symbolically castrated amputees.' *Psychiat. Quart.*, **37**, 518-26.

BLUM, G. S. (1949) 'A study of the psychoanalytic theory of psychosexual development'. *Genet. Psychol. Monogr.*, **39**, 3-99.

BLUM, G. S. (1953) *Psychoanalytic Theories of Personality*. New York: McGraw-Hill.

BLUM, G. S. (1954) 'An experimental reunion of psychoanalytic theory with perceptual vigilance and defence'. *J. Abnorm. Soc. Psychol.*, **49**, 94-8.

BLUM, G. S. (1955) 'Perceptual defence revisited'. *J. Abnorm. Soc. Psychol.*, **51**, 24-9.

BLUM, G. S. (1956a) 'A reply to Charen, J.'. *J. Consult. Psychol.*, **20**, 406.

BLUM, G. S. (1956b) 'Defence preferences in four countries'. *J. Proj. Tech.*, **20**, 33-41.

BLUM, G. S. (1957) 'An investigation of perceptual defence in Italy'. *Psychol. Rep.*, **3**, 169-75.

BLUM, G. S. (1962) 'A guide for the research use of the Blacky Pictures'. *J. Proj. Tech.*, **26**, 3-29.

BLUM, G. S. (1964) 'Defence preferences among university students in Denmark, Germany and Israel'. *J. Proj. Tech. and Personal Assess.*, **28** (1), 13-19.

BLUM, G. S. and HUNT, H. F. (1952) 'The validity of the Blacky Pictures'. *Psychol. Bull.*, **49**, 238-50.

BLUM, G. S. and KAUFMAN, J. B. (1952) 'Two patterns of personality dynamics in male ulcer patients as suggested by responses to the Blacky Pictures'. *J. Clin. Psychol.*, **8**, 273-8.

BLUM, G. S. and MILLER, D. R. (1952) 'Exploring the psychoanalytic theory of the "oral character" '. *J. Pers.*, **20**, 287-304.

BLUMBERG, S. and MAHER, B. A. (1965) 'Trait attribution as a study of Freudian projection'. *J. Soc. Psychol.*, **65**, 311-16.

BOLLES, R. C. (1967) *Theory of Motivation*. New York: Harper & Row.

BORGATTA, E. F. and LAMBERT, W. W. (1968) (eds.) *Handbook of Personality Theory and Research*. Chicago: Rand-McNally.

BOTWINICK, J. and MACHOVER, S. (1951) 'A psychometric examination of latent homosexuality in alcoholism'. *Quart. J. Stud. Alcohol.*, **12**, 268-72.

BOWLBY, J. (1944) 'Forty-four juvenile thieves'. *Int. J. Psychoanal.*, **25**, 1-57.

BOWLBY, J. (1962) (ed.) *Deprivation of Maternal Care*. Geneva: World Health Organisation.

BOWLBY, J. (1969) *Attachment*. Vol. I, *Attachment and Loss*. London: Hogarth Press and Institute of Psychoanalysis.

BOWLBY, J., AINSWORTH, M., BOSTON, M. and ROSENBLUTH, D. (1956) 'The effects of mother-child separation: a follow up study'. *Brit. J. Med. Psychol.*, **29**, 211-47.

BREGER, L. and MCGAUGH, J. L. (1965) 'Critique and reformulation of "learning theory" approaches to psychotherapy and neuroses'. *Psychol. Bull.*, **63**, 338-58.

BRIGGS, K. C. and MYERS, I. B. (1962) *Manual to the Myers-Briggs Type Indicator*. Princeton: E.T.S.

BRONFENBRENNER, U. (1958) 'The study of identification through inter-personal perception'. In TAGIURI, R. and PETRULLO, L. (1958).

BRONFENBRENNER, U. (1960) 'Freudian theories of identification and their derivatives'. *Child Development*, **31**, 15-40.

BROWN, R. (1965) *Social Psychology*. New York: The Free Press.

BROWN, W. C. (1961) *Freud and the Post-Freudians*. Harmondsworth: Penguin.

BROWN, W. P. (1962) 'Conceptions of perceptual defence'. *Brit. J. Psychol.*, *Monogr. Suppl.*, 1962, No: 35.

BRUNER, J. S. and POSTMAN, L. (1947) 'Emotional selectivity in perception and reaction'. *J. Pers.*, **16**, 69-77.

BUCK, J. N. (1948) 'The HTP test'. *J. Clin. Psychol.*, **4**, 151-9.

BUROS, O. K. (1959) (ed.) *The Vth Mental Measurement Year Book*. New Jersey: Gryphon Press.

BUROS, O. K. (1965) (ed.) *The VIth Mental Measurement Year Book*. New Jersey: Gryphon Press.

BYRNE, D. (1964) 'Repression—sensitization as a dimension of personality'. In *Progress in Experimental Personality Research*. Edited by Maher, B. A. New York: Academic Press.

CALDWELL, B. M. (1964) 'The effects of infant care'. In HOFFMAN and HOFFMAN (1964).

CAMERON, P. (1967) 'Confirmation of the Freudian psychosexual stages utilising sexual symbolism'. *Psych. Rep.*, **21**, 1.

CARP. F. M. (1962) 'Psychosexual development of stutterers. *J. Proj. Tech.*, **26**, 4, 388-91.

CARSTAIRS, G. M. and GRYGIER, T. G. (1957) 'Anthropological, psychometric and psychotherapeutic aspects of homosexuality'. *Bull. Brit. Psychol. Soc.*, **32**, 46-7.

CARTWRIGHT, R. D., DYMOND, R. and VOGEL, J. L. (1960) 'A comparison of changes in psychoneurotic patients during matched periods of therapy and no therapy'. *J. Consult. Psychol.*, **24**, 121-7.

CATTELL, P. (1940) *The Measurement of Intelligence of Infants and Young Children*. New York: Psychol. Corp.

CATTELL, R. B. (1946) *Description and Measurement of Personality*. London: Harrap.

CATTELL, R. B. (1957) *Personality and Motivation Structure and Measurement*. Yonkers: New World Book Co.

CATTELL, R. B. (1965) *The Scientific Analysis of Personality*. Harmondsworth: Penguin.

CATTELL, R. B., KNAPP, R. R. and SCHEIER, I. H. (1961) 'Second-order personality factor structure in the objective test realm'. *J. Consult. Psychol.*, **25**, 345-52.

CATTELL, R. B. and LUBORSKY, L. (1947) 'Personality factors in response to humour'. *J. Abnorm. Soc. Psychol.*, **42**, 402-21.

CATTELL, R. B. and LUBORSKY, L. (1952) *The IPAT Humour Test of Personality*. Champaign: IPAT.

CATTELL, R. B. and MUERLE, J. L. (1960) 'The "Maxplane" program for factor rotation to oblique simple structure'. *Educ. Psychol. Meas.*, **20**, 569-90.

CATTELL, R. B. and PAWLIK, K. (1964) 'Third-order factors in objective personality tests'. *Brit. J. Psychol.*, **55**, 1-18.

CATTELL, R. B., PAWLIK, K. and NESSELROADE, J. (1965) 'An examination of the cross-cultural constancy of the personality factors in the 16 PF'. In press.

CATTELL, R. B., PICHOT, P. and RENNES, P. (1961) 'Constance interculturelle des facteurs de personnalité mesures par le test 16 PF. II: Comparaison franco-américaine'. *Rev. Psychol. Appl.*, **11**, 165-96.

CATTELL, R. B. and WARBURTON, F. W. (1967) *Objective Personality and Motivation Tests*. Urbana: Univ. of Illinois Press.

CHAREN, J. (1956a) 'Reliability of the Blacky Tests'. *J. Consult. Psychol.*, **20**, 16.

CHAREN, J. (1956b) 'A reply to Blum, G. S.'. *J. Consult. Psychol.*, **20**, 407.

CHARNES, G. (1953) *The Relative Strengths of Impulse Ego and Superego in Latency, Adolescence and Adulthood.* Ph.D. thesis, Western Reserve Univ.

CHERRY-GARRARD, A. (1970) *The Worst Journey in the World.* Harmondsworth: Penguin.

CHILD, I. L., COOPERMAN, M. and WOLOWITZ, H. M. (1969) 'Esthetic preference and other correlates of active v. passive food preference'. *J. Pers. Soc. Psychol.*, **11**, 75-84.

CHILDERS, A. T. and HAMIL, B. M. (1932) 'Emotional problems in children as related to the duration of breast-feeding in infancy'. *Amer. J. Orthopsychiat.*, **2**, 134-42.

CLARK, R. A. and SENSIBAR, M. R. (1956) 'The relationship between symbolic and manifest projections of sexuality with some incidental correlates'. In ATKINSON, J. W. (1958).

COHEN, A. R. (1956) 'Experimental effects of ego-defence preference on interpersonal relations'. *J. Abnorm. Soc. Psychol.*, **52**, 19-27.

COMREY, A. L. (1961) 'Factored homogeneous item dimensions in personality research'. *Educ. Psychol. Meas.*, **21**, 419-31.

COMREY, A. L. (1962) 'A study of 35 personality dimensions'. *Educ. Psychol. Meas.*, **22**, 543-52.

COMREY, A. L. (1965) 'Scales for measuring compulsion, hostility, neuroticism and shyness'. *Psych. Rep.*, **16**, 697-700.

COMREY, A. L. (1966) 'Comparison of personality and attitude variables'. *Educ. Psychol. Meas.*, **26**, 853-60.

COMREY, A. L. and JAMISON, K. (1966) 'Verification of six personality factors'. *Educ. Psychol. Meas.*, **26**, 945-53.

CONANT, J. B. (1947) *On Understanding Science.* New Haven: Yale Univ. Press.

CORIAT, I. H. (1917) 'Some statistical results of the psychoanalytic treatment of the psychoneuroses'. *Psychoanal. Rev. IV.*, 208-16.

COWEN, E. L. and BEIER, E. G. (1954) 'Threat expectancy, word frequencies and perceptual recognition hypothesis'. *J. Abnorm. Soc. Psychol.*, **49**, 178-82.

CRONBACH, L. J. (1946) 'Response sets and test validity'. *Educ. Psychol. Meas.*, **6**, 475-94.

CRONBACH, L. J. (1950) 'Further evidence on response sets and test design'. *Educ. Psychol. Meas.*, **10**, 3-31.

CRONBACH, L. J. (1955) 'Processes affecting scores on "understanding of others" and "assumed similarity"'. *Psychol. Bull.*, **52**, 177-94.

CRONBACH, L. J. and MEEHL, P. E. (1955) 'Construct validity in psychological tests'. *Psychol. Bull.*, **52**, 281-302.

CROSS, H. J. (1964) 'The outcome of psychotherapy: a selected analysis of research findings'. *J. Consult. Psychol.*, **28**, (5), 413-7.

CROWN, S. (1968) 'Psychoanalysis and problems of scientific method'. In SUTHERLAND, J. D. (1968).

CROWNE, D. P. (1965) 'Review of the IES Test in *VIth Mental Measurement Year Book*'. In BUROS (1965).

CURRAN, D. and PARR, D. (1957) 'Homosexuality: an analysis of 100 male cases seen in private practice'. *Brit. Med. J.*, 797-801.

DAHLSTROM, W. G. and WELSH, G. S. (1960) An *MMPI Handbook*. London: Oxford Univ. Press.

DASTON, P. G. (1956) 'Perception of homosexual words in paranoid schizophrenia'. *Percept. and Mot. Skills*, 6, 45-55.

DAVIS, W. A. and HAVIGHURST, R. J. (1946) 'Social-class and colour differences in child-rearing'. *Amer. Sociol. Rev.*, 11, 698-710.

DAVIS, W. A. and HAVIGHURST, R. J. (1947) *Father of the Man*. Boston: Houghton Mifflin.

DAVIS, H. V., SEARS, R. R., MILLER, H. C. and BRODBECK, A. J. (1948) 'Effects of cup, bottle and breast feeding on oral activities of new born infants'. *Pediatrics*, 2, 549-58.

DELAY, J., PICHOT, P. and PERSE, J. (1962) 'Personnalité obsessionelle et caractère dit obsessionel: étude clinique et psychometrique'. *Rev. Psychol. App.*, 12, 233-62.

DE LUCA, J. N. (1967) 'Performance of overt male homosexuals and controls on the Blacky Test'. *J. Clin. Psychol.*, 23, 497.

DE LUCA, J. N. (1968) 'Psychosexual conflict in adolescent enuretics'. *J. Psychol.*, 68, 145-9.

DEMENT, W. C. (1960) 'The effect of dream deprivation'. *Science*, 131, 1705-7.

DEMENT, W. C. (1963) 'Perception during sleep'. *Proc. Am. Psychopath. Assoc. Symposium on psychopathology of perception*. New York.

DEMENT, W. C., HENRY, P., COHEN, H. and FERGUSON, J. (1967) 'Studies on the effects of REM deprivation in humans and animals'. In *Brain and Behaviour*. Ed. PRIBRAM, K. H. (1967). Harmondsworth: Penguin Books.

DEMENT, W. C., KAHN, E. and ROFFWARG, H. (1965) 'The influence of the laboratory situation on the dreams of the experimental subject'. *J. Nerv. Ment. Dis.*, 140, 119-31.

DEMENT, W. C. and KLEITMAN, N. (1955) 'Incidence of eye motility during sleep in relation to varying EEG pattern'. *Fed. Proc.*, 14, 216.

DEMENT, W. C. and KLEITMAN, N. (1957) 'Cyclic variations in EEG during sleep and their relation to eye movements, bodily motility and dreaming'. *EEG Clin. Neurophysiol.*, 9, 673-90.

DEMENT, W. C., and WOLPERT, E. A. (1958) 'The relation of eye movements, bodily motility and external stimuli to dream content'. *J. Exp. Psychol.*, 53, 543-53.

DENKER, P. G. (1947) 'Results of treatment of psychoneuroses by the general practitioner: a follow up study of 500 cases'. *Arch. Neuro. and Psychiat.*, 57, 504-5.

DESPERT, J. L. (1944) 'Urinary control and enuresis'. *Psychosom. Med.*, 6, 294-307.

DESPERT, J. L. (1946) 'Psychosomatic study of 50 stutterers'. *Amer. J. Ortho-psychiat.*, **16**, 100-132.

DEVEREUX, G. (1947) 'Mohave orality'. *Psychoanal. Quart.*, **16**, 519-546.

DEVEREUX, G. (1951) 'Cultural and characterological traits of the Mohave related to the anal stage of psychosexual development'. *Psychoanal. Quart.*, **20**, 398-422.

DIXON, J. J., DE MONCHAUX, C. and SANDLER, J. (1957) 'Patterns of anxiety: the phobias'. *Brit. J. Med. Psychol.*, **30**, 34-40.

DIXON, N. F. (1958a) 'Apparatus for the continuous recording of the visual threshold by the method of "closed loop control"'. *J. Quart. Exp. Psychol.*, **10**, 62-3.

DIXON, N. F. (1958b) 'Apparent changes in the visual threshold as a function of subliminal stimulation'. *Quart. J. Exp. Psychol.*, **10**, 211-15.

DIXON, N. F. (1960) 'Apparent changes in the visual threshold: central or peripheral'. *Brit. J. Psychol.*, **51**, (4), 297-309.

DIXON, N. F. and HAIDER, M. (1961) 'Changes in the visual threshold as a function of subception'. *Quart. J. Exp. Psychol.*, **13**, 229-35.

DIXON, N. F. and LEAR, T. E. (1962) 'Perceptual regulation and mental disorder'. *J. Ment. Sci.*, **108**, 356-61.

DIXON, N. F. and LEAR, T. E. (1963) 'EEG correlates of threshold regulation'. *Nature*, **198**, 870-2.

DOLLARD, J., DOOB, L. W., MILLER, N. E., MOWRER, O. H. and SEARS, R. R. (1939) *Frustration and Aggression*. New Haven: Yale Univ. Press.

DOLLARD, J. and MILLER, N. E. (1950) *Personality and Psychotherapy*. New York: McGraw Hill.

DOMBROSE, L. A. and SLOBIN, M. S. (1951) *An Approach to the Measurement of Relative Strengths of impulses, Ego and Superego and the Determination of the Effects of Impulses and Superego upon Ego Functions.*' Joint Ph.D. Western Reserve Univ.

DOMBROSE, L. A. and SLOBIN, M. S. (1958) 'The IES Test'. *Percept. & Mot. Skills*, **8**, 347-89.

DUNBAR, H. F. (1954) *Emotions and Bodily Changes*. 4th ed. New York: Columbia Univ. Press.

DURRETT, M. (1959) 'Relationship of early infant regulation and later behaviour in play interviews'. *Child Development*, **30**, 211-16.

DUSS, G. (1940) 'La méthode des fables en psychoanalyse'. In DESPERT, J. L. (1946).

DUTHIE, H. L. and GAIRNS, F. W. (1960) 'Sensory nerve-endings and sensation in the anal region of man'. *Brit. J. Surg.*, **47**, 585-9.

EDWARDS, A. L. (1957) *The Social Desirability Variable in Personality Research*. New York: Dryden.

EHRENZWEIG, A. (1967) *The Hidden Order of Art*. London: Weidenfeld & Nicolson.

ENGESET, A., LYGREN, T. and IDSOE, R. (1963) 'The incidence of peptic ulcer among alcohol abusers and non-abusers'. *Quart. J. Stud. Alcohol.*, **24**, 622-6.

ERIKSEN, C. W. and PIERCE, J. (1968) 'Defence Mechanisms'. Chapter 20 in BORGATTA and LAMBERT (1968).

EVANS, C. and MCCONNELL, J. R. (1951) 'The Minnesota TSE Test'. Princeton: E.T.S.

EYLON, Y. (1967) 'Birth events, appendicitis and appendectomy'. *Brit. J. Med. Psychol.*, **40**, 317.

EYSENCK, H. J. (1947) *Dimensions of Personality*. London: Routledge & Kegan Paul.

EYSENCK, H. J. (1952) 'The effects of psychotherapy: an evaluation'. *J. Consult. Psychol.*, **16**, 319-24.

EYSENCK, H. J. (1953a) *Uses and Abuses of Psychology*. Harmondsworth: Penguin.

EYSENCK, H. J. (1953b) *The Structure of Human Personality*. London: Methuen.

EYSENCK, H. J. (1959) 'Review of the Rorschach Test'. In BUROS, O. K. (1959).

EYSENCK, H. J. (1960a) 'The effects of psychotherapy'. In *Handbook of Abnormal Psychology*. London: Pitman.

EYSENCK, H. J. (1960b) (ed.) *Behaviour Therapy and the Neuroses*. New York: Pergamon Press.

EYSENCK, H. J. (1961) *Handbook of Abnormal Psychology* (also 1960). New York: Basic Books.

EYSENCK. H. J. (1964) 'Principles and methods of personality description, classification and diagnosis'. *Brit. J. Psychol.*, **55**, 284-94.

EYSENCK, H. J. (1965a) *Fact and Fiction in Psychology*. Harmondsworth: Penguin.

EYSENCK, H. J. (1965b) 'The effects of psychotherapy'. *Internat. J. Psychiat.*, **1**, 99-142.

EYSENCK, H. J. (1967a) 'The logical basis of factor analysis'. In JACKSON, D. N. and MESSICK, S. (1967). *Problems in Human Assessment*. New York: McGraw-Hill.

EYSENCK, H. J. (1967b) *The Biological Basis of Personality*. Springfield: C. C. Thomas.

EYSENCK, H. J. and EYSENCK, S. B. (1964) *The EPI*. London: Univ. of London Press.

EYSENCK, H. J. and EYSENCK, S. B. (1969) *Personality Structure and Measurement*. London: Routledge & Kegan Paul.

EYSENCK, H. J. and RACHMANN, S. (1965) *The Causes and Cures of Neurosis*. London: Routledge & Kegan Paul.

FAIRBAIRN, W. R. D. (1938) 'Prolegomena to a psychology of art'. *Brit. J. Psychol.*, **28**, 298-303.

FARBER, M. L. (1955) 'The anal character and political aggression'. *J. Abnorm. Psychol.*, **51**, 486-9.

FARBER, M. L. (1958) 'Anality, political aggression, acquiescence and question-naire construction'. *J. Abnorm. Psychol.*, **56**, 278-9.

FARRELL, B. A. (1951) 'The scientific testing of psychoanalytic findings and theory. III'. *Brit. J. Med. Psychol.*, **24**, 35-51.

FARRELL, B. A. (1961) 'Can psychoanalysis be refuted?' *Inquiry*, **4** (1), 16-36.

FARRELL, B. A. (1964) 'The status of psychoanalytic theory'. *Inquiry*, **7**, 104-22.

FENICHEL, O. (1930) *Ten Years of the Berlin Psychoanalysis Institute.* 1920-30.

FENICHEL, O. (1945) *The Psychoanalytic Theory of Neurosis.* New York: Norton.

FERGUSON, G. A. (1949) 'On the theory of test development'. *Psychometrica*, **14**, 61-8.

FESSARD, A., GERARD, R. W. and KONORSKI, J. (1961) *Brain Mechanisms and Learning.* Oxford: Blackwell.

FIELD, M. J. (1940) *Social Organization of the Ga People.* London: Crown Agents for the Colonies.

FIELD, M. J. (1960) *Search for Security.* London: Faber & Faber.

FINNEY, J. C. (1961a) 'The MMPI as a measure of character structure as revealed by factor analysis'. *J. Consult. Psychol.*, **25**, 327-36.

FINNEY, J. C. (1961b) 'Some maternal influences on children's personality and character'. *Genet. Psychol. Monogr.*, **63**, 199-278.

FINNEY, J. C. (1963) 'Maternal influences on anal or compulsive character in children'. *J. Genet. Psychol.*, **103**, 351-67.

FINNEY, J. C. (1966) 'Relation and meaning of the new MMPI scales'. *Psych.*, **18**, 459-70.

FISHER, C. (1953) 'Studies on the nature of suggestion: I: experimental induction of dreams by direct suggestion'. *J. Amer. Psychoanal. Ass.*, **1**, 222-55.

FISHER, C. (1954) 'Dreams and perception: the role of preconscious and primary modes of perception in dream formation'. *J. Amer. Psychoanal. Ass.*, **2**, 389-445.

FISHER, C. (1960) 'Subliminal and supraliminal influences on dreams'. *Amer. J. Psychiat.*, **116**, 1009-17.

FISHER, C. (1965) 'Psychoanalytic implications of recent research on sleep and dreaming'. *J. Am. Psychoanal. Ass.*, **13**, 197-303.

FISHER, C. and DEMENT, W. C. (1963) 'Studies on the psychopathology of sleep and dreams'. *Amer. J. Psychiat*, **119**, 12, 1160-8.

FISHER, C., GROSS, J. and FELDMAN, M. (1965); Quoted by FISHER, C. (1965).

FISHER, C., GROSS, J. and ZUCH, J. (1965) 'Cycle of penile erection synchronous with dreaming (REM) sleep'. *Arch. Gen. Psychiat.*, **12**, 29-45.

FLANAGAN, D. E. (1930) *The Influence of Emotional Inhibition on Learning and Recall.* Unpub. Master's Thesis, Univ. of Chicago.

FLUGEL, J. C. (1945) *Man, Morals and Society.* London: Duckworth.

FORDHAM, F. (1959) *An Introduction to Jung's Psychology.* Harmondsworth: Penguin.

FOSS, B. M. (1964) 'Mimicry in mynas (Gracula religiosa): a test of Mowrer's theory'. *Brit. J. Psychol.*, **55**, 85-8.

FOULDS, G. A. (1965) *Personality and Personal Illness.* London: Tavistock Publications.

FOULKES, W. D. (1960) *Dream Reports from Different Stages of Sleep*. Unpub. Ph.D. thesis, Univ. of Chicago.

FOULKES, W. D. (1962) 'Dream reports from different stages of sleep'. *J. Abnorm. Soc. Psychol.*, **2**, 65 (1), 14-25.

FOULKES, W. D. (1964) 'Theories of dream formation and recent studies of sleep consciousness'. *Psychol. Bull.*, **62**, 236-47.

FOULKES, W. D. and RECHTSCHAFFEN, A. (1964) 'Pre-sleep determinants of dream content: the effects of two films'. *Paper read at Mid Western Psychological Association*.

FOX, B. (1961) 'The investigation of the effects of psychiatric treatment'. *J. Ment. Sci.*, **107**, 493-502.

FRANKS, C. M. (1969) (ed.) *Behavior Therapy Appraisal and Status*. New York: McGraw Hill.

FRENCH, T. M. and ALEXANDER, F. (1941) 'Psychogenic factors in bronchial asthma'. *Psychosom. Med. Monogr.*, II and IV.

FREUD, A. (1946) *The Ego and the Mechanisms of Defence*. London: Hogarth Press and the Institute of Psychoanalysis.

FREUD, A. and BURLINGHAM, D. T. (1944) *Infants without Families*. New York: Internat. Univ. Press.

FREUD, S. (1966) *The Standard Edition of the Complete Psychological Works of Sigmund Freud*. London: Hogarth Press and Institute of Psychoanalysis.

FREUD, S. (1893) 'On the psychical mechanism of hysterical phenomena: preliminary communication'. Vol. 2, 3.

FREUD, S. (1894) 'The neuro-psychoses of defence.' Vol. 3, 43.

FREUD, S. (1895a) 'A project for a scientific psychology'. Vol. 1, 295.

FREUD, S. (1895b) *Studies in Hysteria*. Vol. 2

FREUD, S. (1895c) 'On the grounds for detaching a particular syndrome from Neurasthenia under the description Anxiety Neurosis'. Vol. 3, 87.

FREUD, S. (1896a) 'Further observations on the neuropsychoses of defence'. Vol. 3, 163.

FREUD, S. (1896b) *The Aetiology of Hysteria*. Vol. 3.

FREUD, S. (1898) 'Sexuality in the aetiology of the neuroses'. Vol. 3, 191.

FREUD, S. (1900) *The Interpretation of Dreams*. Vols. 4-5.

FREUD, S. (1901) *The Psychopathology of Everyday Life*. Vol. 6.

FREUD, S. (1905a) 'Three essays on sexuality'. Vol. 7, 135-243.

FREUD, S. (1905b) *Jokes and their Relation to the Unconscious*. Vol. 8.

FREUD, S. (1905c) 'Fragment of an analysis of a case of hysteria'. Vol. 7, 3.

FREUD, S. (1906) 'My views on the part played by sexuality in the aetiology of the neuroses'. Vol. 7, 271.

FREUD, S. (1908a) 'Character and anal erotism'. Vol. 9, 169.

FREUD, S. (1908b) 'Creative writers and day-dreaming'. Vol. 9, 143.

FREUD, S. (1909a) 'Analysis of a phobia in a five-year old boy'. Vol. 10, 3.

FREUD, S. (1909b) 'Notes upon a case of obsessional neurosis'. Vol. 10, 153.

FREUD, S. (1910a) 'Three contributions to the psychology of love' .Vol. 11, 163.

FREUD, S. (1910b) 'The psychoanalytic view of psychogenic disturbance of vision'. Vol. 11, 211.

FREUD, S. (1911) 'Psychoanalytic notes on an autobiographical account of a case of paranoia (dementia paranoides)'. Vol. 12, 3.

FREUD, S. (1913a) 'Totem and taboo'. Vol. 13, 1.

FREUD, S. (1913b) 'The predisposition to obsessional neurosis'. Vol. 12, 317.

FREUD, S. (1915) 'Repression'. Vol. 14, 143.

FREUD, S. (1916-17) *Introductory Lectures on Psychoanalysis*. Vol. 15 and 16

FREUD, S. (1917a) 'On the transformation of instincts with special reference to anal erotism'. Vol. 17, 127-33.

FREUD, S. (1917b) 'Mourning and melancholia'. Vol. 14, 239.

FREUD, S. (1917c) 'A metapsychological supplement to the interpretation of dreams'. Vol. 14, 219.

FREUD, S. (1918) 'From the history of an infantile neurosis'. Vol. 17, 3.

FREUD, S. (1920) 'Beyond the pleasure principle'. Vol. 18, 7.

FREUD, S. (1923) 'The ego and the id'. Vol. 19, 3.

FREUD, S. (1924a) 'The dissolution of the Oedipus complex'. Vol. 19, 173.

FREUD, S. (1924b) 'Neurosis and psychosis'. Vol. 19, 149.

FREUD, S. (1925) 'Inhibition, symptoms and anxiety'. Vol. 20, 77.

FREUD, S. (1925b) 'Negation'. Vol. 19, 235.

FREUD, S. (1925c) 'Some psychical consequences of the anatomical distinction between the sexes'. Vol. 19, 243.

FREUD, S. (1926) 'The question of lay-analysis'. Vol. 20, 179.

FREUD, S. (1927a) 'Fetishism'. Vol. 21, 149.

FREUD, S. (1927b) 'Humour'. Vol. 21, 161.

FREUD, S. (1928) 'Dostoevsky'. Vol. 21, 175.

FREUD, S. (1931) 'Female sexuality'. Vol. 21, 223.

FREUD, S. (1932) 'The acquisition of control over fire'. Vol. 22, 185.

FREUD, S. (1933) *New Introductory Lectures in Psychoanalysis*. Vol. 22.

FREUD, S. (1935) 'An autobiographical study'. Vol. 20, 7.

FREUD, S. (1939) *Moses and Monotheism*. Vol. 23.

FREUD, S. (1940) 'An outline of psychoanalysis'. Vol. 23, 141.

FREUND, K. (1960) 'Some problems in the treatment of homosexuality'. In EYSENCK, H. J. (1960).

FRIEDMAN, S. M. (1950a) *An Empirical Study of Certain Psychoanalytic Propositions*. Unpub. Ph.D. thesis, Western Reserve Univ.

FRIEDMAN, S. M. (1950b) 'An empirical study of the Oedipus complex'. *Amer. Psychol.*, 5, 304.

FRIEDMAN, S. M. (1952) 'An empirical study of the castration and Oedipus complexes'. *Genet. Psychol. Monogr.*, 46, 61-130.

FROMM, E. (1942) *The Fear of Freedom*. London: Routledge & Kegan Paul.

FROMM, E. (1948) 'The Oedipus complex and the Oedipus myth'. In ANSHEN (1948).

FROMM, E. (1949) *Man for Himself*. London: Routledge & Kegan Paul.

FROMM, E. (1965) *The Heart of Man: its Genius for Good and Evil.* London: Routledge & Kegan Paul.

FULKERSON, F. C. (1957) 'The interaction of frequency, emotional tone and set in visual recognition'. *J. Exp. Psychol.*, 54, 188-94.

GEWIRTZ, J. L. (1969) 'Mechanisms of social learning: some roles of stimulation and behaviour in early human development'. Chapter 2 in GOSLIN, D. A. (1969).

GIBBINS, R. J. and WALTERS, R. H. (1960) 'Three preliminary studies of a psychoanalytic theory of alcohol addiction'. *Quart. J. Stud. Alcohol.*, 21, 618-41.

GILBERT, J. G. and LEVEE, R. F. (1963) 'A comparison of the personality structures of a group of young married and a group of middle-aged married women'. *Percept. Mot. Skills*, 16, 773-7.

GLESER, G. C. and IHILEVICH, D. (1969) 'An objective instrument for measuring defence mechanisms'. *J. Consult. Clin. Psychol.*, 33, 51-60.

GLIXMAN, A. F. (1949) 'Recall of completed and incompleted activities under varying degrees of stress'. *J. Exp. Psychol.*, 39, 281-95.

GLOTTER, A. N. and REECE, M. M. (1962) 'Tactility and sexual symbolism'. *Percept. Mot. Skills*, 14, 302.

GLOVER, E. (1924a) 'Notes on oral character formation'. In GLOVER E. (1956).

GLOVER, E. (1924b). 'The significance of the mouth in psychoanalysis'. In GLOVER, E. (1956).

GLOVER, E. (1949). *Psychoanalysis.* London: Staples Press.

GLOVER, E. (1950). *Freud or Jung?* London: Allen & Unwin.

GLOVER, E. (1956) *On the Early Development of Mind.* London: Mayo Pub. Co.

GOLDBERG, P. A. and MILSTEIN, J. T. (1965) 'Perceptual investigation of psychoanalytic theory concerning latent homosexuality in women'. *Percept. Mot. Skills*, 21, 645-6.

GOLDEN, O. (1954) *Manifestations of Impulse, Ego and Superego in Elementary Schoolboys and Girls.* Unpub. Ph.D. thesis, Western Reserve Univ.

GOLDFARB, W. (1943) 'Effects of early institutional care on adolescent personality'. *J. Exp. Educ.*, 12, 106-29.

GOLDFARB, W. (1944) 'Effects of early institutional care on adolescent personality: Rorschach data'. *Amer. J. Orthopsychiat,.* 14, 441-7.

GOLDFARB, W. (1945) 'Psychological privation in infancy and subsequent adjustment'. *Amer. J. Orthopsychiat.*, 15, 247-55.

GOLDFARB, W. (1947) 'Variations in adolescent adjustment of institutionally-reared children'. *Amer. J. Orthopsychiat.*, 17, 449-57.

GOLDFARB, W. (1949) 'Rorschach test differences between family-reared, institution-reared and schizophrenic children'. *Amer. J. Orthopsychiat.*, 19, 625-33.

GOLDMAN-EISLER, F. (1948) 'Breast-feeding and character formation I'. *J. Pers.*, 17, 83-103.

GOLDMAN-EISLER, F. (1950) 'Breast-feeding and character formation. II: The etiology of the oral character in psychoanalytic theory'. *J. Pers.*, 19, 189-196.

GOLDMAN-EISLER, F. (1951) 'The problem of "orality" and its origin in early childhood'. *J. Ment. Sci.*, **97**, 765-82.

GOLDMAN-EISLER, F. (1953) 'Breast-feeding and character formation'. In KLUCKHOHN, C. and MURRAY, H. A. (1953).

GOLLOB, H. F. and LEVINE, J. (1967) 'Distraction as a factor in the enjoyment of aggressive humour'. *J. Pers. Soc. Psychol.*, **5**, 368-72.

GOMBRICH, E. H. (1963) *Meditations on a Hobby-Horse and other Essays on the Theory of Art*. London: Phaidon Press.

GORER, G. (1943) 'Themes in Japanese culture'. *Trans. New York Acad. Sci.*, **2**, 106-24.

GORSUCH, R. L. and CATTELL, R. B. (1967) 'Second stratum personality factors defined in the questionnaire realm by the 16 PF'. *Multiv. Behav. Res.*, **2**, 211-23.

GOSLIN, D. A. (1969) *Handbook of Socialization Theory and Research*. Chicago: Rand McNally.

GOTTHEIL, E. (1965a) 'Conceptions of orality and anality'. *J. Nerv. Ment. Dis.*, **141**, (2) 155-60.

GOTTHEIL, E. (1965b) 'An empirical analysis of orality and anality'. *J. Nerv. Ment. Dis.*, **141**, 308-17.

GOTTHEIL, E. and STONE, G. C. (1968) 'Factor analytic study of orality and anality'. *J. Nerv. Ment. Dis.*, **146**, 1-17.

GOTTSCHALK, L. A. and GLESER, G. C. (1969) *The Measurement of Psychological States through the Content Analysis of Verbal Behaviour*. Berkeley: Univ. California Press.

GOUGH, H. G. (1957) *The Californian Psychological Inventory*. Palo Alto: Consulting Psychologists Press.

GRANICK, S. and SCHEFLIN, N. A. (1958) 'Approaches to the reliability of projective tests with special reference to the Blacky Pictures Test'. *J. Consult. Psychol.*, **22**, 137-41.

GREENSPOON, J. (1955) 'The reinforcing effect of two spoken sounds on the frequency of two responses'. *Amer. J. Psychol.*, **68**, 409-16.

GREY-WALTER, W. (1961) *The Living Brain*. Harmondsworth: Penguin.

GRIFFITHS, R. (1951) *The Griffiths Mental Development Scale for Testing Babies from Birth to Two Years*. London: Author.

GROSSMAN, S. P. (1967) *A Textbook of Physiological Psychology*. New York: Wiley.

GROTJAN, M. (1957) *Beyond Laughter*. New York: McGraw-Hill.

GRYGIER, P. (1956) 'The personality of student nurses: a pilot study using the DPI'. *Int. J. Soc. Psychiat.*, **2**, 105-12.

GRYGIER, T. G. (1957a) 'Psychometric aspects of homosexuality'. *J. Ment. Sci.*, **103**, 514-26.

GRYGIER, T. G. (1957b) 'A factorial study of insularity'. *Psychol. Rep.*, **3**, 613-14.

GRYGIER, T. G. (1958) 'Homosexuality, neurosis and normality'. *Brit. J. Delinq.* **4**, 59-61.

GRYGIER, T. G. (1961) *The Dynamic Personality Inventory*. London: N.F.E.R.

GUILFORD, J. P. (1956) *Psychometric Methods* (2nd edn.). New York: McGraw-Hill.

GUILFORD, J. P. (1958) *Fundamental Statistics in Psychology and Education*. London: McGraw Hill.

GUILFORD, J. P. (1959) *Personality*. New York: McGraw-Hill.

GUILFORD, J. P. and ZIMMERMAN, W. S. (1949) 'The Guilford-Zimmerman Temperament Survey'. *Manual of Instructions and Interpretations*. Beverly Hills: Sheridan.

HALL, C. S. (1953) *The Meaning of Dreams*. New York: Harper & Row.

HALL, C. S. (1955) 'The significance of the dream of being attacked'. *J. Pers.*, **24**, 168-80.

HALL, C. S. (1963) 'Strangers in dreams: an experimental confirmation of the Oedipus complex'. *J. Pers.*, **31** (3), 336-45.

HALL, C. S. (1964) 'A modest confirmation of Freud's theory of a distinction between the super-ego of men and women'. *J. Abnorm. Soc. Psychol.*, **69**, 440-2.

HALL, C. S. (1966) *The Meaning of Dreams*. New York: McGraw-Hill.

HALL, C. S. and DOMHOFF, B. (1962a) 'Aggression in dreams'. Quoted by HALL and DOMHOFF (1963).

HALL, C. S. and DOMHOFF, B. (1962b) 'Friendliness in dreams'. Quoted by HALL and DOMHOFF (1963).

HALL, C. S. and DOMHOFF, B. (1963) 'A ubiquitous sex difference in dreams'. *J. Abnorm. Soc. Psychol.*, **66**, 3, 278-80.

HALL, C. S. and LINDZEY, G. (1957) *Theories of Personality*. New York: Wiley.

HALL, C. S. and VAN DE CASTLE, R. L. (1963) 'An empirical investigation of the castration complex in dreams'. *J. Pers.*, **33**, (1), 20-9.

HAMMER, E. F. (1953) 'An investigation of sexual symbolism: a study of HTPs of eugenically sterilized subjects'. *J. Proj. Tech.*, **17**, 401-15.

HARMAN, H. H. (1964) *Modern Factor Analysis*. Chicago: Univ. of Chicago Press.

HARRIS, I. (1948) 'Observations concerning typical anxiety dreams'. *Psychiatry*, **11**, 301-9.

HARRIS, I. (1951) 'Characterological significance of the typical anxiety dream'. *Psychiatry*, **14**, 279-94.

HARTMAN, H., KRIS, E. and LOWENSTEIN, R. M. (1947) 'Comments on the formation of psychic structure'. *Psychoanal. Study of the Child*, **11**, 11-38.

HARTSHORNE, H. and MAY, M. A. (1930) *Studies in the Nature of Character*. New York: Macmillan.

HATHAWAY, S. R. and MCKINLEY, J. C. (1951) *The Minnesota Multiphasic Personality Inventory Manual (Revised)*. New York: The Psychological Corp.

HAZARI, A. (1957) *An Investigation of Obsessive-compulsive Character Traits and Symptoms in Adult Neurotics*. Unpub. Ph.D. thesis, University of London.

HELPER, M. M. (1955) 'Learning theory and the self-concept'. *J. Abnorm. Soc. Psychol.*, **51**, 184-94.

N

HENDERSON, D. K. and GILLESPIE, R. D. (1956) *A Text Book of Psychiatry*. 8th edn. London: Oxford University Press.

HENKER, B. A. (1964) 'The effect of adult model relationships on children's play and task imitation'. *Dissert. Abstracts.*, **24**, 4797.

HENRY, J. and HENRY, Z. (1944) 'Doll play of Pilaga Indian children'. *Assn. Inc. Res. Monogr.*, **4**.

HERNSTEIN, M. I. (1963) 'Behavioural correlates of breast-bottle regimes under varying parent-infant relationships'. *Monographs of the Society for Research in Child. Develop.*, **28**, 4.

HERRON, W. G. (1962) 'IES Test patterns of accepted and rejected adolescents'. *Percept. Mot. Skills*, **15**, 435-8.

HETHERINGTON, E. M. and BRACKBILL, Y. (1963) 'Etiology and covariation of obstinacy, orderliness and parsimony in young children'. *Child Development*, **34**, 919-43.

HILGARD, E. R. (1952) 'Experimental approaches to psychoanalysis'. Pp. 3-45 in PUMPIAN-MINDLIN, E. (1952).

HINDE, R. A. (1966) *Animal Behaviour*. New York: McGraw-Hill.

HINNIE, L. E. (1937) (ed.) *Concepts and Problems of Psychotherapy*. New York: Columbia Univ. Press.

HOEFER, C. and HARDY, M. (1929) 'Later development of breast fed and artificially fed infants'. *J.A.M.A.* **92**, 615-19.

HOFFMAN, M. L. and HOFFMAN, L. W. (1964) (eds.) *Review of Child Development Research*. Vol. I. New York: Russell Sage Foundation.

HOLWAY, A. R. (1949) 'Early self-regulation in infants and later behavior in play interviews'. *Amer. J. Orthopsychiat.*, **19**, 612-23.

HORNEY, K. (1937) *The Neurotic Personality of Our Time*. New York: Norton.

HORNEY, K. (1939) *New Ways in Psychoanalysis*. New York: Norton.

HORNEY, K. (1942) *Self Analysis*. New York: Norton.

HORNEY, K. (1945) *Our Inner Conflicts*. New York: Norton.

HOWES, D. H. and SOLOMON, R. L. (1950) 'A note on McGinnies' "Emotionality and perceptual defence" '. *Psychol. Rev.*, **57**, 229-34.

HUSCHKA, M. (1942) 'The child's response to coercive bowel training'. *Psychosom. Med.*, **4**, 301-28.

HSU, F. L. K. (1961) *Psychological Anthropology: Approaches to Culture and Personality*. New York: Dorsey Press.

HYTTEN, F. E., YORSTON, J. C. and THOMSON, A. M. (1958) 'Difficulties associated with breast-feeding'. *Brit. Med. J.*, **I**, 310-15.

INGLIS, J. (1961) 'Abnormalities of motivation and "ego functions"'. In EYSENCK, H. J. (1961).

INMAN, W. S. (1958) 'Clinical thought-reading'. *Internat. J. Psychoanal.*, **38**, 299-304.

INMAN, W. S. (1962) 'Ophthalmic adventure: a story of frustration and organic disease'. *Brit. J. Med. Psychol.*, **35**, 299-309.

ISCOE, I. and STEVENSON, H. W. (1960) (eds.) *Personality Development in Children*. Austin: Univ. of Texas Press.

JACKSON, D. N. and MESSICK, S. (1961) 'Content and style in personality assessment'. *Educ. Psychol. Meas.*, **21**, 771-90.

JACOBS, A. (1954) 'Responses of normals and mental hospital patients to Freudian sexual symbols'. *J. Consult. Psychol.*, **18**, 454.

JACOBS, M. A. *et al* (1965) 'Relationship of oral frustration factors with heavy cigarette smoking in males'. *J. Nerv. Ment. Dis.*, **141**, 161-71.

JACOBS, M. A. *et al.* (1966) 'Orality, impulsivity and cigarette smoking in men. Further findings in support of a theory'. *J. Nerv. Ment. Dis.*, 207-9.

JAHODA, G. (1956) 'Sex differences in preferences for shapes – a cross-cultural replication'. *Brit. J. Psychol.*, **47**, 126-32.

JENSEN, A. R. (1958) *The Reliability of Projective Techniques: Review of the Literature and Methodology*. Amsterdam: North Holland Pub. Co.

JOHNSON, G. B. (1966) 'Penis envy or pencil needing?' *Psychol. Rep.*, **19**, 758.

JOHNSON, H. and ERIKSEN, C. W. (1961) 'Preconscious perception: a re-examination of the Poetzl phenomenon'. *J. Abnorm. Soc. Psychol.*, **62**, 497-503.

JONES, A. (1956) 'Sexual symbolism and the variables of sex and personality integration'. *J. Abnorm. Soc. Psychol.*, **53**, 187-90.

JONES, A. (1961) 'Sexual symbolic responses in prepubescent and pubescent children'. *J. Consult. Psychol.*, **25**, 383-7.

JONES, A. and LEPSON, D. S. (1967) 'Mediated and primary stimulus generalisation basis of sexual symbolism'. *J. Consult. Psychol.*, **31**, 79-82.

JONES, E. (1915) 'Urethalerotik und Ehrgeiz'. *Internat. Z. Psychoanal.*, **3**, 156.

JONES, E. (1923) 'Anal erotic character traits'. In *Papers on Psychoanalysis*. London: Baillière, Tindall & Cox.

JONES, E. (1925) 'Mother-right and the sexual ignorance of savages'. *Internat. J. Psychoanal.*, **6**, 109-30.

JONES, E. (1933) 'The phallic phase'. *Internat. J. Psychoanal.*, **14**, 1-33.

JONES, E. (1936). *Decennial Report of the London Clinic of Psychoanalysis, 1926-36*.

JONES, M. R. (1962) (ed.) *Nebraska Symposium on Motivation*. Lincoln: Univ. of Nebraska Press.

JOUVET, D., VIMONT, P., DELORME, F. and JOUVET, M. (1964) 'Étude de la privation selective de la phase paradoxale du sommeil chez le chat'. *C.R. Soc. Biol. Paris*, **158**, 156-9.

JOUVET, M. (1965) 'Paradoxical sleep: a study of its nature and mechanisms'. In ABERT, K. *et al.* (1965).

JOUVET, M. (1967) 'Neurophysiology of the states of sleep'. *Physiol. Rev.*, **47**, 117-77.

JOUVET, M. and MOUNIER, D. (1960) 'Effets des lésions de la formation réticule pontique sur le sommeil du chat'. *C.R. Soc. Biol. Paris*, **154**, 2301-5.

JUNG, C. G. (1918) *Studies in Word Association*. London: Heinemann.

JUNG, C. G. (1940) *The Integration of the Personality*. London: Routledge & Kegan Paul.

JUNG, C. G. (1949) *Psychological Types*. London: Routledge & Kegan Paul.

JUNG, C. G. (1953) *Two Essays on Analytical Psychology*. London: Routledge & Kegan Paul.

JUNG, C. G. (1955) *Psychology and Alchemy*. London: Routledge & Kegan Paul.

JUNG, C. G. and WILHELM, R. (1931). *The Secret of the Golden Flower*. London: Routledge & Kegan Paul.

KAGAN, J. and PHILLIPS, W. (1964) 'The measurement of identification'. *J. Abnorm. Soc. Psychol.*, **69**, 442-3.

KALES, A., HOEDEMAKER, F. S., JACOBSON, A. *et al.* (1964) 'Dream deprivation: an experimental reappraisal'. *Nature*, **204**, 1337-8.

KAMIJA, J. (1961) 'Behavioural, subjective and physiological aspects of drowsiness and sleep'. In *Functions of Varied Experience*. Edited by FISKE, D. W. and MAODI, S. R. Illinois: Dorsey.

KARACAN, I., GOODENOUGH, D. R., SHAPIRO, A. and STARKER, S. (1966) 'Erection cycle during sleep in relation to dream anxiety'. *Arch. Gen. Psychiat.*, **15**, (2) 183-9.

KARDINER, A. (1945) *The Psychological Frontiers of Society*. New York: Columbia Univ. Press.

KATKOVKSY, W. (1965) 'Review of the IES Test'. In BUROS, O. K. (1965).

KAYE, B. (1962). *Bringing up Children in Ghana: an Impressionistic Survey*. London: Allen & Unwin.

KENT, G. H. and ROSANOFF, A. J. (1910) 'A study of association in insanity'. *Amer. J. Insan.*, **67**, 37-96.

KERLINGER, F. N. (1953) 'Behaviour and personality in Japan: a critique of three studies of Japanese personality'. *Soc. Forces*, **31**, 250-8.

KESSEL, L. and HYMAN, H. T. (1933) 'The value of psychoanalysis as a therapeutic procedure'. *J. Amer. Med. Assoc.*, **19**, 1612-15.

KIESLER, D. J. (1966) 'Some myths of psychotherapy research and the search for a paradigm'. *Psychol. Bull.*, **65**, 110-36.

KIMELDORF, C. and GEWITZ, P. J. (1966) 'Smoking and the Blacky orality factors'. *J. Proj. Tech. and Pers. Assess.*, **30**, 167-8.

KINSEY, A. C., POMEROY, W. B. and MARTIN, C. E. (1948) *Sexual Behaviour in the Human Male*. Philadelphia: Saunders.

KLACKENBERG, G. (1949) 'Thumbsucking frequency and aetiology'. *Pediatrics*, **4**, 418-24.

KLAF, F. S. (1961) 'Evidence of paranoid ideation in overt homosexuals'. *J. Soc. Ther.*, **7**, 48-51.

KLAF, F. S. and DAVIS, C. (1960) 'Homosexuality and paranoid schizophrenia: a survey of 150 cases and controls'. *Amer. J. Psychiat.*, **116**, 1070-75.

KLEIN, H. and HORWITZ, W. (1949) 'Psychosexual factors in the paranoid phenomenon'. *Amer. J. Psychiat.*, **105**, 697-701.

KLEIN, M. (1963) *Étude polygraphique et phylogénique des états de sommeil.* Lyon: Bon Frères.

KLINE, P. (1967a) 'The use of Cattell's 16 PF Test and Eysenck's EPI with a literate population in Ghana'. *Brit. J. Soc. Clin. Psychol.*, **6**, 97-107.

KLINE, P. (1967b) 'Obsessional traits, obsessional symptoms and general emotionality in a normal population'. *Brit. J. Med. Psychol.*, **40**, 153-7.

KLINE, P. (1967c) *An Investigation into the Freudian Concept of the Anal Character.* Unpub. Ph.D. thesis, Univ. of Manchester.

KLINE, P. (1968a) 'Obsessional traits, obsessional symptoms and anal erotism', *Brit. J. Med. Psychol.*, **41**, 299-305.

KLINE, P. (1968b) 'The validity of the Dynamic Personality Inventory'. *Brit. J. Med. Psychol.*, **41**, 307-11.

KLINE, P. (1969a) 'The anal character: a cross-cultural study in Ghana'. *Brit. J. Soc. Clin. Psychol.*, **8**, 201-10.

KLINE, P. (1969b) 'A study of the Oedipus complex and neurotic symptoms in a non-psychiatric population (correspondence)'. *Brit. J. Med. Psychol.*, **42**, 291.

KLINE, P. (1970) 'A projective and psychometric study of the oral character'. *Proc. VII. Internat. Conf. Soc. Rorsch. and Proj. Tech.* Vienna: Hans Huber.

KLUCKHOHN, C. and MURRAY, H. A. (1953) *Personality in Nature, Society and Culture.* New York: Knopf.

KNAPP, P. H. (1963) 'Short-term psychoanalytic and psychosomatic predictions'. *J. Amer. Psychoanal. Assoc.*, **11**, 248-80.

KNIGHT, R. P. (1940) 'The relationship of latent homosexuality to the mechanism of paranoid delusions'. *Bull. Menning Clin.*, **4**, 149-59.

KNIGHT, R. P. (1941) 'Evaluation of the results of psychoanalytic therapy'. *Amer. J. Psychiat.*, **98**, 434-46.

KOHLBERG, L. (1958) *The Development of Modes of Moral Thinking and Choice in the Ten Years to Sixteen.* Unpub. Ph.D. thesis, Univ. of Chicago.

KOHLBERG, L. (1963a) 'Moral development and identification'. In STEVENSON, H. (1963).

KOHLBERG, L. (1963b) 'The development of children's orientation towards a moral order: 1. Sequence in the development of moral thought'. *Vita Humana*, **6**, 11-33.

KOHLBERG, L. (1964) 'Development of moral character and ideology'. In HOFFMAN, M. L. and HOFFMAN, L. W. (1964).

KOHLBERG, L. (1966a) 'Cognitive stages and pre-school education'. *Human Development*, **9**, 5-17.

KOHLBERG, L. (1966b) 'A cognitive developmental analysis of children's sex-role concepts and attitudes'. In MACCOBY, E. E. (1967).

KOHLBERG, L. (1967) 'Moral and religious education and the public schools'. In SIZER, T. (1967).

KOHLBERG, L. (1968) 'Early education: a cognitive developmental view'. *Child Development*, **39**, 1013-62.

KOHLBERG, L. (1969a) 'Stages and sequences: the cognitive developmental approach to socialisation'. Chapter 6 in GOSLIN, D. A. (1969).

KOHLBERG, L. (1969b) *Stages in the Development of Moral Thought and Action.* New York: Holt, Rinehart & Winston.

KRAFKOV, S. V. (1941) 'Colour vision and the autonomic nervous system'. *J. Opt. Soc. Amer.,* **31**, 235-7.

KREITLER, H. and KREITLER, S. (1966) 'Children's concepts of sexuality and birth'. *Child Development,* **37**, 363-78.

KROUT, T. J. (1950) 'Symbol Elaboration Test (SET). The reliability and validity of a new projective technique'. *Psychol. Monogr.,* 1950, **64**, (4).

KROUT, M. H. and KROUT, T. J. (1954) 'Measuring personality in developmental terms'. *Genet. Psychol. Monogr.,* **50**, 289-335.

KUPPUSWAMY, B. (1949) 'Preliminary report of a statistical study of the Oedipus complex'. *Ind. J. Psychol.,* **24**, 23-5.

LA BARRE, W. (1945) 'Some observations on character structure in the Orient: the Japanese'. *Psychiatry,* **8**, 319-42.

LAFFAL, J. (1952) 'The learning and retention of words with association disturbances'. *J. Abnorm. Soc. Psychol.,* **47**, 454-62.

LAFFAL, J. (1955) 'Application of Guttman's scaling method to the TAT'. *Educ. Psychol. Meas.,* **15**, 422-35.

LAMB, C. W. (1968) 'Personality correlates of humour enjoyment following motivational arousal'. *J. Pers. Soc. Psychol.,* **9**, 237-41.

LANDIS, C. A. (1937) 'Statistical evaluation of psychotherapeutic methods'. Pp. 155-9 in HINNIE, L. E. (1937).

LANDY, E. E. (1967) 'Sex differences in some aspects of smoking behaviour'. *Psychol. Rep.,* **20**, 578-80.

LASKY, J. L. and BERGER, L. (1959) 'Blacky Test scores before and after genito-urinary surgery'. *J. Proj. Tech.,* **23**, 57-8.

LAZARE, A., KLERMAN, G. L. and ARMOR, D. J. (1966) 'Oral, obsessive and hysterical personality patterns: an investigation of psychoanalytic concepts by means of factor analysis'. *Arch. Gen. Psychiat.,* **14**, 624-30.

LECKIE, E. V. and WITHERS, R. F. J. (1967) 'A test of liability to depressive illness'. *Brit. J. Med. Psychol.,* **40**, 273.

LEE, S. G. (1958) 'Social influences in Zulu dreaming'. *J. Soc. Psychol.,* **47**, 265-83.

LESSLER, K. (1962) 'Sexual symbols structured and unstructured'. *J. Consult. Psychol.,* **26**, 44-9.

LESSLER, K. (1964) 'Cultural and Freudian dimensions of sexual symbols'. *J. Consult. Psychol.,* **28** (1), 46-53.

LESSLER, K. and ERICKSEN, M. T. (1968) 'Response to sexual symbols by elementary school children'. *J. Consult. Clin. Psychol.,* **32**, 473-7.

LEVIN, R. B. (1966) 'An empirical test of the female castration complex'. *J. Abnorm. Psychol.,* **71**, 181-8.

LEVINE, M. L. and BELL, A. I. (1950) 'The treatment of colic in infancy by use of the pacifier'. *J. Pediat.,* **37**, 750-55.

LEVINGER, G. and CLARK, J. (1961) 'Emotional factors in the forgetting of word associations'. *J. Abnorm. Soc. Psychol.*, **62**, 99-105.

LEVY, D. M. (1928) 'Finger-sucking and accessory movements in early infancy (an etiological study)'. *Amer. J. Psychiat.*, **7**, 881-918.

LEVY, D. M. (1934) 'Experiments on the sucking reflex and social behaviour in dogs'. *Amer. J. Orthopsychiat.*, **4**, 203-24.

LEVY, L. H. (1954) 'Sexual symbolism: a validity study'. *J. Consult. Psychol.*, **18**, 43-6.

LEWIS, H. (1954) *Deprived Children*. London: Oxford Univ. Press.

LIEF, H. I., LIEF, V. F. and LIEF, N. R. (1963) (eds.) *The Psychological Basis of Medical Practice*. New York: Harper & Row.

LINDNER, H. (1953) 'The Blacky Pictures Test: a study of sexual and non-sexual offenders'. *J. Proj. Tech.*, **17**, 79-84.

LINDZEY, G. (1954) (ed.) *The Handbook of Social Psychology*. Reading, Mass: Adison Wesley.

LINDZEY, G. and HALL, C. S. (1965) *Theories of Personality: Primary Sources and Research*. New York: Wiley.

LITTMAN, R. A., NIDORF, L. J. and SUNDBERG, N. D. (1961) 'Characteristics of a psychosexual scale'. *J. Genet. Psychol.*, **98**, 19-27.

LUBIN, A. and LOOS, F. M. (1953) 'The IPAT Humour Test'. In BUROS, O. K. (1953) *IVth Mental Measurement Year Book*. New Jersey: Gryphon.

LUBORSKY, L. (1954) 'A note on Eysenck's article "The effects of psychotherapy: an evaluation"'. *Brit. J. Psychol.*, **45**, 129-31.

LUBORSKY, L. and CATTELL, R. B. (1947) 'The validation of personality factors in humour'. *J. Pers.*, **15**, 283-91.

LUCHINS, A. S. (1950) 'On an approach to social perception'. *J. Pers.*, **19**, 64-84.

LYSTAD, R. A. (1958) *The Ashanti, A Proud People*. New Brunswick, New Jersey: Rutgens Univ. Press.

LYTTON, H. (1969) 'Parent-child interaction studies: an unresolved dilemma?' *Paper at Brit. Psychol. Soc. Annual Conf. 1969*.

MCARTHUR, C., WALDRON, F. and DICKINSON, J. (1958) 'The psychology of smoking'. *J. Abnorm. Soc. Psychol.*, **56**, 267-75.

MCCLELLAND, D. C. (1961) *The Achieving Society*. Princeton: Van Nostrand.

MCCLELLAND, D. C. and FRIEDMAN, G. A. (1952) In NEWCOMB, T.M. and HARTLEY, E. L. (1952) *Readings in Social Psychology*. New York: Holt.

MACCOBY, E. E. (1967) (ed.) *The Development of Sex Differences*. Stanford: Stanford Univ. Press.

MACCOBY, E. E., NEWCOMB, T. M. and HARTLEY, E. L. (1958) (eds.) *Readings in Social Psychology*. 3rd edn. New York: Holt, Rinehart & Winston.

MCCORD, W., MCCORD, J. and GUDEMAN, J. (1959) 'Some current theories of alcoholism: a longitudinal evaluation'. *Quart. J. Stud. Alcohol.*, **20**, 727-49.

MCELROY, W. A. (1950) 'Methods of testing the Oedipus complex hypothesis'. *Quart. Bull. Brit. Psychol. Soc.*, **1**, 364-5.

MCELROY, W. A. (1954) 'A sex difference in preferences for shapes'. *Brit. J. Psychol.*, 45, 209-16.

MCGINNIES, E. (1949) 'Emotionality and perceptual defence'. *Psychol. Rev.*, 56, 244-51.

MCGINNIES, E., COMER, P. B. and LACY, O. L. (1952) 'Visual recognition thresholds as a function of word length and word frequency'. *J. Exp. Psychol.*, 44, 59-65.

MACHOVER, S. and PUZZO, F. S. (1959) 'Clinical and objective studies of personality variables in alcoholism: 1. clinical investigation of the alcoholic personality'. *Quart. J. Stud. Alcohol.*, 20, 505-27.

MACHOVER, S., PUZZO, F. S., MACHOVER, K. and PLUMEAU, F. (1959) 'Clinical and objective studies of personality variables in alcoholism'. *Quart. J. Stud. Alcohol.*, 20, 528-42.

MACKINNON, D. W. (1938) 'Violation and prohibitions'. In MURRAY, H. A. (1938).

MACKINNON, D. W. and DUKES, W. F. (1962) 'Repression'. In POSTMAN, L. (1962).

MACLEAN, P. D. (1949) 'Psychosomatic disease and the "visceral brain"'. *Psychosom. Med.*, 11, 338-53.

MCNEIL, E. B. and BLUM, G. S. (1952) 'Handwriting and psychosexual dimensions of personality'. *J. Proj. Tech.*, 16, 476-84.

MAGOUN, H. W. (1961) 'Darwin and concepts of brain function'. In FESSARD, GERARD and KONORSKI (1961).

MALAN, D. (1959) 'On assessing the results in psychotherapy'. *Brit. J. Med. Psychol.*, 32, 86-105.

MALINOWSKI, B. (1927) *Sex and Repression in Savage Society*. New York: Harcourt Brace.

MARGOLIS, M. (1961) 'The mother-child relationship in bronchial asthma'. *J. Abnorm. Soc. Psychology*, 63 (2), 360-7.

MARKE, S. and NYMAN, E. (1960) *MNT – Skalan*. Stockholm: Skandinaviska Tesforlaget AB.

MARQUIS, D. F., SINNETT, E. R. and WINTER, W. D. (1952) 'A psychological study of peptic ulcer patients'. *J. Clin. Psychol.*, 8, 266-72.

MARTIN. M. (1964) 'Mr Farrell and the refutability of psychoanalysis'. *Inquiry*, 7, 80-98.

MARX, M. H. (1963) (ed.) *Theories in Contemporary Psychology*. New York: Macmillan.

MASLING, J., RABIE, L. and BLONDHEIM, S. H. (1967) 'Obesity, level of aspiration, Rorschach and TAT measures of oral dependence'. *J. Consult. Psychol.*, 31, 233-9.

MASLING, J., WEISS, L. and ROTHSCHILD, B. (1968) 'Relationships of oral imagery to yielding behaviour and birth order'. *J. Consult. Clin. Psychol.*, 32, 89-91.

MASSERMAN, J. H. (1964) (ed.) *Science and Psychoanalysis*. Vol. 7. New York: Grune & Stratton.

MASSERMAN, J. H. and CARMICHAEL, H. T. (1938) 'Diagnosis and prognosis in psychiatry: with a follow-up study of the results of short-term hospital therapy of psychiatric cases'. *J. Ment. Sci.*, **34**, 893-946.

MAURY, A. (1861) *Le Sommeil et Les Rêves*. Paris: Didier.

MAYER-GROSS, W., SLATER, E. and ROTH, M. (1961) *Clinical Psychiatry*. London: Cassell.

MEDAWAR, P. B. (1969) *Induction and Intuition in Scientific Thought*. London: Methuen.

MEDNICK, S. A., GARNER, A. M. and STONE, H. H. (1959) 'A test of some behavioural hypotheses drawn from Alexander's specificity theory'. *Amer. J. Orthopsychiat.*, **29**, 592-8.

MEEHL, P. H. (1955) 'Psychotherapy'. *Amer. Rev. Psychol.*, **6**, 357-78.

MEHLMAN, B. (1952) 'The reliability of psychiatric diagnoses'. *J. Abnorm. Soc. Psychol.*, **47**, 577-8.

MEISSNER, W. W. (1958) 'Affective response to psychoanalytic death symbols'. *J. Abnorm. Soc. Psychol.*, **56**, 295-9.

MENNINGER, W. C. (1943) 'Characterologic and symptomatic expressions related to the anal phase of psychosexual development'. *Psychoanal. Quart.* **12**, 161-93.

MERCHANT, F. C. (1952) *Psychosexual development in stutterers*. Unpub. Ms. quoted by BLUM and HUNT (1952, q.v.).

MESSICK, S. and ABELSON, R. (1956) 'The additive constant problem in multi-dimensional scaling'. *Psychom.*, **21**, 1-15.

MEYER, A. E. (1966) 'Psychoanalytic versus behaviour therapy of male homosexuals: a statistical evaluation of clinical outcome'. *Comprehen. Psychiat.*, **7**, 110-17.

MICHAL-SMITH, H., HAMMER, E. and SPITZ, H. (1951) 'Use of the Blacky Pictures with a child whose Oedipal desires are close to consciousness'. *J. Clin. Psychol.*, **7**, 280-62.

MILES, D. W. (1954) 'The import for clinical psychology of the use of tests derived from theories about infantile sexuality and adult character'. *Genet. Psychol. Monogr.*, **50**, 227-88.

MILES, T. R. (1965) *Eliminating the Unconscious* (a behaviourist's view of psychoanalysis). Oxford: Pergamon Press.

MILLER, N. E. (1948) 'Theory and experiment relating psychoanalytic displacement to stimulus-response generalisation'. *J. Abnorm. Soc. Psychol.*, **43**, 155-78.

MILLER, N. E. and BUGELSKI, R. (1948) 'Minor studies of aggression. II: the influence of frustrations imposed by the in-group on attitudes expressed towards out-groups'. *J. Psychol.*, **25**, 437-42.

MINTURN, L. (1965) 'A cross-cultural linguistic analysis of Freudian symbols'. *Ethnology*, **4**, 336-42.

MISCHEL, W. and GRUSEC, J. (1966) 'Determinants of the rehearsal and transmission of neutral and aversive behaviours'. *J. Pers. Soc. Psychol.*, **2**, 197-205.

MONIZ, E. (1936) *Tentatives Opérations dans le Traitement de Certaines Psychoses*. Paris: Masson.

MOORE, R. A. and SELZER, M. L. (1963) 'Male homosexuality, paranoia and the schizophrenias'. *Amer. J. Psychiat.*, **119**, 743-7.

MOOS, R. and MUSSEN, P. (1959) 'Sexual symbolism, personality integration and intellectual functioning'. *J. Consult. Psychol.*, **23**, 521-3.

MOSAK, H. R. (1955) 'Language and the interpretation of sexual symbolism'. *J. Consult. Psychol.*, **19**, 108.

MOWRER, O. H. (1950) *Learning Theory and Personality Dynamics*. New York: Ronald.

MULLAHY, P. (1948) *Oedipus Myth and Complex*. New York: Hermitage Press.

MULLEN, F. G. (1968) 'Estimation of the universality of Freudian and Jungian sexual symbols'. *Percept. Mot. Skills*, **26**, 1041-2.

MUNN, N. L. (1961) *The Evolution and Growth of Human Behaviour*. London: Harrap.

MURCHISON, C. (1930) (ed.) *Psychologies of 1930*. Worcester, Mass.: Clarke Univ. Press.

MURDOCK, G. P. (1949) *Social Structure*. New York: Macmillan.

MURDOCK, G. P. (1957) 'World ethnographic sample'. *Am. Anthropol.*, **59**, 664-87.

MURPHY, L. B. (1962) *The Widening World of Childhood*. New York: Basic Books.

MURRAY, H. A. (1938) *Explorations in Personality*. New York: Oxford Univ. Press.

MUSSEN, P. H. and DISTLER, L. (1959) 'Masculinity identification and father-son relationships'. *J. Abnorm. Soc. Psychol.*, **59**, 350-6.

NEISSER, U. (1954) 'An experimental distinction between perceptual processes and mental responses'. *J. Exp. Psychol.*, **47**, 399-402.

NELSON, S. E. (1955) 'Psychosexual conflicts and defences in visual perception'. *J. Abnorm. Psychol.*, **51**, 427-33.

NEUMAN, G. C. and SALVATORE, J. C. (1958) 'The Blacky Test and psycho-analytic theory. A factor-analytic approach to validity'. *J. Proj. Tech.*, **22**, 427-31.

NEWSON, J. and NEWSON, E. (1963) *Infant Care in an Urban Community*. London: Allen & Unwin.

NEWTON, N. R. (1951) 'The relation between infant feeding experience and later behaviour'. *J. Pediat.*, **38**, 28-40.

NOBLIN, C. D. (1962) 'Experimental analysis of psychoanalytic character types through the operant conditioning of verbal responses'. *Amer. Psychol.*, **17**, 306.

NOBLIN, C. D., TIMMONS, E. O. and KAEL, H. C. (1963) 'Different effects of positive and negative verbal reinforcement on psychoanalytic character types'. *Amer. Psychol.*, **18**, 412.

NOBLIN, C. D., TIMMONS, E. O. and KAEL, H. C. (1966) 'Differential effects of positive and negative verbal reinforcement on psychoanalytic character types'. *J. Pers. Soc. Psychol.*, **4**, 224-8.

NORMAN, J. P. (1948) 'Evidence and clinical significance of homosexuality in 100 unanalysed cases of dementia praecox'. *J. Nerv. Ment. Dis.*, **107**, 484-9.

NOWLIS, V. (1963) 'Research with the mood adjective check list'. In *Affect, Cognition and Personality*, TOMKINS, S. S. and IZARD, E. C. (eds). New York: Springer.

OBERNDORF, C. P. (1942) 'Results with psychoanalytic therapy'. *Amer. J. Psychiat.*, **99**, 374.

O'CONNELL, W. E. (1960) 'The adaptive function of wit and humour'. *J. Abnorm., Soc. Psychol.*, **61**, 263-70.

O'CONNELL, W. E. (1962) 'Item analysis of the WHAT test'. *J. Soc. Psychol.*, **56**, 271-6.

O'CONNELL, W. E. (1964) 'Multidimensional investigation of Freudian humour'. *Psychiat. Quart.*, **38** (1), 97-108.

O'CONNOR, N. and FRANKS, C. M. (1960) 'Childhood upbringing and other environmental factors'. In EYSENCK, H. J. (1961).

OFFENKRANTZ, W. A. and RECHTSCHAFFEN, A. (1963) 'Clinical studies of sequential dreams'. *Arch. Gen. Psychiat.*, **8**, 497-508.

OHLMEYER, P., BRILMAYER, H. and HISTLSTRUNG, H. (1944) 'Periodische Vorgänge im Schlaf'. *Pflug. Arch. Ges. Physiol.*, **248**, 559.

OHLMEYER, P., BRILMAYER, H. and HISTLSTRUNG, H. (1947) 'Periodische Vorgänge im Schlaf'. II Mitteilung. *Pflug. Arch. Ges. Physiol.*, **249**, 50.

OLDFIELD, R. C. (1955) 'Apparent fluctuations of a sensory threshold'. *Quart. J. Exp. Psychol.*, **7**, 101-15.

O'NEIL, C. W. (1964) 'A cross-cultural study of hunger and thirst motivation manifested in dreams'. *Hum. Develop.*, **8**, 181-93.

ORLANSKY, H. (1949) 'Infant care and personality'. *Psychol. Bull.*, **46**, 1-48.

ORNE, M. (1962) 'On the social psychology of the psychological experiment, with particular reference to demand characteristics and their implications'. *Amer. Psychol.*, **17**, 776-83.

OSWALD, I. (1969) 'Do dreams have a function?' *Paper at Ann. Conf. of Brit. Psychol. Soc.*

PAPEZ, J. W. (1937) 'A proposed mechanism of emotion'. *Arch. Neurol. Psychiat.*, **38**, 725-43.

PARSONS, T. (1955) 'Family structure and the socialization of the child'. In PARSONS and BALES (1955).

PARSONS, T. and BALES, R. F. (1955) *Family, Socialization and Interaction Process*. New York: Free Press.

PASAMANICK, B., DINITZ, S. and LEFTON, M. (1959) 'Psychiatric orientation and its relation to diagnosis and treatment in a mental hospital'. *Amer. J. Psychiat.*, **116**, 127-32.

PAWLIK, K. and CATTELL, R. B. (1964) 'Third-order factors in objective personality tests'. *Brit. J. Psychol.*, **55**, 1-18.

PAYNE, D. E. and MUSSEN, P. H. (1956) 'Parent-child relations and father identification among adolescent boys'. *J. Abnorm. Soc.*, **52**, 358-62.

PEDERSEN, F. and MARLOWE, D. (1960) 'Capacity and motivational differences in verbal recall'. *J. Clin. Psychol.*, **16**, 219-22.

PEIL, M. (1965) 'Ghanaian University students: the broadening base'. *Brit. J. Sociol.*, **16**, 19-28.

PERLOE, S. I. (1958) *An Experimental Test of Two Theories of Perceptual Defence.* Unpub. Ph.D. thesis, Univ. of Michigan.

PERLOE, S. I. (1960) 'Inhibition as a determinant of perceptual defence'. *Percept. Mot. Skills*, **11**, 59-66.

PETERSON, C. H. and SPANO, F. (1941) 'Breast feeding, maternal rejection and child personality'. *Char. and Personal.*, **10**, 62-6.

PETTIT, T. F. (1969) 'Anality and time'. *J. Consult. Clin. Psychol.*, **33**, 170-174.

PIAGET, J. (1948) *The Moral Judgement of the Child.* Glencoe: Free Press.

PICHOT, P. (1954) Cited by CATTELL, R. B. (1957).

PICHOT, P. and PERSE, J. (1967) 'Analyse factorielle et structure de la personnalité'. *Paper in honour of Prof. Essen-Moller.* Lund: Univ. of Lund.

PICKFORD, R. W. (1969) 'Dream-work, art-work and sublimation in relation to art therapy'. *Paper presented at annual Conf. Brit. Psychol. Soc., Edinburgh.*

PINZKA, C. and SAUNDERS, D. R. (1954) 'Analytic rotation to simple structure. II: extension to an oblique solution'. *Res. Bull.*, RB-54-3. Princeton: E.T.S.

POETZL, O. (1917) 'Experimentell erregte Traumbilder in ihren Beziehungen zum indirekten Sehen'. *Ztschr. f.d. Neurol. und. Psychiat.*, **37**, 278-349.

POLLIE, D. M. (1964) 'A projective study of conflict and defence in peptic ulcers and bronchial asthma'. *J. Proj. Tech. and Personal. Assess.*, **28**, 67-77.

POPPER, K. (1959) *The Logic of Scientific Discovery.* New York: Basic Books.

POSTMAN, L. (1953) 'On the problem of perceptual defence'. *Psychol. Rev.*, **60**, 298-306.

POSTMAN, L. (1962) (ed.) *Psychology in the Making.* New York: Knopf.

POSTMAN, L., BRONSON, W. and GROPPER, G. L. (1953) 'Is there a mechanism of perceptual defence?'. *J. Abnorm. Soc. Psychol.*, **48**, 215-24.

POWDERMAKER, H. (1933) *Life in Lesu.* New York: Norton.

PRICE-WILLIAMS, D. R. (1965) 'Displacement and orality in Tiv witchcraft'. *J. Soc. Psychol.*, **65**, (1) 1-15.

PRUGH, D. G. (1954) 'Childhood experience and colonic disorder'. *Amer. N.Y. Acad. Sci.*, **58**, 355-76.

PUMPIAN-MINDLIN, E. (1952) (ed.) *Psychoanalysis as Science.* Stanford: Stanford Univ. Press.

RABIN, A. I. (1957) 'Personality maturity of Kibbutz (Israeli collective settlement) children and non-Kibbutz children as reflected in Rorschach findings'. *J. Proj. Tech.*, **21**, 148-53.

RABIN, A. I. (1958a) 'The Israel Kibbutz (collective settlement) as a "laboratory" for testing psychodynamic hypotheses'. *Psychol. Rec.*, **7**, 111-15.

RABIN, A. I. (1958b) 'Some psychosexual differences between Kibbutz and non-Kibbutz Israeli boys'. *J. Proj. Tech.*, **22**, 328-32.

RABINOWITZ, W. (1957) 'Anality, aggression and acquiescence'. *J. Abnorm. Psychol.*, **54**, 140-2.

RACHMANN, S. (1963) *Critical Essays in Psychoanalysis.* Oxford: Pergamon.

RAMSEY, G. V. (1943) 'The sexual development of boys'. *Amer. J. Psychol.*, **56**, 217-33.

RAMSEY, G. V. (1953) 'Studies of dreaming'. *Psychol. Bull.*, **50**, 432-55.

RAPAPORT, D. and GILL, M. M. (1959) 'The points of view and assumptions of metapsychology'. *Internat. J. Psychoanal.*, **40**, 153-62.

RATTRAY, R. S. (1923) *Ashanti.* London: Oxford Univ. Press.

RECHTSCHAFFEN, A. (1964). In *Science and Psychoanalysis*, Vol. 7. See MAS-SERMAN, J. H. (1964).

RECHTSCHAFFEN, A., VERDONE, P. and WHEATON, J. (1963a) 'Reports of mental activity during sleep'. *Canad. Psychiat. Assoc. J.*, **8**, 409-14.

RECHTSCHAFFEN, A., VOGEL, G. and SHAIKUN, G. (1963) 'Inter-relatedness of mental activity during sleep'. *Arch. Gen. Psychiat.*, **9**, 536-47.

REES, (1959). Cited by HALL, C. S. (1963).

REICH, W. (1945) *Character Analysis.* New York: Orgone Institute.

REPORT OF THE COMMITTEE ON HOMOSEXUAL OFFENCES AND PROSTITU-TION (Wolfenden Report) (1957) London: H.M.S.O.

REST, J. (1968) *Developmental Hierarchy in Preference and Comprehension of Moral Judgement.* Unpub. Ph.D. thesis, Univ. of Chicago.

REYMERT, M. L. (1950) (ed.) *The Second International Symposium on Feelings and Emotions.* New York: McGraw-Hill.

RICHARDSON, M. W. and KUDER, F. (1939) 'The calculation of test-reliability coefficients based upon the method of rational equivalence'. *J. Educ. Psychol.*, **30**, 681-7.

RICKMAN, A. (1940) 'The psychology of ugliness'. *Internat. J. Psychoanal.*, **21**, 294-31.

RITZ, G. H. (1954) *The Relative Strengths of Impulse Ego and Superego in Three Groups of Aged Males.* Ph.D. thesis, Western Reserve Univ.

ROBBINS, L. C. (1963) ' The accuracy of parental recall of aspects of child development and of child-rearing practices'. *J. Abnorm. Soc. Psychol.*, **66**, 261-70.

ROBBINS, S. L. (1962) *Textbook of Pathology.* 2nd edn. Philadelphia: W. B. Saunders.

ROBERTS, E. (1944) 'Thumb and finger sucking in relation to feeding in early infancy'. *Amer. J. Dis.*, **68**, 7-8.

ROFFWARG, H. P., DEMENT, W. C., MUZZIO, J. and FISHER, C. (1962) 'Dream imagery: relationship to rapid eye movements of sleep'. *Arch. Gen. Psychiat.*, **7**, 235-58.

ROGERS, C. R. (1957) 'The necessary and sufficient conditions of therapeutic personality change'. *J. Consult. Psychol.*, **21**, 95-103.

ROGERS, C. R. and DYMOND, R. (1954) *Psychotherapy and Personality Change.* Chicago: Univ. of Chicago Press.

ROGERSON, B. C. F. and ROGERSON, C. H. (1939) 'Feeding in infancy and subsequent psychological difficulties'. *J. Ment. Sci.*, **65**, 1163-82.

ROHEIM, G. (1934) 'The study of character development and the ontogenetic theory of culture'. In *Essays Presented to C. G. Seligman*. (Ed. E. E. Evans-Pritchard *et al*). London: Routledge & Kegan Paul.

ROHEIM, G. (1952) 'The anthropological evidence and the Oedipus complex'. *Psychoanal. Quart.*, **21**, 537-42.

ROKEACH, M. (1960) *The Open and Closed Mind: An Investigation into the Nature of Belief Systems and Personality Systems*. New York: Basic Books.

ROSENSTOCK, I. M. (1951) 'Perceptual aspects of repression'. *J. Abnorm. Soc. Psychol.*, **41**, 304-15.

ROSENTHAL, R. (1964) 'Experimenter outcome-orientation and the results of the psychological experiment'. *Psychol. Bull.*, **61**, 405-12.

ROSENZWEIG, S. (1933) 'The recall of finished and unfinished tasks as affected by the purpose with which they were performed'. *Psychol. Bull.*, **30**, 698.

ROSENZWEIG, S. (1934) 'Types of reaction to frustration'. *J. Abnorm. Soc. Psychol.*, **29**, 298-300.

ROSENZWEIG, S. (1938) 'The experimental study of repression'. In MURRAY, H. A. (1938).

ROSENZWEIG, S. (1954) 'A transvaluation of psychotherapy: a reply to Hans Eysenck'. *J. Abnorm. Soc. Psychol.*, **49**, 298-304.

ROSSI, A. M. and SOLOMON, P. (1961) 'A further note on female Blacky protocols'. *J. Proj. Tech.* **25**, 339-40

SADGER, J. (1929) 'Erfolge und Dauer der psychoanalytischen Neurosenbehandlung'. *Internat. Zeit. Psychoanal.*, **15**, 426-34.

SAMPSON, H. (1965) 'Deprivation of dreaming sleep by two methods. I: Compensatory REM time'. *Arch. Gen Psychiat.*, **13**, 79-86.

SAMUELS, I. (1959) 'Reticular mechanisms and behaviour'. *Psychol. Bull.*, **56**, 1-25.

SANDLER, J. (1954) 'Studies in psychopathology using a self-assessment inventory'. *Brit. J. Med. Psychol.*, **27**, 142-5.

SANDLER, J. and HAZARI. A. (1960) 'The obsessional: on the psychological, classification of obsessional character traits and symptoms'. *Brit. J. Med. Psychol.*, **33**, 113-21.

SAPPENFIELD, B. R. (1965) 'Review of the Blacky Pictures'. In BUROS, O. K. (1965).

SARNOFF, I. (1951) 'Identification with the aggressor. Some personality correlates of anti-Semitism among Jews'. *J. Pers.*, **20**, 199-218.

SARNOFF, I. (1960) 'Reaction-formation and cynicism'. *J. Pers.*, **28**, 129-43.

SARNOFF, I. (1962) *Personality Dynamics and Development*. London: Wiley.

SARNOFF, I. and CORWIN, S. M. (1959) 'Castration anxiety and the fear of death'. *J. Pers.*, **27**, 374-85.

SCHAFER, R. (1954) *Psychoanalytic Interpretation in Rorschach Testing*. New York: Grune and Stratton.

SCHAFFER, H. R. (1958) 'Objective observations of personality development in early infancy'. *Brit J. Med. Psychol.*, **31**, 174-83.

SCHLESINGER, V. J. (1963) *Anal Personality Traits and Occupational Choice – a study of accountants, chemical engineers and educational psychologists.* Unpub. Ph.D. thesis, Univ. of Michigan.

SCHMIDT, H. O. and FONDA, C. P. (1956) 'The reliability of psychiatric diagnosis: a new look'. *J. Abnorm. Soc. Psychol.*, **52**, 262-7.

SCHNEIDER, K. (1958) *Psychopathic Personalities.* London: Cassell.

SCHONBAR, R. A. and DAVITZ, J. R. (1960) 'The connotative meaning of sexual symbols'. *J. Consult. Psychol.*, **24**, 483-7.

SCHWARTZ, B. J. (1955) 'Measurement of castration anxiety and anxiety over the loss of love'. *J. Pers.*, **24**, 204-19.

SCHWARTZ, B. J. (1956) 'An empirical test of two Freudian hypotheses concerning castration anxiety'. *J. Pers.*, **24**, 318-27.

SCODEL, A. (1957) 'Heterosexual somatic preference and fantasy dependence'. *J. Consult. Psychol.*, **21**, 371-4.

SCOFIELD, R. W. and SUN, C. W. (1960) 'A comparative study of the differential effect upon personality of Chinese and American child-training practices'. *J. Soc. Psychol.*, **52**, 221-4.

SCOTT, E. M. (1958) 'Psychosexuality of the alcoholic'. *Psychol. Rep.*, **4**, 599-602.

SEARS, R. R. (1936) 'Experimental studies of projection. I: Attribution of traits'. *J. Soc. Psychol.*, **7**, 151-63.

SEARS, R. R. (1937) 'Initiation of the repression sequence by experienced failure'. *J. Exp. Psychol.*, **20**, 570-80.

SEARS, R. R. (1943) *Survey of Objective Studies of Psychoanalytic Concepts.* Bull. 51, New York: Social Science Research Council.

SEARS, R. R. (1950) 'Personality'. *Ann. Rev. Psychol.*, **1**, 105-18.

SEARS, R. R., MACCOBY, E. E. and LEVIN, H. (1957) *Patterns of Child-Rearing.* Evanston: Row, Peterson.

SEARS, R. R., RAU, L. and ALPERT, R. (1965) *Identification and Child-training.* Stanford: Stanford Univ. Press.

SEARS, R. R., WHITING, J. W. M., NOWLIS, V. and SEARS, P. S. (1953) 'Some child-rearing antecedents of aggression and dependency in young children'. *Genet. Psychol. Monogr.*, **47**, 135-234.

SEARS, R. R. and WISE, G. W. (1950) 'Relation of cup-feeding in infancy to thumb-sucking and the oral drive'. *Amer. J. Orthopsychiat.*, **20**, 123-38.

SEGAL, H. (1964) *Introduction to the Work of Melanie Klein.* London: Heinemann.

SEIDEN, R. H. (1965) 'Onset, age and psychosexual conflict in bronchial asthma'. *Am. Psychol.*, **20**, 548.

SELLS, S. B. (1965) 'The Dynamic Personality Inventory'. In BUROS, O. K. (1965).

SEWARD, J. P. (1950) 'Psychoanalysis, deductive method and the Blacky Test'. *J. Abnorm. Soc. Psychol.*, **45**, 529-35.

SEWELL, W. H. (1952) 'Infant training and the personality of the child'. *Amer. J. Soc.*, **58**, 150-9.

SEWELL, W. H. and MUSSEN, P. H. (1952) 'The effects of feeding, weaning and scheduling procedures on childhood adjustment and the formation of oral symptoms'. *Child Development*, 23, 185-91.

SHERWOOD, M. (1969) *The Logic of Explanation in Psychoanalysis*. New York and London: Academic Press.

SHEVRIN, H. and LUBORSKY, L. (1958) 'The measurement of preconscious perception in dreams and images. An investigation of the Poetzl phenomenon'. *J. Abnorm. Soc. Psychol.*, 56, 285-94.

SIMSARIAN, S. P. (1947) 'Case histories of five thumb-sucking children breast-fed on unscheduled regimes, without limitation of nursing time'. *Child Development*, 18, 180-4.

SIZER, T. (1967) (ed.) *Religion and Public Education*. Boston: Houghton-Mifflin.

SJOBRING. H. (1963) *La Personnalité. Structure et Développement*. Paris: Doin.

SKINNER, B. F. (1954) 'Critique of psychoanalytic concepts and theories'. *Sci. Monogr.*, 79, 300-305. New York.

SMOCK, C. D. (1956) 'Replication and comments: an experimental reunion of psychoanalytic theory with perceptual vigilance and defence'. *J. Abnorm. Soc. Psychol.*, 53, 68-73.

SNIDER, M. (1959) 'On the adequacy of the Krout and Tabin Personal Preference Scale standardization group'. *J. Clin. Psychol.*, 15, 68-70.

SNYDER, F. (1963) 'The new biology of dreaming'. *Arch. Gen. Psychiat.*, 8, 381-91.

SNYDER, F. (1964) 'The REM state in a "living fossil" '. *Paper at Ann. meeting of Assn. Psychophysiol. Stud. Sleep.*

SNYDER, F. (1965) 'Progress in the new biology of dreaming'. *Amer. J. Psychiat.*, 122 (4), 377-91.

SNYDER, F., HOBSON, J. A. and GOLDFRANK, F. (1963) 'Blood pressure changes during human sleep'. *Sci.*, 142, 1313-14.

SPIRO, M. E. (1961) 'An overview and a suggested re-orientation'. In HSU, F. L. K. (1961).

SPITZER, H. M. (1947) 'Psychoanalytic approaches to the Japanese character'. *Psychoanalysis and the Social Services*, Vol. 1. New York: Internat. Univ. Press.

SPRAGUE, R. L. (1959) 'Effects of differential training on tachistoscopic recognition thresholds'. *J. Exp. Psychol.*, 58, 227-31.

STAGNER, R., LAWSON, E. D. and MOFFIT, J. W. (1955) 'The Krout Personal Preference Scale. A factor analytic study'. *J. Clin. Psychol.*, 11, 103-13.

STAGNER, R. and MOFFIT, J. W. (1956) 'A statistical study of Freud's theory of personality types'. *J. Clin. Psychol.*, 12, 72-4.

STARER, E. (1955) 'Cultural symbolism: a validity study'. *J. Consult. Psychol.*, 19, 453-4.

STEIN, M. and OTTENBERG, P. (1958) 'Role of odours in asthma'. *Psychosom. Med.*, 20, 60-65.

STENNETT, R. G. and THURLOW, M. (1958) 'Cultural symbolism: the age variable'. *J. Consult. Psychol.*, 22, 496.

STEPHENS, W. N. (1961) 'A cross-cultural study of menstrual taboos'. *Genet. Psychol. Monogr.*, 64, 385-416.

STEPHENS, W. N. (1962) *The Oedipus Complex Hypothesis: Cross-cultural Evidence*. New York: Free Press of Glencoe.

STEVENSON, H. (1963) (ed.) *Child Psychology*. Chicago: Univ. of Chicago Press.

STOKES, A. (1965) *The Invitation in Art*. London: Tavistock Publications.

STORY, I. A. (1963) *The Relationship between the Effects of Conflict Arousal and Oral Thinking*. Unpub. Ph.D. thesis, Univ. of Michigan.

STORY, I. A. (1968) 'Effects on thinking of relationships between conflict arousal and oral fixation'. *J. Abnorm. Psych.*, **73**, 440-48.

STRASSBURGER, F. (1966) 'The "Steeple effect". Sex differences in marginal perception and fantasy'. *J. Nerv. Ment. Dis.*, **142**, 228-34.

STRAUSS, M. A. (1957) 'Anal and oral frustration in relation to Sinhalese personality'. *Sociometry*, **20**, 21-31.

STREITFIELD, H. S. (1954) 'Specificity of peptic ulcer to intense oral conflicts'. *Psychosom. Med.*, **16**, 315-26.

STRINGER, P. (1970) 'A note on the factorial structure of the Dynamic Personality Inventory'. *Brit. J. Med. Psychol.*, **43**, 1, 95-103.

SUTHERLAND. J. D. (1968) (ed.) *The Psychoanalytic Approach*. London: Hogarth Press and Institute of Psychoanalysis.

TAGIURI, R. and PETRULLO, L. (1958) (eds.) *Person Perception and Interpersonal Behaviour*. Stanford: Stanford Univ. Press.

TAIT, D. (1961) *The Konkomba of Northern Ghana*. London: Internat. African Institute and Univ. of Ghana.

TART, C. T. (1965) 'The hypnotic dream: methodological problems and a review of the literature'. *Psychol. Bull.*, **63**, 87-99.

TAULBEE, E. S. and STENMARK, P. E. (1968) 'The Blacky Pictures Test. A comprehensive annotated and indexed bibliography (1949-67)'. *J. Proj. Tech.*, **32**, 105-37.

TAYLOR, A. (1962) (ed.) *Educational and Occupational Selection in West Africa*. London: Oxford Univ. Press.

THELEN, M. H. (1965) 'Similarities of defence preferences within families and within sex groups'. *J. Proj. Tech. and Person. Assess.*, **29** (4), 461-4.

THOMAS, R. W. (1951) *An Investigation of the Psychoanalytic Theory of Homosexuality*. Unpub. Ph.D. thesis, Univ. of Lexington.

THORNDIKE, E. L. and LORGE, I. (1944) *The Teacher's Word Book of 30,000 Words*. New York: Columbia Univ. Press.

THURSTON, J. R. and MUSSEN, P. H. (1951) 'Infant feeding gratification and adult personality'. *J. Pers.*, **19**, 449-58.

TIMMONS, E. O. and NOBLIN, C. D. (1963) 'The differential performance of orals and anals in a verbal conditioning paradigm'. *J. Consult. Psychol.*, **27**, 383-6.

TINBERGEN, N. (1959) 'Comparative studies of the behaviour of gulls (laridae): a progress report'. *Behav.*, **15**, 1-70.

TRAISMAN, A. S. and TRAISMAN, H. S. (1958) 'Thumb- and finger-sucking: a study of 2,650 infants and children'. *J. Pediat.*, **52**, 566-72.

TRIANDIS, L. M. and LAMBERT, W. W. (1961) 'Pan-cultural factor-analysis of reported socialization practices'. *J. Abnorm. Soc. Psychol.*, **62**, 631-9.

TRILLES, R. P. H. (1912) 'Totémisme chez les Fan'. *Bibliothèque Anthropos.* **1**, 184-205.

TROSMAN, H., RECHTSCHAFFEN, A., OFFENKRANTZ, W. and WOLPERT, E. (1960) 'Studies in the psychophysiology of dreams. IV: relations among dreams in sequence'. *Arch. Gen. Psychiat.*, **3**, 602.

TRUAX, C. B. (1963) 'Effective ingredients in psychotherapy. An approach to unraveling the patient-therapist interactions'. *J. Consult. Psychol.*, **10**, 256-63.

TRUAX, C. B. and CARKHUFF, R. R. (1964) 'Significant developments in psychotherapy research'. In ABT and REISS (eds.) (1964).

TSUJIOKA, B. and CATTELL, R. B. (1965) 'Constancy and difference in personality structure and mean profile in the questionnaire medium from applying the 16 PF Test in America and Japan'. *Brit. J. Soc. Clin. Psychol.*, **4**, 269-86.

UPDIKE, J. (1968) *Couples.* London: André Deutsch.

VALENTINE, C. W. (1960) *The Normal Child and Some of His Abnormalities.* Harmondsworth: Penguin.

VELDMAN, D. J. and BOWN, O. H. (1969) 'Personality and performance characteristics associated with cigarette smoking among college freshmen'. *J. Consult. Clin. Psychol.*, **33**, 109-19.

VENESS, T. (1962) 'An experiment on slips of the tongue and word association faults'. *Lang. and Speech*, **5**, (3) 128-37.

VERNON, P. E. (1953) *Personality Tests and Assessments.* London: Methuen.

VERRILL, B. V., and COSTANZA, V. (1962) 'The IES Test and ward behaviour'. *J. Clin. Psychol.*, **18**, 295-7.

WAELDER, R. (1965) *Psychoanalytic Avenues to Art.* Psychoanalytic Epitomes No. 6. London: Hogarth Press and Institute for Psychoanalysis.

WALLACH, M. A. (1960) 'Two correlates of symbolic sexual arousal: level of anxiety and liking for aesthetic material'. *J. Abnorm. Soc. Psychol.*, **61**, 396-401.

WALLACH, M. A. and GREENBERG, C. (1960) 'Personality functions of symbolic sexual arousal to music'. *Psychol. Monogr.*, **74** (7), 494.

WALLERSTEIN, R. S., ROBBINS, L. L., SARGENT, H. D. and LUBORSKY, L. (1956) 'The psychotherapy research project of the Menninger foundation. Rationale, method and sample'. *Bull. Menning. Clin.*, **20**, 221.

WARBURTON, F. W. (1968) *The Structure of Personality Factors.* Unpub. Ms., Univ. of Manchester.

WATSON, C. G. (1965) 'A test of the relationship between repressed homosexuality and paranoid mechanisms'. *J. Clin. Psychol.*, **21** (4), 380-84.

WAXENBERG, S. E., DICKES, R. and GOTTESFIELD, H., (1962) 'The Poetzl phenomenon re-examined experimentally'. *J. Nerv. Ment. Dis.*, **135**, 387-398.

WEBB, W. B. (1968) *Sleep: an Experimental Approach.* London: Macmillan.

WELLS, W. D. and GOLDSTEIN, R. L. (1964) 'Sear's study of projection: replication and critique'. *J. Soc. Psychol.*, **64** (1), 169-79.

WHITING, B. B. (1963) *Six Cultures: Studies of Child Rearing.* New York: Wiley.

WHITING, J. W. M. (1960) 'Resource mediation and learning by identification'. In ISCOE and STEVENSON (1960).

WHITING, J. W. M. and CHILD, I. L. (1953) *Child Training and Personality.* New Haven: Yale Univ. Press.

WHITING, J. W. M., KLUCKHOHN, H. and ANTHONY, A. (1958) 'The function of male initiation ceremonies at puberty'. In MACCOBY, E. E., NEWCOMB, T. M. and HARTLEY, E. L. (1958).

WHITTAKER, E. M., GILCHRIST, J. C., and FISCHER, J. W. (1952) 'Perceptual defence or response suppression'. *J. Abnorm. Soc. Psychol.*, 47, 732-3.

WHYTE, L. L. (1968) *The Unconscious Before Freud.* London: Tavistock Publications.

WIENER, D. N. (1948) 'Subtle and obvious keys for the MMPI'. *J. Consult. Psychol.*, 12, 164-70.

WIENER, M., (1955) 'Word frequency or motivation in perceptual defence'. *J. Abnorm. Soc. Psychol.*, 51, 214-8.

WIGGINS, J. S., WIGGINS, N. and CONGER, J. C. (1968) 'Correlates of heterosexual somatic preference'. *J. Pers. Soc. Psychol.*, 10, 82-90.

WILKINSON, F. R. and CARGHILL, D. W. (1955) 'Repression elicited by story material based on the Oedipus complex'. *J. Soc. Psychol.*, 42, 209-14.

WILLIAMS, M. (1951) 'Rate of learning as a function of ego-alien material'. *J. Pers.*, 19, 324-31.

WINNICOTT, D. W. (1957) *The Child and the Family.* London: Tavistock Publications.

WINTER, W. D. (1955) 'Two personality patterns in peptic ulcer patients'. *J. Proj. Tech.*, 19, 332-44.

WINTER, W. D. and PRESCOTT, J. W. (1957) 'A cross-validation of Starer's test of cultural symbolism'. *J. Consult. Psychol.*, 21, 22.

WITMER, H. and POWERS, E. (1951) *An Experiment in the Prevention of Delinquency.* New York: Columbia University Press.

WITTENBORN, J. R. (1953) The IPAT Humour Test. In BUROS, O. K. (1953) *IVth Mental Measurement Year Book.* New Jersey: Gryphon.

WOLFENDEN REPORT. See *Report of the Committee on Homosexual Offences and Prostitution.*

WOLOWITZ, H. M. (1964) 'Food preference as an index of orality'. *J. Abnorm. Soc. Psychol.*, 69 (6) 650-4.

WOLOWITZ, H. M. (1965) 'Attraction and aversion to power: a psychoanalytic conflict theory of homosexuality in male paranoids'. *J. Abnorm. Psychol.*, 70, (5) 360-70.

WOLOWITZ, H. M. (1967) 'Oral involvement in peptic ulcer'. *J. Consult. Psychol.*, 31, 418-19.

WOLOWITZ, H. M. and BARKER, M. J. (1968) 'Alcoholism and oral passivity'. *Quart. J. Stud. Alcohol.*, 29, 592-7.

WOLOWITZ, H. M. and WAGONFELD, S. (1968) 'Oral derivatives in the food preferences of peptic ulcer patients. An experimental test of Alexander's psychoanalytic hypothesis'. *J. Nerv. Ment. Dis.*, **146**, 18-23.

WOOD, P. (1962) *Dreaming and Social Isolation*. Unpub. Ph.D. thesis, Univ. N. Carolina. In WEBB, W. B. (1968).

WOODMANSEY, A. C. (1967) 'Emotion and the motions: an enquiry into the causes and prevention of functional disorders of defecation'. *Brit. J. Med. Psychol.*, **40**, 207-23.

WOODWARD, M. (1958) 'The diagnosis and treatment of homosexual offenders'. *Brit. J. Delinq.*, **9**, 44-58.

WOODWORTH, R. S. and SCHLOSBERG, H. (1955) *Experimental Psychology*. New York: Holt, Rinehart & Winston.

WORCHEL, P. (1957) 'Adaptability screening of flying personnel: development of a self-concept inventory for predicting maladjustment'. *USAF Schl. Aviat. Med. Rep.*

WORTHY, M. and CRADDICK, R. A. (1969) 'Semantic differential investigation of sexually symbolic concepts'. *J. Proj. Tech.*, **33**, 78-80.

WYLIE, R. C. (1957) 'Cognitive set and motivational factors in the perception of neutral and threat related stimuli'. *J. Abnorm. Soc. Psychol.*, **55**, 227-31.

WYLLIE, R. W. (1966) 'Ghanaian students: a research note'. *Brit. J. Sociol.*, **17** (3), 306-11.

YARROW, L. J. (1954) 'The relationship between nutritive sucking experiences in infancy and non-nutritive sucking in childhood'. *J. Genet. Psychol.*, **84**, 149-62.

YARROW, L. J. (1961) 'Maternal deprivation: towards an empirical and conceptual re-evaluation'. *Psychol. Bull.*, **58**, 459-90.

ZAMANSKY, H. S. (1958) 'An investigation of the psychoanalytic theory of paranoid delusions'. *J. Pers.*, **26**, 410-25.

ZEICHNER, A. M. (1955) 'Psychosexual identification in paranoid schizophrenia'. *J. Proj. Tech.*, **19**, 67-77.

ZEIGARNIK, B. (1927) 'Über das Behalten von erledigten und unerleditzen Handlungen'. *Psychol. Forsch.*, 1927, **9**, 1-85.

ZELLER, A. F. (1950a) 'An experimental analogue of repression. I: historical summary'. *Psychol. Bull.*, **47**, 39-51.

ZELLER, A. F. (1950b) 'An experimental analogue of repression. II: the effects of individual failure and success on memory measured by relearning. *J. Exp. Psychol.*, **40**, 411-22.

ZUBIN, J., ERON, L. D. and SCHUMER, F. (1965) *An Experimental Approach to Projective Techniques*. London: Wiley.

Author Index

General Index

achievement motivation, 186, 329
Adler's individual psychology, 327-30
aesthetic appreciation, 200-1
affectionless character, 123
aggression, 181, 186, 187, 195
aggressor, identification with. *See* identification
Ai3, 25-8, 37, 58, 59, 85, 86, 280, 281
alchemy, 325
alcoholism, 288-98, 306
anaclitic identification. *See* identification
anal birth, 111
anal character, 2, 6, 8, 10, 11, 17, 22-8, 30, 32-44, 49, 55, 56, 58-61, 66-73, 78, 80, 84-94, 202, 281, 335, 345-7, 350, 354
anal characteristics or traits, 10, 11, 17, 22, 24, 26, 27, 57, 59, 66, 69, 71, 79, 86, 87, 89, 92, 184, 202, 263, 280, 335, 344
anal erotism, 2, 6, 7, 9, 10, 17, 26, 29, 42, 48, 50, 51, 68, 69, 72, 73, 78, 79, 85, 86, 92, 151, 154, 201, 263, 280, 284, 290, 333, 334, 347
anal expulsives, 85
anal factor, 14, 15, 21, 23, 25, 27, 28
anal phase or stage, 6, 7, 15, 55, 85, 154, 220, 261, 263, 282-4, 306
anal retentives, 85
anal sadism, 20, 305
anal scales, 16, 19, 20, 22, 84, 85
anancastic psychopath, 94
anima and animus, 323-5
anorexia nervosa, 291-2, 306
anti-Semitism, 156, 182, 187, 188
anus, 6, 7, 70, 78
anxiety, 7, 33, 36, 152, 155-9, 162, 164, 166, 167, 169, 172, 178, 180, 181, 188, 190, 199, 206, 253, 259, 302, 331
anxiety dreams, 206
anxiety neurosis, 261
appendicitis, 290-1, 306, 346, 350, 356
archetypes, 323, 325, 326, 343, 356
Arnhem Land, 101
arts, the, 190, 192, 200-3, 349
art-work, 201
Ashanti tribe, 59, 186
asthma, 282-4, 288, 306
authoritarian conscience, 337
authoritarian personality, 39, 146, 309
automaton conformity, 338, 339
avoidance, 183

basic anxiety, 341-3
Beethoven, Ludwig van, 201
behaviour therapy, 309, 312, 315, 353, 357, 359
Bell Adjustment Inventory, 16
Beloff scale, 22, 26, 42, 49, 50, 85, 86, 90
biophilous character, 334
birth fantasies, 291, 306, 346, 356
Blacky Pictures, 45, 46, 47, 79-88, 101, 104, 105, 106, 110, 116, 119, 124, 176-7, 179, 180, 182, 266, 267, 274, 275, 278, 279, 281, 283-90, 293, 300-2, 335, 342, 344, 350
blind, dreaming in the, 243
body language, 262
Bosch, Hieronymous, 202
bottle feeding, 47, 62-5, 74, 75
breasts, 91, 202, 331
breast feeding, 47, 62-5, 72-5, 77, 299
Brothers Karamazov, The, 201
budgerigar, 140, 354
buttocks, 92

California Test of Personality, 56, 63, 67
castration anxiety, 99, 102-13, 115, 140, 144, 187, 209, 229, 230, 233, 234, 248, 266, 267, 269, 273, 277, 278, 280, 281, 293, 302, 306, 335, 356
castration complex, 3, 95-9, 101, 103, 105-116, 118, 119, 122, 124, 207, 232-5, 262, 263, 277, 278, 281, 325, 326, 329, 340, 344, 345, 348-50, 353-5, 357-9
Cattell's ergs, 327, 329
Cattell's motivational factors, 131-3
Cattell's objective tests, 31, 32, 131, 133, 134, 138, 318, 348
Cattell's personality factors, 32-6, 43, 44, 348
Cattell 16 PF test, 26, 27, 31, 32-6, 39, 51, 57, 58, 122, 134, 196
censor, 206, 223
ceremonial drinking, 296
ceremonies, 108, 110
Ceylon, 56, 57
change of quality of affect, 155, 156
childhood amnesia, 45
child-rearing procedures, 7, 8, 12, 45-7, 50-2, 54-7, 59-65, 70, 73, 76, 79, 83, 93, 94, 108, 110, 114, 115, 140, 142, 186, 187, 335, 345, 346, 354
China, 57